The Apocalyptic Imagination

John J. Collins

THE APOCALYPTIC IMAGINATION

An Introduction to the Jewish Matrix of Christianity

CROSSROAD · NEW YORK

For Jesse Yarbro
    Sean Ryan
    and
    Aidan Michael

1984

The Crossroad Publishing Company
370 Lexington Avenue, New York, N.Y. 10017

Printed in the United States of America

Library of Congress Cataloging in Publication Data

Collins, John Joseph, 1946–
The apocalyptic imagination

Bibliography: p. 251
Includes index.
1. Apocalyptic literature—History and criticism.
I. Title.
BS646.C65   1984   229'.913   84-17581
ISBN 0-8245-0623-5

47,790

Contents

v

Preface

THIS VOLUME IS the product of more than a decade of study, begun when I was a graduate student at Harvard University. Along the way numerous mentors and friends have informed and corrected my work. Three groups deserve special mention: my teachers at Harvard (Frank M. Cross, Paul D. Hanson, and John Strugnell), the task-force on Forms and Genres of Religious Literature in Late Antiquity, and my colleagues in the Pseudepigrapha Group of the Society of Biblical Literature. Above all my thanks are due to my most constant collaborator, Adela Yarbro Collins. The book is dedicated to our children, who show us how fantastic imagination can be.

I also wish to thank the editors of: *Catholic Biblical Quarterly* for permission to adapt my article "The Apocalyptic Technique: Setting and Function in the Book of the Watchers" (*CBQ* 44 [1982] 91–111); *Journal for the Study of the Old Testament* for permission to adapt my article "Apocalyptic Genre and Mythic Allusions in Daniel" (*JSOT* 21 [1981] 83–100); Eisenbrauns Publishing Co. for permission to adapt my article "Patterns of Eschatology at Qumran" (*Traditions in Transformation*, edited by B. Halpern and J. D. Levenson); Scholars Press for permission to adapt my article "The Heavenly Representative: The 'Son of Man' in the Similitudes of Enoch" (from *Ideal Figures in Ancient Judaism*, edited by G. W. Nickelsburg and J. J. Collins) and to use material from *Semeia* 14; J. C. B. Mohr, Tübingen, for permission to adapt my article "The Genre Apocalypse in Hellenistic Judaism" (from *Apocalypticism in the Mediterranean World and the Near East*, edited by D. Hellholm).

1
The Apocalyptic Genre

Two FAMOUS SLOGANS coined by German scholars may serve to illustrate the ambivalent attitudes of modern scholarship toward the apocalyptic literature. The first is Ernst Käsemann's dictum that "apocalyptic was the mother of all Christian theology."[1] The other is the title of Klaus Koch's polemical review of scholarly attitudes, *Ratlos vor der Apokalyptik*, "perplexed" or "embarrassed" by apocalyptic.[2] Both slogans are, of course, deliberately provocative and exaggerated, but each has nonetheless a substantial measure of truth. Apocalyptic ideas undeniably played an important role in the early stages of Christianity and, more broadly, in the Judaism of the time. Yet, as Koch demonstrated, the primary apocalyptic texts have received only sporadic attention and are often avoided or ignored by biblical scholarship.

The perplexity and embarrassment that Koch detected in modern scholarship has in part a theological source. The word "apocalyptic" is popularly associated with fanatical millenarian expectation, and indeed the canonical apocalypses of Daniel and especially John have very often been used by millenarian groups. Theologians of a more rational bent are often reluctant to admit that such material played a formative role in early Christianity. There is consequently a prejudice against the apocalyptic literature which is deeply ingrained in biblical scholarship. The great authorities of the nineteenth century, Julius Wellhausen and Emil Schürer, slighted its value, considering it to be a product of "Late Judaism" which was greatly inferior to the prophets, and this attitude is still widespread today. In his reply to Käsemann, Gerhard Ebeling could say that "according to the prevailing ecclesiastical and theological tradition, supremely also of the Reformation, apocalyptic—I recall only the evaluation of the Revelation of John—is to say the least a suspicious symptom of tendencies

1

towards heresy."[3] Whatever we may decide about the theological value of
these writings, it is obvious that a strong theological prejudice can impede
the task of historical reconstruction and make it difficult to pay enough
attention to the literature to enable us even to understand it at all. It will
be well to reserve theological judgment until we have mastered the
literature.

Not all the perplexity is theological in origin. In some part it also springs
from the semantic confusion engendered by the use of the word "apocalyptic" as a noun. The word has habitually been used to suggest a world
view or a theology which is only vaguely defined but which has often been
treated as an entity independent of specific texts. Scholars have gradually
come to realize that this "apocalyptic myth" does not always correspond to
what we find in actual apocalypses. Koch already distinguished between
"apocalypse" as a literary type and "apocalyptic" as a historical movement.
More recent scholarship has abandoned the use of "apocalyptic" as a noun
and distinguishes between apocalypse as a literary genre, apocalypticism
as a social ideology, and apocalyptic eschatology as a set of ideas and
motifs that may also be found in other literary genres and social settings.[4]

These distinctions are helpful in drawing attention to the different
things traditionally covered by the term "apocalyptic." The question
remains whether or how they are related to each other: Does the use of the
literary genre imply a social movement? Or does an apocalypse always
contain apocalyptic eschatology? Before we can attempt to answer these
questions we must clarify what is meant by each of the terms involved.

THE GENRE APOCALYPSE

The notion that there is a class of writings that may be labeled
"apocalyptic" has been generally accepted since Friedrich Lücke published
the first comprehensive study of the subject in 1832.[5] Lücke's synthesis was
prompted in part by the recent edition of *1 Enoch* by Richard Laurence
(who also edited the *Ascension of Isaiah*, which Lücke discussed as a Christian apocalypse). The list of Jewish apocalyptic works included Daniel,
1 Enoch, 4 Ezra and the *Sibylline Oracles*, and he adduced this literature
as background for the book of Revelation. Subsequent discoveries have
enlarged the corpus and modified the profile of the genre: 2 and 3 *Baruch*,
2 Enoch, the *Apocalypse of Abraham* and the *Testament of Abraham* were
all published in the later part of the nineteenth century. While there has
been inevitable scholarly dispute about the precise relation of this or that
work to the genre, there has been general agreement on the corpus of
literature that is relevant to the discussion and can be called "apocalyptic"
at least in an extended sense.

Most of the works that figure in discussions of the Jewish apocalyptic literature were not explicitly designated as apocalypses in antiquity. The use of the Greek title *apokalypsis* (revelation) as a genre label is not attested in the period before Christianity. The first work introduced as an *apokalypsis* is the New Testament book of Revelation, and even there it is not clear whether the word denotes a special class of literature or is used more generally for revelation. Both 2 and 3 *Baruch*, which are usually dated about the end of the first century c.e., are introduced as apocalypses in the manuscripts, but the antiquity of the title is open to question. Morton Smith concludes from his review of the subject that "the literary form we call an apocalypse carries that title for the first time in the very late first or early second century A.D. From then on both the title and form were fashionable, at least to the end of the classical period."[6] The subsequent popularity of the title has recently been illustrated by the Cologne Mani Codex, where we read that each one of the forefathers showed his own *apokalypsis* to his elect, and specific mention is made of apocalypses of Adam, Sethel, Enosh, Shem, and Enoch.[7] These apocalypses tell of heavenly ascents. The series concludes with the rapture of Paul to the third heaven.

The ancient usage of the title *apokalypsis* shows that the genre apocalypse is not a purely modern construct, but it also raises a question about the status of early works (including most of the Jewish apocalypses) that do not bear the title. The question is complicated by the fact that some of these works are composite in character and have affinities with more than one genre. The book of Daniel, which juxtaposes tales in chaps. 1–6 and visions in chaps. 7–12, is an obvious example. This problem may be viewed in the light of what Alastair Fowler has called the life and death of literary forms.[8] Fowler distinguishes three phases of generic development. During the first phase "the genre complex assembles, until a formal type emerges." In the second phase the form is used, developed, and adapted consciously. A third phase involves the secondary use of the form—for example, by ironic inversion or by subordinating it to a new context. In historical reality these phases inevitably overlap, and the lines between them are often blurred. It would seem that the Jewish apocalyptic writings that lack a common title and are often combined with other forms had not yet attained the generic self-consciousness of Fowler's second phase, although the genre complex had already been assembled. We should bear in mind that the production of apocalypses continued long into the Christian era.

The presence or absence of a title cannot, in any case, be regarded as a decisive criterion for identifying a genre. Rather, what is at issue is whether a group of texts share a significant cluster of traits that distinguish them from other works. A systematic analysis of all the literature that has been regarded as "apocalyptic," either in the ancient texts or in modern scholarship, was undertaken by the Society of Biblical Literature Genres Project and the results were published in *Semeia* 14 (1979).[9] That analysis will serve as our point of departure. The purpose of *Semeia* 14 was to give precision to the traditional category of "apocalyptic literature" by showing the extent and limits of the conformity among the allegedly apocalyptic texts.

The thesis presented in *Semeia* 14 is that a corpus of texts that has been traditionally called "apocalyptic" does indeed share a significant cluster of traits that distinguish it from other works. Specifically, an apocalypse is defined as: *"a genre of revelatory literature with a narrative framework, in which a revelation is mediated by an otherworldly being to a human recipient, disclosing a transcendent reality which is both temporal, insofar as it envisages eschatological salvation, and spatial insofar as it involves another, supernatural world."*

This definition can be shown to apply to various sections of *1 Enoch*, Daniel, *4 Ezra*, *2 Baruch*, *Apocalypse of Abraham*, *3 Baruch*, *2 Enoch*, *Testament of Levi* 2-5, the fragmentary *Apocalypse of Zephaniah*, and with some qualification to *Jubilees* and the *Testament of Abraham* (both of which also have strong affinities with other genres). It also applies to a fairly wide body of Christian and Gnostic literature and to some Persian and Greco-Roman material.[10] It is obviously not intended as an adequate description of any one work, but rather indicates what Klaus Koch has called the *Rahmengattung* or generic framework.[11] The analysis in *Semeia* 14 differs, however, from Koch's "preliminary demonstration of the apocalypse as a literary type." Koch listed six typical features: discourse cycles, spiritual turmoils, paraenetic discourses, pseudonymity, mythical imagery, and composite character.[12] He did not claim that these are necessary elements in all apocalypses. In contrast, the definition above is constitutive of all apocalypses and indicates the common core of the genre[13] More important, it constitutes a coherent structure, based on the systematic analysis of form and content.

The form of the apocalypses involves a narrative framework that describes the manner of revelation. The main means of revelation are visions and otherworldly journeys, supplemented by discourse or dialogue and occasionally by a heavenly book. The constant element is the presence of an angel who interprets the vision or serves as guide on the otherworldly journey. This figure indicates that the revelation is not intelligible without supernatural aid. It is out of this world. In all the Jewish apocalypses the human recipient is a venerable figure from the distant past, whose name is used pseudonymously.[14] This device adds to the remoteness and mystery of the revelation. The disposition of the seer before the revelation and his reaction to it typically emphasize human helplessness in the face of the supernatural.

The content of the apocalypses, as noted, involves both a temporal and a spatial dimension, and the emphasis is distributed differently in different works. Some, such as Daniel, contain an elaborate review of history, presented in the form of a prophecy and culminating in a time of crisis and eschatological upheaval. Others, such as *2 Enoch*, devote most of their text to accounts of the regions traversed in the otherworldly journey. The revelation of a supernatural world and the activity of supernatural beings are essential to all the apocalypses. In all there are also a final judgment and a destruction of the wicked. The eschatology of the apocalypses differs from that of the earlier prophetic books by clearly envisaging retribution beyond death. Paraenesis occupies a prominent place in a few apocalypses (e.g., *2 Enoch*, *2 Baruch*), but all the apocalypses have a hortatory aspect, whether or not it is spelled out in explicit exhortations and admonitions.

Within the common framework of the definition, different types of apocalypses may be distinguished. The most obvious distinction is between the "historical" apocalypses such as Daniel and 4 Ezra and the otherworldly journeys. Only one Jewish apocalypse, the *Apocalypse of Abraham*, combines an otherworldly journey with a review of history, and it is relatively late (end of the first century C.E.). It would seem that there are two strands of tradition in the Jewish apocalypses, one of which is characterized by visions, with an interest in the development of history, while the other is marked by otherworldly journeys with a stronger interest in cosmological speculation. These two strands are interwoven in the Enoch literature. Two of the earliest "historical" apocalypses, the Animal Apocalypse and the Apocalypse of Weeks are found in *1 Enoch*. These books presuppose the Enoch tradition attested in the Book of the Watchers (*1 Enoch* 1–36) and may in fact presuppose Enoch's otherworldly journey, although they do not describe it. The Similitudes of Enoch also shows the influence of both strands, although it does not present an overview of history. *1 Enoch* as we now have it is a composite apocalypse embracing different types. Yet we can find an apocalypse such as 4 Ezra (late first century) which sharply rejects the tradition of heavenly ascent and cosmological speculation, whereas *2 Enoch* and *3 Baruch*, from about the same time, show no interest in the development of history.

Within the otherworldly journeys it is possible to distinguish subtypes according to their eschatology: (a) only the *Apocalypse of Abraham* includes a review of history; (b) several (Book of the Watchers, Astronomical Book, and Similitudes in *1 Enoch*; *2 Enoch*; *Testament of Levi* 2–5) contain some form of public, cosmic, or political eschatology; (c) a number, *3 Baruch*, *Testament of Abraham*, and *Apocalypse of Zephaniah* are concerned only with the individual judgment of the dead. No apocalypse of this third subtype is likely to be earlier than the first century C.E. The distribution of the temporal and eschatological elements may be illustrated as follows:

	otherworldly journeys								"historical" apocalypses						
	Apoc. Zephaniah	T. Abraham	3 Baruch	T. Levi 2–5	2 Enoch	Similitudes	Astronomical Book	1 Enoch 1–36	Apoc. Abraham	2 Baruch	4 Ezra	Jubilees	Apoc. of Weeks	Animal Apocalypse	Daniel
Cosmogony					x				x	x					
Primordial events		x			x			x	x	x	x				
Recollection of past									x	x	x				x
Ex eventu prophecy									x	x	x	x	x	x	x
Persecution						x			x	x	x			x	x
Other eschatological upheavals				x			x	x	x	x	x	x	x	x	x
Judgment/destruction of wicked	x	x	x	x	x	x	x	x	x	x	x	x	x	x	x
Judgment/destruction of world	x?				x			x?	x		x?	x		x	
Judgment/destruction of other-worldly beings					x	x	x?	x				x	x	x	x
Cosmic transformation				x	x	x	x	x	x	x	x	x?	x	x	x
Resurrection						x				x	x	x?		x	x
Other forms of afterlife	x	x	x?	x	x	x	x	x	x				x	x?	x?

[This grid is adapted from *Semeia* 14, p. 28, where a more complete form may be found.]

The study of the genre is designed to clarify particular works by showing both their typical traits and their distinctive elements. It is not intended to construct a metaphysical entity, "apocalyptic" or *Apokalyptik* in any sense independent of the actual texts. The importance of genres, forms, and types for interpretation has been axiomatic in biblical studies since the work of Hermann Gunkel and the rise of form criticism. It is also well established in literary and linguistic theory and in philosophy and hermeneutics.[15] E. D. Hirsch, Jr., a literary critic, has expressed the essential point well.[16] Understanding depends on the listener's or reader's expectations. These expectations are of a type of meaning rather than of a unique meaning "because otherwise the interpreter would have no way of expecting them." Consequently, utterances must conform to typical usages if they are to be intelligible at all. Even the unique aspects of a text (and every text is unique in some respect) can only be understood if they are located relative to conventional signals. As Hirsch has lucidly shown "the central role of genre concepts in interpretation is most easily grasped when the process of interpretation is going badly, or when it has to undergo revision." An interpreter always begins with an assumption about the genre of a text. If our expectations are fulfilled, the assumptions will need no revision. If they are not fulfilled, we must revise our idea of the genre or relinquish the attempt to understand. There can be no understanding without at least an implicit notion of genre.

The generic framework or *Rahmengattung* indicated in the definition of apocalypse above is important because it involves a conceptual structure or view of the world. It indicates some basic presuppositions about the way the world works, which are shared by all the apocalypses. Specifically, the world is mysterious and revelation must be transmitted from a supernatural source, through the mediation of angels; there is a hidden world of angels and demons that is directly relevant to human destiny; and this destiny is finally determined by a definitive eschatological judgment. In short, human life is bounded in the present by the supernatural world of angels and demons and in the future by the inevitability of a final judgment.

This conceptual structure already carries some implications for the function of the genre, since it provides a framework for viewing the problems of life. The appeal to supernatural revelation provides a basis for assurance and guidance. The prospect of a final judgment creates a context for the clarification of values. The specific problems may vary from one apocalypse to another, and so may the specific guidance and demands. Two apocalypses such as 4 Ezra and *2 Baruch* may disagree on particular issues, but their differences are articulated within the framework of shared presuppositions. If we say that a work is apocalyptic we encourage the reader to expect that it frames its message within the view of the world that is characteristic of the genre.

The literary genre apocalypse is not a self-contained isolated entity. The conceptual structure indicated by the genre, which emphasizes the supernatural world and the judgment to come, can also be found in works that are not revelation accounts, and so are not technically apocalypses. Furthermore, the generic framework is never the only factor that shapes a text. The visions of Daniel, for example, must be seen in the context not only of the genre but also of the tales in Daniel 1–6 and of the other literature inspired by the persecution of Antiochus Epiphanes. Consequently there is always a corpus of related literature that is relevant in varying degrees to the understanding of a particular text. Any discussion of apocalyptic literature must also take account of oracles and testaments, which parallel the apocalypses (especially the "historical" ones) at many points. Yet the definition is important for providing a focus for the discussion and indicating a core to which other literary types may be related.

OTHER VIEWS OF THE GENRE

It may be useful to contrast the view of the genre presented here and in *Semeia* 14 with other views that have been recently advocated. On the one hand, E. P. Sanders has proposed a return to an "essentialist" definition of Jewish apocalypses as a combination of the themes of *revelation* and *reversal* (of the fortunes of a group, either Israel or the righteous).[17] The attractiveness of this proposal lies in the simplicity with which Sanders can then view the social function of the genre as literature of the oppressed. However, the proposal suffers from two crucial disadvantages. First, the combined themes of revelation and reversal are characteristic of the whole tradition of biblical prophecy, as well as of the political oracles of the ancient Near East. All of this literature is, of course, related on a very broad level (the genre apocalypse is a subgenre of "revelatory literature"); but a definition that fails to distinguish between Amos and Enoch is obviously of limited value. Second, it takes no account at all of the cosmological and mystical tendencies in the apocalypses, which have been repeatedly emphasized in recent studies.[18] It may also be that Sanders's view of the social function is too simple. While several major Jewish apocalypses (especially those of the historical type) can be viewed as literature of the oppressed, this is seldom evident in otherworldly journeys, although the latter type frequently bore the label "apocalypse" in antiquity.[19]

On the other hand, a number of scholars have argued that definitions of "apocalypse" or "apocalyptic" should make no mention of eschatology.[20] So an apocalypse might be defined simply as a revelation of heavenly mysteries.[21] Such a definition is unobjectionable as far as it goes. It would of course cover a much wider corpus than the definition given above, but it is certainly accurate for all apocalypses. If one wishes to give a more descriptive definition of the literature that has been traditionally regarded as apocalyptic, then the question arises whether some revelations of heavenly mysteries are distinguished from others by their content. The issue here has usually centered on eschatology. It is true that the scholarly literature has been preoccupied with eschatology to a disproportionate degree and that it is by no means the only concern of the apocalypses. Yet an approach that denies the essential role of eschatology is an overreaction and no less one-sided.

APOCALYPTIC ESCHATOLOGY

The debate over the definition of the genre leads us back to the question of apocalyptic eschatology. The touchstone here must be the kind of eschatology that is found in the apocalypses. Two problems have been raised. First, some have questioned whether the apocalypses exhibit a consistent eschatology.[22] We must bear in mind that as there are different types of apocalypses, there are correspondingly different types of apocalyptic eschatology. The common equation of "apocalyptic" with the scenario of the end of history is based only on the "historical" type like Daniel, and scholars have rightly objected that this is not typical of all apocalypses. All the apocalypses, however, involve a transcendent eschatology that looks for retribution beyond the bounds of history. In some cases (*3 Baruch, Apocalypse of Zephaniah*) this takes the form of the judgment of individuals after death, without reference to the end of history. We should bear in mind, however, that retribution after death is also a crucial component in a "historical" apocalypse like Daniel and constitutes a major difference from the eschatology of the prophets.[23] The fact that apocalyptic eschatology has often been erroneously identified with the "historical"type in the past does not justify the denial that there is any apocalyptic eschatology at all.

Second, neither the judgment of the dead nor even the scenario of the end of history is peculiar to apocalypses: hence the objection that there is no *distinctive* apocalyptic eschatology.[24] Insofar as this objection bears on the definition of the genre, we must note that visions and heavenly journeys are not distinctive either. The genre is not constituted by one or more distinctive themes but by a distinctive combination of elements, all of which are also found elsewhere. A more significant problem arises if we wish to speak of apocalyptic eschatology outside of the apocalypses, for example, in the Gospels or Paul. What is at issue here is the affinity between the eschatological allusions and the scenarios which are found in more elaborate form in the apocalypses. Affinities vary in degree, and, although the label "apocalyptic eschatology" may be helpful in pointing up the implications of some texts, we should always be aware that the adjective is used in an extended sense.

APOCALYPTICISM

We may now return to the relation between the apocalypses and apocalypticism. Koch's "preliminary demonstration of apocalyptic as a historical movement" singled out eight clusters of motifs: (1) urgent expectation of the end of earthly conditions in the immediate future; (2) the end as a cosmic catastrophe; (3) periodization and determinism; (4) activity of angels and demons; (5) new salvation, paradisal in character; (6) manifestation of the kingdom of God; (7) a mediator with royal functions; (8) the catchword "glory."[25] Koch does not claim that all these elements are found in every apocalypse, even in his rather limited list, which essentially corresponds to the "historical" apocalypses of *Semeia* 14. It is apparent, however, that these characteristics do not correspond at all to an apocalypse like *2 Enoch* and that they ignore much of the speculative material that is prominent even in the earliest works of the Enoch tradition. So Michael Stone has argued that "there are some of the books which are conventionally regarded as apocalypses which are for all practical purposes devoid of apocalypticism," and that "truly apocalyptic apocalypses are the exception rather than the rule."[26] Hence the conclusion that a clear distinction must be maintained between apocalypses and apocalypticism.

It is obvious that there are indeed distinctions to be made, but to speak of apocalypses that are not apocalyptic can only compound the semantic confusion. We may begin by clarifying the valid distinctions and then try to sort out the terminology. Insofar as apocalypticism is a historical movement or "refers to the symbolic universe in which an apocalyptic movement codifies its identity and interpretation of reality,"[27] it is not simply identical with the content of apocalypses. There are apocalypses that are not the product of a movement in any meaningful sense. Equally, there are movements, such as the sect of Qumran and early (pre-70 C.E.) Christianity, which did not produce apocalypses but are nonetheless commonly regarded as apocalyptic. The question remains, however, when a movement can appropriately be called apocalyptic. Since the adjective apocalyptic and the noun apocalypticism are derived from "apocalypse," it is only reasonable to expect that they indicate some analogy with the apocalypses. A movement might reasonably be called apocalyptic if it shared the conceptual framework of the genre, endorsing a world view in which supernatural revelation, the heavenly world, and eschatological judgment played essential parts. Arguably, both the Qumran community and early Christianity are apocalyptic in this sense, quite apart from the production of apocalypses. We should remember, however, that the argument depends on analogy with the apocalypses and the affinity is always a matter of degree.

If the word apocalypticism is taken to mean the ideology of a movement that shares the conceptual structure of the apocalypses, then we must recognize that there may be different types of apocalyptic movements, just as there are different types of apocalypses. Koch's list of features corresponds well enough to the "historical" type. We must also allow for mystically oriented movements which are "apocalyptic" insofar as they correspond to the "heavenly journey" type of apocalypse. We are only beginning to explore the historical setting in which Jewish mysticism developed.

The debate over the relation between apocalypses and apocalypticism arises from the fact that previous scholarship has been preoccupied with the "historical" apocalypses and neglected those that incline to mysticism and cosmic speculation. One of the more significant developments of recent years has been the rediscovery of the mystical side of apocalyptic literature. The mystical component cannot be neatly isolated from the historical, but is an integral factor in all apocalyptic literature. A comprehensive understanding of the genre apocalypse in its different types also calls for a more complex view of the social phenomenon of apocalypticism.

APOCALYPTIC LANGUAGE

Up to this point we have been concerned with the generic framework that enables us to identify the apocalypses as a distinct class of writings. We must now turn to two other aspects of the genre that were not examined in *Semeia* 14: the nature of apocalyptic language and the question of setting and function.

The literary conventions that determine the manner of composition and the nature of the literature are no less important than the generic framework. On this issue we may distinguish two fundamentally different approaches, one of which is associated with the name of R. H. Charles and the other with that of Hermann Gunkel. This is not, of course, to suggest that the approaches of these scholars were always incompatible with each other or that every subsequent scholar can be neatly aligned with one or the other. They do, however, represent two divergent tendencies in the study of apocalyptic literature.[28]

The Influence of R. H. Charles

The study of apocalyptic literature in the English-speaking world has to a great extent been influenced by R. H. Charles. His textual editions, translations, and notes have remained standard reference works down to the present, and his knowledge of the material was undeniably vast.[29] Yet such a sober critic as T. W. Manson wrote that "there was a sense in which the language of Apocalyptic remained a foreign language to him. He could never be completely at home in the world of the Apocalyptists. And this made it impossible for him to achieve that perfect understanding which demands sympathy as well as knowledge."[30] Charles's lack of empathy with the material is apparent in two characteristics of his work. First, he tended to treat the texts as compendia of information and paid great attention to identifying historical allusions and extracting theological doctrines. In contrast, he gave little attention to such matters as literary structure or mythological symbolism. The second characteristic is related to this. Since he assumed that the original documents presupposed a doctrinal consistency similar to his own and that the canons of style that governed them were similar to those of his own day, he posited interpolations and proposed emendations rather freely. So F. C. Burkitt wrote in his obituary of Charles: "If he came to have any respect for an ancient author he was unwilling to believe that such a person could have entertained conceptions which to Charles's trained and logical western mind were 'mutually exclusive,' and his favorite explanation was to posit interpolations and a multiplicity of sources, each of which may be supposed to have been written from a single and consistent point of view."[31]

Of course Charles was a child of his age. The principles of literary/source criticism typified by J. Wellhausen were still dominant in biblical studies when he wrote. It is to Charles's credit that he did not share Wellhausen's negative evaluation of apocalypticism. The underlying assumptions of this type of approach have continued to play a prominent part in the study of apocalyptic literature. In large part this has been due to the persistence of a tradition which "has tended towards clarity and simplicity, and . . . has tended to lose from sight the essential problem of understanding the apocalyptic books as literary texts with their own strange form and language."[32] This tendency has been especially, though not exclusively, evident in British scholarship. The two most comprehensive and widely read books on "apocalyptic" in the last half century were by British authors—H. H. Rowley and D. S. Russell.[33] Both books contain much that is still valuable, but as James Barr has pointed out, they are characterized by the "reduction of the very enigmatic material to essentially simple questions."[34] It is also significant that Charles, Rowley, and Russell all sought the sources of apocalyptic language primarily in OT prophecy. While prophecy may indeed be the single most important source on which the apocalyptists drew, the tendency to assimilate apocalyptic literature to the more familiar world of the prophets risks losing sight of its stranger mythological and cosmological components.

The problem with the source-critical method is obviously one of degree. No one will deny that it is sometimes possible and necessary to distinguish sources and identify interpolations. We have learned, however, that the apocalyptic writings are far more tolerant of inconsistency and repetition than Charles and his collaborators realized. Consequently, we must learn the conventions that are actually employed in the text rather than assume that our own criteria of consistency are applicable. In short, our working assumptions should favor the unity of a document, unless there is cogent evidence to the contrary. The burden of proof falls on the scholar who would divide a text into multiple sources.

The methodological assumptions that posit sources and interpolations to maintain an ideal of consistency are frequently coupled with a lack of appreciation of symbolic narratives. The tendency of much historical scholarship has been to specify the referents of apocalyptic imagery in as unambiguous a manner as possible. This enterprise has indeed contributed much to our understanding of passages like Daniel 11. Yet Paul Ricoeur has rightly protested against the tendency to identify apocalyptic symbols in too univocal a way.[35] This tendency misses the element of mystery and indeterminacy which constitutes much of the "atmosphere" of apocalyptic literature. In short, Ricoeur suggests that we should sometimes "allow several concurrent identifications *play*" and that the text may on occasion achieve its effect precisely through the element of uncertainty. It has been common to assume that apocalyptic symbols are mere codes whose meaning is exhausted by single referents. So Norman Perrin contrasted the rich and multidimensional use of the "kingdom of God" in the teaching of Jesus (a "tensive" symbol) with what he conceived to be the one-dimensional usage of the apocalypses ("steno-symbols").[36] Such a contrast shows little appreciation for the allusive and evocative power of apocalyptic symbolism, but we must admit that Perrin's approach was consistent with much English-language scholarship.

THE INFLUENCE OF HERMANN GUNKEL

Hermann Gunkel, who pioneered so many creative developments in biblical study, also pointed the way to a more satisfactory appreciation of the apocalypses.[37] Much of Gunkel's work on apocalyptic literature was directed to the recovery of traditional, and especially mythological, materials embedded in the apocalypses. On the one hand, this work suggested that the various seams detected by the so-called literary critics (e.g., when an interpretation ignores some elements in a vision) need not point to multiple authorship but only to the use of traditional material by a single author. In short, authors who work with traditional material do not conform to the standards of consistency and coherence presupposed by Charles and Wellhausen but may well allow loose ends and even contradictions to stand in their work. On the other hand, by pointing to the mythological roots of much apocalyptic imagery, Gunkel showed its symbolic and allusive character. Apocalyptic literature was not governed by the principles of Aristotelian logic but was closer to the poetic nature of myth.

Gunkel's critique of the principles of "literary" criticism was long neglected by students of apocalyptic literature but has been repeatedly vindicated in recent study. The insight that the apocalypses did not aspire to

conceptual consistency but could allow diverse formulations to comple-
ment each other is especially important. The juxtaposition of visions and
oracles, which cover essentially the same material, with varying imagery
is a feature of a great number of apocalypses and related writings—Daniel,
Sibylline Oracles, Similitudes of Enoch, 4 Ezra, *2 Baruch*, Revelation. This
phenomenon cannot be adequately explained by positing multiple sources,
since we should still have to explain why sources are consistently combined
in this way. In fact, repetition is a common literary (and oral) convention
in ancient and modern times. A significant parallel to the apocalypses is
found in the repetition of dream reports—for example, the multiple
dreams of Joseph or of Gilgamesh. The recognition that such repetition is
an intrinsic feature of apocalyptic writings provides a key to a new understanding of the genre.

Biblical scholarship in general has suffered from a preoccupation with
the referential aspects of language and with the factual information that
can be extracted from a text. Such an attitude is especially detrimental to
the study of poetic and mythological material, which is expressive language, articulating feelings and attitudes rather than describing reality in
an objective way. The apocalyptic literature provides a rather clear
example of language that is expressive rather than referential, symbolic
rather than factual.[38]

TRADITIONAL IMAGERY

The symbolic character of apocalyptic language is shown especially by
its pervasive use of allusions to traditional imagery. Like much of the
Jewish and early Christian literature, the apocalypses constantly echo
biblical phrases. This point has been demonstrated especially by the
Swedish scholar Lars Hartman. The title of Hartman's basic book,
Prophecy Interpreted, may be somewhat misleading, if it is taken to suggest that the use of the biblical material is primarily exegetical. To be sure,
the direct interpretation of older prophecies is a significant factor in apocalyptic writings: the interpretation of Jeremiah's prophecy in Daniel 9 is an
obvious example. In many cases, however, the use of older texts consists
only in the use of a phrase that brings a biblical passage to mind without
claiming to interpret it in a definitive way. So the opening chapter of
1 Enoch is a patchwork of biblical phrases, alluding *inter alia* to Balaam's
oracle in Numbers 23–24.[39] This allusiveness enriches the language by
building associations and analogies between the biblical contexts and the
new context in which the phrase is used. It also means that this language
lends itself to different levels of meaning and becomes harder to pin down
in a univocal, unambiguous way.

The importance of biblical allusions in apocalyptic literature is generally admitted. Far more controversial is the use of mythological allusions. In part, the controversy arises from the notorious diversity of ways in which the word myth is used: sometimes as a genre label, sometimes as a mode of thought, sometimes implying an association with ritual, and sometimes even as a derogatory term for what is false or "pagan."[40] A case can be made, I believe, for using "myth" as a genre label (on a broader level than apocalypse) in any of a number of senses—for example, as a paradigmatic narrative (à la M. Eliade) or as a story that obscures or mediates the contradictions of experience (à la C. Lévi-Strauss). In view of the ambiguity of the word, however, such a generic use of "myth" is scarcely helpful. The word is used in biblical studies primarily to refer to the religious stories of the ancient Near East and the Greco-Roman world. When we speak of mythological allusions in the apocalyptic literature we are referring to motifs and patterns that are ultimately derived from these stories.

The importance of Near Eastern mythology for understanding the apocalyptic literature was forcefully suggested by Gunkel in his famous book *Schöpfung und Chaos in Urzeit und Endzeit* in 1895. The insight was kept alive by writers of the "myth and ritual" school such as S. H. Hooke and especially by A. Bentzen and S. Mowinckel.[41] In English-language scholarship it has been revived especially by Paul D. Hanson, building on the work of Frank M. Cross.[42] Whereas Gunkel sought his mythological parallels in the Babylonian material then available and subsequent scholars posited vast Persian influence, more recent scholarship has looked to the Canaanite-Ugaritic myths—especially in the case of Daniel.

There is still widespread resistance to the idea that Jewish apocalypses use mythological motifs.[43] In large part this resistance is theological, when the myths are viewed as "false" or "pagan." In fact, however, Canaanite motifs had been domesticated in the religion of Israel from very early times.[44] In some measure, the resistance arises from misconceptions. The Ugaritic texts come from the middle of the second millennium B.C.E., more than a thousand years before the earliest apocalypses. However, no one would claim that the authors of Daniel or Enoch had before them the exact texts we now have. We have very little documentation of the Canaanite religious tradition. The Ugaritic myths provide examples of a tradition that is largely lost. They are not the immediate sources of the apocalyptic imagery, but they illustrate the traditional usage that provides the context for the allusions. Before the Ugaritic texts were discovered, Gunkel appealed primarily to the Babylonian myths. The Ugaritic parallels now appear more adequate at some points. Future discoveries may yield even better comparative material. Gunkel was not wrong to appeal to the

Babylonian material, since the issue is not the exact derivation but the kinds of allusions involved.

It should also be clear that a mythological allusion does not carry the same meaning and reference in an apocalyptic context as it did in the original myth. If the "one like a son of man" who comes on the clouds in Daniel 7 alludes to the Canaanite figure of Baal, this is not to say that he is identified as Baal, or that the full story of Baal is implied. It merely suggests that there is some analogy between this figure and the traditional conception of Baal. In the same way, the "Son of Man" passage in Mark 13:26 alludes to Daniel, but the figure in Mark does not have the same reference as it had in Daniel, and the full narrative of Daniel 7 is not implied. Mythological allusions, like biblical allusions, are not simple copies of the original source. Rather they transfer motifs from one context to another. By so doing they build associations and analogies and so enrich the communicative power of the language.

THE QUEST FOR SOURCES

The recognition of allusions, and of the sources from which they derive, is an important factor in the study of apocalyptic literature. Yet it is important to distinguish the *generic* approach advocated here from the *genetic* approach which has long been dominant in this field of study.

An extraordinary amount of the scholarly literature has been devoted to the quest for the "origins of apocalyptic." For much of this century opinion was divided between those who viewed "apocalyptic" as the child of prophecy (e.g., Rowley) and those who regarded it as a "foreign" adaptation of Persian dualism. [45] More recently Gerhard von Rad suggested that it was derived from wisdom. [46] The renewed interest in mythological, especially Canaanite, sources is usually combined with the derivation from prophecy.

Much of this quest must be considered misdirected and counterproductive. Any given apocalypse combines allusions to a wide range of sources. The book of Daniel has obvious continuity with the prophets in the vision form and the use of Jeremiah's prophecy among other things. Yet we will argue that Canaanite imagery plays a crucial role in Daniel 7, and the schema of the four kingdoms is borrowed from the political propaganda of the Hellenistic Near East. While the importance of Persian dualism was greatly exaggerated in the past, it cannot be dismissed entirely. It is widely admitted in the Qumran scrolls and is quite compatible with the extensive use of Israelite traditions. Ultimately the meaning of any given work is constituted not by the sources from which it draws but by the way in which they are combined.

The quest for sources has often led scholars to view apocalypticism as a derivative phenomenon, a product of something other than itself. This tendency reflects a theological prejudice, inherited from the Wellhausen era, which views the apocalyptic writers (and postexilic Judaism in general) as inherently inferior to the prophets. In fact, the designation of sources has often been used as a covert way of making theological judgments. If "apocalyptic" is the child of prophecy it is legitimate; if it is a Persian import it is not authentically biblical. This logic is patently defective. The sources from which ideas are developed do not determine the inherent value of those ideas. Many of the central biblical ideas were in any case adapted from the mythology of the Canaanites and other Near Eastern peoples.

The designation of sources also sometimes serves as an indirect way of expressing the character of the phenomenon. Scholars who relate the apocalyptic literature exclusively to prophecy tend to concentrate on the eschatology and neglect the cosmological and speculative concerns that are also found in the apocalypses. Von Rad's theory that apocalypticism is derived from wisdom sought to correct that emphasis, but the issues have been confused by the genetic formulation of his thesis. The apocalypses do indeed present a kind of wisdom insofar as they, first, offer an understanding of the structure of the universe and of history, and, second, see right understanding as the precondition of right action. This wisdom, however, is not the inductive kind that we find in Proverbs or Sirach, but is acquired through revelation. The wisdom of Daniel and Enoch has close affinities with the *mantic* wisdom of the Babylonians.[47] The quest for higher wisdom by revelation is well attested in the Hellenistic age,[48] and it is significant that the biblical wisdom book that shows most correspondence with the apocalypses is the Hellenistic (deuterocanonical) Wisdom of Solomon.[49] There is also an analogy between the wisdom literature and some apocalypses on the level of the underlying questions, insofar as both are often concerned with theodicy or the problem of divine justice. The use of the dialogue form in 4 Ezra recalls the book of Job in this regard, although the culminating revelations in the two books are very different.[50] The relation to wisdom is seldom a matter of derivation but concerns the way we perceive the nature of the apocalypses. The most fruitful effect of von Rad's proposal has been to redirect attention to those aspects of the apocalypses which are cosmological and speculative rather than eschatological.

THE SETTINGS OF THE GENRE

The study of the apocalyptic genre rejects the genetic orientation of previous scholarship and places its primary emphasis on the internal coherence of the apocalyptic texts themselves. It is apparent that the apocalypses drew on various strands of tradition and that the new product is more than the sum of its sources. There is, however, a different genetic question that must be considered, concerning the historical and social matrix of the genre. In 1970 Klaus Koch could still assume that "if there was really a community of ideas and spirit between the different books which we now call apocalypses, these books must go back to a common sociological starting point; they must have a comparable *Sitz-im-Leben*."[51] Koch went on to complain that "the secondary literature shows an unsurpassed jumble of opinions" and concluded that apocalypse is a genre whose *Sitz im Leben* we do not yet know.

More recent study has shown that this formulation of the problem is inadequate. In an important critique of Old Testament form criticism in 1973, Rolf Knierim argued that "the conclusion seems unavoidable that 'setting' in the sense biblical form criticism has understood it, cannot be regarded indispensably as one of the factors that constitute genres."[52] The reason is not only the obvious practical one that we often do not have the necessary information to establish the setting of a text. More fundamental is the realization that settings are of different sorts, and so there is need of a typology of settings. The "jumble of opinions" about which Koch complains is due in large part to the lack of such a typology.

It is generally agreed that apocalypse is not simply "a conceptual genre of the mind"[53] but is generated by social and historical circumstances. On the broadest level "the style of an epoch can be understood as a matrix insofar as it furnishes the codes or raw materials—the typical categories of communication—employed by a certain society."[54] Much of the traditional debate about the sources of apocalypticism is relevant here insofar as the "codes and raw materials" are thought to be provided by late prophecy, Persian dualism, etc. On another level we may consider Philip Vielhauer's thesis that "the home of Apocalyptic is in those eschatologically excited circles which were forced more and more by the theocracy into a kind of conventicle existence."[55] A more specific variant of this type of setting would assign the apocalypses to a particular party, such as the Hasidim or the Essenes. A different type of setting is reflected in Vielhauer's further claim that the apocalypses "were frequently written out of actual distresses and for the strengthening of the community in them."[56] There is no necessary assertion about the existence of apocalyptic groups on this level. Yet another type of setting concerns the manner of composition. Do apocalypses reflect authentic visionary experience? Are they products of learned scribes? Or do they articulate popular beliefs? Finally, one may discuss the function of a text without specifying a social or historical setting at all. Recently Lars Hartman and David Hellholm have focused on the *illocution* of a text, or that which it does *in* saying what it says.[57] Hartman suggests that exhortation and consolation are typical illocutions of apocalypses. Even on this level, the function of a text may be more or less specific. Exhortation to pacifism is distinctly different from exhortation to violence, and either may be the function of a given text. We should also note that a text remains in existence and may be reused in various settings at different times.

THE GENERAL MATRIX

POSTEXILIC PROPHECY

We may begin with the question of the matrix of the genre on the most general level. In an influential study published in 1975, Paul Hanson argued that "the dawn of apocalyptic" should be located in postexilic prophecy in the late sixth century B.C.E.[58] Hanson was well aware that the main corpus of apocalyptic literature comes from a much later time. His point was that the basic configuration of apocalyptic thought can already be found in the late prophetic texts.

Hanson distinguishes two parties in the postexilic community: the hierocratic party represented by Haggai, the early chapters of Zechariah and Ezekiel 40–48 and the visionary heirs of Second Isaiah, represented by Isaiah 56–66, Zechariah 9–14, and a number of other passages, most notably Isaiah 24–27.[59] The closest formal analogies to the apocalypses are found in the "hierocratic" literature, especially in the visions of Zechariah that are interpreted by an angel.[60] On the other hand, Hanson sees in the visionary literature the dawn of apocalyptic eschatology, which he associates with the eclipse of human instrumentality in the divine intervention in history. The oracles of Isaiah 56–66 are written out of a growing sense of alienation from the hierocracy. The prophet calls on God to "rend the heavens and come down" (64:1). Divine intervention is necessary to set the situation right. The vision of the future is a new creation, new heavens and a new earth. In addition to the hope for a transcendent future, these oracles anticipate the use of mythological language in the apocalypses. The most striking illustrations are found in Isaiah 24–27. God will swallow up Death forever (25:8, an allusion to the figure of Mot or Death in Canaanite mythology) and will punish Leviathan and slay the dragon that is in the sea (27:1). Further, the social and historical matrix of these oracles has significant affinities with that of at least some later apocalypses. The sense of alienation from the present order is fundamental to many apocalypses, especially the historical type.

Hanson has indeed shown that there is significant continuity between the apocalypses and the prophetic tradition, and especially that the apocalyptic use of mythological imagery has ample biblical antecedents.

Yet some major defining characteristics of apocalyptic thought are lacking in these oracles. One is the interest in the heavenly world. Angels play some part in Zechariah, but scarcely any in the so-called visionary literature. Nothing in these books prepares for the mystical and speculative aspects of the Enoch literature. The eschatology too is rather different from the later apocalypses. In the "new earth" of Isaiah 65 "the child shall die a hundred years old and the sinner a hundred years old shall be accursed" and "like the days of a tree shall the days of my people be." Life will be transformed, but it will still be distinctly this-worldly ("they shall plant vineyards and eat their fruit"). It will also be finite, however lengthened it may be. This conception is quite different from the expectation of resurrection or of the judgment of the dead as we find it in Daniel and *Enoch*. When the goal of life is located beyond death, then there is evidently a greater impulse also to speculation about the world beyond and to the mystical elements in the apocalyptic literature.

While postexilic prophecy shares some significant features of the apocalypses, it still lacks the generic framework of apocalyptic thought.[61] The so-called Apocalypse of Isaiah in Isaiah 24–27 comes closer to the later literature than the other oracles. Isaiah 25 speaks of the destruction of Death, and Isa 26:19 of the resurrection of the dead. From the context it would seem that this language is metaphorical for the restoration of Israel, as is explicitly the case in Ezekiel's vision of the dry bones (Ezekiel 37). The dead who shall live are contrasted with the lords who ruled over Israel, who are gone without remembrance.[62] Yet the use of such language is a significant factor in the development of apocalyptic thought. An intriguing passage in Isa 24:21–22 speaks of a day when God will punish "the host of heaven in heaven and the kings of the earth on the earth" and they will be shut up in prison for many days until they are punished. This passage, like all of Isaiah 24–27, remains enigmatic, but it suggests an underlying mythology that is more elaborate than anything expressed in the texts, and which may well have been significant for the development of apocalyptic eschatology.[63]

THE EARLIEST APOCALYPSES

Postexilic prophecy undoubtedly supplied some of the codes and raw materials utilized by the later apocalypses. However, if we wish to examine the matrix in which the configuration of the genre emerged, we must surely begin with the earliest actual apocalypses, rather than with their partial antecedents.

The earliest apocalypses, by the definition given above, are found in *1 Enoch*. Substantial fragments of the Book of the Watchers and the Astronomical Book have been found at Qumran in manuscripts from the early

second or even late third century B.C.E., and the antiquity of these works
is also corroborated by allusions in the book of *Jubilees*.[64] The early date
of this Enoch material is significant for our perception of the genre, since
the contrast with the prophetic literature is much greater than in the case
of Daniel. The noncanonical apocalypses can no longer be dismissed as
"second-rate imitators" of Daniel. Both the Book of the Watchers and the
Astronomical Book involve otherworldly journeys and a good deal of
cosmological speculation.

The place of composition of these documents is far from certain. There
has been a general tendency to assign them to Palestinian Judaism. There
are indeed some references to Palestinian geography: Enoch is located in
"Dan which is southwest of Hermon" (13:7) and the description of the
"middle of the earth" in *1 Enoch* 26 is in fact a description of Jerusalem
and its surroundings.[65] Yet it is doubtful whether this evidence necessarily
requires that the author lived in the homeland. Several scholars have noted
the prominence of Babylonian lore in both the Book of the Watchers and
the Astronomical Book.[66] The possibility that this literature originated in
the eastern Diaspora cannot be discounted. It is noteworthy that the tales
in Daniel 1-6 are set in Babylon. There again a Diaspora origin is possible,
although the visions in Daniel 7-12 were certainly composed in Judea. In
no case can we point to an apocalyptic writing that was definitely composed in Babylon or the eastern Diaspora, nor can we assume that all were
definitely composed in Judea. Later we will find that some apocalyptic
writings also originated in the Hellenistic Diaspora.

A BABYLONIAN MATRIX?

In view of the manifest associations of the earliest Enoch and Daniel
literature with Babylon, we must consider whether the apocalyptic genre
owes its distinctive shape to a Babylonian matrix. Our question here is not
whether the earliest apocalypses were written in the eastern Diaspora,
since this possibility cannot be decisively verified at present. Rather the
question is to what extent were the "codes and raw materials" of the
apocalypses Babylonian in origin.

Several scholars have noted affinities between apocalyptic revelation and
the "mantic wisdom" of the Chaldeans.[67] Daniel in the tales (Daniel 1-6)
operates as a Babylonian wise man, skilled in the interpretation of dreams.
The figure of Enoch is to some degree modeled on Enmeduranki, founder
of the guild of *bārûs*, or Babylonian diviners. There is also a general similarity between the methods of apocalyptic revelation and of divination,
insofar as both involve the interpretation of mysterious signs and symbols,
and both carry overtones of determinism. Yet it must also be said that the
apocalyptic visions of Daniel 7-12 and the actual revelations of Enoch are

quite different from the literature of divination and omen collections.[68] Some scholars have tried to find a mediating link in the Akkadian prophecies, which have only come to light in recent years.[69] This genre has been described as follows by A. K. Grayson: "An Akkadian prophecy is a prose composition consisting in the main of a number of 'predictions' of past events. It then concludes either with a 'prediction' of phenomena in the writer's day or with a genuine attempt to forecast future events. The author, in other words, uses *vaticinia ex eventu* to establish his credibility and then proceeds to his real purpose, which might be to justify a current idea or institution, or, as it appears in the Dynastic prophecy, to forecast doom for a hated enemy."[70] Five exemplars of the genre have been recognized ranging in date from the twelfth century to the Seleucid era: the Marduk and Shulgi prophetic speeches, Text A, the Uruk prophecy, and the Dynastic prophecy. The Marduk and Shulgi speeches provide early examples of pseudonymity. The affinity of these prophecies with the Jewish apocalypses lies primarily in their "predictions" of past events, or *vaticinia ex eventu*. The cryptic manner in which these predicitons are presented ("A prince will arise . . . another man who is unknown will arise") has rightly been compared to Daniel 11, or Daniel 8:23-25.[71] More extensive parallels can be found in the *Sibylline Oracles*. In this respect at least the Akkadian prophecies provide noteworthy precedents for a prominent characteristic of the historical apocalypses. Yet the Babylonian prophecies fall far short of providing a comprehensive model for the apocalypses, even for the historical type. The extant evidence provides no parallel for the apocalyptic reception of revelation in a vision or heavenly tour and has no suggestion of an eschatology involving the judgment of the dead. In all, they seem closer to such political prophecies as the *Sibylline Oracles* than to the apocalypses. We will have occasion to discuss them further in connection with Daniel.

No one would argue that the Babylonian material provides a complete or sufficient matrix for the apocalyptic genre. It must, however, be seen as a significant contributing factor, especially insofar as apocalyptic revelation resembles divination in the decoding of mysterious signs.[72] To be sure, divination and dream interpretation were not exclusively Babylonian phenomena. There are obvious parallels between Daniel and Joseph, while Enoch is implicitly compared with Balaam in *1 Enoch* 1. In view of the Babylonian associations of both Enoch and Daniel, however, it is reasonable to assume that the affinities between apocalyptic revelation and mantic wisdom are due in some part to Babylonian influence.

Persian Apocalypticism

For much of the twentieth century Jewish apocalypticism was widely assumed to have been heavily influenced by Persian thought.[73] Such influence is still often admitted in the case of the Qumran scrolls, at least in the dualism of light and darkness. In general, however, scholars have become reticent on this subject because of the notorious difficulty of dating the Persian material. The Zoroastrian scripture, the Avesta, consists of writings from diverse periods which were collected in the Sassanian period (221–642 c.e.). The Gathas are believed to derive from Zoroaster himself, but the other components of the Avesta (the Younger Avesta) cannot be dated with precision. Moreover, only about one quarter of the original Avesta has survived. Much old material is preserved in the Pahlavi books, but these, in their present form, date chiefly from the ninth century c.e. The most important documents of Persian apocalypticism and eschatology belong to this Pahlavi literature. The difficulty lies in determining how far this Pahlavi literature preserves material from the pre-Christian era.[74]

The potential significance of Persian apocalypticism can be seen from a consideration of one of these Pahlavi works, the Zand-ī Vohuman Yasn, or *Bahman Yasht*.[75] This work is allegedly a "zand" or interpretation of a lost book of the Avesta, the *Vohuman Yašt*. The lost Yašt is also widely thought to have influenced other Persian apocalyptic writings and, perhaps, some non-Persian oracles, such as the Egyptian *Potter's Oracle*. The Zand also claims (1:1) to depend on the lost *Stûtkar Nask* of the Avesta.

According to the Zand, chap. 1, Zarathustra asked for immortality from Ahura Mazdā but was granted instead "wisdom of all-knowledge." He then saw a tree with four branches, one of gold, one of silver, one of steel, and one of mixed iron. Ahura Mazdā explained the vision, saying that the four branches were four kingdoms of which the last is ruled by the "dīvs who have disheveled hair." The fourth kingdom is said to come when the tenth century, or millennium of Zarathustra is at an end. Chapter 3 of the Zand contains an extended version of this incident, in which Zarathustra sees seven branches which are again interpreted as kingdoms, and concludes with the "dīvs" of disheveled hair and the end of the millennium of Zarathustra. In chap. 4 Zarathustra inquires about the signs of the tenth century and end of the millennium, and Ahura Mazdā replies by describing a long series of upheavals and disturbances, both political and cosmic. Chapters 7–9 prophesy what will happen when Zarathustra's millennium will end and Aûsîtar's will begin (8:8). Near the end of the second millennium Pêsyôtan son of Vistâšp will appear as a savior figure who will destroy the dīvs. The millennium of Aûsîtarmāh follows, when men will not even die because they "will be so versed in medicine" (9:12). Then at the end of this millennium "Sôsîyôs will make the creatures pure again" and the resurrection will follow (9:23).

The *Bahman Yasht* is a full-blown apocalypse of the historical type. It is in fact the only extant Persian work that combines the apocalyptic manner of revelation with the elaborate periodization of history and eschatology.

There is no doubt that periodization and the succession of millennia, with the attendant sense of determinism, is an integral feature of Persian theology. The classic expression of this view of cosmic history is found in the *Bundahišn*, a late (twelfth-century) compendium of traditional teaching. There the course of history is divided into twelve thousand years. The last nine thousand involve a conflict between Ahura Mazdā and Ahriman. Three thousand years pass according to the will of Ahura Mazdā, three thousand according to the will of both, and in the final three thousand Ahura Mazdā triumphs. The *Bundahišn* contains also an account of the resurrection and the purification of the world by fire (chap. 34).

It is by no means certain that the full schema of history and eschatology that we find in the *Bundahišn* was already developed in the Hellenistic period.[76] We do have a brief early account of Persian religion in Plutarch's treatise *On Isis and Osiris* (47).[77] There we are told that Ahura Mazdā (Horomazes) and Ahriman (Areimanus) have an ongoing struggle: "for three thousand years alternately the one god will dominate the other and be dominated, and that for another three thousand years they will fight and make war, until one smashes up the domain of the other. In the end Hades will perish and men shall be happy." It is not clear whether this schema should be understood as corresponding to the last nine thousand years of the *Bundahišn* or whether it represents a different, earlier system. It is also not certain how far Plutarch's account was representative of Persian theology. Plutarch ascribes this account to Theopompus, who flourished in the fourth century B.C.E. Although much is uncertain, the passage in Plutarch corroborates the idea that the dualistic struggle of Ahura Mazdā and Ahriman and the division of world history into set periods were at home in Persian thought at the beginning of the Hellenistic age. We know from Theompompus that the belief in resurrection was also developed by this time.[78]

Another witness to Persian apocalyptic thought that can be dated to pre-Christian times is found in the *Oracle of Hystaspes*.[79] References to this oracle are found in Justin, Clement, and Aristokritos, but our main source is the *Divine Institutions* of Lactantius. The nature of the oracle can be seen from *Div. Inst.* 7.15: "A wonderful dream, upon the interpretation of a boy who uttered divinations, announcing long before the Trojan nation that the Roman name would be taken from the world." The manner of revelation is reminiscent of Daniel 2. The content is political upheaval, but there is also a reference to the destruction of the world by fire (Justin *Apol.* 1.20). Other features of the oracle may be gathered from passages in Lactantius where Hystaspes is not explicitly mentioned but appears to be used. In *Div. Inst.* 7.16 there is a description of the signs of the end that shows several parallels with the *Bahman Yasht*, and to a lesser extent with the *Bundahišn*. In *Div. Inst.* 7.17 there is a reference to a "great king" who has been variously identified as Mithras, Sošiyans, or a national king.[80] Further, Aristokritos, in the passage that refers to Hystaspes, indicates that "the fulfillment would take place after the fulfillment of 6,000 years." Lactantius (*Div. Inst.* 7.14) says that six saecula would elapse before the reign of Christ. Presumably, then, Hystaspes had a schema of six thousand (or seven thousand) years, in contrast to the twelve thousand of the *Bundahišn*. The *Oracle of Hystaspes* has been dated to the first, or possibly the second, century B.C.E.[81] It is not an apocalypse in form, but it throws important light on Persian eschatology, in a pre-Christian form.

It appears then that several key features of the historical apocalypses were paralleled in Persian writings already in the Hellenistic age, notably the periodization of history, eschatological woes, resurrection, and the supernatural forces of good and evil.[82] Further, the *Bahman Yasht* presents its overview of history in a revelation that is interpreted by a divine being, and in the form of an *ex eventu* prophecy. If this accurately represents the Avestan Yasht, then it may well be that the generic framework or *Rahmengattung* had already been developed by the Persians and was adapted by the Jews. In view of the problems of dating, this can be no more than a possibility. Even if it were true, we should still have to allow for considerable freedom in the Jewish adaptations, since the Persian conception of a sequence of millennia is quite different from what we find in the Jewish apocalypses. The *Bahman Yasht* itself cannot be regarded as the prototype of any Jewish apocalypse, although it is certainly relevant to the discussion of Daniel.

Persian analogues can also be found for the second type of apocalypse which involves a heavenly journey. Here again there is a full-blown apocalypse in the *Book of Arda Viraf*, but it dates from the ninth century.[83] Viraf was a priest who drugged himself to release his spirit to explore the fate of the dead. The book describes his visions of heaven and hell, attended by interpreting angels. The name Viraf occurs in the Avesta, and the book has been thought to have an old kernel; but, of course, any earlier form is hypothetical. The motif of the ascent of the soul is certainly old in Persian tradition.[84] Here again the general outline of this type of apocalypse may have had Persian precedents, but we cannot be certain, because of the dating problem.

The Persian parallels to the apocalyptic genre are more comprehensive in nature than what we find in either postexilic prophecy or the Babylonian prophecies.[85] Yet even if the Persian apocalypses could be dated securely to the Hellenistic age, the Jewish genre cannot be regarded as a simple borrowing, since it is adapted to the needs of Jewish monotheism. Some features of the apocalypses, such as the periodization of history, do indeed seem to be Persian in origin, but the actual motifs in which the Jewish revelations are expressed are drawn predominantly from Jewish tradition. In short, whatever was taken over from Persian apocalypticism was thoroughly reconceived and integrated with other strands of thought.

THE HELLENISTIC MILIEU

Neither the Babylonian nor the Persian material can be conceived as an exclusive matrix for Jewish apocalypticism. There was some interpenetration of Persian and Babylonian ideas in any case, and both circulated widely in the Hellenistic world.[86] The division of history into a set number of periods is attributed to the pagan sibyl of Cumae in Italy, and the famous schema of four kingdoms, which may also be Persian in origin, is attested in several Roman sources.[87] Chaldean astronomy and astrology enjoyed widespread currency in the Hellenistic age.[88] Analogous material is found in the astrological oracles of Nechepso and Petosiris from Egypt in the second century B.C.E. In the broadest sense the matrix of the Jewish apocalypses is not any single tradition but the Hellenistic milieu, where motifs from various traditions circulated freely.[89]

The affinities of the apocalypses with widespread Hellenistic conceptions can be seen by considering two clusters of texts, the first involving otherworldly journeys, the second, eschatological prophecy. The motif of the otherworldly journey, both ascent to heaven and descent to the netherworld, was widespread in antiquity and is found already in Homer's *Odyssey*, Book 11.[90] The motif was sufficiently widespread in the early third century B.C.E. to inspire the satire of Menippus of Gadara (in Palestine). In Plato's Myth of Er (*Republic*, Book 10) the journey motif is used to convey a revelation about the judgment of the dead, and Plato's work served as a model for Cicero in the *Somnium Scipionis* and Plutarch (*De genio Socratis* 21–22 and *De sera numinis vindicta* 22–31).[91] This classical tradition is marked by strong philosophical interests, which are quite different from what we find in the Jewish apocalypses, but the similarities in the conceptual structure are nonetheless noteworthy. Another, less philosophical kind of otherworldly journey is found in Virgil's *Aeneid*, Book 6, where Aeneas is accompanied to Hades by the sibyl. In this case there is also a "prophecy" of the future greatness of Rome. The parodies of Lucian, based on those of Menippus, would suggest that the motif of the otherworldly journey must have been well known in the Greco-Roman world. It is of interest that in the *Nekyomanteia*, Menippus is said to go to Babylon to find a magus to accompany him on his descent. It is possible that the Greek use of this motif was influenced by eastern prototypes to some extent, although it was developed in a thoroughly Hellenistic way.

These otherworldly journeys provide parallels for the apocalypses which deal primarily with personal eschatology or life after death. The most noteworthy similarities are found in the Diaspora apocalypses, such as 2 *Enoch* and the *Testament of Abraham*, which probably date from the first century c.e. There are, of course, significant diffierences in detail—for example, the belief in reincarnation. Plato's Myth of Er is quite alien to the Jewish tradition. Yet the interest in the judgment of the dead is one of the motifs that clearly distinguish the Jewish apocalypses from the earlier biblical tradition. It is noteworthy that belief in afterlife was widespread in the Hellenistic age in many forms, from Plato's adaptation of the Orphic myths to popular notions of astral immortality.

The second cluster of relevant texts consists of eschatological prophecies.[92] We have already noted the use of *ex eventu* prophecy in the Babylonian tradition. An early Hellenistic example of this phenomenon is found in the *Alexandra* of Lycophron, an obscure learned poem that purports to be the prophecy of Cassandra or Alexandra.[93] Its purpose is apparently to glorify the Trojans and their descendants, the Romans. The four-kingdom schema apparently originated in the context of Near Eastern resistance to Greek and Roman rule, but it was then adapted by the Romans for their purpose. The most significant parallels to the Jewish apocalypses are found in the anti-Hellenistic oracles of various Near Eastern traditions. Here mention should be made of the Babylonian *Dynastic Prophecy* and the Persian *Oracle of Hystaspes* (and possibly *Bahman Yasht*). In Egypt there was an ongoing tradition of such prophecy, which had its native antecedents in ancient works such as the "Admonitions of Ipuwer" and the "Vision of Neferrohu."[94] From the Hellenistic period we have the *Demotic Chronicle*, which is written as a "pesher"-like commentary on ancient oracles. The commentary provides *ex eventu* prophecies of the oppression of Egypt by Persians and Greeks and prophesies a future king who will set things right.[95] Another Demotic text, the *Oracle of the Lamb to Bocchoris*, predicts an invasion of Egypt from Syria, followed by nine hundred years of oppression, but ending with a restoration. The most famous example of Hellenistic Egyptian prophecy is the *Potter's Oracle*, which is preserved in, and was probably composed in, Greek.[96] It contains a "prophecy" of Greek domination, followed by cosmic and social chaos and a war with a king from Syria. Finally, Alexandria will be laid waste and a king will come from the sun, sent by the great goddess Isis, to restore Egypt. It has been argued that a later redaction of this text speaks of cosmic renewal rather than national restoration.[97]

These political prophecies typically claim to have been issued in an ancient time—the *Demotic Chronicle* under Pharaoh Tachos, the *Potter's*

Oracle under King Amenhotep, etc. They also draw on ancient traditions. The *Potter's Oracle* draws on the structure of Egyptian creation myths and echoes the prophecy of Neferty from the twentieth century B.C.E. Naturally, an Egyptian oracle draws on primarily Egyptian traditions, but the implication is that even when the Jewish apocalypses draw on biblical or Canaanite traditions, such retrieval of ancient imagery is a common phenomenon of the Hellenistic age.[98]

These Hellenistic parallels do not argue that the apocalyptic genre is derived from Hellenistic culture or that the Jewish apocalypses lack their own originality and integrity. In Rolf Knierim's terms, the Hellenistic world furnishes some of the codes that are used in the apocalypses. It remains true that the apocalypses draw heavily on biblical tradition and that common Hellenistic motifs take on a distinctive appearance in a Jewish context. The pseudonymous authors of the apocalypses are, predominantly, patriarchs and leaders from biblical history, and the ancient traditions to which the Jewish writers looked were predominantly their own. It is equally true, however, that Jewish tradition is adapted in ways that are broadly typical of the Hellenistic age. It is important that several of the most prominent aspects of the apocalypses involve modifications of biblical tradition that are in accord with widespread ideas of the Hellenistic age: pseudepigraphy, periodization, *ex eventu* prophecy, heavenly journeys, interest in the heavenly world, judgment of the dead. In the earliest Jewish apocalypses these motifs are woven together with considerable originality, and indeed variety, into a composite structure that was distinctively Jewish but was also strikingly new, as over against the earlier biblical tradition.

The Hellenistic parallels may be explained by two factors. First, the conquests of Alexander brought changes that were common to the entire Near East. The network of Hellenistic cities facilitated the spread of ideas. Hence we get the sense of a *Zeitgeist*, of a common atmosphere of ideas and attitudes, even when they are not clearly articulated and when we cannot document specific borrowings. Second, the spread of Hellenism changed the political and social circumstances of the Near East. The Jews had lost their native kingship at the time of the Babylonian exile. Now the Egyptians and Babylonians had lost theirs too. When the *Potter's Oracle* anticipates the coming of an ideal king, we need not suppose that it has been influenced by Jewish messianism or vice versa. Similar circumstances could produce similar effects in traditions that had considerable similarity to begin with.[99] The Hellenistic age was marked by widespread nostalgia for the past and alienation from the present. In a broad sense this "Hellenistic mood" may be considered a matrix for the apocalyptic literature.

THE SOCIAL SETTINGS

The more specific social and historical matrices of the apocalyptic literature will be discussed in relation to the specific texts. Older scholarship in this area has suffered from excessive hastiness because of the tendency to assume that the setting of one or two well-known apocalypses is representative of the whole genre. We will refrain deliberately from applying a sociological or anthropological model.[100] Such models may well prove to be illuminating, but if they are to be used validly they must presuppose an adequate literary understanding of the apocalypses. We cannot assume a priori that the Enoch literature attests the same phenomenon that anthropologists, on the basis of very different evidence, call a millenarian movement or "apocalyptic religion."

When we approach the question of social setting inductively, it is apparent that some commonplace assumptions are in need of qualification. There is no basis for the assumption that all the apocalyptic literature was produced by a single movement.[101] We may speak of apocalyptic movements in specific cases such as Qumran and early Christianity. There are also clusters of texts, such as the early Enoch books, which belong to a common tradition. In those cases we may assume some social and historical continuity on the part of the authors. It is not apparent, however, that the authors of Daniel belonged to the same circles as those of *1 Enoch*. *4 Ezra* and *2 Baruch* represent a very different theological tradition from the Enoch literature. It is misleading, then, to speak of "the apocalyptic movement"[102] as though it were a single unified social phenomenon.

P. Vielhauer's thesis that the apocalypses were conventicle literature finds some support in the case of Qumran (where the sectarian literature is "apocalyptic" in a broader sense, though not in the form of apocalypses). It is possible, but only hypothetical, that the Enoch literature originated in conventicles. The thesis would have to be modified somewhat for a work like Daniel and has no apparent justification in the case of 4 Ezra or *2 Baruch*. The "conventicle" theory of apocalypticism is at best an unwarranted generalization.

Vielhauer's broader thesis, that the apocalypses were "written out of actual distresses" holds true, if we allow that the distresses may be of various kinds.[103] Daniel 7–12 was written in the heat of persecution, but this seems to be rather exceptional. 4 Ezra and 2 and 3 *Baruch* reflect the aftermath of the destruction of Jerusalem after a considerable interval. The kind of division within the community which Hanson posits as the matrix of postexilic prophecy may have been generative in the case of the Qumran community, but it is by no means a constant factor. In some cases, such as the Book of the Watchers, we cannot specify the underlying crisis with any confidence. We must also reckon with the fact that what is perceived as a crisis by an apocalyptic author cannot always be accepted as objective reality.[104]

THE COMPOSITIONAL SETTING

The apocalyptic literature is a "scribal phenomenon,"[105] a product of learned activity rather than popular folklore. The pseudonymous authors are frequently identified as wise men or scribes—Enoch, Daniel, Ezra, Baruch.[106] The pervasive allusions to biblical and other traditional lore most probably reflect systematic study. Our clearest illustrations of the use of scripture in this period are found in the Qumran writings, which reflect the constant study of the sacred writings that was practiced by the members of the community. This literature was esoteric insofar as it was produced by the learned few, but it was not necessarily designed to be kept secret. The wise in Daniel were to instruct the masses, presumably by divulging their revelations. Even in 4 Ezra 14, where we are told that seventy books are reserved for the wise among the people, it would seem that the time has come to make this material available to the larger public.

A more difficult question concerns the authenticity of the visionary experiences recorded in the apocalypses. On the one hand there are manifold resemblances between the vision accounts and the experience of visionaries and shamans elsewhere (e.g., the visionaries often fast or make other preparations for reception of visions).[107] On the other hand the phenomenon of pseudonymity complicates the issue, since we do not hear elsewhere of pseudonymous shamans.

Pseudonymity was very widespread in the Hellenistic age.[108] It is attested in Babylonian, Persian, and Egyptian prophecy, and in various Greek and Latin genres. It cannot be explained simply as a consequence of the decline of Israelite prophecy,[109] although it does imply a heightened veneration of the past. The theory that it was intended to shelter the real authors from persecution is also unsatisfactory:[110] not all the apocalypses would have provoked persecution, and some apocalyptic writers would in any case have welcomed martyrdom (compare Daniel 11). There is no doubt that a pseudonym such as Enoch or Abraham enhanced the authority of a writing. It also augmented a sense of determinism, especially in the "historical" apocalypses, by affirming that the course of history or the structure of the cosmos was determined long ago. In many cases, the presumed analogy between the situations of the ancient sage and the real author helped to provide perspective on the present. In view of the extent of the phenomenon, we must assume that the authors of this literature were conscious of its conventional character. At the same time, the effectiveness of the device presupposes the credulity of the masses.[111]

To say that pseudonymity was a device is not to say that it was used arbitrarily. The pseudonym had to be appropriate for the subject matter. So heavenly revelations could aptly be ascribed to Enoch, but a wisdom book was more appropriate to Solomon. How far the real author can be said to have identified with his pseudonymous counterpart is more difficult to say. C. Rowland appeals to J. Lindblom's discussion of visionary psychology for the view that "frequently the visionary distinguishes between two persons representing himself; the one being his everyday *ego*, the other the extraordinary *ego*,"[112] but he admits that this phenomenon is still some distance from the pseudonymity of the apocalypses. The psychology of pseudonymity is closely related to the question of the authenticity of the visions. Rowland suggests that many (not necessarily all) apocalyptic visions were experienced in the context of reflection on scripture. In general it would seem that the underlying problems addressed in the visions were not exegetical but concerned historical and existential matters. The scriptures provided at most the occasion of the revelation. The contrast between "authentic religious experience" and literary activity may be overdrawn. The composition of highly symbolic literature involves a vivid use of the imagination, which may be difficult to distinguish from visionary experience in any case. Similarly, the apocalyptists may have felt an intense and emotional kinship with their pseudonymous counterparts, while still being aware of the fiction involved. It is worth bearing in mind that even shamans have to learn the cosmology and mythology of their ascents before they can "experience" them in ecstasy.[113]

THE LITERARY FUNCTION

From the preceding discussion it is apparent that the settings of the apocalyptic genre present complex problems and that generalizations are of limited value. It is possible, however, to speak of the illocution or literary function of a text apart from the social setting. David Hellholm has proposed that the definition of apocalypse in *Semeia* 14 be emended by the following addition: "*intended for a group in crisis with the purpose of exhortation and/or consolation by means of divine authority.*"[114]

The reference to a "group in crisis" is appropriate for many apocalypses, though scarcely for all; but it is perhaps too suggestive of the conventicle theory of apocalypticism. It is true, however, that all apocalypses address some underlying problem. It is obvious enough that the manner of revelation is designed to lend supernatural authority to the message (the divinity is not always directly invoked). The main problem with specifying the function in the definition is that even on this general level the purpose of a text may be a matter of dispute. Is the function of 4 Ezra to console or to instruct and refute? Even if we concluded that its purpose was refutation (of a heretical party represented by Ezra, as some have claimed), 4 Ezra would surely be still an apocalypse.

In fact, however, the illocutionary functions of exhortation and consolation can generally be maintained for the Jewish apocalypses.[115] Two qualifications must be kept in mind. First, the nature of the exhortations may vary. The Animal Apocalypse in *1 Enoch* encourages support for the Maccabean revolt. The message of Daniel, in the same setting, is quite different. Second, the literary function must be seen to be integrally related to form and content in what may be called the "apocalyptic technique." Whatever the underlying problem, it is viewed from a distinctive apocalyptic perspective. This perspective is framed spatially by the supernatural world and temporally by the eschatological judgment. The problem is not viewed simply in terms of the historical factors available to any observer. Rather it is viewed in the light of a transcendent reality disclosed by the apocalypse. The transcendent world may be expressed through mythological symbolism or celestial geography or both. It puts the problem in perspective and projects a definitive resolution to come. This apocalyptic technique does not, of course, have a publicly discernible effect on a historical crisis, but it provides a resolution in the imagination by instilling conviction in the revealed "knowledge" that it imparts. The function of the apocalyptic literature is to shape one's imaginative perception of a situation and so lay the basis for whatever course of action it exhorts.

2
The Early
Enoch Literature

THE PUBLICATION of the Ethiopic *Book of Enoch* in the early nineteenth century was a major stimulus to the modern study of apocalyptic literature, in recent years the publication of the Aramaic fragments of *Enoch* from Qumran has intensified interest in the subject and changed our conception of its history. In fact, *1 Enoch* is not just one work, but is a major collection of apocalyptic writings. Five separate compositions have long been distinguished: the Book of the Watchers (chaps. 1–36), the Similitudes (chaps. 37–71), the Astronomical Book (chaps. 72–82), the Book of Dreams (chaps. 83–90) and the Epistle of Enoch (chaps. 91–108). Within the Epistle, the Apocalypse of Weeks (93:1–10; 91:11–17) stands out as a distinct unit.[1] The full corpus of *1 Enoch* is only extant in Ethiopic.[2] Substantial portions of the first and fifth parts and a passage from the fourth have been discovered in Greek.[3] In recent years Aramaic fragments of all parts except the Similitudes have been found at Qumran. In the Qumran scrolls the Book of Giants was copied in the place of the Similitudes. The editor of the Aramaic fragments, J. T. Milik, argued that the five books that make up *1 Enoch* constituted an Enochic pentateuch, which was a counterpart of the Mosaic pentateuch.[4] The Astronomical Book, however, was copied on a separate scroll. There is no textual evidence that the Enochic corpus was conceived as a pentateuch or correlated with the Mosaic Torah. A more plausible suggestion is that the order of the collection reflects the sequence of Enoch's supposed career.[5]

Charles was already aware that the earliest sections of *1 Enoch* were written before the Maccabean revolt. The discoveries at Qumran considerably strengthened the evidence. The earliest manuscript of the Astronomical Book is dated by Milik to "the end of the third or the beginning of the second century."[6] The oldest fragments of the Book of the Watchers are ascribed to the first half of the second century. Since the compositions are presumably somewhat older than the earliest fragments, and since the Book of the Watchers shows evidence of multiple stages of composition, it is probable that both these works were extant in some form already in the third century B.C.E.[7] Indeed Milik has argued that both the Astronomical Book and the Book of the Watchers are presupposed in Genesis 5-6. It seems clear enough that Genesis is alluding to some more extensive traditions, but the correspondences between the biblical text and *1 Enoch* can be more satisfactorily explained on the assumption that Genesis is prior. The link between Enoch and the fallen angels is neither made nor presumed in Genesis, but rather seems to have been suggested by the juxtaposition of these episodes in the biblical story. No section of *1 Enoch* as we have it can be dated prior to the Hellenistic age, although it undoubtedly draws on older traditions.

THE FIGURE OF ENOCH

The figure of Enoch is a highly enigmatic one in the biblical text. In Gen 5:18-24 we read that Enoch was the son of Jared and the father of Methuselah. "Thus, all the days of Enoch were three hundred and sixty-five years. Enoch walked with God; and he was not, for God took him."[8] Evidently this brief notice does not imply the full account of Enoch's otherworldly journeys which we find in *1 Enoch*, but is rather the seed from which later speculation grew. We do not know how elaborate a story is presupposed in Genesis. The biblical allusion does, however, contain some intriguing indications of the context in which Enoch speculation developed.[9]

Enoch is listed in Genesis as seventh in line from Adam. In the Sumerian King List, the seventh king is Enmeduranki or Enmenduranna. Sippar, the city ruled by this king, was a center of the cult of Shamash, the sun god. Enoch is associated with the solar calendar: his age is given as 365 years in Genesis and the Astronomical Book presupposes a calendar of 364 days. Enmeduranki was also the founder of a guild of diviners and a recipient of revelations. His enthronement is described as follows:[10]

> Šamaš in Ebabbarra [appointed]
> Enmeduranki, [king of Sippar]
> the beloved of Anu, Enlil [and Ea].
> Šamaš and Adad [brought him in] to their assembly.
> Šamaš and Adad set him on a large throne of gold;
> they showed him how to observe oil on water,

a mystery of Anu, they gave him
the tablet of the gods, the liver,
a secret of heaven [and the underworld],
they put in his hand the cedar (rod), beloved of the great gods."

This text is of interest in view of the elevation of Enoch, and especially in view of his identification with the "Son of Man" figure in *1 Enoch* 71. Enoch's wisdom is derived from "the heavenly vision . . . the words of the holy angels and . . . the tablets of heaven" (93:2). Evidently the biblical seventh man emulates the Mesopotamian seventh king.

Other Mesopotamian analogies can be found for the figure of Enoch. Utuabzu, the seventh sage, a contemporary of Enmeduranki, was said to have been taken up to heaven.[11] A noteworthy parallel to the translation of Enoch (by which "God took him") is found in the epic of Gilgamesh. There, after the flood had subsided, the god Enlil declared to Utna-pishtim/Atrahasis, the flood hero:

"Hitherto Utnapishtim has been but human.
Henceforth Utnapishtim and his wife shall be like us gods.
Utnapishtim shall reside far away, at the mouth of the rivers!"
Then they took me and made me reside far away,
At the mouth of the rivers.[12]

The biblical equivalent of Utnapishtim is Noah, but it is Enoch, not Noah, who is "taken" by God. It is also noteworthy that Ea "let Atrahasis see a dream and he perceived the secret of the gods"[13]—specifically the imminent flood. We might compare Enoch's dream-vision of the destruction of the earth in *1 Enoch* 83. Enoch had also acquired some features of the Mesopotamian flood hero.

We should not attempt to identify one Mesopotamian figure as the sole, sufficient prototype of Enoch. Rather the Jewish figure picks up and combines elements associated with various mythical heroes. The purpose of the development of this Enoch legend vis-à-vis Mesopotamian legend is clear enough. The peoples of the ancient Near East engaged in what might be called "competitive historiography" to show how their national heroes outshone the heroes of other peoples or were the true and most ancient founders of culture.[14] The Babylonian Berossus and the Egyptian Manetho produced national histories in Greek in the third century which stressed the antiquity of their own peoples. A fragment of a Samaritan work that Eusebius incorrectly ascribed to Eupolemus claims that Enoch, not the Egyptians, invented astrology and that he was really identical with Atlas, to whom the Greeks ascribe the invention.[15] The parallels between Enoch and the legendary Mesopotamian figures suggest that Enoch was developed as a Jewish counterpart of such heroes as Enmeduranki—no less than them in antiquity, status, or access to divine knowledge. Insofar as he combined traits of various heroes he might be said to be superior to any of them. The most natural setting for the development of the figure of Enoch, with its strong Babylonian associations, was surely the eastern Diaspora, although the extant Enoch books may still have been composed in Judea, and some of them certainly were.

The figure of Enoch, then, might be viewed from one aspect as an answer to the heroes for whom the Babylonians claimed great wisdom and revelatory power. The figure was also of significance within the Jewish tradition. Since Enoch was mysteriously "taken" by God, he was well qualified to be the revealer of heavenly mysteries. Further, he was more ancient than Moses and was associated with primordial history. There is no necessary opposition between Enoch and Moses, but Enoch could serve as the authority for a revelation over and above that of Moses. We should also note that Enoch is not associated with the distinctive history of Israel but with the primordial history of all humanity.

THE BOOK OF THE WATCHERS

The Book of the Watchers may serve as our introduction to the Enoch literature, since it is one of the oldest, pre-Maccabean Enochic works and gives the most explicit elaboration of the story of Enoch. It has received extensive attention in recent years.[16] Much of the discussion has focused on smaller units within *1 Enoch* 1–36: chaps. 6–11, 6–16, or 6–19. There is no doubt that the book is composite in origin, although it is questionable whether we can separate the strands exactly or profitably discuss the date and provenance of the components. It is also clear that the various sources have been woven together into a unified whole. The earliest fragments, 4QEn[a] extend from 1:1–6 to 12:4–6. The apparently distinct unit of chaps. 6–11 was already integrated into a larger whole. The full book of chaps. 1–36 is fragmentarily represented in manuscripts from the first century C.E. but seems to be presupposed already in the book of *Jubilees* in the mid second century B.C.E.[17] Milik maintains that the Qumran manuscripts "allow us to establish that from the first half of the second century onwards the *Book of the Watchers* had essentially the same form as that in which it is known through the Greek and Ethiopic versions."[18]

The book may be divided into three main sections: chaps. 1–5, 6–16, and 17–36.

THE INTRODUCTION

Chapters 1–5 constitute an introduction. The book is characterized as "the words of the blessing of Enoch according to which he blessed the chosen and righteous who must be present on the day of distress (which is appointed) for the removal of all the wicked and impious" (1:1). The "chosen" and "righteous" are stereotyped designations in the Enoch literature. We will return below to the question whether they indicate a distinct group or movement. The term "blessing" recalls the Blessing of Moses in Deuteronomy 33. It evidently refers to the destiny of the righteous on "the day of distress." Already from the opening verse, the book has an eschatological horizon: it is ultimately concerned with the final judgment of righteous and wicked. The second verse adds a second characterization which is more obviously appropriate: "a holy vision in the heavens which the angels showed to me." Although Enoch is described in terms reminiscent of Balaam's oracle ("whose eyes were opened") the manner of revelation goes beyond the conventions of the prophets and is typically apocalyptic. Since Enoch is supposed to have lived in primordial times, his revelation is inevitably "for a distant generation."

The initial characterization of the book is followed by a prophecy of God's coming in judgment, reminiscent of the theophanies in Deuteronomy 33, Judges 5, Habakkuk 3, Micah 1, etc.[19] In Deuteronomy 33, God comes *from* Sinai. Here he comes from "his dwelling" and will tread from there upon Mount Sinai. The slight change is significant. Sinai has a place in Enoch's revelation, but it is not the ultimate source. The Watchers, whose story is told in *1 Enoch* 6–16 are said to shake at the revelation of God. The story of the Watchers, then, is clearly oriented toward this eschatological horizon. finally, we note that "he comes with ten thousand holy ones." A similar, even greater, angelic entourage will surround the Ancient of Days in Daniel. This angelic world forms the backdrop for the human action in both books.

The remainder of the introduction, chaps. 2–5, sets the scene for the judgment in a different manner. Here the idiom is closer to the wisdom literature. The reader is invited to contemplate and consider all the works of nature, how "they do not transgress their law." In contrast "you have not persevered, nor observed the law of the Lord." As a result, Enoch pronounces curses on the wicked, but predicts a blessed state for the "chosen."

The reference to "the law of the Lord" is of some importance for understanding the Book of the Watchers. Lars Hartman has argued at length that the "referential background" of *1 Enoch* 1–5 is the Mosaic covenant.[20] This is indicated, for Hartman, by the allusion to Mount Sinai, the terminology of the denouncement speech, the echoes of the last chapters of

Deuteronomy, and the constellation of blessing and curse motifs. These motifs are indeed present, but they are placed in a new context here. The most obvious "law of the Lord" in chaps. 2–5 is not the law of Moses, which was unknown in the fictive time of Enoch, but the law of nature. The sinfulness of the wicked is demonstrated in contrast to the orderliness of nature, not by the special revelation of Sinai. To be sure, there is no suggestion that Sinai is at variance with the laws of nature, but the ultimate authority is older than Moses and applies not only to Israel but to all humanity. The contrast between the order of nature and the disorder of sinful humanity forms the backdrop for the eschatological judgment.

1 Enoch 1–5 is not very explicit about the eschatological rewards of the chosen: "for the chosen there will be light and joy and peace and they will inherit the earth" (5:7). The impression given is of a utopian life on earth "in eternal peace all the days of their life" (5:9). We might compare the "new creation" in Isa 65:17–25, where "the child shall die a hundred years old." This picture will be complemented in the later chapters. Constitutive of the blessed state is the gift of wisdom: "when wisdom is given to the chosen, they will all live, and will not again do wrong" (5:8). Wisdom here is a gift that is given only through supernatural revelation. The attainment of such wisdom is a recurring goal of apocalyptic literature.

The Story of the Watchers

The second section, chaps. 6–16, is an elaboration of the story of the "sons of God" in Genesis 6. The main story is in chaps. 6–11; chaps. 12–16 are transitional chapters that introduce Enoch and provide the point of departure for his revelatory journey. As transitional chapters they provide a key to the way in which the parts of the book are connected. Enoch is introduced specifically in response to the crisis caused by the Watchers, and he acts as an intermediary between them and heaven. As the text now stands, all Enoch's heavenly revelation is narrated to the Watchers—not only the unrelenting judgment of God on the Watchers themselves but also the travels in chaps. 17–36.

The story of the Watchers is itself complicated by the interweaving of distinct traditions. In one tradition the leader of the Watchers is Šemiḥazah, and the primary sin is marriage with humans and procreation of giants; in another tradition the leader is 'Aśa'el, and the primary sin is improper revelation.[21] The fact that these distinct traditions are allowed to stand in a certain degree of tension is already significant for our understanding of the function of the book. It is readily obvious that both stories have allegorical potential. Yet, unlike some other apocalyptic allegories such as Daniel, the story of the Watchers does not have a clearly identifiable referent. The situation is confused to a considerable degree by the tension between the 'Aśa'el and the Šemihazah material, but even the separate traditions are quite evasive. George Nickelsburg emphasizes the violence that pollutes the earth and ingeniously detects in the Šemihazah material a reflection of the wars of the Diadochi, the Hellenistic princes who succeeded Alexander the Great. The suggestion is attractive in view of the pretensions to divinity on the part of the Hellenistic princes and their irruption into the Near East as aliens from outside. The instruction motif in the 'Aśa'el tradition could also be easily applied to Hellenistic culture. An alternative view emphasizes the sexual sin in the Šemihazah material and adduces passages from the *Testament of Levi* and the *Damascus Document* from Qumran (CD) in support of an application to the Jerusalem priesthood.[22] These proposals need not be seen as mutually exclusive, and indeed Nickelsburg also sees polemic against the priesthood in chaps. 12–16, which he regards as a separate redactional stage.[23] At least the citations from *T. Levi* 14:1–8 and 4QTLevi[a] show that this myth could indeed be applied to the Jerusalem priesthood in the second century B.C.E. whether it was originally composed for that purpose or not.[24] Even if Nickelsburg is right that the Watchers originally referred to Hellenistic princes, we cannot confine the application of the myth to the periods of outright warfare. It could apply to the general conditions of Hellenistic rule in the east at any point in the third century. In any case the myth as it now stands, in combination with the 'Aśa'el story, must have been reapplied to other situations after the wars of the Diadochi.

APOCALYPTIC MULTIVALENCE

What we touch on here is the essential multivalence of apocalyptic symbolism. We may reasonably claim that the myth of the Watchers, both in the separate Šemihazah and 'Aśa'el traditions and in their combined form reflects some kind of crisis. The pollution of the earth is a figurative expression in any case, but the story suggests violence and lawlessness. Even here we should beware of drawing too firm a conclusion about social reality from symbolic description. *1 Enoch* 6–11 records *perceived* crises, whether the perception was generally shared or peculiar to a small group. We have no hard evidence about the historical specificity of the crises. The author chose not to refer explicitly to the wars of the Diadochi or to the Jerusalem priesthood. Instead, the problem—whatever it was—is transposed to a mythological plane. By telling the story of the Watchers rather than of the Diadochi or the priesthood, *1 Enoch* 1–36 becomes a paradigm which is not restricted to one historical situation but can be applied whenever an analogous situation arises.

In the Book of the Watchers, as in all the Jewish apocalypses, the situation of the historical author is concealed. This is effected in part through the use of the pseudonym Enoch, which imposes the setting of the fictive author on the historical situation. A typological view of history is thereby implied. The crises of the Hellenistic age are presumed to bear some analogy to the story of Enoch and the Watchers. In other Jewish apocalypses the Babylonian crisis of the sixth century often provides the filter through which later crises are viewed. The emphasis is not on the uniqueness of historical events but on recurring patterns, which assimilate the particular crisis to some event of the past whether historical or mythical.

The transposition of situations involved in apocalyptic symbolism is in itself part of the solution for the problem generating the text. By concealing the historical specificity of the immediate situation beneath the primeval archetype, the apocalyptic symbolism relieves anxiety. The resolution of the ancient conflict generated by the Watchers emerges with an inevitability that guarantees a similar resolution to the conflicts of the Hellenistic age. The superhuman status of the actors takes the action out of the sphere of human control and places the immediate situation in a deterministic perspective which also serves to relieve anxiety. This transposition of situations has been aptly illuminated by application of C. Lévi-Strauss's discussion of the effectiveness of symbols by analogy with psychotherapy.[25] The apocalyptic "cure" is effected by reexperiencing and working through the past. We might also compare Lévi-Strauss's theory on the function of myth. The perplexing problems of the present are "mediated" or obscured and so are overcome by the superimposition of the myth.[26] We should note, however, that the fear and anxiety caused by violence and lawlessness are not merely avoided. They are aroused on a grander scale by the story of the Watchers and giants, but then they are all the more effectively allayed.

The Mission of Enoch

The allegorization of the crisis is not the only way in which the apocalypse provides a therapy. The more obvious and elaborate response is found in the mission of Enoch and his heavenly journey. Whatever the stages of composition of the Book of the Watchers, the heavenly revelation is now presented in the context of Enoch's address to the Watchers. Only a brief part of that address is concerned with the divine response to their petition. The journeys of Enoch are related to the story of the Watchers insofar as they present a proper revelation, in contrast to the improper revelation of the Watchers.

To appreciate the coherence of the heavenly revelation with the story of the Watchers, we must observe that the two strands of tradition associated with Šemiḥazah and 'Aśa'el are not merely juxtaposed but are carefully intertwined. Thus, we read in chap. 7, after the Watchers had chosen wives, "And they began to go in to them and were promiscuous with them. And they taught them charms and spells, and showed to them the cutting of roots and trees. And they became pregnant and bore large giants. . . ." It is true that the instruction here breaks the sequence between the sexual union and the pregnancy, but we should not too easily assume editorial carelessness. The sexual sin of the giants is immediately associated with the improper revelation. Further, chap. 7 concludes with the violence caused by the giants, which evokes the complaint of the earth. In chap. 8, violence and fornication result from the revelations of the Watchers, and again the earth cries out. The complaint of the angels in chap. 9 puts the sin of 'Aśa'el first and says that Šemihazah revealed spells before mentioning the illicit union with women. Moreover, the sexual sin appears in chap. 9 as the occasion of the revelation: the Watchers "lay with these women, and became unclean, and revealed to them these sins" (9:8). The divine judgment in chap. 10 gives first and longest attention to Šemihazah's revelation of a mystery. In chap. 15 the main indictment is directed against the sexual sin of the Watchers, but the conclusion of chap. 16 returns to the "worthless mystery" that they made known to the women.[27]

The cry of the earth is caused by pollution[28]—mainly through violence but also through fornication. Two accounts of the source of that violence are interwoven side by side. If recent critics are correct in holding that the 'Aśa'el/revelation material was added latest we must consider whether the redactor wished to offer a reinterpretation of the sexual myth in terms of inappropriate revelation. Given the long traditional usage in the Hebrew prophets of fornication as a metaphor for religious infidelity, it is even possible to take the story of the descent of the Watchers as a metaphorical expression of illicit revelation. The understanding of the sin of the Watchers as improper revelation provides the obvious counterpart of the proper revelation of Enoch in the rest of the book. In view of these considerations, it would seem that the 'Aśa'el tradition was not merely added but significantly influenced the final shape of the book.

THE THRONE VISION

The heavenly revelation of Enoch occupies more than half the entire Book of the Watchers. The revelation begins with Enoch's ascent to heaven in 14:8. He then proceeds through a house that was "hot as fire and cold as snow" and then another, larger house that was built of a tongue of fire. Here he sees a high throne, beneath which flow rivers of burning fire. On it sat "He who is great in glory" whose "raiment is brighter than the sun and whiter than any snow." Ten thousand times ten thousand stood before him and the Holy Ones who were near him did not depart from him. This divine figure then gives Enoch his response for the Watchers: "You ought to petition on behalf of men, not men on behalf of you . . . (15:2). You were in heaven, but (its) secrets had not yet been revealed to you and a worthless mystery you knew." Say to them therefore "you have no peace" (16:4).

This throne vision has recently attracted attention as "the oldest Merkavah vision we know of from the literature outside of the canonical Scriptures."[29] The vision raises intriguing questions about the development of Jewish mysticism. The detailed observations on the heavenly "house," its effect on Enoch, and the throne itself go beyond the biblical prototypes and surely presuppose mystical speculation.[30] The vision also illustrates the mystical component in apocalyptic literature. The correspondences to Daniel 7 in the appearance of the divinity, the rivers of fire beneath the throne, and the entourage of Holy Ones (ten thousand times ten thousand) suggest that even the more historically oriented apocalypses drew on mystical traditions.[31] The context of the vision here must also be noted. While the scene is not specifically a court scene, as in Daniel, it is the setting for the divine condemnation of the Watchers. The numinous elements in the vision such as the repeated fire imagery and the careful observation of Enoch's terrified reaction ("fear covered me and trembling took hold of me," 14:13) acquire added significance in this context. If the vision is so awesome that even the righteous Enoch shakes and trembles, how much more should those who face condemnation be terrified. The primary purpose of the vision, however, is surely to establish Enoch's authority. Enoch's acceptance into the presence of God inevitably enhances the status of his entire revelation.

THE OTHERWORLDLY JOURNEY

In chap. 17 Enoch begins his tour, guided by the angels. The places he visits are mostly located at the extremities of this world, but they are accessible to no other human.[32] What he sees are the foundations of the universe, from the water of life to the mouth of the deep. Again, this material surely draws on a learned tradition of cosmological speculation. In the context in *1 Enoch* 1–36, however, the speculation is by no means disinterested. The first stage of the tour culminates with "the prison for the stars of heaven and the host of heaven" (18:14), where they are kept until the great judgment day. If the book at one time ended at 19:3,[33] the point of the tour in chaps. 17–19 would seem to be to reinforce the certainty of the judgment by showing that the place of judgment is "really" there, thereby amplifying the fear of God.

As it now stands, however, the tour is prolonged in chap. 21. The extension in chaps. 21–23 is primarily eschatological. Chapter 22 describes the places where the "spirits of the souls of the dead" will be kept until the day of judgment. These are in three compartments: the righteous, the wicked who were not punished on earth, and sinners who were killed.[34] The eschatological interest persists in chap. 25 with a discourse about a fragrant tree that will be given to the righteous when God "comes down to visit the earth for good," and in chaps. 26–27 with a description of Gehenna. Only in chaps. 28–36 is explicit eschatological material lacking. These chapters fill out the comprehensive tour of the ends of the earth and include the Garden of Eden in chap. 32.

Even if the eschatological material of chaps. 21–23 is an extension of the original book, it is only making explicit what was implied all along. The judgment of the Watchers is paradigmatic for human sinners. These chapters do, however, add a dimension to the eschatology of the book by addresssing the judgment of the dead. Chapter 5 had spoken of the life of the righteous in a rather this-worldly manner reminiscent of the prophets. In chaps. 10–11 the resolution of the crisis with the Watchers provides a prototype for the eschatological judgment. On the one hand, the angel Raphael is told to "bind Azazel by his hands and his feet, and throw him into the darkness. And split open the desert which is in Dudael and throw him there. And throw on him jagged and sharp stones, and cover him with darkness; and let him stay there forever, and cover his face, that he may not see light and that on the great day of judgment he may be hurled into the fire" (10:4–6, trans. Knibb). Correspondingly, Šemiḥazah and his followers are bound "under the hills of the earth until the day of their judgment and of their consummation, until the judgment which is for all eternity is accomplished. And in those days they will lead them to the abyss of fire; in torment and in prison they will be shut up for all eternity" (10:12–13). On the other hand, Raphael is also told to "restore the earth which the angels have ruined" (10:7). This is further explicated in 10:16–22: "And let the plant of righteousness and truth appear . . . and now all the righteous will be humble, and will live until they beget thousands; and all the days of their youth and their sabbaths they will fulfil in peace." The resolution of the crisis with the Watchers, then, has two aspects: the confinement of the sinners until the final judgment, and the present healing of the earth. In view of chaps. 21–22 it appears that the final judgment is not only for the Watchers. The spirits of the dead, both righteous and wicked, are also kept for a day of judgment. This judgment of the dead is not clearly correlated with the hope that the earth will be healed. In chaps. 10–11 the earthly restoration is "for all the generations of eternity," but then in 10:10 "eternal life" is synonymous with "five hundred years." In short, it is not clear whether the earthly restoration is terminated or at all affected by the final judgment. The author of the Book of the Watchers is not attempting to give a precise account of eschatological developments.

It is apparent that he looks for a restoration on earth, which will be definitively satisfying, whether it lasts forever or not. It is also clear from chap. 22 that he looks for a judgment of the dead beyond this life, where the destiny of righteous and wicked is ultimately decided.

Enoch's journey has no close parallel in the Hebrew scriptures, and it does not appear to be closely modeled on a nonbiblical source either. Partial analogies abound. We have noted Enoch's affinities with the Mesopotamian heroes Enmeduranki and Utuabzu, both of whom were said to ascend to heaven. Enoch's journeys are in a limited way reminiscent of the journeys of Gilgamesh. Both Babylonian and Greek motifs are used in the description of the abodes of the dead in chap. 22.[35] The widespread motif of heavenly ascent provides a general backdrop, but Enoch's development of the motif is distinctive. The Book of the Watchers is even significantly different from the ascents we find in later Jewish apocalypses, which describe a more orderly ascent through a set number of heavens. We must acknowledge, then, a considerable degree of originality here in the way that various traditional motifs are combined. The possibility that the author had a mystical experience cannot be discounted, but we can more profitably discuss the work as a literary product, and consider its function and effect.

One model for understanding Enoch's journey has been derived from ancient Near Eastern diplomacy as illustrated in 2 Kings 20, where Hezekiah displays his treasures to the Babylonian envoys.[36] The function of the display is to impress and intimidate. This proposal is helpful up to a point in clarifying the rationale for the tour. The heavenly realm is often modeled on the conventions of royalty in Near Eastern mythology—hence such conceptions as the divine council, the celestial guardians, and perhaps also the treasuries. Yet the analogy with royal diplomacy does not adequately account for some fundamental aspects of the Enoch story. It is of crucial importance that Enoch's journey takes him outside the world that is normally accessible to humanity. His successful and appropriate elevation to the heavenly world provides the counterpart of the disastrous descent of the Watchers. It is because of the supernatural location of his journey that his revelation qualifies as a "mystery" surpassing the worthless mystery of the giants. The elements of mystery and mysticism in the ascent and journey are not clarified by the diplomatic practice reflected in 2 Kings 20. Again, the story in 2 Kings provides no explicit analogy for the correlation of cosmology and judgment, which not only is essential to 1 Enoch but also is typical of other apocalypses. Even the details of the tour are necessarily concerned with cosmological marvels of a different order from the splendors of an earthly kingdom.

Yet the tour does indeed display God's wisdom and power. It also establishes the wisdom of Enoch, but this wisdom depends on divine revelation and so on the power and wisdom of God. This dependence is made very explicit also in Daniel and is indeed typical of apocalyptic literature. The intimate connection of power and wisdom is shown also in the equivalence of the "tablets of wisdom" and the "tablets of destiny" in Mesopotamian texts. [37]

The demonstration of power has a clear enough purpose. On the level of communication internal to the text it invites the Watchers to look on the mighty works of God and despair. On the external level, the readers too must share Enoch's awe before the mysteries of creation and judgment. The emotion aroused by Enoch's journey is primarily awe—including a strong component of fear but also of hope and reassurance.

The demonstration of wisdom is no less important. On one level it convinces the Watchers of the reality of the judgment, since the place of judgment is already prepared. On the other level it enables the human beings who are submerged by the violence and corruption expressed in the story of the Watchers to believe that there is another dimension to the world. The sufferings of the present can be viewed from the perspective of ultimate transcendence. What is offered is not only hope but also knowledge, guaranteed by supernatural revelation. Its certainty is established by the wealth of cosmological detail. The comprehensive tour of the cosmos is designed to show that the destiny of humanity is not left to chance but is built into the structure of the universe. The eschatological focus is shown by the climactic location of the prison of the Watchers in chaps. 18–19 and the amount of space devoted to eschatology in chaps. 21–27. It is true that eschatology is only one component in the comprehensive view of the cosmos, but it is an essential component and is fully integrated with the cosmological speculations.

More definitively than the allegorization in chaps. 6–16, the otherworldly journey provides the response to the crisis evoked by the Watchers. Enoch's tour of the hidden regions of the cosmos provides a frame within which human problems are seen in a new perspective. Whatever crisis pollutes the earth, the foundations of the cosmos, its outer regions and the places of judgment remain intact, as of course does the heavenly court. The frame is both spatial and temporal: it refers both to the hidden regions traversed by Enoch and to the coming judgment. The Book of the Watchers does not convey the sense of an imminent ending that is characteristic of some apocalypses. It is sufficient that there is an eventual judgment. It is also important that the places of judgment are there in the present and can be contemplated through the revelation of Enoch.

THE SETTING

Our interpretation of the Book of the Watchers has proceeded on the assumption that the crisis of the fallen angels is an allegory for some crisis of the Hellenistic age. This assumption is well founded by analogy with other apocalypses. We cannot determine precisely what crisis it was that generated the Book of the Watchers, and in any case the allegory could be reapplied in several different situations. We should note that there is no indication that religious persecution is envisaged here. The original crisis may have been of a rather general nature, such as the spread of Hellenistic culture in the east.

The Book of the Watchers in itself gives us little clear indication of its specific setting. We will return below to the question of its relation to the early Enoch tradition. It casts considerable light, however, on the literary technique of an apocalypse. Whatever crisis generated this text, it is viewed from a distinctive apocalyptic perspective. The situation is transposed to the mythical time of Enoch by the device of pseudonymity. It is not described directly but is covered by the allegory of the Watchers. In this way the outcome of the crisis is already known and so is guaranteed. At the same time, the human situation is placed in perspective by the other-worldly geography, where the places of judgment are already prepared. The Book of the Watchers, then, does not explicitly address any crisis of the Hellenistic age or advocate specific conduct. Rather it provides a lens through which any crisis can be viewed. By evoking a sense of awe and instilling conviction in its revelation of the transcendent world and the coming judgment, the apocalypse enables the faithful to cope with the crises of the present and so creates the preconditions for righteous action in the face of adversity.

THE ASTRONOMICAL BOOK

The Astronomical Book, *1 Enoch* 72–82, is attested in fragments of four manuscripts from Qumran. The earliest of these dates from the end of the third or the beginning of the second century and so is the earliest of the Enoch manuscripts. The Aramaic work represented in these fragments was much longer than the text that survived in Ethiopic. Milik surmises that those who translated the Aramaic into Greek (on which the Ethiopic was based) "were at pains to shorten the voluminous, prolix and terribly monotonous original."[38]

The beginning of the book has not been preserved in Aramaic. In the Ethiopic it is introduced as:

> The book of the revolutions of the lights of heaven, each as it is, accord-
> ing to their classes, according to their (period of) rule and their times,
> according to their names and their places of origin and according to
> their months, which Uriel, the holy angel who was with me and is
> their leader showed to me; and he showed me all their regulations,
> exactly as they are, for each year of the world and forever, until the
> new creation shall be made which will last for ever. (72:1)

There is no account of the actual process of revelation, such as we usually find in an apocalypse, through the description of a vision or of a heavenly journey. We are given the content of a revelation rather than a report of the revelation itself. (This is also true of the Apocalypse of Weeks.) Yet a heavenly tour is clearly implied. Uriel is the accompanying angel or tour guide. Enoch ranges all over the heavens to the ends of the earth (76:1). In 81:5 he is brought back to earth by "three holy ones," who set him before the door of his house. This passage appears to be a secondary addition to the Astronomical Book, but the presumption of a heavenly journey is consistent with the preceding chapters.

The content of the revelation is primarily cosmological and concerned with the movements of the sun, moon, and stars. The astronomical observations are primitive in relation to Babylonian and Hellenistic knowledge, although the conception of the world definitely shows Babylonian influence.[39] The descriptions are highly mythological. The heavens are peopled with angels: "the leaders of the heads of thousands who are in charge of the whole creation and in charge of all the stars . . ." (75:1). Uriel is the leader of the lights of heaven.

The lengthy descriptions of the heavenly bodies are in part a celebration of the order of the universe. They also have an immediate purpose. They support the contention that "the year amounts to exactly three hundred and sixty-four days" (72:32). The solar calendar of 364 days is also a subject of interest in the book of *Jubilees* and in the Qumran scrolls. It is at variance with the 354-day luni-solar calendar of the rabbinic period and has usually been taken as a sign of sectarian provenance, since the calendar determined the proper observance of the festivals.[40] The Astronomical Book, however, does not make an issue of the festivals and does not polemicize against the 354-day calendar. Instead it attacks a 360-day calendar which fails to include the four additional days (75:1-2; 82:4-6), although we do not know that such a calendar was ever used in Judaism.[41] We will return below to the possible implictions of the 364-day calendar for the social setting of the Enoch literature.

Although most of the Astronomical Book is devoted to cosmological speculation, the eschatological horizon is also present. At the outset the heavenly regulations are said to hold "until the new creation" (72:1). Eschatological concerns emerge more clearly in chap. 80: "in the days of the sinners the years will become shorter. . . . And many heads of the stars in command will go astray . . . and the entire law of the stars will be closed to the sinners and the thoughts of those who dwell upon the earth will go astray over them . . . and will think them gods. And many evils will overtake them and punishment will come upon them to destroy them all." These disruptions are in marked contrast to the order of the heavens in the preceding chapters.[42] We are reminded of the contrast between orderly nature and sinful humanity in *1 Enoch* 1-5. Here the transgressions originate with the heads of the stars. Earthly sinfulness has a supernatural cause, just as it has in the story of the Watchers. The correlation of stars and angelic beings was old in Israel (see Judg 5:19-20; Job 38:7) and was ultimately derived from the belief in astral divinities which is condemned here.

Chapter 81 stands apart from the rest of the work because of its lack of cosmological interest. Here Enoch derives his explanation from "the tablets of heaven" and the book where the deeds of men are recorded. Enoch's response, "Blessed is the man who dies righteous and good . . . ," implies some form of afterlife. Milik points out that the reference to "three holy ones" who bring Enoch back to earth in 81:5 presupposes the reference to three angels in 87:3 in the Animal Apocalypse; 81:9 ("and those who practise righteousness will die because of the deeds of men") suggests a time of persecution. Chapter 81 then was probably an addition to the Astronomical Book. It serves a twofold purpose in its present context. It explains how Enoch is given one year after his heavenly journeys to impart his wisdom to Methuselah before he is finally taken up, and it gives Enoch's revelation an ethical orientation.

Chapter 82 is in the form of a parting address to Methuselah. Accordingly it illustrates the overlap between apocalypse and testament, although the dominant form in this case is clearly the revelation. The exhortation in chap. 82 is more specific than that in 81 and is integrally related to the revelations about the sun and moon: "Blessed are all those who walk in the way of righteousness and do not sin like the sinners in the numbering of all their days." The chapter goes on to elaborate the law of the stars and the names of the angels who lead them.

The address to Methuselah underlines the primary purpose of the Astronomical Book: to prevent sin by calendrical error. The purpose here is far more specific than in the Book of the Watchers, but the technique is rather similar. Right observance is determined by an understanding of the heavenly world. What Enoch conveys is wisdom, but a "wisdom which is beyond their thoughts" (82:2), which must be obtained through revelation.

The alleged experience of Enoch evokes a sense of awe at the workings of the heavenly bodies, under their angelic leaders, and instills conviction in the understanding he imparts. The revelation provides assurance "in the days of the sinners" and this assurance is confirmed, in the present form of the book, by the eschatological revelation in chap. 81.

THE APOCALYPSE OF WEEKS

The Apocalypse of Weeks in *1 Enoch* 93 has long been recognized as a distinct apocalypse.[43] It is also well known that its conclusion is found in *1 Enoch* 91. The Aramaic fragments from Qumran have provided confirmation that the verses in chap. 91 are displaced in the Ethiopic tradition. In one fragment (En^g) 91:11-17 follows directly on 93:9-10. Accordingly, the Apocalypse may be confidently delineated as 93:1-10 + 91:11-17. The Apocalypse of Weeks is a self-contained unit, but opinion is divided on whether it actually circulated separately. Milik sees no evidence that it was ever independent of the Epistle of Enoch (chaps. 92-105). Matthew Black finds signs of redaction in the Apocalypse and infers that it is older than its context.[44] Like the Book of the Watchers, both the Apocalypse of Weeks and the Epistle avoid explicit reference to historical figures and events, and so frustrate the desire to date them precisely. Charles tentatively dated the Apocalypse of Weeks before the Maccabean revolt because "there is in it no reference to the persecution of Antiochus," but he located the Epistle under the Hasmoneans in the early first century.[45] A major factor in dating these books is the fact that the book of *Jubilees* apparently alludes to both the Apocalypse of Weeks and the Epistle. According to *Jub.* 4:18 "he was the first to write a testimony, and he testified to the sons of men among the generations of the earth and recounted the weeks of the jubilees. . . ." The theme of testifying is more prominent in the Epistle than in any other Enochic writing (see also 105:1). If the reference to Enoch's testimony is in fact a reference to the Epistle, this would require a date before 160 B.C.E.[46] The Apocalypse of Weeks may still have been an independent composition, but it is not necessarily significantly older than its context.

THE SCHEMATIZATION OF HISTORY

Although Enoch's ascent is presupposed in the Apocalypse of Weeks, it is not described, and there is no allusion to a heavenly tour. Enoch's revelation is imparted as an address to his children, but he claims to have received this revelation in typical apocalyptic fashion: "that which appeared to me in the heavenly vision, and (which) I know from the words of the holy angels and understand from the tablets of heaven." Again, he imparts understanding or wisdom—but a wisdom that is accessible only through revelation. It is also a *mediated* revelation, given in "the books" and tablets of heaven and conveyed to Enoch by angels.

The substance of this apocalypse is made up not by heavenly cosmology but by an overview of history. The history is highly schematized and organized into periods of "weeks." Ultimately there are ten periods specified, but the crucial transition occurs in the seventh week with the election of the "chosen righteous." The division of history into ten periods is most probably derived from the Persian idea of the millennium. It is common in the *Sibylline Oracles* and is a major structuring element in *Sib. Or.* 1 and 2 and *Sib. Or.* 4. It is found in the Melchizedek scroll from Qumran, and Milik cites two fragments of a "commentary on the (book of) periods created by God" (4Q*180* and *181*), where there are ten weeks from Noah to Abraham.[47] Multiples of seven also figure prominently in eschatological texts. Already in *1 Enoch* 10:12 the Watchers are bound under the earth for seventy generations. *T. Levi* 16:1 says that the descendants of Levi will err for seventy weeks, but claims to have learned this from the book of *Enoch*. In Daniel 9 the seventy weeks of years are tied to the prophecy of Jeremiah (Jer 25:11–12 and 29:10). In the Animal Apocalypse in *1 Enoch* 85–90, the "sheep" (Israel) are subjected to seventy shepherds in the period after the exile. The ten jubilees of 11QMelchizedek are also equivalent to seventy weeks of years. In the "pesher on the periods" (4Q*180-181*) Azazel and the angels lead Israel astray for seventy weeks, and Milik reports another apocalypse of ten jubilees in the unedited fragments from cave 4. Underlying all of this is the notion of the sabbath and of sabbatical and jubilee years, expounded in the priestly laws of the Torah (Leviticus 25). Moreover, Enoch was said to be seventh from Adam while the flood, which terminated the first epoch of history, was in the tenth generation.

The division of history into a set number of periods is a common feature of the "historical" type of apocalypse. One effect of this periodization is the impression of an ordered universe where everything proceeds in a predetermined manner. There is an analogy between the set number of periods here and the set number of heavens that will be seen in later apocalypses. Periodization also makes it possible to locate the present in an overall schema of history. In the case of the Apocalypse of Weeks the time of the real author is evidently to be situated in the seventh week, before the "root of iniquity" is cut off in the eighth. The schematization of history then shows that the greater number of periods has already elapsed and that the turning point is at hand. The use of an ancient pseudonym like Enoch permits a *vaticinium ex eventu*, a review of past history as if it were future, and so adds to the impression that all is determined in advance, and under divine control.

The treatment of history in the Apocalypse of Weeks is not exhausted by the division into periods. There is also a pattern of sin and salvation.[48] In the first week "justice and righteousness still lasted." In the second, "great wickedness will arise" but "in it a man will be saved." The reference is to Noah. After this God "will make a law for sinners," presumably the covenant with Noah. The third week is marked by the election of Abraham: "a man will be chosen as the plant of righteousness forever." The fourth includes the giving of the law "for all generations" and the gift of the land. In the fifth "a house of glory and sovereignty will be built forever." In the sixth week all will be blinded, but a man will ascend, presumably Elijah. This week concludes with the destruction of the temple and the exile. The seventh week is dominated by an apostate generation, but at its end "the chosen righteous from the eternal plant of righteousness" will be chosen. The pattern that emerges is that periods of wickedness culminate in the separation of the elect. At the end of the second generation Noah is saved; in the sixth Elijah is taken up. After the flood, Abraham is chosen as the plant of righteous judgment. After the corrupt seventh generation, the "chosen righteous from the eternal plant of righteousness" are elected. The election of this group thus becomes a focal point of the whole schema. It is prefigured in the case of Abraham, and to some extent in Noah and Elijah. The eighth, ninth, and tenth weeks provide the eschatological finale. The eighth week is "that of righteousness" when sinners are destroyed by the sword. In the ninth the righteous judgment will be revealed to the whole world, and "the world is written down for destruction." Then in the tenth week "the eternal judgment will be executed on the Watchers." Then the first heaven will pass away and a new heaven will appear. After this "there will be many weeks without number forever in goodness and righteousness."[49]

In view of the reference to the Watchers it would seem that the whole schema of history here is an elaboration of the seventy generations of *1 Enoch* 10. The culmination is reminiscent of Isaiah 65, where the new heaven and new earth are interpreted as a transformed state where successive generations live in peace. The Enochic text is more explicit that this world is written down for destruction. Matthew Black argues that some of the original ending has been lost in the Ethiopic.[50] The Qumran text, En^g, has a passage before 91:18 of which only one or two words are decipherable, but which occupied roughly four lines. Milik identifies this verse with 91:10. Black reconstructs it on the basis of 92:3. In either case it would contain a reference to resurrection. This reference would bring the eschatology of the apocalypse more explicitly into line with the full Book of the Watchers and the expectations of other apocalypses. It is not certain, however, that this verse was actually part of the Apocalypse of Weeks.

The emphasis in the Apocalypse of Weeks is primarily on the historical axis: the assurance that time is measured out and under control. Even here the heavenly world is not lacking. Enoch's revelation is received through the angels and at the end angels (and the Watchers) figure in the new creation. The control of history is in the hands of supernatural agents. The overview of history and the cosmic judgment provide encouragement for the "chosen righteous" and, more basically, confirm their special status in the design of God.

THE EPISTLE OF ENOCH

The Apocalypse of Weeks is embedded in a longer composition generally known as the Epistle of Enoch. This is said to be "written by Enoch the scribe" for "all my sons who dwell upon the earth and for the last generations who will practise uprightness and peace." It bears some resemblance to a testament, although it lacks the usual third-person narrative of a deathbed scene. Enoch asserts his authority by such formulas as "I say to you" or "I swear to you," but he also appeals to his knowledge of the heavenly realm: "I swear to you that I understand this mystery. And I have read the tablets of heaven and seen the writing of the holy ones . . ." (103:1-2). Enoch's heavenly revelation is presupposed throughout, but the dominant form is paraenesis.

The bulk of the Epistle is taken up with woes against the sinners and exhortations for the righteous. The accusations against the wicked are of two types. On the one hand, the sinners are accused of blasphemy (94:9; 96:7) and idolatry (99:7). On the other hand, the majority of the accusations are social in character: "Woe to those who build their houses with sin, for from their whole foundation they will be thrown down, and by the sword they will fall; and those who acquire gold and silver will quickly be destroyed in the judgment" (94:8). "Woe to you who devour the finest in the wheat and drink the best of the water and trample upon the humble through your power" (96:5). Such explicit concern with social issues is exceptional in the early Enoch literature. The class divisions reflected in the woes were not peculiar to any one period, but they are thoroughly intelligible against the background of the Hellenization of Palestine in the period before the Maccabean revolt, as illustrated by the story of the Tobiads in Josephus.[51]

We have noted that Charles saw in the Epistle a reflection of disputes between Pharisees and Sadducees. Milik points out that the accusation of idolatry could scarcely be applied to the Sadducees.[52] The woes could be applied more appropriately to hellenizing Jews in the period before the revolt. Twice Enoch denounces those who "alter and distort the words of truth" and "write books in their (own words)," (104:10; 98:15). This could be read as a rejection of those authors who attempted to present the Jewish tradition in Greek dress. The concern with the sea in 101:4-9 has been taken to suggest provenance in a maritime town.[53] All of this is, of course, extremely tentative. The highly general language in which the Epistle is couched lent itself to application in several different settings. In view of the apparent allusion in *Jubilees*, a date before 160 B.C.E. is plausible.

We should emphasize, however, the uncertainty of the historical location of the Epistle, and even of its relation to the other early Enoch literature. Although the Epistle preserves major motifs of Enoch's revelation, there is at least one striking discrepancy. In 98:4 Enoch declares that as "a mountain has not, and will not, become a slave, nor a hill a woman's maid, so sin was not sent on the earth, but man of himself created it." This pronouncement would seem to contradict the explanation of the origin of evil in the story of the Watchers.[54] This discrepancy may reflect a revision within a unified tradition, or it may be indicative of a different provenance for the Epistle. In the absence of some more specific evidence we cannot be certain.

The exhortations in the Epistle resemble the apocalypses in their argumentation. At the outset the righteous are assured that "the Holy Great One has appointed days for all things, and the righteous man will rise from sleep, will rise and will walk in the path of righteousness" (92:3). In 104:2-6 they will shine like the lights of heaven and be associates of the host of heaven. The angels will gather the sinners for judgment (100:4). The wicked "will be given into the hand of the righteous and they will cut your throats and kill you and not have mercy on you" (98:12). The wisdom imparted in the Epistle, which is derived from the heavenly tablets, is primarily concerned with the eschatological judgment.[55] In short, Enoch appeals to the authority of heaven to show that the righteous who are oppressed in this world can hope for salvation outside it and that the present world order will eventually be reversed. An apocalyptic view of the world provides consolation and the basis for perseverance in the seemingly unprofitable ways of righteousness.

THE ANIMAL APOCALYPSE

One other apocalypse of Enoch, the Animal Apocalypse, is attested at Qumran. It can be dated on internal grounds to the Maccabean revolt.[56] This apocalypse is itself part of the Book of Dreams (chaps. 83-91). Enoch recounts to Methuselah "two visions I saw before I took a wife." The first was a simple vision of cosmic destruction, how the earth "is about to sink into the abyss and be utterly destroyed." We are reminded of Jer 4:23-26: "I looked on the earth, and lo, it was waste and void, and to the heavens and they had no light." This brief vision is a paradigm of judgment, a reminder that the whole world could be destroyed. It implies the contingency of the world, its dependence on its Maker. It need not refer to any particular crisis.

The second vision in chaps. 85–91 is a complex allegory. The figures of biblical history are represented by animals. Adam is a white bull. Cain and Abel are black and red bullocks. Seth and his descendants are white bulls. The descent of the Watchers is expressed in chap. 86 as the descent or fall of stars from heaven, in accordance with the common identification of stars with angels or heavenly beings. The giants begotten by them are "elephants, camels, and asses." Then "there came from heaven beings who were like white men." These are the angels who bind the Watchers and imprison them. Three angels also lift Enoch up to a high place from which he can view the course of history. Enoch does not undertake a heavenly tour, but his vision is assisted by the angels.

Noah, like Adam, is a white bull. The key to his salvation is that he is taught a mystery by the angels. He then "became a man." This development does not contradict the general symbolism by which humans are represented as animals and angels as humans. Noah is transformed to an angel-like state.[57] The sons of Noah "began to beget wild animals and birds, so that there arose from them every kind of species" (89:10). As in Ezekiel 34, the nations are represented by the wild creatures. From these Abraham emerges as a white bull. Isaac is also a bull, but Jacob is a sheep—which marks the transition from the patriarchal period to the history of Israel. The imagery for the nations is also nuanced. The Ishmaelites to whom Joseph is sold are asses, but the Egyptians are wolves. The exodus is narrated at some length. Moses is a sheep at first, but he, like Noah, "became a man" (89:36, 38). The kings are represented as rams.

The account of the kingdoms is similar to the sixth week in the Apocalypse of Weeks. The sheep are blinded and go astray. The ascension of Elijah is noted. God delivers the sheep into the hands of the wild animals. Then seventy shepherds are appointed to watch over the sheep and destroy some of them while "another" is told to record what the shepherds do.

Charles regarded the seventy shepherds as "the most vexed question in Enoch," but he showed conclusively that they are the angelic patrons of the nations.[58] They are later grouped with the fallen angels at the judgment, while "another" who records their deeds is clearly an angel in chap. 90. The background of this conception is found in Deuteronomy 32, where God divided the nations according to the number of the sons of God.[59] The conception figures prominently in Daniel 10. The number seventy corresponds to Daniel's seventy weeks of years and the common division of history into seventy generations, which we have noted above. Both the number seventy and the "shepherd" imagery are found in Jeremiah 25.[60]

The reign of the seventy shepherds is divided into four periods, which are allotted 12, 23, 23, and 12 shepherds respectively. This division roughly corresponds to the periods of Babylonian, Persian, Ptolemaic, and Seleucid rule, but the correlations are not explicit. Neither does Enoch correlate it with a four-kingdom schema such as we find in Daniel. The division conveys a sense of order and providential control. The first period culminates in the rebuilding of the temple. Here we are told that all the bread offered in the new temple was unclean and not pure. This verdict on the Jewish restoration is quite compatible with the Apocalypse of Weeks, which simply refers to an "apostate generation." We need not infer that the Second Temple was rejected in principle, but that the actual cult of the early restoration period was regarded as impure.

At the end of the third period (90:6) "small lambs were born from these white sheep, and they began to open their eyes." This development corresponds to the emergence of the "chosen righteous" in the Apocalypse of Weeks. 1 Enoch 90:8 describes how "one of these lambs" was killed. This has been taken as a reference to the murder of the high priest Onias III.[61] No other plausible referent is known. If this is correct, the rejection of the Second Temple must be modified. There is no doubt that the great horn that grew on one of those sheep in 90:9 is Judas Maccabee. Eventually the recording angel goes down to help Judas, a probable reference to the tradition that an angel appeared at the battle of Beth-Zur.[62] Beyond this point the apocalypse is no longer describing history but rather is describing its anticipated conclusion. God himself comes down and sets up his throne for judgment. A sword is given to the "sheep" as it was given to the righteous in the Apocalypse of Weeks. Then the Watchers and the seventy shepherds are destroyed but also the "blind sheep" or apostate Jews. Then the "old house" is replaced and all the nations bow down to the Jews. Those that had been destroyed are brought back, presumably by resurrection, and all are transformed into "white bulls"—the condition of Adam and the early patriarchs. The "wild animals" are also gathered in the new "house," but it is not clear that they are transformed. In view of 90:30 they are clearly subject to the Jews. The final transformation then is located in the land of Israel, but since God has come down and lives among them we may speak of heaven on earth, just as the new Jerusalem comes down from heaven in Revelation 21. The "house" here may indeed refer to Jerusalem, since the temple is represented as a "tower."

The technique of the Animal Apocalypse is similar to the other Enoch writings we have considered. The work is addressed to the crisis that led to the Maccabean revolt. This crisis is put in perspective by being located in an overview of all history. The history is treated allegorically, so the emphasis is on the typical rather than the particular. It is also measured out and said to be under supernatural control. The eschatological finale is integrated into the sequence of history and so gains credibility from the accurate detail of the preceding "prophecy." The message is ultimately that the judgment is at hand and that the heavenly angels will dispose of the Gentile rulers as they originally disposed of the Watchers. Unlike what we will find in Daniel, this apocalypse affirms a militant role for the righteous. Yet the victory is in the hands of God and his angels and the resolution involves a resurrection beyond this life, even if it is located on earth. The Animal Apocalypse then provides the "elect" with an understanding of their situation which not only can relieve anxiety but also can be an effective support for their action.

AN APOCALYPTIC MOVEMENT?

The four apocalypses of Enoch that we have considered show literary continuity in the reuse of the legend of Enoch's ascent and, in the Apocalypse of Weeks and the Animal Apocalypse, the allusions to the Watchers. It is reasonable to suppose that there was also some historical and social continuity and to ask whether these books are the product of a single movement or group.

Evidence that the Enoch literature articulates the ideology of a movement can be found in the Apocalypse of Weeks and in the Animal Apocalypse. We have noted above that a major focus of the Apocalypse of Weeks is the emergence of "the chosen righteous from the eternal plant of righteousness."[63] The apocalypse is introduced (93:2) as "concerning the sons of righteousness and concerning the chosen of the world and concerning the plant of righteousness and uprightness." The plant of righteousness appears in the third generation as the descendants of Abraham. The "chosen righteous from the eternal plant of righteousness," which is chosen in the seventh generation, is then an offshoot of the people of Abraham. This special elect group will be given "sevenfold teaching concerning his whole creation." The movement is not entirely pietistic, however. It evidently endorses the use of the sword against the wicked: "And after this the roots of iniquity will be cut off and the sinners will be destroyed by the sword" and, in the eighth generation, "the sinners will be handed over into the hands of the righteous." These statements can be read as purely future expectation, since the author's own time is most probably located in the climactic seventh week. Yet the ideology they reflect is obviously compatible with that of the Maccabean revolt.

A few other items in the Apocalypse of Weeks may be indicative of group identity. The "chosen righteous" will be given "sevenfold teaching concerning his whole creation" (93:10). They are possessors of some special wisdom. Then, at the end of the eighth week "they will acquire houses because of their righteousness." Both of these points relate the apocalypse to the Epistle of Enoch. There we are told "that books will be given to the righteous and wise" (104:12). We might infer that the "righteous" are a scribal class, and the inference may be corroborated by the description of Enoch as a "scribe of righteousness" in the Book of the Watchers (12:4). The Epistle complains more than once about those who "build their houses with sin" (94:7) or "with the toil of others" (99:13) and consoles the righteous with the hope of an angelic afterlife. The Apocalypse provides for some material compensation, within the context of cosmic transformation.[64] The Epistle shares the militant note of the Apocalypse (95:3; 96:1; 98:12) but lacks the reference to the "chosen" as a group designation. The righteous are still to testify to the sons of the earth about the wisdom in them (105:1). They are not, then, closed off from the society around them.[65] There would seem to be some progression between the Epistle and the Apocalypse of Weeks toward clearer definition of a group, but the evidence is very slight.

Both the Epistle and the Apocalypse of Weeks draw sharp contrasts between the righteous and the wicked. The sinners in the Epistle are accused of idolatry and oppression. They are evidently a wealthy class, but the extent of their role in Jewish society is unclear. The Apocalypse of Weeks, in contrast, dismisses the whole postexilic period as "an apostate generation." There is no mention of the rebuilding of the temple until the eighth week in the eschatological period. It is unclear whether the sweeping characterization of the postexilic period expresses a total rejection of the restoration or should be regarded as a hyperbolic reaction to the circumstances at the time of composition.

The emergence of the "chosen righteous" can be correlated with the "small lambs" which "began to open their eyes" in the Animal Apocalypse. Here there is clear support for the Maccabean revolt, but Judas is not said to be one of the lambs, but one of the sheep. We may infer from this that he was not part of the original movement. The Animal Apocalypse also implies that the lambs had taken up arms and been defeated (by the "ravens," 90:9) before the rise of Judas.

In this apocalypse the foreign rulers of Israel are the primary enemies. We have noted the apparent rejection of the worship of the Second Temple in 89:73, which must be modified if the high priest Onias III is regarded as "one of the lambs" in 90:8.

Neither the Book of the Watchers nor the Astronomical Book, which appear to be the oldest Enochic writings, attests a particular group identity in its terminology. In *1 Enoch* 10:16 the plant of righteousness and truth is apparently Israel, and we are not told of any other offshoot. The story of the Watchers may have reflected a division within the people, by criticism of the priesthood, but party lines are not clearly drawn. It has been suggested that the punishment of 'Aśa'el/Azazel in 1 Enoch 10 is an adaptation of the scapegoat ritual in Leviticus 16 and constitutes an implicit rejection of the official ritual of atonement.[66] In the Aramaic fragments from Qumran, however, the name of the Watcher is 'Aśa'el, not Azazel, and so it is doubtful whether there was any allusion to Leviticus 16.[67] Even if the association with Leviticus 16 were established, the cult would not necessarily be devalued. The scapegoat ritual might simply be given a new level of reference.

The Astronomical Book makes the usual Enochic distinction between righteous and sinners in chap. 81. The main indicator of group identity in this writing, however, is the allegiance to the 364-day calendar. This has often been taken as a sign of sectarian provenance. The issue is clouded, however, by a number of factors. First, there is no direct evidence concerning what calendar was officially in use in Judaism in the third or the early second century. It is generally assumed that the lunisolar calendar of later Judaism was already in force,[68] but some have argued that the solar calendar was offical, even down to the the time of Antiochus Epiphanes.[69] The latter position is open to some objection: Antiochus is known to have disrupted the Jewish festivals, but it is doubtful whether a change in the calendar regulating the traditional festivals could have resulted from his actions.[70] Yet the fact remains that we are ill-informed about the official calendar in pre-Maccabean times.[71] Second, as already noted, the Astronomical Book does not polemicize against a lunar or solilunar calendar, but only against a 360-day calendar, which was never official.[72] In the light of this, the Astronomical Book does not seem to have been generated by a conflict with the Jerusalem temple. It is difficult to see how the authors of this book could have functioned in a temple regulated by a lunar calendar. This problem would be avoided if the Astronomical Book was composed in the eastern Diaspora, where actual use of the temple was not an immediate issue. The 364-day calendar is explicit only in the Astronomical Book in the Enochic corpus, but the Book of the Watchers lists the path of the moon among the harmful teachings of the Watchers (1 Enoch 8:3). The solar calendar is not contradicted in the other early Enoch books and is probably presupposed, but the evidence is lacking.

The internal evidence for an apocalyptic movement in 1 Enoch, then, is less than complete. If we may assume that all these works come from an ongoing tradition (which is plausible though not certain) then we have a movement that had its roots in the third century. In the earliest writings, the group identity is not prominent. The authors were presumably scribes, like Enoch, who had a mission to their fellow Jews and to humanity at large. While its calendar may have differed from that of the Jerusalem temple, it was not involved in polemics against mainline Judaism. The Apocalypse of Weeks and the Animal Apocalypse show a heightened group identity, apparently reflecting the recent emergence of a stronger group formation. They are also more militant and more directly critical of the temple and of the Jewish leadership. It is of interest that in these apocalypses, written in a time of conflict, the cosmological interests of the apocalyptic genre recede, and the historical interests come to the fore.

The movement or group that is clearly attested in the Apocalypse of Weeks and the Animal Apocalypse must be correlated with some analogous developments in *Jubilees* and the *Damascus Document* (CD). In *Jubilees* 23, after a period of suffering at the hands of the Gentiles, "the children shall begin to study the laws and to seek the commandments and to return to the paths of righteousness" (23:26). Life will then be transformed, so that their days will be close to a thousand years and "there shall be no Satan or any evil destroyer." At that time the servants of the Lord will "rise up and see great peace and drive out their adversaries." *Jubilees* does not use a specific group designation such as "chosen righteous." A relationship with Enochic circles is suggested, however, by *Jubilees*' defense of the solar calendar, which in this case is directly opposed to a lunar system (*Jub.* 6:32–38). *Jubilees* still insists on the use of the temple (e.g., the Passover must be celebrated there, 49:16). How this relates to the actual temple cult at the time when *Jubilees* was written is unclear.

The opening column of the so-called *Damascus Document* (CD) also describes the rise of a movement and, like *1 Enoch*, uses the metaphor of "plant" to describe it:

> For when they were unfaithful and forsook Him, He hid His face from Israel and His Sanctuary and delivered them up to the sword. But remembering the Covenant of the forefathers, He left a remnant to Israel and did not deliver it up to be destroyed. And in the age of wrath, three hundred and ninety years after He had given them into the hand of king Nebuchadnezzar of Babylon, He visited them, and He caused a plant root to spring from Israel and Aaron to inherit His Land and to prosper on the good things of His earth. And they perceived their iniquity and recognized that they were guilty men, yet for twenty years they were like blind men groping for the way. And God observed their deeds, that they sought Him with a whole heart, and He raised for them a Teacher of Righteousness to guide them in the way of His heart. (CD 1:3-11)[73]

The figure of 390 years is presumably derived from Ezek 4:5 and cannot be taken as chronologically exact, but it requires a lapse of several hundred years after the exile. CD 1 then distinguishes three developments in the postexilic period: first, the "remnant," which apparently refers to all Jews who survived the destruction of Jerusalem; second, the "plant root," an off-shoot that arose several hundred years later and was a penitential movement; and, third, the arrival of the Teacher of Righteousness, who is generally regarded as the founder of the Qumran community. On the basis of the archaeology of Qumran the latter development is usually placed in the mid second century B.C.E., and the chronological data of CD are perfectly compatible with this view.

Objections have been raised against the reliability of CD 1, because the chronological data disrupt the metric arrangement and so appear to be added as glosses.[74] Even glosses, however, must still be explained. At the very least, CD 1 gives us a redactor's view of the origin of the sect, at a time no later than the early first century B.C.E. The burden of proof must fall on any modern scholar who contends that this view is inaccurate. The objection to the chronology that is explicit in CD 1 has been based on a theory that locates the origin of the sect in the exile, shortly after the fall of Jerusalem. Support for this theory has been drawn from CD 3:12-13, where God establishes a covenant and makes revelations to "those who adhered to the commandments of God, who were left over of them." This statement follows directly on the destruction of the members of the first covenant, and so has been taken to refer to the exilic generation.[75] In fact, however, CD 3:12-13 gives no indication of the date of this covenant and revelation. Unlike the remnant in 1:4, this group is specified as "those who held fast to the law." The redactor of CD 1 evidently thought that the new development was several hundred years after the destruction and the elliptic data of CD 3 are not incompatible with this view.[76]

The failure of CD to acknowledge the sixth-century restoration is paralleled in several documents of the Hellenistic age, notably the Apocalypse of Weeks, but also *Jubilees* 1; whereas Daniel 9 still looks for the fulfillment of Jeremiah's prophecy, even though it acknowledges the return in the Persian period. The Animal Apocalypse disputed the validity of the Second Temple.[77] The statements of CD on developments after the destruction of Jerusalem must be read in this light.[78] In effect a reference to an "exilic generation" provides no chronological information if the exile is thought to persist for several hundred years.

The focus of CD is on "the new covenant in the land of Damascus," which is mentioned several times (6:19; 7:21; 19:34; 20:12). As the document now stands, this covenant is associated with the Teacher of Righteousness and is generally assumed to be the covenant of the Qumran community. Correspondingly, Damascus is usually taken as a code name for Qumran, although some have argued that it originally referred to Babylon.[79] Recently the view has been put forward that the Qumran covenant is only introduced as a late redactional stage in CD, and that the original "covenant in the land of Damascus" was formulated in the Babylonian exile.[80] The distinction of two "Damascus covenants" relies heavily on CD 20:12, which refers to "the covenant and the pact which they made in the land of Damascus, that is the new covenant." In view of the usage of the "new covenant" elsewhere in CD, however, the distinction here is surely between the "new covenant in the land of Damascus" and the "old" preexilic covenant; that is, "the covenant in the land of Damascus" and "the new covenant" are identical. CD provides no warrant for positing an earlier Damascus covenant. The precise significance of Damascus is still debatable. In addition to the references to the new covenant, it occurs in CD 6:5 and in the Amos–Numbers midrash in col. 7. CD 6:5 is translated by Vermes as: "The Well is the Law, and those who dug it were the converts of Israel who went out from the land of Judah to sojourn in the land of Damascus." The word translated "converts," *šby*, is ambiguous. It has been taken as a participle of *šûb*, but also as the noun *šby*, "captivity."[81] The participle has also been translated as "returnees,"[82] but "the returnees who went out" is a singularly awkward expression. "The captivity of Israel who went out" makes much better sense, although we should expect a singular participle for went out, rather than the plural. It must be said, however, that the evidence of CD taken as a whole favors the translation "converts" or "penitents."[83] Not only is there a clear analogy with *šby pš'*, "those who repent of sin" (2:5; 20:17); but also the "plant root" in CD 1 is clearly described as a penitential movement. Even if the expression were translated "captivity," this would not necessarily have to be read as a reference to the Babylonian exile, given the patently symbolic sense of other terms in the passage, including Damascus. Equally, Judah cannot be given a strictly geographical connotation. Damascus here signifies a place (or even state?) of exile. It is also the location of the new covenant, and presumably it refers to the habitation (or habitations) of the sect.[84] CD provides no reason to posit a settlement at "Damascus" before the time of the Teacher of Righteousness. The hypothesis of a Babylonian origin of the community is not entirely impossible, but it lacks positive evidence to support it.

CD is written from the perspective of the Teacher's community. We will consider it further in the context of the Qumran scrolls. Its relevance to the Enoch literature lies in the information that the "plant root" preceded the arrival of the Teacher by some twenty years and at this time was not so clearly organized as the later Qumran community. The relevance to the Enoch literature is strengthened by the fact that the revelations associated with the new covenant in 3:14 concern "His holy sabbaths and His glorious festivals"—in short, the calendar.

Martin Hengel has suggested that the Apocalypse of Weeks, the Animal Apocalypse and the *Damascus Document* refer to the formation of a group that is mentioned in 1 Maccabees 2 as the "assembly of the pious" or Hasidim (*synagōgē asidaiōn*).[85] Hengel also attributes the book of Daniel to this group. He then takes the Hasidim as the forerunners of the Qumran community. This hypothesis is attractive in drawing together diverse pieces of evidence from the early second century, but it also presents some problems.[86]

The Hasidim are mentioned three times in the books of Maccabees. In 1 Macc 2:42 they are "mighty warriors of Israel" who join the Maccabees after the slaughter of a group of pious Jews on the sabbath. In 1 Macc 7:12–13 they seem to be identified with a group of scribes who sought peace with the high priest Alcimus but who were taken by surprise, so that sixty of them were killed. In 2 Macc 14:6 Alcimus reports to the Syrian king Demetrius that "those of the Jews who are called Hasideans, whose leader is Judas Maccabeus, are keeping up the war and stirring up sedition and will not let the kingdom attain tranquility." While Judas Maccabee's relation to the Hasidim may be overstated in the latter passage, it is clear that they did support him, at least for a time, and that they participated actively in the military campaign. These three references are the only evidence for an organized party of Hasidim in Maccabean times. References to the "assembly of the pious" or Hasidim in Psalm 149, the Qumran Psalm Scroll (11QPs[a] 154, 155) and in the *Psalms of Solomon* (4:1; 17:16) cannot be taken as evidence for such a party.

Our evidence for the Hasidim, then, is extremely scanty. One of the few things we can say of them with confidence is that they participated in the revolt in support of Judas Maccabee. They were not quietists or pacifists. This point should enable us to correct at least one element in Hengel's reconstruction. The book of Daniel reflects a quietistic ideology and cannot be ascribed to the militant Hasidim. Victor Tcherikover has argued persuasively that the Hasidim were the initiators of the revolt.[87] According to his reconstruction, they had rebelled against Jason, the Hellenizing high priest, and ousted him from Jerusalem. This disturbance led to the intervention of Antiochus Epiphanes and then to the persecution. The martyrs in the wilderness in 1 Maccabees 2, who let themselves be slaughtered rather than break the sabbath, were not pacifists, but militants who were strict observers of the law. Tcherikover identifies the Hasidim as "the chief scribes."[88] 1 Macc 7:12–13 does indeed support the view that they were scribes, but there is no evidence for their status among the people.

The Apocalypse of Weeks, the Animal Apocalypse, and *Jubilees* are all compatible with what we know of the Hasidim, although the allusions in 1 and 2 Maccabees give no hint of the range of concerns in those books. The Animal Apocalypse is especially intriguing in the light of Tcherikover's reconstruction, since it implies that the "lambs" took up arms before the rise of Judas. The Apocalypse of Weeks and *Jubilees* are not so clearly tied to the Maccabean revolt but still make good sense in that context. The relation of the *Damascus Document* to the other texts is less clear. It contains no reference to militant action and refers rather to a penitential movement. Yet the metaphor of planting forms a link with the Enoch literature. Moreover, the 364-day solar calendar of *1 Enoch* and *Jubilees* was also observed at Qumran. CD has much in common with *Jubilees* in their common adherence to priestly traditions. The Enoch books and *Jubilees* were preserved at Qumran. Yet it would be too simple to suppose that all these books attest a single movement that later settled at Qumran.[89] There are significant differences between the eschatology of the scrolls, which lack a belief in resurrection and emphasize messianic expectation and that of the Enoch literature. It is possible, of course, that the term Hasidim is used broadly in the Maccabean books to refer to a class of people (as we might use the term "conservatives") rather than to an organization. In this sense, "Hasidim" might serve as a loose umbrella term for the different developments attested in these books, which were still closely related to each other. The label "early Essenism" is hardly justified. Even in the case of the "plant root" of CD before the arrival of the Teacher we should probably speak rather of pre-Essenes.

Our reconstruction of the social matrix of the Enoch tradition must remain very tentative. Fundamental matters, such as the status of the 364-day calendar in the third century, remain quite uncertain. We may say with some confidence that this literature was produced by scribes who were distressed by the encroachments of Hellenism and the consequent erosion of traditional customs and aggravation of class divisions. We may also say that the tradition involved separatist tendencies from the start, by its appeal to the higher revelation of Enoch, over and above the Mosaic Torah. It does not appear, however, that the bearers of the Enoch tradition before the Maccabean revolt were separated from the rest of Judaism in the manner of the later Qumran community. They could at least make common cause with other strands of Judaism at the time of the revolt.

APPENDIX:
THE BOOK OF JUBILEES

We have already had occasion to note some of the affinities of the book of *Jubilees* with the early Enoch literature, of which the most notable is the calendar. *Jubilees* clearly presupposes the Book of the Watchers and the Astronomical Book and possibly alludes to the Book of Dreams, the Apocalypse of Weeks, and the Epistle.[90] Even in the use of material derived from Enoch, significant variations occur. According to *Jubilees* the initial descent of the angels was so "that they should instruct the children of men, and that they should do judgment and justice on earth" (4:15). In short, there was no rebellion in heaven. Their initial sin was with the daughters of men. Later, after the flood, one-tenth of their offspring are allowed to remain with Mastema (Satan) to afflict mankind (10:11). In *1 Enoch* 15:9-12 the spirits of the giants will rise against humanity, without limitation. The eschatology of *Jubilees* is less elaborate than that of the Enoch books and of course *Jubilees* has extensive areas of interest that are not paralleled in Enoch at all. In short, the conformity between *Jubilees* and the Enoch literature is not complete. Both *Jubilees* and the Enoch literature may derive from the Hasidim, but we must allow that the movement embraced some differences in opinion and theological tradition.[91]

The book of *Jubilees* is introduced as "the history of the division of the days of the law and of the testimony, of the events of the years, of their (year) weeks, of their Jubilees throughout all the years of the world, as the Lord spoke to Moses on Mount Sinai when he went up to receive the tables of the law and of the commandment." In fact it is an expansionistic paraphrase of the book of Genesis and, more briefly, of Exodus down to the revelation of Sinai. The focus of the work is on halakic matters that regulate the Jewish way of life. So the account of creation highlights the sabbath in chap. 2, and the book concludes with instructions for the sabbath in chap. 50. Great attention is paid to the festivals and to rituals such as circumcision. A major concern of the work is to defend the 364-day calendar and to warn against "the feast of the Gentiles" and the aberration of the moon (6:32-38). The biblical narrative is expanded to show how the patriarchs observed the Torah. The practical concerns of the book may be illustrated from the deathbed speech of Abraham in chaps. 20-22. Abraham warns his sons to practice circumcision, renounce fornication and uncleanness, refrain from marriage with Canaanite women, avoid idolatry, eat no blood, and perform washings before and after sacrificing. Marriage with Gentiles is emphatically forbidden in the story of the destruction of Shechem (*Jubilees* 30).[92]

Some special emphases of *Jubilees* acquire added point with reference to the period of the Maccabean revolt. The story of Adam and Eve is taken as showing that "they should cover their shame and not uncover themselves as the Gentiles uncover themselves" (3:31). Nudity in the gymnasium had been a major scandal in Jerusalem on the eve of the revolt (1 Macc 1:14-15). Making war on the sabbath is explicitly forbidden in 50:12. In 1 Maccabees

2 we read of those who were slaughtered because they refused to defend themselves on the sabbath. Thereafter the Hasidim joined Mattathias, who had decided to make an exception to this law. *Jubilees* would seem to represent a purist position on the issue.

Detailed discussion of the halakic positions and exegetical techniques of *Jubilees* falls outside the scope of our present study. Rather, our concern is with the apocalyptic dimension of the book. The content of the book is evidently quite different from what we usually find in an apocalypse. Yet the work as a whole is presented as a revelation communicated to Moses by the angel of the presence.[93] The laws are often said to be written "on the heavenly tablets" (3:10, 31; 4:5, 32; etc.).[94] Although there is no description of a vision or a heavenly journey, the manner of revelation is distinctly apocalyptic.

Moses, rather than Enoch, is the recipient of revelation here. More clearly than the Enoch books, *Jubilees* works within Mosaic tradition. Yet the choice of Moses as the recipient should not obscure the fact that *Jubilees* is rewriting the Mosaic law and modifying it at several points. It is significant that the speaker—and ultimately the authoritative figure here—is not Moses, but the angel.[95] *Jubilees* can correct the traditional law by appealing to the words of the angel and the heavenly tablets.

The angel's revelation is presented as an account of the *Jubilees*. We may compare the role of jubilees in the Apocalypse of Weeks, Daniel 9, and 11QMelch. In *Jubilees*, the account extends only as far as the Sinai revelation. Yet in the introduction the account is said to cover "all the years of the world, and until God descends to dwell among them for all eternity" (1:26). We have no reason to believe that the account was ever completed,[96] but *Jubilees* does envisage history as a whole, with an eschatological conclusion. There are a few anticipatory glances toward the end of history, which may satisfy the claim of the introduction.

The eschatological finale of history is developed especially in two places. *Jub.* 1:23-29 anticipates a time when the Jews will turn to God and he will live among them for all eternity. There will be a new creation, and heaven and earth shall be renewed "and all the luminaries (will) be renewed for healing and for peace and for blessing for all the elect of Israel." The other passage in *Jubilees* 23 is more explicit. Here we get a rapid overview of all generations from the time of Abraham. There is an extended account of the decline of humanity and the abuses of "an evil generation" (23:14) of the Hellenistic age. One of the charges against this generation is that it has forgotten "feasts and months and sabbaths and jubilees"—a possible reference to a change of calendar. But then (23:26) "the children shall begin to study the laws" and the transformation will begin. They will drive out their adversaries and live in peace. Finally, "their bones shall rest in the earth and their spirits will have much joy"—an apparent reference to after-life without resurrection.[97]

Although *Jubilees* does not conclude with eschatological prediction, the prospect of a final judgment is of crucial importance throughout: "the judgment of all is ordained and written on the heavenly tablets in righteousness" (5:13). This formulation highlights another typically apocalyptic aspect of *Jubilees*—its determinism. Already in 1:29 we hear of "the tables of the divisions of the years," an indication that the course of the future is inscribed in advance. In 32:21 Jacob is allowed to read from heavenly tablets all that would befall him and his sons through the ages. Yet it is apparent that the deterministic framework functions as a hortatory device. If "the judgment of all is ordained and written in the heavenly tablets in righteousness," this is especially a warning for "all who depart from the path" that "if they walk not therein, judgment is written down for every creature and for every kind" (5:13). The inevitability of judgment is the ultimate sanction for the laws of *Jubilees*.

The eschatological horizon is, then, crucial for *Jubilees*, as it is for any apocalypse. The heavenly world is no less important. *Jubilees* does not pursue the speculative interest of the early Enoch books, but it is nonetheless interested in the order of nature. The account of creation (2:2) lists the angels of the spirits of the elements. The world of *Jubilees* is as thoroughly supervised by angelic beings as that of the Astronomical Book of Enoch. In addition to the angels of the elements there are angels of the presence and of sanctification. These interact with humanity by transmitting messages and by protecting the elect from their demonic adversaries. The latter are constituted by the descendants of the Watchers and are led by Mastema or Beliar (1:20). As a result, humanity is torn between two ways, each controlled by supernatural powers, in a manner similar to what we will find at Qumran.[98]

Jubilees represents a borderline case for the apocalyptic genre. Confusion about its genre is reflected in the various titles used for the book: *Jubilees*, which suggests a treatment of history; the *Little Genesis*, which suggests a biblical paraphrase (sometimes loosely called midrash); but also the *Apocalypse of Moses*.[99] Testuz regarded the work as of composite genre, combining historical, legal, chronological, apocalyptic, and testamentary aspects.[100] *Jubilees* differs from other apocalypses in its close reliance on the biblical narrative and its halakic interests, and these factors should be given due weight in a full description of its genre. It remains true, however, that the *Rahmengattung* or generic framework of *Jubilees* is an apocalypse.[101] It is a revelation mediated by an angel to a venerable figure of the past. The laws it presents are reinforced by the inevitabilitiy of the pre-determined judgment and are guidelines for the conflict between the angels and the demons. The apocalyptic ideas of revelation, eschatology, and the good and evil spirits constitute the view of the world within which the laws of *Jubilees* are vitally important. We may compare the role of the apocalyptic framework here with the Astronomical Book of Enoch. The specific message of the Astronomical Book concerns the observance of the 364-day calendar, which is not in itself distinctively apocalyptic. In both *Enoch* and *Jubilees*, however, the calendrical and halakic ideas are given a supporting structure, in a view of the cosmos and of history which is distinctively apocalyptic.

Jubilees is not related to a historical crisis in as obvious a manner as the Animal Apocalypse or Daniel. Yet it too is a product of the Maccabean era. One clue to the date of the book is found in the eschatological section of chap. 23. As we have noted above, the "children" who begin to study the laws and rise up and drive out their adversaries can be plausibly identified with the Hasidim or a wing of that party, and the prohibitions against nudity, marriage with Gentiles, and fighting on the sabbath make good sense in that context. It has been argued that "possibly in one instance, *Jub.* 34:2-9, and almost certainly in another, 37:1-38:14, *Jub.*'s author has composed accounts of battles whose inspiration was the victories of Judas Maccabeus."[102] A further indication of date is found in the relation of *Jubilees* to the Qumran scrolls.[103] It is well known that *Jubilees* shares key doctrines and observances with Qumran: the calendar, determinism, dualism (ethical and angelic), and an eschatology that lacks the idea of resurrection. Yet *Jubilees* lacks any indication of organization in a separate community and is concerned with the full nation of Israel, although the "children" who study the laws are a distinct group within it. In view of these considerations *Jubilees* has been thought to come from a pre-Qumran stage of a movement that culminated in the Essenes and should be associated with the Hasidim.[104] The date should be set about 160 B.C.E., certainly before the Maccabees took over the high priesthood.[105] *Jubilees*, then, is a product of the Maccabean crisis. The crisis perceived in *Jubilees*, however, is not the political crisis or the persecution, which dominates the book of Daniel. It is rather the crisis of piety, occasioned by the neglect of the solar calendar and disregard for the laws. The crisis is primarily within the Jewish community: hence the appeal to the authority of Moses and the attempt to rewrite the law to incorporate *Jubilees*' special interests. *Jubilees* responds to the crisis not only by reaffirming the law of Moses and ascribing its own disputed laws to him (or rather, beyond Moses, to the angel and the heavenly tablets). It also provides a view of the cosmos and of history where the good angels and their followers will prevail and the sinners will be doomed to an inevitable judgment.

3
Daniel

THE BOOK OF DANIEL contains the only full-blown example of apocalyptic literature in the Hebrew Bible. Consequently it has received far more attention than any other Jewish apocalypse,[1] but its special status has not always been beneficial. On the one hand, there has been a tendency to treat Daniel as the paradigmatic apocalypse, although in fact it is representative of only one type. On the other hand, there is even now the agonized attempt to disassociate the canonical book from the rest of the (disreputable) genre. Attempts to dismiss the noncanonical apocalypses as Daniel's "second-rate imitators" should by now be discredited. There are, however, differences between Daniel and the Enoch tradition, some apparent and some real, which require consideration.

THE FIGURE OF DANIEL

The most obvious difference between Daniel and *1 Enoch* is that the visions of Daniel are prefaced by a collection of tales that purport to describe his career. Unlike the prediluvian Enoch, Daniel is presented as a figure from the relatively recent past. Details of the stories could, in principle, be verified from historical sources, and conservative scholars have labored unceasingly, and in vain, to do so.[2] The tales in Daniel bristle with historical problems.[3] The famous case of Darius the Mede may serve as an illustration. The conqueror of Babylon was Gobryas, governor of Gutium, a general of Cyrus, king of Persia. No such person as Darius the Mede is known in history. The successor of Cyrus as king of Persia was named Darius. The author of Daniel inherited a schema of four kingdoms in which Media preceded Persia, and it seems highly probable that he created the figure of Darius the Mede to fit this schema. Similarly, there is a wide consensus that the tale of Nebuchadnezzar's madness was developed from a tradition that orginally concerned the later Babylonian king Nabonidus.[4]

What is at issue in all this is not the veracity of "the word of God," as literalists usually construe it, but a question of genre. An assumption that the "word of God" must be factual historical reporting, and cannot be literary fiction, is theologically unwarranted. Whether or not a given passage is historically accurate is a question of relative probability in view of our total evidence. Nothing is gained by straining credibility in the hope of saving the historical appearances.[5]

The fact that Daniel is located in the historical setting of the exile rather than in primordial antiquity is no indication of historical reliability. Other apocalypses are ascribed to Ezra and Baruch, whose historical existence is beyond doubt, but the books attributed to them in the first century C.E. are nonetheless fictions. We should also expect the tales in Daniel to contain historical reminiscences and local color of the Persian and even the Babylonian period, but these are only the building blocks of the stories. Even if one were to prove the historical existence of both Daniel and Darius the Mede, one would not thereby verify the story of the lions' den.

In fact, the figure of Daniel may be more akin to Enoch than to Ezra or Baruch. The Bible contains no reference to a prophet by this name outside the actual book of Daniel. In the book of Ezekiel (an actual prophet of the exile) we do, however, have two references to Daniel. Ezek 14:14 says that when a land sins against God "even if these three men, Noah, Daniel and Job, were in it, they would deliver only their own lives." Ezek 28:3 taunts the king of Tyre: "Are you wiser than Daniel?" It would appear from these references that Daniel was the name of a legendary wise and righteous man. Further, the name appears (*Dnil*) in the Ugaritic story of Aqhat. Daniel is the father of Aqhat and is conspicuous for offering oblations to the gods and judging the case of the widow and the fatherless. The motif of judging is implied in the name Daniel and is found again in the story of Susanna. At the other end of the biblical period we read in *Jub.* 4:20 that Enoch married "Edni, the daughter of Dânêl, the daughter of his father's brother." We are given no further information about this Dânêl, but the association with Enoch of a name so similar to Daniel, and possibly identical with it, is intriguing.

It is distinctly possible that the same traditional figure underlies the Daniel of Ugarit and Ezekiel, and the Dânêl of *Jubilees*.[6] It is in any case clear from Ezekiel that the name carried traditional associations that could only enhance the authority of the biblical book. The tales in Daniel 1–6, however, give this hero a new identity. The differences with Enoch become more significant at this point. Enoch's wisdom was derived primarily from his ascent. Daniel is at first an interpreter of dreams. Later, in Daniel 7–12, he is the dreamer himself. Obviously the difference here is not absolute. Enoch too has dream visions and in some apocalypses is, like Daniel, preoccupied with the course of history. The difference emerges mainly in contrast to the Book of the Watchers and the Astronomical Book. Daniel lacks the interest in cosmological speculation, which is characteristic of much of the Enoch tradition.

THE DATE AND UNITY OF DANIEL

The crucial argument on the date of Daniel was already formulated by the Neo-Platonic philosopher Porphyry in the third century.[7] Porphyry argued that Daniel was not written in the course of the Babylonian exile but in the time of Antiochus Epiphanes. His basic point was that Daniel "predicted" accurately the course of events down to the time of Antiochus Epiphanes but not beyond it. This argument has stood the test of time. The issue is not "a dogmatic rejection of predictive prophecy" as conservatives like to assert, but a calculation of probability. Everyone recognizes that the predictions of Enoch are after the fact. The same logic holds in the case of Daniel.

The second-century date for the visions of Daniel (chaps. 7–12) is accepted as beyond reasonable doubt by critical scholarship.[8] The dating of the tales in chaps. 1–6 is less evident and is keenly debated. Doubts about the unity of the book arise from several factors. To begin with, the book is written in two languages: Hebrew (1:1–2:4a; chaps. 8–12) and Aramaic (2:4b–7:28). Second, there is the formal distinction between the tales in chaps. 1–6, in which Daniel appears in the third person, and the first-person accounts of revelations in chaps. 7–12.[9] Third, there is the fact that further additions were made to Daniel, which are not found in the Hebrew Bible. The Prayer of Azariah and the Song of the Three Young Men are inserted in Daniel 3 in the Greek translations. The stories of Susanna and of Bel and the Dragon are added on in the Greek versions. These additions attest the ongoing accumulation of Danielic material, although they do not necessarily tell us anything about the composition of the Hebrew/Aramaic book. The so-called Prayer of Nabonidus (4QPrNab), discovered at Qumran, throws more light on the manner in which the tales developed.[10] This document is obviously related to the story of Nebuchadnezzar's madness in Daniel 4, although the relationship is not one of literary dependence in either direction. 4QPrNab suggests that Daniel 4 drew on an old tradition that was preserved and adapted in various ways.[11]

The existence of these related documents may suggest that the book of Daniel was in part a compilation of traditional materials. The crucial argument, however, against the original unity of Daniel comes from the indications of date. The visions in Daniel 7–12 clearly refer to the persecution of Antiochus Epiphanes. There is no clear allusion to this period in the tales. To be sure, these stories were found relevant to the time of persecution and many elements (such as Nebuchadnezzar's madness) could be applied very well in that setting.[12] Nothing in these chapters, however, requires a Maccabean date, and it does not appear that they were composed in the time of Antiochus. However arrogant the kings may be in the tales, they are not without hope of reform. In contrast, in chaps. 7–12 the Gentile kings have acquired a near demonic status. In chaps. 3 and 6 the faithful Jews are rescued alive. In chap. 12 they must look beyond death to a resurrection. The aggravated sense of crisis and negative attitude toward the Gentile kings coincide with the formal transition from tales to visions. One of the puzzles of the book of Daniel is the fact that the formal division does not coincide with the transition between the two languages.

Various explanations have been put forward for the problem of the two languages. There is a consensus that chaps. 2–6 were composed in Aramaic. Some scholars hold that an earlier form of chap. 7 completed the Aramaic Daniel. Some also hold that chaps. 8–12 were composed in Aramaic and then translated into Hebrew.[13] The evidence for the latter point is not compelling, nor is it apparent why only these chapters should have been translated. Chapter 1 may have been composed as an introduction either to the tales, in Aramaic, or to the whole book, in Hebrew.

The key to this problem seems to lie in the fact that an author of the Maccabean period wished to incorporate the collection of Aramaic tales, but himself preferred to write in Hebrew. Although the tales were not composed with the Maccabean situation in mind, the author now wished to integrate them into a new unity. This was accomplished not by rewriting the tales but by binding them to the visions through editorial devices.[14] Daniel 7 was composed in Aramaic (perhaps at a slightly earlier time than chaps. 8–12). Since this vision was thematically related to Daniel 2, it completed a symmetrical arrangement in which chaps. 3 and 6 and chaps. 4 and 5 were closely related pairs.[15] In this way, chap. 7 was associated with the foregoing tales. However, the chronological dating of the chapters associates 7 rather with 8–12. Chapters 2, 3, and 4 are set in the time of Nebuchadnezzar. Chapter 5 refers to the transition from Belshazzar to Darius the Mede. Chapter 6 is set under Darius but ends with a reference to Cyrus of Persia. The sequence of Nebuchadnezzar, Belshazzar, Darius, and Cyrus is not, of course, historical, but it corresponds to the traditional schema of the four kingdoms, in which Persia was preceded by Media. Chapter 7, however, does not continue this sequence but reverts to the reign of Belshazzar. The sequence is then repeated with Darius (chap. 9) and Cyrus (chap. 10) and a reference to the coming "prince" of Greece (10:20). In short, the book of Daniel presents two sequences of dates, and chap. 7 is linked with chaps. 8–12. In this way chap. 7 is associated with both halves of the book and forms a bridge between them. The Hebrew chap. 1 serves to form an enclosure with the later Hebrew chapters. Whether it was specially composed for this purpose is uncertain. The concern for purity in this chapter is not repeated in the tales. Yet chap. 1 sets the scene for chaps. 2–6 but does not anticipate the concerns of chaps. 7–12. It seems somewhat more probable that it was originally an introduction to the tales, presumably in Aramaic.

The unity of Daniel, then, is a secondary unity, achieved through the integration of older tales. We should not think, however, that the connection between tales and visions is purely external. Rather, they represent the continuity of a tradition. The characterization of Daniel and his friends is significant for the author of the visions and his circle. The continuity is indicated by the fact that Daniel and his friends are said to be *maśkîlîm bĕkŏl hŏkmâ* (1:4) ("skillful in all wisdom"), whereas the heroes of the Antiochan persecution in chap. 11 are called *maśkîlîm* (wise teachers). The theme of Jewish relations to Gentile kings runs through both tales and visions. The tales anticipate the crisis of persecution in the stories of the fiery furnace and the lions' den. Most important, however, is the understanding of wisdom and revelation developed in the tales, since it shows the background of one strand of tradition that led into the apocalyptic literature.

We cannot attempt a full discussion of the tales of Daniel here.[16] We will take Daniel 2 as our illustration because it is the most complex of the tales and the one which has the most obvious affinities with the apocalyptic visions.

DANIEL 2

On one level, the story in Daniel 2 can be read as an adaptation of a traditional folktale, in which a person of lower status is called on by a superior to solve an apparently insoluble problem, succeeds in doing so, and is rewarded.[17] This type of tale is widely known. Important Near Eastern precedents include the tale of Ahikar and the biblical story of Joseph. In this case, Daniel is a Jewish exile at the Babylonian court, and his challenge is to tell the king not only the meaning of his dream but also the dream itself, when all the Babylonian wise men have failed. This formulation of the story rings some changes on the traditional folktale. On the one hand, a prominent theological element is introduced. Daniel does not solve the problem by his own wits but by praying to his God for a revelation. The recourse to God is necessitated by the sheer impossibility of the king's demand. The contrast between Daniel and the unsuccessful Chaldeans is a consequence of the contrast between their respective gods. Even the Babylonian king attests the theological implications of the story: "Truly your God is God of gods and Lord of kings, and a revealer of mysteries, for you have been able to reveal this mystery" (2:47).[18] On the other hand, the story has obvious political and ideological implications. Daniel has been said, justifiably, to be a model for "a life-style for the Diaspora." He illustrates how strict Jewish piety is not only compatible with success at a foreign court, but is precisely the key to such success.[19]

The portrayal of Daniel is significant not only as a model for the Diaspora but also as background for the understanding of the apocalyptic visionary in chaps. 7–12. Daniel is presented as a colleague of the Chaldean wise men whose functions include, conspicuously, the interpretation of dreams.[20] Throughout the ancient world dreams were regarded as an important means of communication between the gods and humanity. They are regarded ambivalently in the Bible,[21] but their validity is assumed here. Daniel does not use the traditional Babylonian devices of divination. The point is that he has a superior means of access to revelation, by prayer to his God. Yet it is noteworthy that revelation is given in the veiled symbolism of dreams and so is a mystery (*raz*) which is in need of interpretation (*pesher*). Both these terms, *raz* and *pesher* are prominent in the Qumran scrolls. In the apocalypses, as already in Daniel 7, the mystery is heightened by the fact that the interpretation is given by an angel but the structure of mystery and interpretation persists. Related to this is a sense of determinism. The course of events is already decided. All one can do is understand and take one's position accordingly. In view of this emphasis on understanding, G. von Rad made his famous proposal that the apocalyptic understanding of revelation is more closely akin to wisdom than to prophecy. It is important, however, that the wisdom of Daniel is mantic wisdom, concerned with dreams and mysteries, not proverbial wisdom, which set little store by such obscure phenomena.[22] There was a biblical precedent for mantic wisdom in the story of Joseph, but the context in Daniel is the Babylonian interest in dream interpretation, which confronted the Jews in the eastern Diaspora. It is significant that the Joseph story is also set in a place of exile, in Egypt.

The test of Daniel's wisdom, and that of his God, is the revelation of Nebuchadnezzar's dream. Because of its famous prophecy of the four kingdoms, the dream has been more intensively studied than any other part of the tales. Yet, as the chapter now stands, the emphasis is not on the content of the dream but on the fact that Daniel is able to reveal it. Nebuchadnezzar is apparently oblivious to the implied demise of the Babylonian kingdom and even does homage to Daniel. The king's apparent disregard for the future of his kingdom has been explained as an illustration of the staying power of the old motifs of the folktale, which requires that the hero, Daniel, be rewarded at the end.[23] Yet it is clear that the content of the interpretation carries political implications that strain the conventions of the folktale. If the story had been composed as a vehicle for a prophecy of the kingdom of God we should expect that the traditional motifs would have been adapted to reflect this emphasis at the end.

THE FOUR KINGDOMS

The actual dream and the interpretation are of considerable interest for the background of the apocalyptic view of history. Two complexes of traditional ideas are involved. The statue is made of metals of declining value: the head of gold, breast and arms of silver, belly and thighs of bronze, legs of iron, feet partly iron and partly clay. This succession is strikingly reminiscent of Hesiod's *Works and Days*, 106–201, which speaks of the declining ages of men—first golden, then silver, third bronze, and finally iron.[24] It is probable that Hesiod was already adapting a traditional source, which may have originated in the east, possibly in Persia.[25] It is unlikely that Daniel depended directly on Hesiod. More probably they drew on a common tradition. The significance of Hesiod for our present purpose is that he makes quite explicit the logic of the sequence, which is one of gradual decline. Hesiod also implies that there is something better to follow the generation of iron.

The second complex of traditional ideas involves a schema of four kingdoms followed by a fifth of definitive character. This schema is attested in a fragment of the Roman chronicler Aemilius Sura, who wrote in the early second century B.C.E.: "The Assyrians were the first of all races to hold power, then the Medes, after them the Persians and then the Macedonians. Then, when the two kings Philip and Antiochus, of Macedonian origin, had been completely conquered, soon after the overthrow of Carthage, the supreme command passed to the Roman people."[26] The schema is evidently of eastern origin, since the Assyrians and Medes never ruled over the west. The inclusion of the Medes suggests an origin in Media or Persia. Before the Greek, Macedonian, kingdom was added to the list, the sequence of Assyria, Media, and Persia was already attested in Herodotus and Ctesias. Aemilius Sura adapted the sequence to support the definitive status of Roman rule.

The schema is also found in the fourth *Sibylline Oracle* (*Sib. Or.* 4:49–101). Here again the kingdoms are identified as Assyria, Media, Persia, and Macedonia. The schema of the four kingdoms is combined with a division of world history into ten generations. Six generations are attributed to the Assyrians, two to the Medes, and one each to the Persians and the Macedonians. The Macedonian kingdom is the last of the sequence and coincides with the last generation. In the present form of the fourth

Sibyl there follows an oracle on Rome, but this is not integrated into the numerical sequence and is apparently added to update the oracle. Rome is not envisaged as a definitive or lasting empire. The oracle concludes with cosmic destruction and resurrection of the dead.

The present form of *Sib. Or. 4* is a Jewish oracle from the late first century C.E. The original four-kingdom oracle must have been written before the rise of Rome, probably before the battle of Magnesia in 190 B.C.E., in which the Romans defeated Antiochus the Great of Syria.[27] We cannot be sure how the original oracle concluded, whether with the expectation of a fifth kingdom, as in Daniel 2, or with cosmic destruction. We cannot even be sure whether it was Jewish. In any case, the Sibyl has no pro-Roman sympathies, but it is clear that the fourth kingdom, that of the Greeks, would be destroyed. Accordingly, the four-kingdom oracle could represent the hopes of any Near Eastern people for an end to Hellenistic rule.[28]

An intriguing instance of a four-kingdom schema is provided by the Persian *Zand-ī Vohuman Yasn* or *Bahman Yasht*, which combines the four kingdoms with a sequence of metals in a manner similar to Daniel. The opening chapter of the Zand describes a dream in which Ahura Mazdā showed Zarathustra a tree with four branches, one of gold, one of silver, one of steel, and one of mixed iron. These branches are explained as four periods: the first is the time of Zarathustra and king Hystaspes, the second and third are the reigns of later, Sassanian kings, and the fourth is the sovereignty of the "divs" with disheveled hair, when the tenth century of Zarathustra will be at an end. Despite the inclusion of later kings, many scholars have held that the original schema dates from Hellenistic times and that the "divs" were originally identified with the Greeks, the first conquerors of Persia.[29] The schema of four periods illustrated by metals (gold, silver, steel, and mixed iron) is also found in *Dēnkard* 9.8. Both the *Dēnkard* and the *Bahman Yasht* draw on old Avestan tradition.

It is evident, then, that the dream and interpretation in Daniel 2 draw on traditional motifs but use them in a distinctive way. In a Jewish context, the final kingdom set up by the God of heaven must inevitably be read as a Jewish kingdom. Since this point receives no emphasis in the conclusion of the story, there is reason to question whether the dream was composed for its present context. Various suggestions have been made concerning the extent and meaning of the original dream. One suggestion is that the interpretation in Daniel 2, which specifies that the dream refers to four kingdoms, is secondary.[30] The original statue in the dream would have symbolized Nebuchadnezzar and his successors, Amel-Marduk, Neriglissar, and Nabonidus. The iron mixed with clay might refer to the coregency of Belshazzar with Nabonidus. The declining value of the metals would then symbolize fading power. The point of the dream would be the imminent collapse of the Babylonian empire, symbolized by the whole statue, and the dream would have an anti-Babylonian character. The stone that became a great mountain could then be understood as a messianic Jewish kingdom or conceivably, in a non-Jewish context, the Persian empire. The extant interpretation would have been added in the Hellenistic age to update the oracle.

Alternatively, the interpretation in terms of four kingdoms may have been originally attached to the dream.[31] The first kingdom is the Babylonian kingdom of Nebuchadnezzar. The combination of the sequence of metals with the four-kingdom schema implies a gradual decline in the political situation. The oracle was presumably written under the fourth kingdom and regarded it as the nadir of history. The reign of Nebuchadnezzar is looked on as a golden age. We may compare the contrast between the golden age of Hystaspes and the evil sovereignty of the "divs" in the *Bahman Yasht*. It seems unlikely that this prophecy was Jewish in origin. Nebuchadnezzar was not so fondly remembered in Jewish tradition.[32] In contrast, Babylonians of the Hellenistic age looked back nostalgically to the age of Nebuchadnezzar and developed his exploits to surpass those of Alexander the Great and Seleucus.[33] The identification of Nebuchadnezzar with the head of gold appears far more appropriate for a Hellenistic Babylonian than for a Jew of any period.

Daniel 2 does not specify the identities of the other kingdoms. The fourth, which is "strong as iron" and breaks and shatters all, is surely the Hellenistic kingdom. Since the first is Babylon, the second and third must then be the Median and Persian empires. This sequence of kingdoms is in fact presupposed throughout Daniel (hence the introduction of Darius the Mede). It is not a historical sequence but is adapted from the traditional schema of Assyria, Media, Persia, and Greece by substituting Babylon for Assyria. The inclusion of Media can be explained only by reference to the schema. According to this interpretation the stone that shatters the entire statue must be viewed as part of the Jewish redaction. The original dream might have ended with the description of the statue, as the dream in *Bahman Yasht* chap. 1 simply describes the tree. The anticipated final kingdom would be a Babylonian restoration.

Our knowledge of Babylonian prophecy is still very fragmentary, although it has increased substantially in recent years. A. K. Grayson identifies five main compositions in the genre, ranging in date from the twelfth century B.C.E. to the Hellenistic era.[34] These are all predictions after the event. They are concerned with the succession of reigns. No names are mentioned, but the references can often be identified, much in the manner of what we will find below in Daniel 11. The latest of these, the *Dynastic Prophecy* has been adduced in the discussion of Daniel 2, since it apparently describes a sequence of four kingdoms.[35] According to Grayson, "Each of the first three columns contains a description of a change or fall of a dynasty (column i: fall of Assyria, rise of Babylonia; column ii: fall of Babylonia, rise of Persia; column iii: fall of Persia, rise of Macedonia."[36] Column iv is badly preserved. Grayson suggests that it may refer to the capture of Babylon by Seleucus I. These reigns are alternatively good and bad: those at the ends of columns i and iii are good, those in ii and iv (presumably) bad. The text is fragmentary and many details are uncertain.

The *Dynastic Prophecy* is of some, though limited, relevance to Daniel 2. It provides an instance of Babylonian political prophecy from the Hellenistic age. If Grayson is correct in his interpretation, the prophecy ends with a prediction of the downfall of the Seleucids. It is, then, a rare illustration of the use of prophecy for political propaganda in Hellenistic Babylonia.[37] It is doubtful, however, whether the prophecy can be said to attest a four-kingdom schema. Given the fragmentary character of the text, we cannot be sure that the number four is regarded as definitive. It cannot be regarded as a prototype for Daniel, since it omits Media.[38] It could possibly be an adaptation of the four-kingdom schema discussed above, substituting Babylonia for Media, but this is far from certain.

Unfortunately the conclusion of the *Dynastic Prophecy* is fragmentary, and so its significance remains ambiguous. We should note, however, that the idea of an everlasting kingdom is attested in Babylonian prophecy. The Uruk prophecy, which apparently refers to the time of Nebuchadnezzar II, says: "After him, his son will arise as king in Uruk and rule the entire world. He will exercise authority and kingship in Uruk and his dynasty will last forever. The kings of Uruk will exercise authority like the gods."[39] This Babylonian hope is ironically subverted in the Jewish redaction of the oracle in Daniel 2. The kingdom which will be set up by the God of heaven and which will never pass to another people is surely Jewish, but its identity is not made explicit for Nebuchadnezzar.

The interpretation in Daniel 2 clearly requires a date in the Seleucid period since it refers to the unsuccessful intermarriage of the Ptolemaic and Seleucid houses (2:43). It is, of course, difficult to be sure at what point particular verses were added. In any case, the use of the four-kingdom schema points to a date after the conquest of Alexander.

Any reconstruction of the original oracle that has been used in Daniel 2 must be tentative and hypothetical. It is, nevertheless, apparent that the dream in Daniel 2 is drawn from the world of political prophecy, and the interpretation in terms of four kingdoms reflects the Near Eastern resistance to Hellenism in the era after Alexander. This interest in political prophecy is obviously an important strand in the traditions that nourished the apocalyptic literature.

Taken in itself, Nebuchadnezzar's dream and its interpretation imply a theology of history. The context in Daniel 2, however, highlights not the development of history or the prediction of a messianic kingdom but the superior wisdom of Daniel's God. The image of the stone that crushes the statue ignores the element of chronological sequence. The destruction of the statue here must be viewed in the light of the references to statues and metals elsewhere in the tales. In Daniel 3 Nebuchadnezzar sets up an image of gold. The Jewish youths are prepared to die rather than worship it. In Daniel 5 Belshazzar comes to grief because "you have praised the gods of silver and gold, of bronze, iron, wood and stone" (5:23). In this light, the destruction of the statue in Daniel 2 is primarily an affirmation of the transcendent power of God to destroy all idols and the kingdoms that worship them. This power goes hand in hand with the divine ability to reveal all mysteries. As in the Book of the Watchers, the themes of wisdom and power are closely related.

Despite the destructive conclusion of the dream, Daniel 2 does not reject pagan rule. Rather, this too is viewed as part of God's providential design. The message of the chapter is summed up succinctly in 2:20–23. God has wisdom and might. He removes kings and sets up kings and he gives wisdom to the wise. The orderly sequence of four kingdoms suggests that this is, after all, a managed universe. The fall of the pagan empires will come at its appointed time. For the present, Daniel's fidelity to his own God is in no way incompatible with his service to the king. Rather, his God-given wisdom makes him preeminent among the sages of Babylon. Throughout the tales we find a strikingly optimistic attitude. Good Gentile kings will come to acknowledge the God of the Jews. The arrogant will be chastened. Despite the political supremacy of the Gentiles, God's in his heaven and all's well with the world.

THE APOCALYPTIC VISIONS: DANIEL 7

When we turn to the second half of the book of Daniel we find ourselves in a very different atmosphere. To be sure there is continuity. These chapters, too, are concerned with God's control of the destinies of all peoples. His sovereignty is not publicly evident; it is seen through special revelations by the wise and through exceptional acts of deliverance. These are themes that run through the whole book. Even these themes, however, take on a new coloring in the face of the persecution by Antiochus Epiphanes in 167 B.C.E.[40] The Gentile kingdoms were no longer seen as potential servants of God. Instead they were rebellious monsters that could only be destroyed. The aspiration of the faithful Jews was no longer to rise to high position in the Gentile court but to shine like the host of heaven in the afterlife.

THE BEASTS FROM THE SEA

Daniel 7, like Daniel 2, presents a dream-vision that concerns a schema of four kingdoms, but the context and the specific imagery are quite different. The contest of wisdom between Chaldean and Jew is no longer a factor in chap. 7, nor is there any question of winning the approval of a Gentile king. Now Daniel himself is the dreamer and he has need of an interpreter, in the person of an angel. The dream-vision has become an apocalypse, where the mysterious revelation must be explained by a supernatural being. Daniel's vision has older formal precedents, most notably in the early chapters of Zechariah, where the interpreting angel is introduced.[41] We might also compare the *Bahman Yasht* chap. 1, where Zarathustra's dream vision about four kingdoms is explained by Ahura Mazdā.[42] The change from the human interpreter of Daniel 2 to the angel of chap. 7 expresses a deeper sense of mysteriousness in the later vision.

Like Nebuchadnezzar's dream in chap. 2, Daniel 7 draws freely on traditional motifs. In this case the schema of the four kingdoms is combined with the imagery of beasts coming up out of the sea. The Hebrew Bible contains several scattered allusions to sea-monsters, which are defeated or slain by Yahweh, although there is no explicit account of such a battle. Sometimes this mythic conflict is linked with creation, as in Job 26:7–13:

> He stretches out the north over the void
> and hangs the earth upon nothing . . .
> By his power he stilled the sea,
> by his understanding he smote Rahab.
> By his wind the heavens were made fair,
> his hand pierced the fleeing serpent.

At other times it is linked with the Exodus, as in Isa 51:9–10:

> Was it not thou that didst cut Rahab in pieces
> that didst pierce the dragon?
> Was it not thou that didst dry up the sea,
> the waters of the great deep;
> that didst make the depths of the sea a way
> for the redeemed to pass over?

Yet again, in late prophecy the struggle could be projected into the future: "In that day the Lord with his hard and great and strong sword will punish Leviathan, the fleeing serpent, Leviathan, the twisting serpent, and he will slay the dragon that is in the sea" (Isa 27:1). From all this it is clear that the biblical writers were familiar with mythological traditions, which are much more extensive than what we now find in the Bible and which are highly relevant for Daniel 7.[43] Much light has been thrown on these traditions by the discovery of the Ugaritic myths.

In the Ugaritic myths, the Sea, Yamm, appears as a god who challenges the sovereignty of Baal.[44] They fight, and Baal destroys him. Elsewhere we read that Baal "smote Lotan, the ancient dragon, destroyed the crooked serpent, Shilyat with the seven heads." In a variant of the myth we read that Anat smote "the beloved of El, Sea," destroyed El's river Rabbim, muzzled the dragon and smote the crooked serpent, Shilyat of the seven heads. In this conflict between Baal and the Sea we evidently have a proto-type of Yahweh's battle with the sea-monsters in biblical poetry.

Against this background we can appreciate the evocative power of Daniel's vision. The reference to the winds of heaven stirring up the great sea may be said to echo the primordial scene in Gen 1:2,[45] but here the winds serve to arouse chaos rather than subdue it. Daniel sees a world engulfed by disorder. The beasts of the sea, the traditional "dragons on the waters" (Ps 74:13) and the "dragon that is in the sea" (Isa 27:1) are let loose upon the world. Specifically, chaos takes the form of Gentile rule, expressed by the traditional schema of four kingdoms. Subsequently we are told that "these four great beasts are four kings that will arise out of the earth" and again that the fourth beast represents a "kingdom." It should be apparent that this interpretation does not exhaust the significance of the vision. It gives the reference of the four beasts. It does not give their expressive value.[46] The vision of terrible beasts rising out of the sea does not merely give factual information that four kings or kingdoms will arise. It paints a picture of these kingdoms as monstrous eruptions of chaos, in order to convey a sense of terror far beyond anything suggested by the flat statement of the interpretation. The impact is more profound when we recognize the mythological overtones of the imagery. The kings are not merely human but are manifestations of the primordial force of chaos. As Paul might say: "our struggle is not against flesh and blood but against principalities and powers."

The terror of the beasts is aroused only to be allayed. In 7:9 the scene changes to one of divine majesty. Thrones are placed and the Ancient of Days takes his seat. The divine throne, surrounded by myriad angels and a stream of fire recalls Enoch's vision in *1 Enoch* 14:22 and suggests that the apocalyptic visionaries drew on common traditions. A judgment follows in accordance with the heavenly books (also a common motif in Enoch). The fourth beast is slain and burned in the fire, while the others lose their power. Then follows the famous apparition of "one like a son of man" coming with the clouds of heaven, and dominion, glory, and kingdom are conferred on him.

ONE LIKE A SON OF MAN

The meaning or identity of the "one like a son of man" is perhaps the most celebrated question in all the apocalyptic literature. We must distinguish two levels of the problem: the traditional associations of the imagery and its reference in its present context.

Many scholars have noted that in traditional biblical usage the rider of the clouds is Yahweh.[47] Yet here the one who comes with clouds is clearly subordinate to the Ancient of Days. This imagery is not readily explicable from the Hebrew Bible. However, the Hebrew depiction of Yahweh as rider of the clouds is itself adapted from the older Canaanite storm imagery of the theophanies of Baal.[48] Baal is repeatedly called "rider of the clouds" in the Ugaritic texts. He is, of course, a divine figure, but in the Canaanite pantheon he is subordinate to El, the father of gods and human beings. El is called *abu shanima* in a Ugaritic text, a phrase that is most plausibly interpreted as "father of years" and suggests that El is indeed the prototype for the Ancient of Days.[49]

Since the visions of the Ancient of Days and one like a son of man stand out from their present context, some have regarded them as fragments of ancient sources.[50] This is possible, but they cannot be divorced from the earlier vision of beasts rising from the sea. The exaltation of the Baal-like rider of the clouds over the sea-monsters must be related to Baal's triumph over Yamm in the Canaanite myths.[51] Of course, Daniel does not give an exact reproduction of the Ugaritic myth.[52] To begin with, the Ugaritic myths are more than a thousand years older than Daniel, and the traditions must inevitably have undergone some change. Besides, the tradition provides the building blocks for Daniel's vision, and he adapts it for his own purpose. So the judicial scene replaces the violent conflict of the myth. Yet the juxtaposition of the sea and its monsters with the rider of the clouds shows that we have here more than a borrowing of isolated motifs. Daniel is adapting the structure, or pattern of relationships, of the Canaanite myth.

The use of traditional imagery here should not be confused with the reference of the vision. Daniel is not talking about Baal or Yamm but is characterizing the situation of the Jews under Antiochus Epiphanes. The purpose of the traditional imagery is to bring out the meaning of that situation by analogy. There is some fundamental similarity between the arrogance of the Gentile kings, especially the "little horn" Antiochus, and the raging of Yamm (Sea). The use of this imagery obscures the historical particularity of the present crisis and assimilates it to a cosmic pattern. For this reason Daniel's vision could be reinterpreted and reapplied in subsequent situations (as we find in 4 Ezra 12 and in the New Testament). No names are named. There would be other arrogant beasts after the demise of Antiochus. The effect of the imagery is twofold. On the one hand, it articulates the terror and revulsion evoked by Gentile rule in the light of the persecution. On the other hand, the use of a traditional pattern carries the assurance that the outcome is inevitable. The monsters of chaos will be overcome not, of course, by Baal but by the one like a son of man, who takes his place.

As we have noted, there is no doubt that Daniel 7 is describing the persecution of the Jews under Antiochus Epiphanes. The exaltation of the one like a son of man represents the triumph of the Jews. What is at issue in the scholarly debate over the one like a son of man is the manner in which that triumph is conceived and symbolized. The corporate interpretation holds that the one like a son of man is merely or purely a symbol, whose meaning is exhausted by the identification of its referent.[53] Other views see a more complex relation between this figure and the Jewish people. The traditional view, that the one like a son of man is the messiah is still occasionally defended.[54] This view draws support from the fact that the beasts in the vision are said to be kings and that there is a fluid relationship between the king and the kingdom that he represents. However, it suffers from the fact that there is no clear reference to the messiah elsewhere in Daniel. The main alternative to the corporate interpretation is the view that this figure is the angelic leader of the heavenly host.[55]

Several considerations support the view that the one like a son of man is an angelic being. There is an obvious contrast between this human-like figure and the beasts. The beasts are not mere steno-symbols for corporate entities. They represent kings as well as kingdoms, but in addition they symbolize the chaotic power that these kingdoms embodied. The exalted appearance of the figure who comes with clouds suggests that the righteous Israelites too have supernatural support. The supernatural backdrop of the struggle is made fully explicit in Daniel 10–12. There we are told that behind the human conflicts of the Hellenistic age there is an ongoing battle in heaven between Michael, the patron angel of Israel (assisted by Gabriel), and the angelic "princes" of Persia and Greece. At the end of the conflict Michael will "arise" in victory. In view of the parallelism between Daniel 7 and 10–12 it is apparent that the conflict is not envisaged in purely human terms. It is unlikely that the one like a son of man is merely a corporate symbol for the Jews. Rather we should expect him to represent their angelic or supernatural counterpart. In fact, similar expressions are used elsewhere in Daniel to refer to angels. Gabriel is "like the appearance of a man" (8:15, 10:18), has the voice of a man (8:16), is "like the resemblance of the sons of man" (10:16). Angels are simply "men" at 9:21; 10:5; 12:6, 7. (Compare the symbolism of the Animal Apocalypse, where men represent angels or humans transformed to an angelic state.) Furthermore, the adaptation and reinterpretation of the "Son of Man" figure through the New Testament period is invariably in the individual sense.[56] In *1 Enoch* 46:1 the "Son of Man" has the appearance of a man and his face was full of graciousness like one of the holy angels." In the New Testament the Son of Man is repeatedly associated with the angels (Matt 13:41; 16:27; 24:31; 25:31; Mark 8:38; 13:27, 41; Luke 9:26). In Rev 14:14 "one like a son of man" appears, seated on a cloud, who is evidently an angel and is not identified with Christ. This development of the tradition is most readily intelligible if the expression was originally understood to refer to an angel.

THE HOLY ONES OF THE MOST HIGH

In 7:18 the interpreting angel informs Daniel that "the holy ones of the Most High shall receive the kingdom and possess the kingdom for ever, for ever and ever." Since the kingdom was given to the "one like a son of man" in the vision, this figure and the holy ones are obviously correlative—although they are not necessarily identical without remainder. The expression "holy ones," used substantively, in the Hebrew Bible refers to angels or supernatural beings in the great majority of cases.[57] The evidence is not entirely conclusive, since the term "his holy ones" in Ps 34:10 presumably refers to the Israelites. Again, in the Qumran scrolls "holy ones" usually refers to angels. In 1QM 10:10 "the people of the holy ones" is clearly Israel, but this phrase may be equivalent to "the people of the angels" (analogous to "the people of God"). A number of occurrences in the Qumran scrolls are ambiguous, including the closest parallel to Daniel's "holy ones of the Most High" in CD 20:8: "Let no man agree with him in property or work for all the holy ones of the Most High have cursed him." It may be argued, however, that the extension of the term "holy ones" to human beings at Qumran is mediated by the belief that the community enjoyed fellowship with the angels.

Although the philological evidence is not conclusive, it must be held to create a balance of probability. The probability is strengthened by the fact that the unambiguous occurrences in the book of Daniel itself (4:10, 14, 20; 8:13)[58] refer to angels, and the "holy ones" in *1 Enoch* 14:22-23, a passage closely related to Daniel 7, are also clearly angelic.

Objections to taking the holy ones as angels have been raised mainly on the basis of 7:21 ("the horn made war on the saints and prevailed over them") and 7:25 ("He shall speak words against the Most High, and shall wear out the holy ones of the Most High").[59] It is not, of course, disputed that the experiential datum that gives rise to these assertions is the persecution of the Jews by Antiochus. The issue, again, is how that conflict is conceptualized and symbolized. We have seen that the battle between angelic forces is explicit in Daniel 10–12. In 11:36 we read that Antiochus will exalt and magnify himself above every god and "speak astonishing things against the God of gods." In a parallel passage in 8:10 the little horn "grew great, even to the host of heaven; and some of the host of the stars it cast down to the ground and trampled upon them." Here the horn quite explicitly fights with the heavenly host.[60] The stars, which are cast to the ground, were commonly identified with angels or gods both in Israel and elsewhere in the ancient Near East.[61] In the light of this passage the objection to the angelic interpretation in 7:21 and 25 cannot be sustained.

We should emphasize that the interpretation of the holy ones as the angelic host does not in any case exclude reference to the persecuted Jews. Scholars who reject this interpretation have failed to grasp the nature of the homology between the heavenly and earthly worlds in ancient Near Eastern thought.[62] In modern thinking we assume the priority of human experience and see the mythological world of the gods as a projection.[63] In the ancient world, in contrast, the priority of the world of the gods is assumed, and earthly affairs are regarded as reflections of the greater reality. This homology is quite explicit in Daniel 10, where the struggle between Jews and Greeks is viewed as a battle between their angelic patrons. The link between the holy ones and the Jewish people is clarified in Dan 7:27, which says that "the kingdom and the dominion and the greatness of the kingdoms under the whole heaven shall be given to the people of the holy ones of the Most High." The genitival relationship of the people to the holy ones is analogous to that of the holy ones to the Most High.[64] Dan 7:27 complements 7:18, where the holy ones receive the kingdom. In view of the homology between the people and the holy ones, a kingdom that is given to one is given to both.

The interpretation of the holy ones as angels fits naturally with the identification of the one like a son of man as Michael, leader of the heavenly host. The relation between this figure and the holy ones, then, is not identity, but representation. The three formulations of Dan 7:14, 18, and 27, in which the one like a son of man, the holy ones of the Most High, and the people of the holy ones are said in turn to receive the kingdom, represent three levels of a multidimensional reality. A closely similar conception is found in the Qumran *War Scroll*, where God "will raise up the kingdom of Michael in the midst of the gods, and the realm of Israel in the midst of all flesh" (1QM 17:6–8).[65]

Daniel 7 does not mention Michael by name, as indeed it does not mention any proper names. The suppression of proper names lends an air of mystery to the whole vision. The specific identification of the one like a son of man is not of ultimate importance. What matters is that there is a heavenly savior figure who represents the righteous community on the supernatural level. This figure is specified in various ways in different texts. Michael is named explicitly in Daniel 10-12 and 1QM. Melchizedek in 11QMelch, "that son of man" in the Similitudes of Enoch, the man from the sea in 4 Ezra 13, and the Son of Man in the New Testament all fill this function with varying nuances. Apocalyptic thought allows for considerable fluidity in its mythological conceptions. Although there is now general agreement that Son of Man was not a title in pre-Christian Judaism, the mysterious figure in Daniel represents a type that is widespread in the apocalyptic literature.[66]

The "kingdom" that is conferred in Daniel 7 is also characterized by indeterminacy. There is no attempt to specify a manner of administration. We are not told the extent to which it will be continuous with previous history or how great a transformation it will entail. In the light of our interpretation of the "holy ones" we should expect it to have both a heavenly and an earthly dimension. Daniel is not concerned with giving us information about this future kingdom. He is, however, quite definite that the kingdoms of the Gentiles will come to an end. As in Daniel 2 this judgment is pronounced on all at once, without regard for chronological sequence. Daniel is less concerned with the sequential development of history than with the confrontation with Gentile power in the critical moment of the present.

THE PARALLEL VISIONS

Daniel 7 does not stand alone. Its picture of the Antiochan crisis is complemented by three parallel revelations that go over the same events in slightly different ways. Some scholars have argued that these chapters are the work of different authors.[67] Even if this were so, we should have to assume that the additional authors belonged to the same circle and wrote within a very short time of each other. We should also have to assume that a member of this circle imposed an editorial unity on the book by repeating the sequence of Babylonian, Median, and Persian empires in chaps. 7-12, to parallel that of chaps. 1-6. The authors' circle must in any case have been bilingual, since Hebrew and Aramaic are allowed to stand in juxtaposition. It is surely simpler to suppose that these chapters, which are woven so closely together, are the work of a single author.

In fact, the juxtaposition of complementary revelations is a typical feature of apocalyptic literature. It can be seen in the Similitudes of Enoch, 4 Ezra and 2 *Baruch*. An elaborate example is found in the book of Revelation. In none of these cases can the multiplicity of revelatory units be taken as evidence of multiple authorship. Repetition of a structural pattern with variations of specific detail is a basic means of communication, well attested in myth and folklore as well as in modern communication theory. The English anthropologist Edmund Leach has explained this phenomenon by the analogy of electronic communications.[68] If a message has to be communicated in the face of distractions or "noise," the communicator must use "redundance" by repeating the message several times in slightly different ways. In this way the basic structure of the message gets through. No one formulation exhausts the total message. This use of redundance is crucially important for our understanding of apocalyptic language. It implies that the apocalypses are not conveying a "literal" or univocal truth that can be expressed precisely in one exclusive way. Rather, they share the poetic nature of myth and allude symbolically to a fullness of meaning that can never be reduced to literalness.

DANIEL 9

The parallel revelations in Daniel 8–12 consist of a vision in chap. 8 which closely resembles chap. 7,[69] the interpretation of Jeremiah's prophecy of seventy weeks in Daniel 9, and an angelic discourse in Daniel 10–12. Daniel 9 stands out from the rest insofar as it is explicitly formulated as an interpretation of older biblical texts. The passages in question are found in Jer 25:11–12; 29:10, and say that the dominion of Babylon will last for seventy years, after which time the Jews will be restored. Historically, this prophecy was not accurate. Less than seventy years elapsed before the Jewish restoration. More seriously, the "desolations of Jerusalem" were not then brought to an end, as was painfully obvious in the Maccabean era. Accordingly, the biblical text is treated as a mystery, just as the symbolic visions were. The interpretation must be provided by an angel, in apocalyptic fashion.

Before proceeding to the interpretation, Daniel 9 places a lengthy prayer on the lips of Daniel. In many ways this prayer seems incongruous in its present context. It is not a prayer for illumination, by an individual, as we might expect. It is rather a communal prayer of confession, of a type widely used in the postexilic period.[70] The fluency of its Hebrew is in marked contrast to the rest of Daniel 8–12. Most important, the theology of the prayer contrasts sharply with the apocalyptic framework of Daniel. The logic of the prayer is that the affliction of Jerusalem is a punishment for sin and will be removed if the people repent and pray. Yet when the angel arrives he tells Daniel that the response was sent forth at the beginning of his supplication (in effect without waiting to hear it) and he emphasizes that the end is decreed. In short, events will follow their predetermined course, irrespective of prayer and repentance. Whether this prayer was deliberately placed here by the author to show this contrast[71] or was inserted by a later redactor, it neatly highlights a fundamental difference between the apocalyptic view of history and the traditional Deuteronomic theology. In the apocalyptic view, the course of events is predetermined. This does not mean that there is no room for human freedom. People can determine their own destiny by their reactions, but they cannot change the course of events.

The angel explains that the seventy weeks of Jeremiah are really seventy weeks of years. It is assumed that the biblical number can be regarded as a symbol and interpreted allegorically. The seventy weeks of years, 490 years, are not the product of any chronological calculation. Rather they reflect a traditional schema, ultimately inspired by the idea of the jubilee year (Leviticus 25) and may be taken as an instance of "sabbatical eschatology."[72] We have seen similar schemata in connection with the Apocalypse of Weeks, the seventy generations in *1 Enoch* 10, and the seventy shepherds in the Animal Apocalypse. At least some of the Enochic passages are older than Daniel and show that Daniel drew on traditions that were shared by other apocalyptic writings.

The first seven weeks represent the period "from the going forth of the word to restore and build Jerusalem" (at the time of Daniel's prayer, 9:23) to the coming of an anointed one, a prince (either Zerubbabel or, more probably, Joshua, the first postexilic high priest). Then sixty-two weeks pass virtually without comment. The focus of the prophecy is on the last week, the real time of the author. This is marked by the murder of an anointed one (Onias III, see 2 Macc 4:34) and the profanation of the temple. The point of the prophecy is that all this is determined in advance, and an end is decreed. Daniel gives only a vague indication of what may follow this "end": transgression will be ended, everlasting righteousness established, and the holy place anointed (9:24). His main concern is not in speculating on the future but in providing an assurance that the predetermined period of Gentile sovereignty is coming to an end.[73]

DANIEL 10–12

The most elaborate revelation in the book of Daniel extends from 10:1 to 12:4. The introductory verse alludes to a vision but does not describe it. The apparition of the interpreting angel, presumably Gabriel, is described in detail, so as to emphasize its overpowering effect.[74] The revelation itself has two dimensions. First, the angel explains the supernatural backdrop of the Hellenistic wars. There is an ongoing battle between Michael, "one of the chief princes," and the princes of Persia and Greece. Second, in chap.

11, he outlines the course of the Hellenistic wars in terms of human actions.

The supernatural backdrop is of crucial importance for Daniel's conception of history, as we have already seen in connection with Daniel 7. It is rooted in a common mythological assumption that whatever happens on earth is a reflection of a celestial archetype.[75] A battle between two earthly powers is a reflection of a battle between their respective gods. This conception is vividly illustrated in Isa 36:18-20 (2 Kgs 18:32-35) in the words attributed to the commander of the Assyrian army: "Beware lest Hezekiah mislead you by saying 'The Lord will deliver us.' Has any of the gods of the nations delivered his land out of the hand of the king of Assyria? Where are the gods of Hamath and Arpad? Where are the gods of Sepharvaim? Have they delivered Samaria out of my hand? Who among all the gods of these countries have delivered their countries out of my hand, that the Lord should deliver Jerusalem out of my hand?" Behind every nation stands a god who does battle on behalf of his people. The "princes" of Daniel 10 are clearly an adaptation of this idea. Their significance is that they add a dimension of depth to the record of events. The course of history is not in human hands but is determined by forces beyond our control.

The "prophecy" of Hellenistic history mentions no names, but the people and events can be readily identified.[76] The struggles of the kings of the south (Ptolemies) with the kings of the north (Seleucids) are swiftly reviewed, reaching a preliminary crescendo with the career of Antiochus III (the Great).[77] The main focus of attention is Antiochus IV Epiphanes, to whose reign more than half the chapter is devoted. The preceding review of Hellenistic history bridges the gap between the supposed time of Daniel and the actual composition of the book. It is presented as a prediction and follows the cryptic style of prophecy. In this way it suggests that the course of history has been determined in advance. It also lends credibility to the real prophecy with which the passage concludes. If the "predictions" are known to have been accurate down to the present, then they are likely to be reliable for the future too. In fact, the concluding prophecy of the death of the king was not fulfilled, and so Daniel 11 provides a clear indication of the time when the book was composed.

The technique of Daniel 11 presupposes a willingness to believe that this prophecy had been written by Daniel, some hundreds of years before. We must assume that the immediate circles of the apocalyptic writers were aware of the fiction of pseudonymity, but, although this literature was produced by scribes of considerable learning, it was addressed to the masses at large. Its general effectiveness was undoubtedly enhanced by the willingness of common people to accept the ancient authorship of newly promulgated books.

Daniel 11 provides a rare insight into the nature and goals of the author and his circle. In 11:32 we are told that Antiochus will "seduce with flattery those who violate the covenant," a reference to the Hellenizing Jews who supported his policies. In contrast to these "the people who know their God" will stand firm and take action, and the wise teachers of the people (literally "those who make the people wise") will make the masses understand. Some of these teachers will be killed. They will receive "a little help," although many will join them insincerely. Their deaths are said to refine and purify them until the appointed end.

There is no doubt that the author of Daniel belonged to these wise teachers (the *maśkîlîm*), who are portrayed here as the true heroes of the persecution and in chap. 12 are singled out for special honor at the resurrection. They are portrayed as activists, but they are not said to fight. Their activism lies in making the masses understand. The understanding they convey is presumably the revelation contained in the book of Daniel. The thesis of the visions is that the true meaning of events is not publicly evident but is known to the wise, through revelations. The real struggle is being fought between the angelic princes. Its course and eventual outcome are already predetermined. This knowledge provides a perspective that enables the faithful Jews to bear up under persecution. Further, it gives them a rationale for laying down their lives, since by so doing they will be purified and will be assured of their reward at the resurrection. We are reminded of the story in 1 Maccabees 2 of the martyrs who let themselves be massacred rather than violate the sabbath. We will find a similar stance in the *Testament of Moses*.

This passage throws an interesting light on the alleged esotericism of apocalyptic literature. It is true that the perspective conveyed in the visions is not publicly accessible but requires special, apocalyptic revelation. Yet the whole purpose of this revelation, in the case of Daniel, is to make the masses understand. The command of the angel in Dan 12:4 to "shut up the words and seal the book" must be regarded as a consequence of pseudonymity—it explains why the revelations of Daniel had not been circulated before the Maccabean era. It is possible that some other apocalyptic writings were intended for a restricted group, but at least Daniel is addressed to the *rabbim* or populace at large.

In this light we can also see the location of Daniel within the Jewish community. There is a division within Israel between "those who violate the covenant" and "those who know their God." The commitment of the masses appears uncertain. The *maśkîlîm*, then, constitute a distinct group. Yet they are oriented outward, and they function within the larger community. There is no evidence of separate organization, such as we find at Qumran. The temple and central institutions of the religion are evidently not rejected, although for the present they are defiled.

Many scholars have held that the *maśkîlîm* of Daniel are identical with the Hasidim.[78] This theory does not warrant the consensus it has received. One of the few things we know about the Hasidim is that they were militant supporters of Judas Maccabee. There is no evidence that Daniel supports such a stance. The reference to "a little help" in Dan 11:34 has traditionally been taken as a slighting reference to the Maccabees. In fact it is doubtful whether the author of Daniel would have considered the militant Maccabees to be a help at all. For him, the objective of the wise was to make others understand and to purify themselves. The battle could be left to Michael and his angels.

It is apparent that Daniel lacks the enthusiasm for the Maccabean revolt that characterizes the Animal Apocalypse of Enoch. We must conclude that the group from which Daniel emerged was different from that which developed the Enoch literature, although they occasionally draw on common traditions. The apocalyptic literature was not the product of a single unified movement.

THE RESURRECTION

The angel's revelation reaches its climax in 12:1–3. There we read that when Michael will arise all the people whose names are inscribed in the book will be delivered. Then "many of those who sleep in the land of dust will awake, some to eternal life and some to shame and everlasting contempt. The wise teachers will shine like the glory of the firmament and those who make the masses righteous will be like the stars for ever and ever." Daniel does not envisage a general resurrection.[79] Many, not all, will arise, presumably the very good and very bad. The *maśkîlîm* are singled out for special honor. Shining like the stars should not be dismissed as a mere metaphor. We have noted above that the stars often represent the heavenly host and are used in that sense in Dan 8:10. The significance of the reference in Daniel 12 can be seen clearly in the light of a parallel in *1 Enoch* 104. There the righteous are promised that they "will shine as the lights of heaven and the portals of heaven will be opened to you" (vs. 2) and a few verses later that they will "become companions to the host of heaven" (vs. 6). In this case it is quite clear that to "shine like the stars" is to join the angelic host. This conception is found also in other apocalyptic texts. In the Similitudes of Enoch (39:5) "the dwelling places of the righteous are with the holy angels." In Mark 12:25 (and parallels) Jesus tells the Sadducees that when men rise from the dead they are like the angels in heaven. In the Qumran scrolls the members of the community mingle with the angels even before death. In Daniel 12, too, the identification of stars and angels is implied. The wise teachers, who derive their wisdom from angelic revelations throughout the book, hope to mingle with the angels after their death. In view of this hope we can appreciate the full significance of the triumph of the holy ones in Daniel 7.

The most obvious function of the resurrection in Daniel 12 is to lend support to those who had to lay down their lives if they refused to betray their religion. In the perspective of Daniel, martyrdom makes sense. Belief in vindication beyond death undercuts the greatest threat at the disposal of the tyrant. Yet the function of the resurrection should not be understood exclusively with reference to the persecution. Daniel 12:3 does not say that only the martyred *maśkîlîm* will shine like stars. Presumably this is the destiny of all the wise teachers. Fellowship with the angels is the fulfillment of a life of wisdom and purity.

Daniel 12 says nothing of a kingdom. It does not exclude the continuation of life on earth, and, in the light of Daniel 7 and 9 we must assume that it is implied. However, the earthly fulfillment is not the goal of the *maśkîlîm*. Rather, their attention is focused on the higher world from which the affairs of this life are directed. While Daniel is directly concerned with political affairs, and not with cosmological speculation such as we found in parts of *1 Enoch*, the mystical side of apocalyptic thought is important here too.

SETTING AND FUNCTION

The book of Daniel is related to a specific historical crisis to a degree that is unusual in an apocalyptic book. The sharp reduction in speculative material relative to *1 Enoch* can probably be attributed to the urgency of that crisis. In fact there is little speculative material in the Enochic Apocalypse of Weeks and Animal Apocalypse, which may have been written about the same time. The heat of persecution also underlies the attempts in Daniel to specify the number of days until the end. Such attempts are rare in the apocalypses. Even in Daniel, the fact that contradictory numbers were allowed to stand side by side (Dan 12:11, 12) shows that they were not taken with absolute literalness. [80]

The visions of Daniel are not, of course, mere reflections of the historical crisis. They are highly imaginative constructions of it, shaped as much by mythic paradigms as by the actual events. Fundamental to the perspective of Daniel is the belief that events are guided by higher powers, expressed through the mythological symbolism of the beasts and the rider of the clouds in chap. 7 and, more directly, as angelic princes in chap. 10. A concomitant belief is the idea that the course of history is predetermined and that its end is assured. The destiny of the wise lies beyond this life in a resurrection and pertains to the world of the angels. Since life is thus bounded by a supernatural world, the revelation mediated by the angels acquires crucial importance.

This imaginative construction enables the persecuted Jews to cope with the crisis of the persecution, first by bringing its enormity to expression so that it can be clearly recognized, second by providing assurance that the forces of evil will inevitably be overcome by a higher power, and ultimately by providing a framework for action since it furnishes an explanation of the world that supports those who have to lay down their lives if they remain faithful to their religion. It provides a basis for nonviolent resistance to Hellenistic rule, even in the throes of the Maccabean rebellion.

It is apparent that some elements of the world view of the visions are derived from the tales about Daniel preserved in Daniel 1-6. There too the sovereignty of the God of the Jews is hidden in the present but revealed to the wise. The tales show how Jews could work in the service of Gentile kings and still maintain the purity of their religion. They posit compatibility between the kingdom of God and the Gentile kingdoms. That compatibility was shattered by the persecution of Antiochus Epiphanes. In the light of that crisis the tradents of the Daniel stories sought a new genre that could symbolize more fully the forces behind events—which seemed beyond human control—and could also articulate a hope that transcended what is possible in this life. Daniel 7-12 adapts various traditional patterns and forms in a distinctive and original way, but its basic structure conforms to the apocalyptic genre, which we have already seen exemplified in various ways in *1 Enoch*.[81]

4
Related Genres: Oracles and Testaments

I. ORACLES

The "historical" apocalypses, which view the course of history from the perspective of supernatural forces and the coming judgment, first emerge clearly in the period of the Maccabean revolt. There is obvious continuity with biblical prophecy, especially in the case of Daniel, in the use of the vision form and the expectation of decisive divine intervention. We have seen, however, that there were also important lines of continuity with the political oracles of the Hellenistic age. This Hellenistic background is more immediately obvious in another genre, that of sibylline oracles, which is closely related to the historical apocalypses and appears in Judaism about the same time.

THE SIBYLLINE ORACLES

The genre of sibylline oracles had a long tradition behind it before it was taken over by the Jews.[1] Heraclitus, in the fifth century B.C.E., was already familiar with the figure of the sibyl as an ecstatic woman who uttered prophecies of a predominantly gloomy nature. In the Hellenistic period several sibyls were known, of whom the best known were those of Erythrea (in Asia Minor) and Cumae (in Italy). The most famous collection of sibylline oracles was the official one at Rome.[2] Only fragments of the pagan sibylline oracles have survived.[3] We know that they were often concerned with prodigies but also that they were interpreted with reference to historical and political occurrences. So Plutarch argues that "the prophecies have witnesses to testify for them in the numerous desolations and migrations of Grecian cities, the numerous descents of barbarian hordes and the overthrow of empires. And these recent and unusual occurrences near Cumae and Dicaearcheia, were they not recited long ago in the songs of the Sibyl?" (*De Pythiae Oraculis* 9 [398]). One of the surviving sibylline fragments prophesies that the land of Italy and the Latins will always be subject to Rome. The Cumean sibyl, according to Virgil's *Fourth Eclogue*, foretold a final age, or *ultima aetas,* and a later commentary on the *Eclogue* by Servius says that the sibyl divided the ages according to metals and foretold who would rule over each.[4] It would seem, then, that some pagan sibylline prophecy attempted to encompass the course of history in a manner similar to what we find in the Jewish oracles.

The Roman sibylline oracles were not regarded as different in kind from those associated with other locations. When the temple of Jupiter was burned down in 83 B.C.E. and the sibylline books were destroyed, oracles were gathered from various places, especially Erythrea.[5] The Erythrean sibyl was credited with "foreseeing on behalf of men all hardships difficult to endure."[6] Such oracles played a serious role in the political propaganda of the Hellenistic age.[7] Their importance is reflected in the fact that Augustus had two thousand oracles destroyed and even edited the Roman sibylline books.[8]

The sibylline oracles must be viewed in the wider context of the oracles of the Hellenistic age and especially the political oracles. There was a tradition of prophecy in Egypt which looked for the restoration of native Egyptian rule and the demise of the Greeks.[9] The most important examples are the *Demotic Chronicle* and the *Potter's Oracle.* We have already had occasion to refer to the Persian *Bahman Yasht* because of its affinities with Daniel. From a slightly later period, the *Oracle of Hystaspes* also exhibits the interest in periodization of history and eschatological upheaval that is characteristic of both the historical apocalypses and the Jewish *Sibylline Oracles.*[10] It is against this general background that we must understand the Jewish adaptation of the sibylline form. Unlike the apocalypses of Enoch and Daniel, which are ascribed to figures of the Israelite tradition, the oracles are attributed to the pagan sibyl, and so enter explicitly into the world of Hellenistic propaganda.

The Jewish and Christian *Sibylline Oracles* are preserved in a standard collection of twelve books (conventionally numbered 1–8 and 11–14).[11] Of these, books 3–5 and 11–14 are entirely Jewish (except for minor interpolations), whereas books 1–2 and 8 contain a Jewish substratum. Only books 6 and 7 are original Christian compositions. The latest material, in book 14, extends down to the Arab conquest of Egypt. Books 3–5, however, date from the period between the Maccabees and Bar Kokhba. *Sib. Or.* 3 is generally recognized as the oldest of the Jewish books, and it will be the subject of our attention here. Books 4 and 5 will be considered in a later chapter.

THE THIRD SIBYL

Sib. Or. 3 is itself a complex composition which collects material from a span of two centuries.[12] The main corpus in vss. 97–349 and 489–829 consists of a loosely structured collection of oracles. This material can be dated to the middle of the second century B.C.E. The oracles against various nations in vss. 350–488 are diverse in origin, and at least some of them derive from the first century B.C.E. The oracles in vss. 1–96 are also diverse in origin. These have been thought to be displaced here and to have been originally the conclusion of a different book.[13]

The initial oracle of the main corpus, vss. 97–161, stands apart from the rest of the book. It describes the fall of the tower of Babylon (vss. 97–104) and the war of the Titans against Cronos and his sons (vss. 105–55). It then concludes with a list of world kingdoms (vss. 156–61). The account of Cronos and the Titans is euhemeristic—it "demythologizes" the gods and treats them as figures of ancient history.[14] Such concern with pagan mythology is exceptional in the Jewish sibyllines. Here it establishes a major theme of the sibyl: the struggle for kingship and sovereignty, a struggle that had gone on from the dawn of history. The list of world kingdoms in vss. 156–61 specifies eight, but we should supply the initial kingdom of Cronos and probably also a final kingdom to come. A list of ten kingdoms is a common feature of sibylline oracles.[15]

Four other oracles in *Sib. Or.* 3 may be said to display a common pattern, in which sin (usually idolatry) leads to disasters and tribulations, which are ended by the advent of a king or kingdom:[16] vss. 162–95; 196–294, 545–656 and 657–808. The second of these (vss. 196–294) describes the Babylonian exile and restoration. In the other sections, the king or kingdom is expected in the future. In 162–95 the king who brings the disasters to an end is identified as the seventh king of Egypt from the Greek dynasty. In vss. 545–656 he is a "king from the sun." In the final oracle the reference is to a kingdom that will be raised up by God.

The Seventh King

The interpretation of *Sib. Or.* 3 depends heavily on our understanding of this future king or kingdom, and this in turn is closely bound up with the date and setting of the book. The "seventh king of Egypt" is mentioned not only in vs. 193 but also in vss. 318 and 608. According to vs. 318 Egypt will be torn by strife in the seventh generation of kings, but then war will cease. In vss. 606–8, men will throw away idols when "the young seventh king of Egypt rules his own land, numbered from the dynasty of the Greeks." While seven is admittedly an ideal number, these passages could scarcely have been written after the death of seventh Ptolemy.[17] Some confusion was possible on the enumeration of the Ptolemies, since Ptolemy VI Philometor and Ptolemy VIII Euergetes II (Physcon) were coregents in the years 170–164. Philometor also shared the throne with his son, Ptolemy VII (Neos Philopator) in the last year of his reign, and the youth reigned very briefly after his father's death. On any reckoning, the date of composition cannot be later than the end of Physcon's reign (117 B.C.E.). Since the seventh king is still anticipated as future, a date in the reign of Philometor is more likely, especially in view of the good favor of that Ptolemy toward the Jews.[18] Such a date fits well with the other indications in the book. Vss. 175–93 contain a vigorous attack on Rome, which is said to cause evils in many places, but especially in Macedonia. This can only refer to the Roman conquest of Greece in the mid second century B.C.E.[19] The sibyl's negative attitude toward Rome probably reflects the attitude of Philometor, who lost the support of Rome from 161 B.C.E. on.[20] It stands in marked contrast to the good relations between Rome and the Maccabees in this period.

The statement in vss. 315–18 that Egypt would be torn by civil strife has been usually taken as a reference to the civil war between Philometor and Physcon. In vs. 611, in a passage that follows immediately on an allusion to the seventh king, we read that a king will come from Asia and destroy Egypt. This destruction becomes the occasion of the conversion of the Egyptians. Many scholars have identified the king from Asia as Antiochus Epiphanes who invaded Egypt in 170 and again in 169.[21] In fact the king from Asia was a traditional enemy of Egypt, a tradition that went back to the time of the Hyksos.[22] In v. 611, the invasion would seem to be a future, eschatological event. However, if this allusion was triggered by the recent experience of the invasion of Epiphanes we have a further indication of a date in the time of Philometor. The "young" seventh king could be Philometor himself[23] or, more plausibly, his anticipated successor, Neos Philopator.

The King from the Sun

The passages that refer to the seventh king do not depict him as an active savior figure, but they say that a crucial turning point will come in his reign. In vv. 652–56 the expected king is portrayed in more active terms: "Then God will send a king from the sun, who will stop the whole earth from evil war, killing some, imposing oaths of fidelity on others. He will not do all these things by his own plans, but in obedience to the noble teachings of the great God." This "king from the sun" has been the subject of much controversy. The phrase has been commonly rendered "king from the east" and has been presumed to refer to a Jewish messiah,[24] but there is no precedent either for a simple equation of "sun" with "east" or for a messiah from the east. The closest parallel for the expression is found not in a Jewish work at all but in the Egyptian *Potter's Oracle*. There we read "and then Egypt will increase, when the king from the sun, who is benevolent for fifty-five years, becomes present, appointed by the greatest goddess Isis." Here "king from the sun" is an old pharaonic title. The *Potter's Oracle* is predicting a native Egyptian king who would overthrow the Ptolemies. However, the Ptolemies could also adopt the pharaonic titles for their own purposes. Ptolemaic kings are elsewhere said to be "chosen by the sun" and "son of the sun, to whom the sun has given victory."[25] In *Sib. Or.* 3, the "king from the sun" cannot be divorced from "the seventh king of Egypt from the line of the Greeks." The king who will stop the earth from war must be presumed to be the same as the one in whose reign war will cease, especially since there is no evidence against the identification. The "king from the sun," then, must be identified with the seventh Ptolemy, either Philometor or his anticipated successor.

If this interpretation is correct, it follows that *Sib. Or.* 3 hails a Ptolemaic king as a virtual messiah. Precedent for such a positive attitude to a Gentile king can be found in Isa 45:1, where Cyrus is hailed as "my messiah" or "my anointed one." Precisely this analogy is brought to mind by *Sib. Or.* 3:286–94. There we read:

> And then the heavenly God will send a king and will judge each man in blood and the gleam of fire. There is a certain royal tribe whose race will never stumble. This too, as time pursues its cyclic course, will reign, and it will begin to raise up a new temple of God. All the kings of the Persians will bring to their aid gold and bronze and much-wrought iron. For God himself will give a holy dream by night and then indeed the temple will again be as it was before.

The mention of the "kings of the Persians" makes clear that the reference is to the restoration from the exile in the fifth century. The "king" who is sent is not an eschatological messiah, but Cyrus, who released the Jews. The passage might, however, be said to provide a typology for the eschatological time. The typology would suggest that the well-being of the Jews depends on the power of a benevolent Gentile king.[26] In fact, the Jews had been loyal subjects throughout the postexilic period. Before the Maccabean revolt there was a significant division between those who supported the Seleucids of Syria and those who favored the Ptolemies.[27] At a time when Judea was locked in deadly combat with the Seleucids, it was natural that some Jews, especially those in Egypt, should look to the Ptolemies for deliverance.

The Judaism of the Sibyl

Naturally, *Sib. Or.* 3 is not simply propaganda for a Ptolemaic king. The eschatological sections, including the predictions of the seventh king, serve as a frame for the religious and ethical message of the book. In several passages the sibyl specifies the kinds of conduct that lead to destruction and those that lead to deliverance. The religious stance might be characterized as "covenantal nomism."[28] The Jews are praised for "fulfilling the word of the great God, the hymn of the law" (vs. 246) and "sharing in the righteousness of the law of the Most High" (vs. 580). They can fail, on occasion, and be punished, as is shown by the example of the Babylonian exile, but they are restored if they keep their trust in the laws (vss. 283-84). Yet the sibyl treats the law in practice as if it were natural law. Other nations can be condemned for failing to observe it (vss. 599-600). The main requirements that are emphasized are not the distinctive Jewish laws, such as circumcision or dietary restrictions, but the common ethic which the Diaspora Jews hoped to share with enlightened Gentiles.[29] Idolatry is the chief sin. Sexual abuses, especially homosexuality, are repeatedly denounced. There are warnings against arrogance and greed. A more distinctive position is taken in the unequivocal condemnation of astrology, augury, and divination. The central points of the ethical teaching are summed up in vss. 762-66: "Urge on your minds in your breasts and shun unlawful worship. Worship the Living One. Avoid adultery and indiscriminate intercourse with males. Rear your own offspring and do not kill it, for the Immortal is angry at whoever commits these sins."

There is, however, another important aspect of the sibyl's teaching. In an address to the Greeks in vss. 545-72 she specifies that the rejection of idolatry entails offering sacrifices in "the temple of the great God." The future ideal is the restoration of pious men who not only keep the law but fully honor the temple of the great God with all kinds of sacrifices (vs. 575). In the final utopian state the Jews will all live peacefully around the temple, and the Gentiles will be moved to "send to the temple" and ponder the law of God (vss. 702-31). The Jerusalem temple is of vital importance for the true religion and should become a place of worship for all nations. Apart from sending gifts there, the Gentiles are warned to keep their hands off Jerusalem: "But wretched Greece, desist from proud thoughts. Do not send against this city your planless people which is not from the holy land of the Great One" (vss. 732-35). The Greeks who in fact sent armies against Jerusalem in this period were the Seleucids, and the admonition is addressed to them. It is apparent, however, that it would also apply if a

Ptolemy were to attack Jerusalem. The sibyl includes a fantasy, reminiscent of Psalms 2 and 48, in which the kings of the Gentiles assemble to attack Jerusalem but are judged by God (vss. 657–68).

The Ptolemaic king is not exalted for his own sake. Rather, his role is to facilitate and pave the way for a utopian Jewish state centered on Jerusalem. This was also the role of the "messiah" Cyrus in Deutero-Isaiah. The fact that a Ptolemaic king has a role in this scenario is a significant indication of the political perspective from which the sibyl wrote.

The Provenance of Sib. Or. 3

We may now inquire which circles in Judaism in the mid second century B.C.E. would have produced a document such as this.[30] The combination of Jewish law and temple cult, on the one hand, and enthusiasm for a Ptolemaic king, on the other, could plausibly be attributed to Onias III, the last legitimate high priest before the Maccabean revolt. 2 Maccabees presents Onias as a man of great piety, especially devoted to the temple cult. His father, Simon the Just, was pro-Seleucid, but Onias himself seems to have inclined toward the Ptolemies. This may be inferred from the fact that the pro-Ptolemaic Hyrcanus, son of Tobias, deposited funds in the Jerusalem temple, and also from the readiness of Antiochus Epiphanes to displace Onias. After the Maccabean revolt, Onias's son, Onias IV, sought refuge in Egypt. There he attained distinction in the service of Philometor and was allowed to build a temple at Leontopolis. The hypothesis that *Sib. Or.* 3 was composed in circles close to the younger Onias accounts satisfactorily for all aspects of the work. The enthusiasm for the Ptolemaic house is more readily intelligible among the supporters of the warrior priest than in any academic circles in Alexandria. Such a provenance would also explain the strange silence of *Sib. Or.* 3 on the Maccabean revolt.[31] Onias was no supporter of the Maccabees. Yet he never actively opposed them either.

Sib. Or. 3 is definitely oriented toward the Jerusalem temple. This fact should not militate against the view that its author was associated with Leontopolis. The Leontopolis temple was probably not founded until several years after Onias arrived in Egypt.[32] The oracles may have come from the earlier period. It is improbable that Leontopolis was ever intended as a rival of Jerusalem. Its remote location makes such a role unlikely.[33] Although the Jews of the land of Onias continued to play a prominent part in Egyptian Judaism, their temple was never a bone of contention. We know from the example of Qumran that rejection of the current priesthood did not necessarily exclude the hope for an ultimate restoration of Jerusalem.[34]

Sib. Or. 3, then, is a highly propagandistic document. It presents Judaism to the Hellenistic world in terms that are primarily ethical:

avoidance of idolatry, superstition, and sexual misconduct. This view of Judaism is integrated into a political vision where the Ptolemaic kingship would continue to play a role. The use of the sibyl's name was intended to lend the weight of a venerable pagan authority to this view. The suggestion of determinism in the oracular form, enhanced by the frequent use of *ex eventu* prophecy, lent an air of inevitability to the sibyl's message. In all, then, this was a medium well suited for Jewish propaganda in the Hellenistic world.

THE SIBYLLINES AND THE APOCALYPSES

Philip Vielhauer wrote that "the Sibyllines represent the Apocalyptic of Hellenistic Diaspora Judaism (from which only one real Apocalypse is known, slav. Enoch)."[35] He went on to elaborate on the ambivalence of this remark. The oracles do indeed share some prominent features with the historical apocalypses: pseudonymity, historical reviews, expectation of a definitive kingdom. Vielhauer distinguished the two genres primarily in terms of their function. He regarded the apocalypses as "conventicle literature," whereas the sibyllines were outward-directed "missionary propaganda." We have seen already that Vielhauer's understanding of the function of the apocalypses requires some modification. The function of the sibyllines is also less clear-cut when we consider *Sib. Or.* 5 in a later chapter. It is true, however, that no Jewish apocalypse serves the function of propaganda to the Gentile world in the way we have found in *Sib. Or.* 3. It is not apparent that an apocalypse could not be used in that way, but in fact it does not seem to have been. The function of these documents is variable, however, on the level of social function which Vielhauer has in mind. Other differences are more deeply rooted in the structure of the genres themselves. We have seen that the sibyl, like the apocalypses, uses the eschatological horizon as a frame to lend urgency to an ethical and political message. In the sibyllines, however, the supporting framework is all on the horizontal axis—the authority of the sibyl, the allusions to historical events, the expectation of a kingdom. The vertical axis of the apocalypses is missing. There is no interest in angels and demons or in the cosmology of the heavenly world. Consequently, the oracles lack the mystical dimension of the apocalypses, and this difference is reflected in the eschatology. *Sib. Or.* 3 contains no hint of a judgment of the dead; all is on a political, earthly level. The later sibyllines, to be sure, acquired an interest in the judgment of the dead, but this interest was not an intrinsic part of the sibylline genre.

ORACLES FROM THE FIRST CENTURY B.C.E.

Sib. Or. 3 inaugurated a tradition of sibylline prophecy in Egyptian Judaism. In its present form the book contains a number of oracles from the first century B.C.E. The most notable of these is found in vss. 350–80. It predicts the vengeance of Asia on Rome, which will be exacted by a lady, a *despoina*. The lady in question should be identified as Cleopatra, who also represented Egypt, as its queen, and the goddess Isis, whom she claimed to incarnate.[36] The oracle must have been written shortly before the battle of Actium and the decisive fall of Cleopatra. This oracle lacks the ethical and religious convictions characteristic of the earlier oracles of *Sib. Or.* 3, but the enthusiasm for the Ptolemaic house is carried on. Such enthusiasm might well be expected in the military colony of the land of Onias. The oracle continues a vein of anti-Roman polemic that was already present in *Sib. Or.* 3:175–90 and came to play an increasing part in the later Jewish sibyllina.

A quite different attitude to Cleopatra is found in two brief oracles in vss. 46–62 and 75–92, both of which were written in the aftermath of Actium. Both reflect the disillusionment of Cleopatra's supporters after her defeat. The hope for a glorious kingdom is replaced by the expectation of a day of destruction. This is marked by brimstone from heaven in vss. 60–61, by the collapse of the heavens and a stream of fire in vss. 80–85. The "lady" Cleopatra, of whom so much is expected, is now the "widow" (vs. 77) who brings desolation to the world. It is significant that the decline of the confident hopes in the Ptolemaic house is accompanied by an increasing use of the imagery of cosmic destruction, familiar from the historical apocalypses. This tendency is even more strongly evident in *Sib. Or.* 3:63–74, which says that "Beliar will come from the Sebasteni." This should be read as an allusion to Nero, from the house of the Augusti. Nero becomes a central figure in several later sibylline books. The mythic portrayal of the emperor as Beliar marks a further rapprochement with apocalyptic imagery.

Not all the sibylline oracles are devoted to political upheavals. *Sib. Or.* 11 is an early oracle, most probably written in the early first century C.E.[37] It shares the political interests of the other sibyllines, but is pro-Roman in stance and predicts no political upheaval. This dispassionate attitude is also in evidence in the later Jewish books 12–14. These books show that the oracles, like the apocalypses, could be used in more than one way, in the service of more than one ideology. In fact there are a few oracles in *Sib. Or.* 3:1–45 and the *Sibylline Fragments* that are not concerned with history or politics at all, but with a highly spiritual philosophy.

We will return in a later chapter to examine *Sib. Or.* 4 and 5, books written in the disastrous period between 70 and 132 C.E. In these works the affinities with the historical apocalypses are closer than in *Sib. Or.* 3. The entire sibylline tradition remains, however, important background for the apocalypses, since it illustrates a strand of political prophecy that had a considerable impact on one aspect of apocalyptic thought.

II. THE TESTAMENTARY LITERATURE

Another literary genre that is closely related to the apocalypses and appears in the Hellenistic age is the testament. A testament is a discourse delivered in anticipation of imminent death. The speaker is typically a father addressing his sons or a leader addressing his people or his successor. The narrative framework describes, in the third person, the situation in which the discourse is delivered and ends with an account of the speaker's death. The actual discourse is delivered in the first person.[38]

Biblical prototypes can be found in the "blessings" of Jacob (Genesis 49) and Moses (Deuteronomy 33-34).[39] The genre was also known, though poorly attested, in the Hellenistic world.[40] The Jewish and Christian pseudepigrapha include testaments of the twelve patriarchs, Isaac, Jacob, Moses, and Job, and the so-called *Visions of Amram* from Qumran cave 4 and the *Testament of Adam* (in part) are close to the testamentary form.[41] Only the testaments of Moses and Job and the *Visions of Amram* can be regarded as Jewish in their present form, but all the others contain substantial Jewish material. In addition, testaments occur as subsidiary forms in several Jewish works: Tobit 14; 1 Macc 2:49-70; *Jubilees* 21, 36; Pseudo-Philo's *Biblical Antiquities* 19, 23-24, 33; *2 Enoch* 39-55; *2 Baruch* 43-47.

THE TESTAMENT OF MOSES

The affinities of testaments with apocalypses are most readily obvious in the *Testament of Moses*. This work is known from a single Latin manuscript, published by A. Ceriani in 1861 and identified as the *Assumption of Moses*.[42] In fact, however, this document does not refer to the assumption of Moses but is a prophecy delivered before his death. Accordingly, the dominant opinion of scholars is now that this text corresponds to the work known in antiquity as the *Testament of Moses*, not the *Assumption*.[43] Since the conclusion of the text is missing, it is possible that it originally contained an assumption of Moses too. We should expect that it at least referred to his death.

The *Testament* begins by having Moses summon Joshua and commission him as his successor, since his own death is at hand. Chapters 2-9 then give an extensive prophecy of the history of Israel. Chapter 2 very rapidly surveys the period from the conquest to the exile; chap. 3 deals with the exile as a punishment for sin. Then in chap. 4 "one who is over them" enters to intercede, and the restoration follows. Chapter 5 refers to the rise of kings "who share in their guilt and punish them," and chap. 6 to "kings bearing rule" who will call themselves high priests of God and work iniquity in the holy of holies, followed by "an insolent king," who is evidently Herod. Chapter 7 describes a time of impious and treacherous men, followed in chap. 8 by a persecution. Then a man named Taxo, with his seven sons, resolve to purify themselves and die rather than break the laws. Chapter 10 prophesies how God's kingdom will then appear. The book concludes with an interchange between Moses and Joshua.

DATE

In its present form the *Testament of Moses* dates from the early years of the first century C.E.[44] Chapter 6 clearly refers to the Hasmoneans (the kings who will call themselves priests), Herod, and the campaign of Varus in 4 B.C.E. (6:8–9: "cohorts and a powerful king of the west will come, who will conquer them, and he will take captives, and burn a part of their temple with fire, and crucify some around their colony"). Yet the account that follows in chap. 8 is reminiscent of the persecution of Antiochus Epiphanes: Jews are persecuted because of their circumcision and are forced to participate in idolatry and blasphemy; circumcision is disguised by medical means. Although the correspondence with other accounts of the persecution is not exact, it is more specific than we should expect if this passage were intended as a prophecy of purely future events.[45] Accordingly, R. H. Charles proposed that chaps. 8 and 9 originally stood before chap. 6 and so fitted into the chronological sequence of the book.[46] This proposal is now universally rejected. Not only has it no textual basis, but it also violates the logic of the book, which requires that chap. 10 follow as a response to chaps. 8 and 9.[47] Most probably we should reckon with two stages in the composition of *T. Moses*. The first culminated in the crisis under Antiochus Epiphanes. The second updated the historical review by inserting the references to the Hasmoneans and Herod in chap. 6 and culminated in the partial destruction of the temple by Varus.[48]

THEOLOGY

The basic theology of the book is consistent throughout. God created the world on behalf of his people but did not manifest his purpose, in order to confound the Gentiles (1:12–13). The work may be viewed somewhat loosely as a rewriting of Deuteronomy 31–34.[49] The announcement of Moses' death, the commissioning of Joshua, and instructions to preserve the books are all paralleled in Deuteronomy 31. Deuteronomy 32 has a schematic review of history, although it is much less extensive than what we find in *T. Moses* and is not presented as a prediction. Deuteronomy 33, the blessing of Moses, may be said to have eschatological implications for the destiny of Israel, and the account of Moses' death in Deuteronomy 34 was presumably adapted in the lost conclusion of the *Testament*. It is true in any case that history in *T. Moses* is governed by a Deuteronomic pattern of sin and punishment. History falls into two cycles. The first, in chaps. 2–4 extends from the conquest to the Babylonian exile. Although some southern kings broke the covenant, the main sin of this period was the apostasy of the northern tribes, which broke with the Jerusalem temple. Accordingly, the southern tribes complain "inasmuch as ye have sinned we too are led away with you." The restoration follows from the intercession of "one who is over them."[50] The second cyle then concerns the postexilic period. Again there is a period of sin (chaps. 5, 7), followed by punishment in the form of persecution. This time Taxo intervenes as mediator, and the eschatological kingdom of God is ushered in .[51] This theology might also be aptly described as covenantal nomism. Salvation comes through membership of the Jewish people and requires observance of the law. The pattern of sin and punishment is affirmed even in the face of persecution where the righteous are killed.

TAXO

The story of Taxo and his sons plays a crucial role in the *Testament of Moses*, since it marks the transition from the persecution to the revelation of God's kingdom. Taxo resolves: "Let us fast for the space of three days and on the fourth let us go into a cave which is in the field, and let us die rather than transgress the commands of the Lord . . . for if we do this and die, our blood will be avenged before the Lord" (9:6–7). The logic of this resolution is supplied by Deut 32:35–43: "Vengeance is mine, and recompense . . . for the Lord will vindicate his people . . . for he avenges the blood of his servants and takes vengeance on his adversaries." The way to bring about a change in the course of history is not by violent rebellion but by moving God to action—specifically by letting oneself be killed rather than break the law. Then God will consecrate an angel to take vengeance on the enemy and will himself rise from his throne and punish the Gentiles.[52] Nature will be thrown into upheavals. Satan will be no more, and Israel will be exalted to the heaven of stars and look down on its enemies in Gehenna. This astral exaltation recalls the destiny of the *maśkîlîm* in Daniel and clarifies the willingness of Taxo to submit to death. The pious Jew can afford to lose his life, if by so doing he ensures his future happiness with the heavenly host.

The attitude represented by Taxo is reminiscent of the story in 1 Macc 2:29–38 of the martyrs who refused to defend themselves on the sabbath but resolved: "Let us all die in our innocence; heaven and earth testify for us that you are killing us unjustly." (The allusion to heaven and earth again recalls Deuteronomy 32.) We have seen in chap. 3 above that this attitude is close to the stance of Daniel, where the *maśkîlîm* are prepared to lay down their lives in the hope of future glory. It stands in sharp contrast to the model of Phinehas the zealot (Num 25:6–15), which is invoked to justify the action of Mattathias in 1 Maccabees 2. *T. Moses* evidently advocates a policy of nonviolence which emphasizes purity and fidelity to the law, even at the price of death.

RELATION TO THE APOCALYPSES

The affinity of *T. Moses* with the apocalypses is most obvious in comparison with Daniel. A major purpose of the *Testament* is to assure the faithful Jews that the world is created for them, despite the contrary appearances in the present. In Daniel too the course of history is mysterious and is only revealed through special revelation. In both documents, the culmination of history is the revelation of a heavenly kingdom, and in both an angel plays a key role in bringing it about. In both books the overview of history is designed to support a stance of martyrdom. The outcome of history will be achieved on the supernatural level. The task of the Jew is one of piety, not militance.

The literary form of the Testament is different from that of an apocalypse: it is prophecy uttered by Moses, not an angelic revelation received by him. Even here there are also similarities. One is the use of pseudonymity. The *Testament*, like the apocalypses, is given a weight of authority by its association with a venerable figure of the past. The schematic review of history is also a typical feature of the "historical" apocalypses and conveys the sense that there is indeed a divine design. Yet there is also a significant theological difference between *T. Moses* and either Daniel or *1 Enoch*. The choice of Moses as pseudonym is significant. *T. Moses* is deeply rooted in the covenantal theology of Deuteronomy. Consequently, it is less deterministic than the apocalypses. In both Daniel and the Enochic apocalypses the course of history is set. Humanity can only understand and react. In *T. Moses* the course of history can be changed by human intervention, in the case of the mediator in chap. 4 and of Taxo in chap. 9. True, humanity does not change the course of events directly, but can only persuade God to do so. Yet the *Testament* preserves the interaction of human and divine initiative, which is at the heart of the Deuteronomic theology. This theological difference is not entailed by the literary genres of apocalypse and testament in themselves. Testaments are not necessarily bound to covenantal theology. Rather, the difference reflects the ways in which these genres were actually used in the second century B.C.E.

THE REDACTION OF THE TESTAMENT OF MOSES

The theology of the *Testament of Moses* is not modified by the updating insertion of chap. 6, which denounces the Hasmoneans and Herod.[53] The pacifistic tendency of the work is probably more evident in the later edition. The figure of Taxo suggests a contrast with the portrayal of Mattathias in 1 Maccabees 2.[54] Both are from priestly families. Both are loyal to the law and their fathers and deplore the impiety of the Gentiles. Both exhort their sons to die rather than be guilty of apostasy. However, Mattathias advocates militant resistance. His sons number five, Taxo has the perfect number seven. Mattathias looks to Judas for vengeance, Taxo looks to God. It is not clear how far this contrast would have been evident at the actual time of the revolt, although the basic contrast between militance and martyrdom was inevitable. At the turn of the era, when 1 Maccabees had been long in circulation, the full contrast was surely apparent. We know that the Maccabees served as prototypes for Jewish revolutionaries in the later period.[55] Taxo could now serve as an antitype. The stance of nonviolent resistance flourished in Judaism side by side with the impulse to zealotry throughout the period leading up to the war with Rome.[56]

THE LOCATION IN JUDAISM

The *Testament of Moses* evidently presupposes a division within Israel between those who observe the law and those who do not (12:10-11). It is not apparent that the righteous are organized in a distinct community.[57] In 4:8 we read that after the restoration "the two tribes will continue in their prescribed faith, sad and lamenting because they will not be able to offer sacrifices to the Lord of their fathers." This statement has usually been read as a rejection of the worship of the Second Temple, an attitude that finds possible parallels in the Apocalypse of Weeks, the Animal Apocalypse (*1 Enoch* 89:73) and *T. Levi* 16:1.[58] It is possible that the passage refers to those of the two tribes who remain in exile and so are prevented by distance from offering sacrifices.[59] In view of the elliptic nature of the text it is not possible to be certain.

THE TESTAMENTS OF THE TWELVE PATRIARCHS

The most extensive corpus of testamentary literature from the ancient world is the *Testaments of the Twelve Patriarchs*. This work is certainly Christian in its present form but there is also no doubt that it incorporates Jewish material. The history of composition is one of the most controversial issues in the current study of the pseudepigrapha. The traditional view that the *Testaments* were Christian gave way in the nineteenth century to a theory of Jewish composition with Christian interpolations.[60] The dissertation of M. de Jonge in 1953 revived the theory of Christian authorship.[61] De Jonge and his students have strenuously defended this position in recent years,[62] but most scholarly publications continue to espouse some variant of the interpolation theory.[63] In the wake of the discovery of the Qumran scrolls a number of scholars proposed that the *Testaments* were Essene documents.[64] This proposal has won little acceptance, but we are still far from a consensus on the history of composition.[65]

JEWISH TRADITIONS

The use of Jewish traditions in the *Testaments* is shown by the existence of parallel materials. The exploits of Judah in *T. Judah* 3-7 are paralleled in *Jub.* 34:1-9 and *Midrash Wayissa'u*, but the similarities appear to derive from a common tradition rather than from direct dependence.[66] A Hebrew *Testament of Naphtali* has been known since the end of the last century. This is definitely not the source of the Greek testament but is a much later document. It is possible that both Greek and Hebrew depend on a common source.[67] A further parallel to *T. Naphtali* 1:6-12, in Hebrew, has been found at Qumran. Aramaic parallels to *T. Levi* from the Cairo Geniza were discovered at the beginning of the century.[68] These fragments provide a partial parallel to *T. Levi* 8-13 and a remote parallel to *T. Levi* 6. There are also two Greek additions that are inserted into a Mount Athos manuscript of *T. Levi* of the *Testaments of the Twelve Patriarchs* at 2:3 and 18:2. The Greek insert at 18:2 shows extensive agreement with the Aramaic Geniza fragments. An Aramaic fragment from Qumran has been found which corresponds to the Greek addition at 2:3.[69] The Qumran fragments have been held to represent "essentially the same document"[70] as the Aramaic fragments from the Geniza and also show other points of contact with the Greek text of the *Testaments of the Twelve Patriarchs*.[71] From all this it appears that there was an original Aramaic Levi apocryphon which served as a source for the *Testament of Levi*. It is not certain, however, whether the Aramaic Levi material or the Hebrew Naphtali material was in the form of a testament. If the Qumran Naphtali material represents a *Testament of Naphtali*, then we should suppose that there was a Hebrew *Testaments of the Twelve Patriarchs* in the second century B.C.E., since Naphtali was such an obscure patriarch.[72] It is possible that the Qumran material had a different literary form. Even if the Qumran fragments represent an original *Testaments of the Twelve Patriarchs*, it is apparent that this original document did not correspond exactly to the Greek text that has come down to us. In some respects the original text was apparently longer. On the other hand, no Semitic parallels for the extensive homiletic material in the *Testaments* have been published. Many scholars hold that this material was originally composed in Greek, possibly in the Hellenistic Diaspora.[73] So, while it is clear that the *Testaments* incorporate pre-Christian Jewish material, it is also apparent that the Jewish elements can only be identified tentatively and with caution.

THE CONTENT OF THE TESTAMENTS

The *Testaments of the Twelve Patriarchs* display a consistent pattern which involves three basic elements:[74] (1) historical retrospective, in the form of a narrative about the patriarch's life (*T. Asher* is the only exception); (2) ethical exhortation; and (3) prediction of the future (these predictions often display the so-called sin–exile–return pattern,[75] which is typical of Deuteronomic theology). These elements are logically related. The ethical exhortation is supported by the example of the patriarch's life (which can be a negative example) and by the threats and promises of the future predictions. This logic of persuasion has often been compared with the traditional, Deuteronomic covenant form, where the stipulations of the covenant are given motivation by the recollection of the mighty acts of Yahweh and by the blessings and curses.[76] In the *Testaments*, however, the "historical" segment is replaced by the individual example of the patriarchs, and the ethical sections are oriented toward individual virtues (e.g., chastity, simplicity) rather than the societal emphases of the Pentateuchal laws. The covenantal nomism of the *Testaments* is most obvious in the so-called sin–exile–return passages, which posit a strict correlation between obedience to the law and prosperity in the land.[77] This pattern, too, has an evident hortatory purpose. The *Testaments of the Twelve Patriarchs* are vehicles for paraenesis in a much more explicit way than was the *Testament of Moses*, where the exhortation is conveyed indirectly through the review of history and the story of Taxo. In the *Testaments of the Twelve Patriarchs* the ethical message is made fully explicit, and at great length. Hence some scholars have argued that the *Testaments* can be viewed as an offshoot of the wisdom literature.[78]

THE APOCALYPTIC ELEMENTS

The *Testaments* are clearly not apocalypses in form. Their framework is the address of a father to his sons, not the transmission of supernatural revelation by an angel. The covenantal theology of the *Testaments of the Twelve Patriarchs* is rather different from what we have found in *1 Enoch* and Daniel, although the theological difference is not necessarily required by the genres. In *1 Enoch* and Daniel the course of events is set and cannot be changed. In the *Testaments* the course of events is determined by human actions. The extent of the explicit hortatory material in the *Testaments* is also without parallel in the apocalypses. Yet there are also noteworthy similarities, beginning with the obvious use of pseudonymity, by which a name from venerable antiquity is used to lend authority to the message.

Although the instruction of the patriarch is usually based on his own experience, there are occasional appeals to higher authority. Prophecies of the future, especially of the sins of the Israelites, are often said to be derived from the writings of Enoch. Allusions to Enoch are found in approximately half the *Testaments*. [79] Correspondence with the actual book of *Enoch* is never precise, [80] but there are enough prophecies of wickedness in all the early Enoch writings to provide a general context for the allusions. An allusion to Enoch has been found in an Aramaic Levi fragment from Qumran that is dated by its editor to the end of the third century. [81] Accordingly the appeal to Enoch is present in the tradition of the *Testaments* from a very early stage. It is noteworthy that what is attributed to the Enoch literature is primarily historical and eschatological prediction.

THE ASCENT OF LEVI

The patriarchs can also claim on occasion to be recipients of revelation themselves. So Asher claims to know what is written in the tablets of heaven (2:10; 7:5) and Naphtali has two visions in which he learns about the future. The main instances of apocalyptic revelation are found in *T. Levi*. In chaps. 2–5 we find a full-blown apocalypse. The heavens were opened and an angel of God called on Levi to enter. This ascent-vision has been thought to be based on the ascent of Enoch in *1 Enoch* 14–16. [82] It differs from that vision markedly by enumerating the heavens. The cosmology has evidently undergone a process of growth. In chap. 2 Levi sees three heavens and is promised that he will see four more. Chap. 3 speaks of seven heavens, but the highest heaven, where God resides, is mentioned fourth in the sequence. [83] Chap. 3, in particular, is close to the orderly sequence of heavens that we will later find in *2 Enoch* and *3 Baruch*. There is little evidence of Christian influence in these chapters. [84] The Aramaic Levi apocryphon from Qumran is relevant to the context in chap. 2, but does not contain the enumeration of the heavens. Consequently, we cannot be sure how much of this material was derived from the Aramaic source. Our other Jewish attestations of a numbered sequence of heavens are thought to come from the Diaspora in the first century C.E. It is quite possible that Levi's ascent also attained its final form in the Diaspora.

T. Levi 3 is atypical of the *Testaments* in its interest in cosmological speculation and the angelic world. Even here an eschatologial focus is also present. In the third heaven are the heavenly armies, drawn up for the day of judgment to do vengeance on Beliar and the spirits of deception. Chapter 4 describes the cosmic upheaval of the day of judgment. Levi is separated from injustice and made a son and servant of God. In chap. 5 he is commissioned as priest in a supplementary vision, "until I come and dwell in the midst of Israel." Then he is given a sword to punish Shechem for the rape of Dinah.

It would appear that the primary purpose of this little apocalypse is to legitimate Levi as priest and one chosen by God. The legitimation presumably extends to his successors, and so elevates the office of the priest-hood. Another vision that describes the investiture of Levi as priest by seven angelic "men" follows in *T. Levi* 8. In view of the complex history of the development of the *Testaments* it is difficult to determine the historical setting for which these visions were designed, especially since, as we have seen, there is evidence of multiple layers in chap. 3. A clue to one possible setting is provided in 5:3, when the angel brings Levi back to earth, gives him a sword, and tells him to take vengeance on Shechem. We are further told that the destruction of the sons of Hamor had been written on the heavenly tablets. This heavenly justification of the destruction of Shechem must be seen in the context of Jewish-Samaritan hostility, which cul-minated in the destruction of Shechem and Mount Gerizim by John Hyrcanus. R. H. Charles regarded this passage as evidence of a pro-Hasmonean ideology and as a clue to the date of the *Testaments.*[85] This view now seems less likely, because of the links of *T. Levi* with Qumran. The sectarians would hardly have been receptive to Hasmonean propa-ganda. In fact hostility to the Samaritans was not peculiarly Hasmonean. Ben Sira 50:26 already refers to "the foolish people that lives in Shechem," a phrase that is echoed in *T. Levi* 7:2. The biblical story of the sack of Shechem is retold in several Jewish sources, from *Jubilees* 30 to Josephus (*Antiquities* 1.21.1-2 [§§337-41) and is always justified.[86] The *Testaments* show many points of contact with *Jubilees,* where the sack of Shechem is also associated with the priesthood of Levi.[87] Much light would be thrown on the setting of this apocalypse if we knew the full extent of the Levi apocryphon from Qumran. It is apparent that this Aramaic work con-tained some form of the heavenly vision and that Levi is given some royal traits.[88] In the Qumran setting, Levi is presumably the prototype for the eschatological priestly messiah. Later, in the final Christian redaction, he is a figure for Christ. Whatever the original setting of *T. Levi* 2-5 may have been, the text evidently lends itself to legitimating the institution of the priesthood and the use of violence—against Shechem in particular or, by analogy, against unbelievers. It is noteworthy that an apocalyptic vision can thus be used to support the use of power, just as well as to express rebellion or dissent.

The Eschatological Sections

Significant analogies with the historical apocalypses are also found in the passages in the *Testaments* which involve future predictions. As we have noted, the sin–exile–return passages are firmly rooted in the Deutero-nomic tradition. However, they typically culminate in an eschatological scenario that involves Beliar, messianic expectation, and the resurrection of the dead.

Beliar is mentioned in every testament except *T. Gad,* and Satan is mentioned there. Over against Beliar stands the angel of peace. In *T. Judah* 20:1 two spirits lie in wait for man, that of truth and that of error. These spirits are primarily the agents of an ongoing ethical dualism, but they also have eschatological roles: "The ends of men show their righteousness when they encounter the angels of the Lord and of Satan. For if the soul departs troubled, it is tortured by the evil spirit, which it also served, . . . but if it is peacefully and joyfully greeted by the angel of peace, he will summon it to life" (*T. Asher* 6:4-6). In *T. Levi* 18:12 Beliar will be bound by the eschatological priest. In *T. Judah* 25:3 he will be cast into fire forever.

The resemblance to the apocalypses in all of this lies in the idea that supernatural forces direct and influence human actions. In Daniel, this role was filled by the patron angels of the nations and by the contrasting symbols of the beasts and "one like a son of man." In *1 Enoch*, the Watchers and the angels were such supernatural powers. In the *Testaments* the forces of evil come to a focus in the single figure of Beliar, who attains a greater universality than the historically specific beasts of Daniel. The closest parallels to the *Testaments* are found in the Qumran scrolls, where the *Community Rule* (1QS) contrasts the Spirit of Light and the Spirit of Darkness and the *War Scroll* prepares for an eschatological battle between Belial, leading the Sons of Darkness, and Michael, leading the Sons of Light. The *Testaments* lack the strong deterministic note that we will find in the scrolls. *T. Asher* emphasizes that men are free to choose between the two ways. The Qumran *Community Rule* suggests that humanity is already divided into two lots, although in practice a choice would still seem to be required.

We cannot be sure at what point this metaphysical dualism was introduced into the *Testaments*. Similar conceptions are found in early Christianity, notably in *Barnabas* 18-21, where the angels of God and the angels of Satan preside over the ways of Light and Darkness.[89] The role of Beliar does not tie the *Testaments* directly to the Qumran sect but illustrates how such ideas were diffused in ancient Judaism and early Christianity. The dualistic contrast of supernatural forces can indeed be viewed as a development of the mythological symbolism of the early apocalypses. It was given a distinctive expression at Qumran, where, as we shall see, Persian influence was also possible. In the case of Qumran this dualism carried deterministic overtones. The *Testaments* show that it could also be used to undergird a vigorous ethic of free choice.

MESSIANIC EXPECTATION

The most striking characteristic of the expectation of the *Testaments* is the association of the messiah with both Levi and Judah.[90] These two patriarchs have a leading role throughout.[91] They are ranked first and second in the resurrection (*T. Judah* 25:1) and elsewhere (e.g., *T. Reuben* 6:7; *T. Gad* 8:2; *T. Issachar* 5:7). Not all passages that speak of the leadership of Levi and Judah are messianic. Some affirm Levi's priesthood and Judah's kingship. Others speak of salvation which is to come from Levi and Judah (*T. Dan* 5:10; *T. Naphtali* 8:2). Others refer more explicitly to messianic expectation. In *T. Simeon* 7:2 the Lord "will raise up from Levi as it were a chief priest and from Judah as it were a king, god and man. He will save all the nations and the race of Israel." Similarly in *T. Joseph* 19:6 the children of Joseph are to honor Levi and Judah because from them will arise the Lamb of God who will save all the nations and Israel by grace. *T. Levi* 18 focuses on the priestly figure. He will be a "new priest," but his star will rise in heaven like a king. He will open the gates of paradise and bind Belial. *T. Judah* 24 speaks of a man from the seed of Judah. The heavens will be opened for him and no sin will be found in him. He will save all who call upon the Lord among the Gentiles. Christian influence is obvious in these messianic passages.

In their final form the *Testaments* envisage one messiah, who is associated with both Levi and Judah and is evidently identified as Christ. Since the messiah is associated with both these tribes and they are both singled out for leadership, it is probable that the *Testaments* adapt an earlier Jewish expectation of two messiahs. The main parallel for such a conception is found in the Qumran scrolls, which speak of messiahs from Aaron and Israel. Precedent for such dual leadership is found in the organization of the early postexilic community, as attested by the two "sons of oil" in Zechariah 4. Already in Zechariah, and throughout the postexilic period, the chief priest played the predominant role, and this is also the case in the *Testaments*.[92] Levi always takes precedence. *T. Judah* 21:2 explicitly says that God made the kingship subordinate to the priesthood. In the Aramaic Levi apocryphon royal as well as priestly terminology is applied to Levi,[93] a fact that suggests that the dual leadership of Levi and Judah may have been a later development.

Messianic expectation plays scarcely any role in the early apocalypses, which rely rather on angelic deliverance. (Only in the Animal Apocalypse does a human leader have a prominent role.) The primary expectation of a priestly messiah in the *Testaments* would seem to have arisen in reaction to the corruption of the priesthood in the Maccabean era. The great prophecy of the "new priest" in *T. Levi* 18 comes at the end of a prophecy that divides history into seventy weeks, or seven jubilees, a schema that corresponds to the first seven weeks in the Apocalypse of Weeks. The seventh jubilee is marked by the sins of the priests: idolatry, violence, greed, licentiousness. It is not clear from *T. Levi* whether the entire postexilic period is corrupt, but at least the final jubilee stands out from the rest. At its end the old priesthood will lapse and God will send the new priest, who will also be the recipient of revelation and have attributes of judge and king.[94] We know that some form of these chapters was contained in the Aramaic Levi apocryphon. Unfortunately we do not know the full extent of that work, and consequently any discussion of the emergence of the priestly messiah in the second century must remain inconclusive. It has been suggested that the dual leadership of Levi and Judah was developed in protest against the combination of priestly and religious power by the Hasmonean priest kings.[95] This rationale may also have inspired the distinction of the messiahs of Aaron and Israel at Qumran.

A number of the *Testaments* conclude with a prediction of resurrection.[96] Although the earliest clear attestations of afterlife and resurrection in Judaism are found in the apocalypses of Enoch and Daniel, the belief became widespread and does not necessarily imply the full apocalyptic world view. Nonetheless, these passages constitute another point of similarity between the *Testaments* and the apocalypses.

Our discussion of the *Testaments of the Twelve Patriarchs* is necessarily inconclusive in view of the uncertainty of the history of composition. The final, Christian *Testaments* evidently incorporated material from various sources. Some of this material might be designated "apocalyptic" because of its similarity to what we find in the apocalypses, and *T. Levi* even includes an apocalypse in the account of Levi's ascent. Moreover, some sources of the *Testaments*, including the Aramaic Levi apocryphon, were closely related to the Enoch literature and *Jubilees* and to the Qumran scrolls. These early sources are of considerable importance for the development of Jewish messianism. We can only hope that more light will be thrown on this obscure area by the full publication of the Qumran material.

MESSIANISM IN THE PSALMS OF SOLOMON

The "new priest" is complemented in the *Testaments* by the man from Judah, the star that will arise from Jacob according to Balaam's oracle in Numbers 24. This figure has rightly been identified as the Davidic messiah.[97] Scholars have generally assumed that such a figure was a standard object of Jewish expectation. In fact clear messianic references are rare in the so-called intertestamental literature before the turn of the era. Apart from the complex evidence of the *Testaments* and the Qumran scrolls, the only passage from this period that deals with the Davidic messiah is found in the *Psalms of Solomon* 17–18.[98]

The *Psalms of Solomon* are only remotely related to the apocalyptic literature, and so are of marginal interest in this study. They contain nothing of the apocalyptic manner of revelation and show no interest in the angelic or heavenly world. They attest a belief in afterlife (3:12; 13:11; 14:3; 14:13; 16:1–3), but the primary focus of the eschatology is on the restoration of Jerusalem, which will be brought about by the Davidic messiah. The *Psalms* were written in the wake of Pompey's conquest of Jerusalem in 63 B.C.E. In part the figure of the messiah is a counter to the Roman general (who is given a mythical connotation by being called a dragon in 2:25). However, the *Psalms* also insist that Jerusalem was punished because of the sins of the Jews: "From the chief of them to the least of them the people were in complete sinfulness. The king was in transgression, the judge in disobedience, and the people in sin" (17:20). Those that "loved the synagogues of the pious" (presumably the circles that produced the psalms) had to flee from this wickedness. The *Psalms* repeatedly castigate the arrogance of the rich. Not least among their crimes was the fact that they set up a king who was not from the Davidic line (17:6–7). It appears that the hope for a Davidic messiah was inspired in large part by opposition to the Hasmonean monarchy (as may also be true in the *Testaments* and at Qumran). Because of their general theology the *Psalms* are usually ascribed to Pharisaic circles.[99]

The portrait of the messiah echoes the language of the canonical Psalms (especially Psalm 2) and Isaiah.[100] He will at once subdue and save the nations. The traditions embodied in this picture are largely independent of the apocalyptic literature. In the first century C.E., however, this traditional picture of the messiah was increasingly integrated into the apocalyptic scenario, as we will find in the Similitudes of Enoch, 4 Ezra and 2 Baruch.

5
Qumran

THE DISCOVERY OF THE Dead Sea Scrolls has shed new light on several aspects of postbiblical Judaism, not least on the area of Jewish apocalypticism. This new light has been twofold. On the one hand, the early Enoch manuscripts have revised our understanding of the origin and early development of apocalyptic literature. On the other hand, there are obvious similarities between the newly discovered sectarian documents and what we find in the apocalypses, especially in their interest in the angelic world and in their eschatology. So Qumran has been dubbed "an apocalyptic community" and held to offer a unique opportunity to study the institutional setting of apocalyptic thought.[1]

Three reservations are in order at the outset. First, the material found at Qumran has not been fully published. Hence all conclusions are tentative to a degree. This point should not be exaggerated, since any conclusions about the ancient world are subject to revision in the light of new discoveries. Second, not all the documents found at Qumran were products of that community or of the Essene sect. Apart from biblical texts, some apocryphal and pseudepigraphic works are older than the Qumran settlement and were also transmitted independently of the scrolls. These include the oldest Enoch literature and *Jubilees*. Even works that were not known before the discovery of the scrolls are not necessarily sectarian in origin. The *Genesis Apocryphon* and the *Words of the Heavenly Luminaries* are cases in point. In other cases, notably the *Temple Scroll*, we must admit a gray area, where there is no consensus on the question of provenance.[2] Third, and most significant for the present context, there is no clear example of an actual apocalypse that was composed at Qumran. A few works are too fragmentary to permit a definitive decision either on their genre or on their provenance. These include the *Book of Giants* and the

Visions of the New Jerusalem.[3] None of the major documents of the community is in the form of an apocalypse. Hence, Qumran throws no light on the setting in which apocalypses were produced. If it is called "an apocalyptic community" the adjective can only connote similarity to the apocalypses, although these similarities are nonetheless significant.

THE HISTORY OF QUMRAN

The history of the Qumran community involves complex questions that cannot be fully treated here. We may take as established the identification of the community as an Essene settlement.[4] We may also accept the scholarly consensus that the community took up residence at Qumran about the middle of the second century B.C.E.[5] On the evidence of the *pesharim* it would seem that the origin involved a dispute between the founder, the Teacher of Righteousness, and the Wicked Priest, who evidently had control of the Jerusalem temple.[6] The occasion of this rift is often thought to have been the assumption of the high priesthood by the Maccabees. The Wicked Priest has been identified as either Jonathan or Simon Maccabee.[7] The fact that the sectarian calendar differed from the official one in the Hasmonean period may also have been a factor in the breach. More specific proposals about the origin of the community, that it was composed of returnees from Babylon or that the Teacher of Righteousness was high priest in the period between 162 and 152, are possible but extremely hypothetical, and no weight can be placed on them.[8] Attempts to identify the Teacher of Righteousness with a known figure such as Judah the Essene fail for lack of specific evidence, and some suggestions (Jesus, John the Baptist) are wildly implausible.[9] There is as yet no consensus on the import of the so-called *Temple Scroll* for the origin of the sect.[10]

Even the widely held view that the Hasidim of the Maccabean era were the precursors of the community has no sure foundation. As we have seen, the "plant root" of the *Damascus Document* is closely related to the developments attested in *Enoch* and there are marked similarities between *Jubilees* and the scrolls, but there are also significant points of continuity with Daniel.[11] It is by no means certain, however, that all this material pertains to a single movement or that its relation to the scrolls is necessarily genetic.

The major periods of the Qumran settlement are well known. A modest beginning in the middle of the second century was followed by significant expansion in the reign of John Hyrcanus (134–104 B.C.E.). There may have been an intermission in the occupation of the site after the earthquake of 31 B.C.E.[12] The settlement was destroyed during the revolt of 66–70 C.E., but the Essene movement may have continued thereafter.[13]

The identification of the community depicted in the scrolls as the Essenes depends on the notices about that sect in ancient literature.[14] Pliny the Elder reported that the Essenes dwelled on the west side of the Dead Sea, north of Engedi. He described them as "a solitary people, the most extraordinary in the world since there are no women (they renounce all sexual desire), they have no money, and they enjoy only the society of the palm-trees." He marvels at the survival of these people among whom no one is born "through thousands of ages." Pliny wrote after 70 c.e., but it is generally assumed that his information reflects an earlier period.

Both Josephus and Philo say that the Essenes were not confined to one settlement but lived in many towns. Both emphasize the customs of the sect, especially celibacy, community of property, and communal meals. Josephus, in the longest account, also mentions an order of Essenes who marry (*War* 2.8.13 §§160–61). Hence modern scholars have distinguished between "monastic" and "lay" Essenes.[15] It is apparent that the accounts of both Josephus and Philo are based primarily on the "monastic" kind. Josephus provides the most specific information. Noteworthy features of his account include the four-stage process of admission to the sect, provisions for expulsion, concern for purification, interest in the writings of the ages, reverence for the lawgiver, strict observance of the sabbath, secrecy regarding the books of the sect and the names of the angels, and a peculiar position on sacrifice.[16] Neither Josephus nor Philo describes the ideas of the Essenes in detail. Josephus emphasizes their fatalism but also gives an interesting account of their beliefs about life after death (*War* 2.8.11 §§154–58). Hippolytus (*Refutatio omnium haeresium* 9.27) claims that they also believed in the resurrection of the body, cosmic destruction, and world judgment.[17]

Josephus and Philo have their own emphases, which are likely to distort their accounts of the Essenes—for example, Josephus's patent desire to emphasize similarities with "the sons of Greece" (*War* 2.8.11 §155). Yet there are enough points of contact with the scrolls to assure us that they are indeed describing the same sect. The affinities with the *Community Rule* (1QS) are most important. These include the stages of admission,[18] community of goods, and injunctions to secrecy and to hatred of the unjust. The description of the belief in afterlife, which provides for the punishment of the damned in a murky and tempestuous dungeon, finds its closest parallel in 1QS 4.

The distinction between two orders of Essenes appears to be reflected in the scrolls by the existence of two rule books, the *Community Rule* (1QS) and the *Damascus Document* (CD).[19] CD provides for people who "live in camps according to the rule of the land, marrying and begetting children . . ." (CD 7:6). There is no question of community property. CD also provides a rule for the assembly of the camps (col. 12). In contrast, 1QS appears to be the rule for a particular community. Marriage is not mentioned. Membership is achieved by a free act of adults—there is no provision for children. 1QS also envisages some communal control of property, although private property is not entirely eliminated.[20] In all, 1QS appears more typical of the Essenism described by Josephus than is CD, although there are also some parallels in the latter case (e.g., regarding the strict observance of the sabbath).

There is no evidence that the distinction between the two orders of Essenes involved a schism in the sect. CD looks back to the Teacher of Righteousness as a founder figure,[21] and he is generally regarded as the founder of Qumran. There is no reason to suppose that he was rejected by any group of Essenes or that the apostates who are denounced in CD 19-20 were still members of the sect. The rule "for the camps" was still preserved at Qumran in multiple copies. Vermes has plausibly argued that Qumran was the headquarters of the sect. He suggests that the "assembly of all the camps" was an annual convention to renew the covenant at Qumran and that the Guardian of the Qumran community was also Guardian of all the camps.[22] The "monastic" community at Qumran may have had some more detailed and esoteric doctrines than those shared by all Essenes, but there is no evidence that one order rejected the doctrines of the other.

Despite the compelling evidence for the identification of the Qumran community with the Essenes, the picture given by the scrolls is very different from that of Philo and Josephus. Naturally, we should expect the community's own documents to be more complete. Philo and Josephus were outsiders,[23] and their reports were by no means objective. So the priestly character of the community emerges much more clearly from the scrolls. More significant for our purposes, the eschatological concerns of the sect now appear far more important than had been suspected from the Greek accounts. Although Josephus emphasized the importance of immortality for the Essenes, neither he nor Philo mentioned messianic beliefs, nor any kind of public, national, or cosmic eschatology. This again should not surprise us. Both these authors were concerned with presenting the Essenes in such a way as to win the respect of Gentiles. This effect could only be jeopardized by a discourse on the war of the Sons of Light with the Sons of Darkness. The omission of any reference to the dualism of the sect is more surprising, but both Philo and Josephus are concerned with the practices of the sect rather than its ideas. In any case we cannot assume that the Greek authors describe the beliefs of the Essenes outside of Qumran. As we have seen, their accounts are generally closer to 1QS than to CD and pertain chiefly to the celibate order of Essenism. It should also be said that the eschatology of the Essenes as described by Josephus is closer to that in 1QS than to that in other related pseudepigrapha such as *Jubilees* or the *Testament of the Twelve Patriarchs.*

We proceed, then, on the assumption that both orders of the Essene sect lived in harmony with each other and that documents such as CD or 1QSa, which allow for marriage and children, were still representative of the same sect that inhabited Qumran.[24] We cannot attempt here to discuss all aspects of the sect's theology but only those that bear on its apocalyptic character—the idea of revelation, eschatology, and the angelic world. It should be noted, however, that these are by no means incidental areas but provide a conceptual framework for the *halakah* or prescriptive rules of the community.[25]

We can say little of the evolution of apocalyptic ideas within the Essene movement. The issue here is not the a priori likelihood of such evolution but the limitation of our actual evidence. The major documents of the sect were composed early on and continued to circulate throughout the history of Qumran. The oldest copies of 1QS date to the first quarter of the first century B.C.E. and those of CD to the first half of that century.[26] None of these copies are autographs. Both documents were probably completed by 100 C.E., perhaps much earlier. The *Hodayot* or Thanksgiving Hymns are widely thought to be the work of the Teacher himself, at least in part, although the scroll dates from the first century C.E.[27] The manuscript of the *War Scroll* also comes from the Herodian period but various scholars date one or other segment to a much earlier time, and it is possible that the framework of the document dates from a very early period in the history of the sect.[28] Only in the case of the *pesharim* is there general consensus on a fairly late date (mid first century B.C.E.) and even here the assumption that all the *pesharim* were composed at the same time is not beyond question.[29]

Attempts to bolster evolutionary theories by the use of source criticism must be viewed with caution for several reasons. First, the procedure is notoriously subjective: elements that do not fit a preconceived theory are too easily excised as "additions."[30] Second, many of the supposed sources are very brief, and probably incomplete. Arguments from the *omissions* of such sources have no value—for example, the fact that dualism is not explicit in a passage of a few verses does not prove that this is a "non-dualistic" source.[31] Third, even where different sources can validly be distinguished, adequate evidence for their chronological sequence is often lacking. The Instruction of the Two Spirits in 1QS 3-4 may well have been an independent composition, but there is nothing to indicate that it was composed at a later time than the so-called manifesto in 1QS 8.[32]

We may assume that there was a process of development, at least in the formative period of the sect, although we only rarely find solid evidence of it. [33] There is little doubt, however, that such documents as 1QS and CD continued to function as authoritative documents after they reached their present form, and indeed were in their present form for most of the history of the Qumran settlement. Too much weight should not be placed on speculative theories about the prehistory of these texts or of the origin of the community. We must also respect the coherence of the way in which their various components have been put together.

REVELATION

Fundamental to the idea of revelation at Qumran is the belief that all things are regulated according to "the mysteries of God." [34] The term for "mystery" (*raz*) is found also in Daniel 2 and 4. The idea is closely bound with the belief in providential control, despite the evidence of evil in the world. All that is and is to be comes from the God of knowledge. Before ever they existed he established their design, and they accomplish their task without change. Even the sins caused by the Angel of Darkness are in accordance with the mysteries of God, but also "in the mysteries of his understanding and in his glorious wisdom" God has appointed an end to falsehood (1QS 3-4). These mysteries concern not only the course of history and human affairs. They involve angels as well as men: "for great is your majestic plan and your marvelous mysteries on high, for raising up to you from the dust and casting down angels" (1QM 14:14). They can also involve the workings of the cosmos: "the heavenly lights according to their mysteries, the stars to their paths . . . and the perfect treasuries (of snow and hail) according to their purposes . . ." (1QH 1:11-12). All is graven before God with the graving tool of the reminder (1QH 1:21-25) as surely as all was inscribed for Enoch on the heavenly tablets.

What is crucially important here is the manner in which these mysteries are revealed. From 1QS 3-4 one might expect that the Spirits of Truth and Falsehood play the roles of revealers, but this is not specified. The author of the *Hodayot* claims to be the recipient of direct revelation: "These things I know by the wisdom which comes from Thee for Thou hast unstopped my ears to marvelous mysteries" (1QH 1:21). The common idea that the speaker here is the Teacher of Righteousness is supported by the *pesher* on Habbakuk, 7:3-4: "And when it says, So that he can run who reads it, the interpretation of it concerns the Teacher of Righteousness to whom God made known all the mysteries of the words of his servants the prophets."

It appears that the Teacher of Righteousness was the official mediator of revelation for the community, and we are not told that he needed the services of an interpreting angel.[35] In this regard, the scrolls depart from the conventions of the apocalypses, although the concept of mystery is very similar. The characteristic compositions of Qumran are not revelation accounts, but rules (*Serek*), hymns, and *pesharim*. The rules and hymns attest a more direct form of communication, where the author appears to have more confidence in his own authority than was the case with the authors of the pseudonymous apocalypses. This phenomenon may arise from the structure of authority within the community and may be analogous to the revival of prophecy in early Christianity.

The *pesharim* are perhaps the category of literature at Qumran that comes closest to the apocalyptic manner of revelation.[36] There is obvious similarity between their interpretation of prophecy and the interpretation of Jeremiah in Daniel 9. The affinity with Daniel's dream interpretation is underlined by the common use of the word *pesher*. In the Qumran *pesharim* the words of scripture are treated as mysteries that refer not to the time of their author but to the end time, which is now being fulfilled in the history of the community. So "for the wicked surround the righteous" (Hab 1:4) is taken as a reference to the Wicked Priest and the Teacher of Righteousness. "Where the lion went to enter" (Nah 2:12) is interpreted as "Demetrius, king of Greece, who sought to enter Jerusalem." This style of interpretation has its roots in the mantic wisdom and divination of the ancient Near East but also has analogues in the Hellenistic world, notably in the Egyptian *Demotic Chronicle*. Presumably the task of interpretation was handed on to others in the community after the death of the original Teacher.

Pesharim are not apocalypses. Not only do they differ in their manner of revelation, but their content is not properly eschatological. It refers rather to the historical experience of the community. They also pursue the biblical texts in a manner far more systematic than anything we find in the apocalypses.[37] Yet they bear some resemblance to apocalyptic revelation. The sources of revelation, including scripture, are mysterious. There is need of a special interpretation, which was itself revealed to the Teacher of Righteousness. The scriptural text requires a higher revelation. This is true of the Qumran texts in general. These texts are more directly interested in the Torah and the scripture than is usual in the apocalypses. Yet they too rely on a higher revelation. In the *Community Rule* the ceremony of the renewal of the covenant takes on a new character in view of the discourse of the two spirits, which is in effect an exposition of the underlying mystery. This reliance on a higher revelation is an important modification of the Torah-centered piety of Qumran.[38]

ESCHATOLOGY

Usually those who have designated Qumran as an apocalyptic community have had in mind the eschatology of the scrolls rather than the idea of revelation. In fact, the scrolls provide a complex set of conceptions and formulations which throw valuable light on the nature of eschatological language, however we evaluate their affinities with the apocalypses.[39]

Jewish eschatology in the Second Temple period has traditionally been divided into two main types. In the words of Sigmund Mowinckel: "The one side is national, political, this worldly, with particularistic tendencies, though univeralistic when at its best. The other is super-terrestrial, other-worldly, rich in religious content and mythological concepts, universalistic, numinous, at home in the sphere of the 'Holy' and the 'wholly Other.'"[40] The expectations of the early *Sibylline Oracles, Testaments of the Twelve Patriarchs,* and *Psalms of Solomon* may be classified roughly under Mowinckel's first type. In contrast, the early Enoch apocalypses and Daniel fall with the second. The two types have often been associated with the figures of "messiah" and "Son of Man" respectively; but, as we have seen, the early apocalypses do not necessarily focus on a single savior figure, and "Son of Man" was not an established title in this period. The eschatology of the scrolls embraces both of these types, even within a single document in the case of 1QS. We will find that this fusion of different types is increasingly common in the later apocalypses.

MESSIANIC EXPECTATIONS

The aspect of Qumran eschatology that has received most scholarly attention is Mowinckel's "national, political, this-worldly" eschatology. Much of the discussion here has focused on the peculiarity that the scrolls refer to not one but two messiahs.[41] The so-called *Damascus Document* (CD) refers in several places to the coming of the messiah of Aaron and Israel.[42] When this document was first discovered in the Cairo Geniza at the beginning of this century, Louis Ginzberg realized that it implied two messiahs rather than one.[43] This interpretation was supported by the reference in 1QS 9:11 to the coming of a prophet and the messiahs of Aaron and Israel. The scriptural basis for this expectation is laid out in 4QTestimonia, where we find juxtaposed the prediction of a prophet like Moses (Deut 18:18-19), Balaam's oracle in Num 24:15-17 ("a star shall come out of Jacob and a sceptre shall rise out of Israel") and the blessing of Levi in Deut 33:8-11 ("Give thy Thummim to Levi"). The texts suggest, respectively, the coming of an ideal prophet, king, and priest.[44] Finally, in 1QSa, the rule for the community "at the end of days," we read that "the priest" will take precedence over "the messiah of Israel." Here again the priest is clearly the messiah of Aaron and a dual messiahship is envisaged. Although the terminology of CD could, grammatically, refer to either one or two messiahs,[45] there is no reason why a single messiah should be said to come from both Aaron and Israel unless a dual messiahship had been envisaged at an earlier stage. There is no evidence that CD is later than the texts that explicitly refer to two messiahs. Accordingly, the references in CD must be understood in the dual sense.

The expectation of two messiahs is not such an anomaly as it first appeared. We have seen that the *Testaments of the Twelve Patriarchs* imply belief in some Jewish circles in a messiah from Levi and a messiah from Judah. The biblical precedent for such dual messiahship is found in Zech 4:14, which speaks of two "sons of oil," the governor Zerubbabel and the high priest Joshua. Already in Zechariah, the priest is the more prominent figure, and the priestly messiah takes precedence both in the *Testaments* and in the scrolls. The idea of dual leadership would seem to have been revived in the second century B.C.E., the ideal priest in reaction to abuses of the priesthood, the duality of leadership in reaction to the Hasmonean combination of priestly and political power. Yet insofar as it had a biblical precedent it may be called "restorative" eschatology.[46] It is modeled on a situation of the past, looks for an idealized fulfillment of that situation, but is not entirely different from it. There is nothing to suggest that the messiahs are other than human. They will fill institutional roles within the community. They are eschatological figures, in the sense that they imply a definitive change in the course of history, but they do not imply an end of the historical process. S. Talmon has perceptively noted that the difference between the dual messiahship of Qumran and the single messiahship of Christianity is qualitative as well as quantitative.[47] What is involved at Qumran is an ideal community structure. There is no emphasis on the personalities of the messiahs as savior figures. In fact, the scrolls are tantalizingly reticent on the activities of the messiahs and in most cases merely assert that they will arise. The activity of the messiahs in 1QSa takes place within the eschatological age and is not envisaged as saving action that brings that age into being. The focus is on the community of which the messiahs are a part, rather than on the exaltation of the messiahs themselves.[48]

THE DIFFERENT DIMENSIONS OF MESSIANISM

The offices to be filled by the messiahs at the end of days correspond to positions in the historical sect. The "rule for the assembly of all the camps" in CD 14 singles out two authoritative figures: the priest who enrolls the congregation and the "Guardian of all the camps" (*mĕbaqqēr*). The latter is supposed to have "mastered all the secrets of men." On a lower level, CD 13 prescribes that wherever there are ten men there must be a priest, and they shall be ruled by him. He is clearly distinguished from the "Guardian of the camp." While the law of leprosy is to be applied by the priest, the Guardian is to instruct the priest in the interpretation of the law. The Guardian has the task of instructing the congregation and examining all entrants. It appears then that CD provides for dual leadership of the sect, both at the level of the individual camps and at the assembly of all the camps.

1QS also uses the term mĕbaqqēr for the Guardian of the congregation in the "rule for the assembly of the the congregation." This figure is very probably identical with the pāqîd of 1QS 6:14 and also with the maśkîl of 1QS 3 (in view of the similarity of their functions). He is not identified as a priest and is presumably a distinct figure as in CD. According to 1QS 6 any group of ten must include a priest, who presides at the communal meal. The presidency of the priest must also be assumed to apply to the assembly of the congregation.[49] It appears then that both CD and 1QS envisage dual leadership, where the priest takes precedence. There are, to be sure, differences between the two documents in other respects. 1QS does not legislate for "the assembly of all the camps." It also provides for a council of three priests and twelve men (obviously reflecting the twelve tribes of Israel). The dual leadership of the priest and the mĕbaqqēr (Guardian), however, appears to be a constant feature of the organization of the sect.

The roles of the priest and the mĕbaqqēr are clearly analogous to those of the messiahs of Aaron and Israel. The messiahs are still expected in the future and so cannot be identified simply with the present rulers, but the offices they will fill are presumably the same (quite certainly so in the case of the priestly messiah). The ambiguity entailed by this situation becomes clear in 1QSa.[50] This brief document is introduced as "the rule for all the congregation of Israel in the last days." It is largely concerned with the different stages of initiation and authority in the community and restrictions on membership of the assembly. Then in 1QSa 2:11-22 we find instructions for a time "when [God] sends the messiah to be with them."[51] The passage first describes the entry of the congregation in which the priest enters at the head of the Aaronids and then the messiah of Israel and the rest of the congregation.[52] At the common table, the priest is the first to bless the bread and wine, then the messiah of Israel "shall stretch out his hand to the bread and then all the congregation shall give thanks and partake." Thus far the text might be read simply as a prescription for the future messianic age. However, the passage concludes: "And they shall act according to this prescription whenever (the meal) [is arr]anged when as many as ten solemnly meet together." Now if "the priest" and the "messiah of

Israel" were specific (eschatological) individuals they could scarcely be present at every meal at which ten men assembled. We must conclude that the messianic roles could be assumed by the leaders of the community or group. Indeed there is already a close parallel between the messianic meal of 1QSa and the community meal in 1QS 6:4: "and when they prepare the table to eat or the wine to drink, the priest will first stretch out his hand to bless the bread and the wine." All of 1QSa before the introduction of the messiahs is concerned with matters that apply to the present regulation of the community (stages of initiation, restrictions of membership, etc.) We must conclude that the "messianic" rule also reflects the current practice of the sect while projecting it into the future.[53]

It would seem, then, that the expectation of the two messiahs is already actualized in the institutions of the sect. The actualization is undoubtedly proleptic and does not preclude the expectation of further fulfillment in the future. Yet it shows that even the "restorative" eschatology of Qumran is not as univocal as it first appears. The doctrine of the two messiahs refers to a recurring pattern, which can be discerned in Israel's historical past, in the present structure of the community, and will be fully manifest in the future. Even the eschatological fulfillment of the pattern can be encountered, in some degree, in the present ritual of the community.

A similar ambiguity in eschatological language is evident in a controversial passage in CD 6:2-11. The passage applies Num 21:18 to the history of the community and concludes "And the Staff (*mĕhôqēq*) is the expositor of the Law (*dôrēš hattôrâ*) . . . and *the nobles of the people* are those that have come to dig the well with precepts (*mĕhôqĕqôt*) which the Staff laid down, that they might walk in them during the whole epoch of wickedness. Except for them they cannot grasp (the Law) until he who shall teach righteousness arises in the end of days." The "Righteous Teacher" is well known from other passages as the key figure in the founding of the sect.[54] Here, however, he is preceded by an "Interpreter of the Law," who sets out the precepts which are apparently still in force. There are two possible interpretations of this figure. Either he is "a precursor of the Teacher at the earliest beginnings of the sect,"[55] or he is the one elsewhere called the "Righteous Teacher"; and the one who shall teach righteousness here is a messianic figure. It is important that the one who shall teach righteousness here appears to be expected in the future. Elsewhere in CD the Righteous Teacher is always a figure in the past. In CD 20:1, 14 the "unique teacher"[56] is already dead, and in 20:32 the voice of the Righteous Teacher is the normative way to salvation.[57] CD 20 has been thought to be part of a separate, later source, but the Teacher (*mwrh ṣdq*) is also mentioned in CD 1:11 in the account of the origin of the sect. One attempt to resolve the anomaly of the future reference in CD 6:11 has proposed that the document was composed before the rise of the Teacher. The phrase in CD 6:11, then, would refer to a messianic figure, with whom the historical Teacher was subsequently identified.[58] This theory, however, fails to explain the present form of CD, where the "one who teaches righteousness" is still in the future, although the historical Teacher is clearly in the past. The conclusion that CD 6:11 refers to a messianic figure, presumably the messiah of Aaron, is indeed inevitable. There is no warrant, however, for the conclusion that such a figure was expected before the rise of the historical Teacher, or that the Teacher claimed to be a messiah.[59] Rather, the point is that the future messiah will fill the same role in the community as the historical Teacher. Most scholars have correctly seen that the "Interpreter of the Law" in this passage is none other than the historical Teacher.[60] The complexity of the passage is compounded by the ambiguity of the expression "Interpreter of the Law," which clearly refers to a figure of the past in CD 6. In CD 7:18–20, however, the Interpreter is identified with the star of Balaam's oracle, the scepter is the "prince of the whole congregation," and the allusion is most probably messianic.[61] In 4QFlor 1:11–12 the Interpreter is clearly messianic: the "Branch of David" will arise with the Interpreter of the Law in Zion at the end of days. "Interpreter of the Law," then, can refer to a figure of the past or to a messiah, or even in 1QS 6 to a present figure in the community.[62] This ambiguous usage becomes intelligible if we bear in mind that the scrolls are concerned with functions and institutions rather than with personalities.

In summary, then, our examination of messianic expectations shows that the distinction between historical present and eschatological future is blurred at Qumran. The eschatological terminology overlaps with that used to describe the current institutions. In this case the ambiguity arises from the fact that the Essenes attempted to embody their vision of the future in a community structure. We have no evidence of similar organization on the part of the authors of the early apocalypses. However, the Qumran evidence throws some light on the nature of messianic expectation and of the restorative type of eschatology. It arises out of an idealized view of the past and is at least capable of actualization in a historical community.[63]

THE WAR OF LIGHT AND DARKNESS

The expectation of the two messiahs is representative of Mowinckel's "national, political, this-worldly" eschatology. In contrast, the great eschatological tableau of 1QM (the *War Scroll*) fits rather the second, "superterrestrial, other-worldly" type, which "is found particularly in the apocalyptic literature."[64] 1QM anticipates a conflict of cosmic forces, the Sons of Light under the leadership of Michael, and the Sons of Darkness led by

Belial. The atmosphere of the work may be indicated by a passage from 1QM 12:7-8: "Mighty [men and] a host of angels are among those mustered with us, the Mighty One of War is in our congregation, and the host of His spirits is with our steps."[65] The language and concepts of the scroll are clearly drawn from streams of tradition other than those of national eschatology. The difference between the two conceptual worlds is so striking that some scholars have sought to explain 1QM as a late development, owing to the disappointment when messianic expectations failed to materialize.[66] The issue is complicated by the composite character of the *War Scroll*. The practical regulations in cols. 2-9 presuppose a different outline of the war from what we find in cols. 1 and 15-19, where the metaphysical backdrop of the war between Michael and Belial is elaborated. Scholarly opinions have differed as to which of these sections is older, but we should note that the metaphysical backdrop of the supernatural forces has its closest parallels in second-century B.C.E. documents, Daniel and 1QS, and cannot be regarded as a late conception in any case.[67] Consequently, several scholars have argued that at least in these sections the *War Scroll* is one of the earliest of the Qumran documents.[68] As the book now stands, cols. 1 and 15-19 constitute the framework within which the practical regulations of cols. 2-9 are subsumed. Columns 10-14 are closely related to 15-19, although the relationship can be construed in various ways. The eschatological tableau which has significant affinities with the apocalypses is found primarily in the framework.

The outline of the war is set out in col. 1:

> On the day when the Kittim fall there shall be a mighty encounter and carnage before the God of Israel, for that is a day appointed by Him from of old for a battle of annihilation for the Sons of Darkness, on which there shall engage in a great carnage the congregation of angels and the assembly of men, the Sons of Light and the lot of Darkness. . . . In three lots shall the Sons of Light prove strong so as to smite the wicked, and in three the army of Belial shall recover so as to bring about the withdrawal of the lot [of Light] . . . but in the seventh lot the great hand of God shall subdue [Belial and all] angels of his dominion. . . ."

Despite lacunae in the text it is clear from cols. 15-19 that the sons of light and darkness prevail in alternate lots. There too it is clear that Michael is the leader of the Sons of Light, and the counterpart of Belial. This conception of an eschatological battle is indebted to biblical tradition at several points.[69] The names of Michael and Belial are Hebrew.[70] God's triumph in the *seventh* period suggests what has been called "sabbatical eschatology."[71]

The contrast of light and darkness has a biblical history, for example, in Amos 5:18 in connection with the "Day of the Lord." However, the total conception has no real precedent in Israelite tradition. What is peculiar here is that Belial is allowed to triumph in equal periods with Michael, before the final intervention of God. The measured assignment of periods, the balanced dualism, and the terminology of light and darkness in this context, all suggest that Persian influence plays a part here.[72] Persian dualism has long been recognized as a factor in the contrast of the two spirits in 1QS.[73] It should also be recognized here with the qualification that the scrolls do not produce simple replicas of Persian ideas but combine them with Israelite motifs to form a new whole.

The respective roles of Michael and Belial must be seen not only against Persian dualism but also against the apocalyptic view of the Hellenistic wars in Daniel 10-12. In Daniel, Michael did battle with the angelic "princes" of Persia and Greece. In 1QM Michael is no longer simply the prince of Israel but the leader of the Sons of Light. This designation may have been correlated in practice with members of the community, but in principle it was open to broader interpretations and freed from ethnic associations. Belial, too, is no longer the prince of a specific nation. He has a human counterpart in "the king of the Kittim," but his identity is not defined in terms of a single people. Rather he represents evil at large, like Satan or Mastema in the book of *Jubilees*. Michael and Belial are closer here to being spirits of cosmic scope than are any of the angelic figures in Daniel. The less specific terminology lent itself all the more easily to reapplication. The epithet "Sons of Darkness" might refer to the Seleucids in the second century B.C.E. but to the Romans in the first century C.E.

The *War Scroll* is not only concerned with the otherworldly conflict between Michael and Belial. There is a human component on both sides. The Sons of Darkness, the army of Belial, are identified as "the troop of Edom and Moab, and the sons of Ammon, and the army [of the dwellers of] Philistia and the troops of the Kittim of Asshur, and in league with them, the offenders against the covenant" (1:1-2). Edom, Moab, Ammon, and Philistia are all, of course, traditional enemies of Israel. The main item of interest here is "the Kittim of Asshur."[74] The name Kittim is derived from Citium in Cyprus and was applied, according to Josephus (*Antiquities* 1.3.1 §128), to all islands and most maritime countries. In Daniel 11 the Kittim are the Romans, but 1 Maccabees says that Alexander the Great came from the land of Kittim, and calls Perseus, king of Macedonia, "king of the Kittim" (8:5). In the Qumran *pesharim* the Kittim are clearly the Romans, and in the first century C.E. the reference in the *War Scroll* would certainly have been applied to the Romans too. Yet it is clear that "Kittim" could refer to either Romans or Greeks, and the "Kittim of Asshur" may well have been originally the Seleucids (compare the "chief of the kings of Greece," CD 8). The "king of the Kittim" (15:3) would then be a Greek king, not necessarily a historical individual but whoever happened to be king at the time of the final conflict. In the first century C.E. the phrase would have been applied to the Roman emperor.[75] In any case it would appear that the "Kittim" function here like "the nations" in Psalm 2, as the consummation of Gentile hostility in the end-time. Unlike the conflict in Daniel, the battle anticipated in the *War Scroll* is purely future, and so the enemies in question are less historically specific.

It is important that the conceptions of 1QM are not totally incompatible with this-worldly eschatology. The outcome of the battle has two levels: "to raise amongst the angels the authority of Michael and the dominion of Israel amongst all flesh" (1QM 17:7). The state of salvation of the Sons of Light is never clearly described. It will extend "unto all appointed times of [eternity] for peace and blessing, glory and joy, and long life for all Sons of Light" (1:9). The hymnic passage in 1QM 12:11-15 uses a string of biblical phrases to paint a picture of this-worldly glory in Zion. These passages are at least compatible with a this-worldly view of salvation. 1QM envisages the "eternal annihilation of all the lot of Belial" (1QM 1:5), but there is no reference to the destruction of the world and the historical process is not necessarily brought to an end. No mention is made of the messiahs of Aaron and Israel, but the citation of Balaam's prophecy (the star and the scepter) in 1QM 11:6 may be read as a reference either to both messiahs or to the kingly messiah alone. Further, it is possible that the chief priest, who is prominent throughout the scroll and "the Prince of the Whole Congregation" in 1QM 5:1 should be interpreted respectively here as the messiahs of Aaron and Israel. As we have noted, it is difficult to distinguish between the historical leaders of the community and their eschatological successors. The question here is whether the definitive messianic state has arrived in the *War Scroll*. The scroll does not in fact speak of messiahs of Aaron or Israel, but these passages show that 1QM can be correlated with messianic expectations. They also put those expectations in perspective: the messiahs, like the priest and the prince in the eschatological war, can have no more than a subordinate position in a greater system. The victory is not in their hands but in those of God and his angels.

The *War Scroll* envisages a synergism of the earthly and the heavenly. It is concerned with a conflict between the faithful Israelites and their enemies on earth. However, it sees this conflict as only one dimension of a cosmic event. Corresponding to the earthly war—and determining its outcome—is the war between the angelic Sons of Light and Sons of Darkness. This correspondence of earthly and heavenly events is a common feature of ancient Near Eastern thought. In the Bible it is found in the oldest traditions of the "Wars of Yahweh" and again comes to prominence in Daniel 10. This otherworldly dimension of the *War Scroll* cannot be simply reduced to a figurative device for expressing an earthly conflict. There is no exact correspondence between Michael and Belial and their human counterparts. The idea that the war is ultimately controlled by conflicting supernatural powers entails an admission that the human agents are not masters of their fate. Accordingly, the language of the scroll carries with it a sense of determinism that is not suggested by the doctrine of the two messiahs. It also gives expression to a supernatural power of evil, personified in Belial. Since this power is evenly matched with Michael, the "Prince of Lights," until the time of divine intervention, the *War Scroll* presents a dualistic vision of the world which is unparalleled in the biblical tradition. The messiahs of Aaron and Israel could be accommodated within this system, but they evidently could be no more than a subordinate component.

The implications of the terminology used in the *War Scroll* are, however, more far-reaching still. The primary designations used for the adversaries in the war are neither ethnic nor national, nor even social. They are "Sons of Light" and "Sons of Darkness." These terms may be taken as metaphysical or as moral, but in any case they cannot be assumed to coincide with external human distinctions. The sectarians may have tended to assume that the Sons of Light were coterminous with their community, but they allowed for the future conversion of others and made regulations to govern the departure of present members (e.g., 1QS 7:16–27). It follows that the identity of the Sons of Light is not absolutely public and certain at any given time. The term "Sons of Light" expresses not only membership in the community, but more precisely, a certain state of the individual which is presumed to be constitutive of members of the community. The adoption of this terminology in preference to the traditional, national, and social affiliations opens up considerably the range of application of the eschatological language. Specifically, it invites the correlation of the eschatological drama with the state of the individual. The implications of this are seen more fully in 1QS.

THE CONFLICT OF THE SPIRITS IN 1QS

1QS does not speak directly of the battle between Michael and Belial. However, it gives elaborate expression to the dualism of the Sons of Light and Sons of Darkness. Again, the conflict is not simply on the human level. Rather:

> in the hand of the prince of lights is the rule over all the sons of righteousness, and in the ways of light they walk. In the hand of the angel

of darkness is all the rule over the sons of deceit and in the ways of darkness they walk. By the angel of darkness (comes) the aberration of all the sons of righteousness, . . . but Israel's God and His true angel help all the sons of light. (1QS 3:20-25)

The human Sons of Light have a heavenly counterpart in the Prince of Lights, and their adversaries are led by an Angel of Darkness. It is widely recognized that these titles are variants for Michael and Belial, but the variation is significant. The angels in 1QS are "two spirits" in which humanity must "walk until the time of visitation" (1QS 3:18). They are personifications not, or not only, of national or social groups, but of life-styles, characterized on the one hand by such qualities as humility, patience, compassion, goodness, and on the other hand by impiety, falsehood, pride, and haughtiness (1QS 4:2-6, 9-12). Further, "the spirits of truth and deceit struggle in the heart of man. . . . According to his share in truth and righteousness, thus a man hates deceit, and according to his assignment in the lot of deceit (and ungodliness) thus he loathes truth" (1QS 4:22-24). The location of the conflict is now "in the heart of man." The cosmic conflict of the Prince of Light and the Angel of Darkness is now taken to express not only the social antithesis of the Qumran sect and its opponents but also the moral conflict of good and evil within every individual.[76]

The eschatological dimension of the conflict is not entirely suppressed. God "has put down a limited time for the existence of deceit. At the time fixed for visitation He will destroy it for ever, and then the truth of the earth will appear forever" (1QS 4:18-19). The outcome for the Sons of Light involves "healing and great peace in a long life, multiplication of progeny, together with all everlasting blessings, endless joy in everlasting life, and a crown of glory together with a resplendent attire in eternal light" (1QS 4:7-8) and for the Sons of Darkness "eternal perdition by the fury of God's vengeful wrath, everlasting terror and endless shame, together with disgrace of annihilation in the fire of dark regions" (1QS 4:12-13). The contrasting fates of the Sons of Light and the Sons of Darkness are seen as the consistent working out of the dualism inherent in creation, when God created the two spirits (1QS 3:18). The conflict of Light and Darkness is also a feature of creation from the beginning. The full consequences of the division between the two spirits will only be evident at "the time fixed for visitation" (1QS 4:19), but those consequences are already determined for each individual according to "his share in truth" or "his assignment in the lot of deceit" (1QS 4:24).

Here again the distinction between the present of the community and the eschatological future has been blurred. The juxtaposition of the *War Scroll* and 1QS suggests a series of homologies: the dualistic conflict may be envisaged at once on several different levels.[77] The social, and perhaps military, conflict between the sect and its adversaries is only one manifestation of a more fundamental dualism, which is expressed at the cosmic level as the conflict of two spirits or angelic powers. This conflict is also manifested in the moral struggles in the hearts of individuals. The single dualism of light and darkness is found on a series of distinct levels—the individual heart, the political and social order, and the cosmic level embracing earth and heaven. The cosmic conflict of the two spirits may be used to express this dualism on any other level. The resolution of the conflict by the intervention of God to aid the Sons of Light may also indicate the anticipated resolution of the conflict at any level.

There is no doubt that the *Community Rule* is an early document, even allowing for a number of redactional stages, and that it enjoyed authoritative status for most of the community's history. The prominence of the discourse on the two spirits in this document reflects the importance of this doctrine at Qumran. There is no corresponding discourse in the *Damascus Document*. Yet there too we find that error is the work of Belial (4:13-15), who is let loose upon Israel for a period and is also an agent of destruction (8:2). Moreover, in CD 5:18 we are told that Moses and Aaron arose with the help of the Prince of Lights, while Belial raised up Jannes and his brother. In short, although CD does not undertake to expound the dualism of Belial and the Prince of Lights, it presupposes that doctrine.

A further indication of the early development of dualism is found in the so-called *Testament of Amram*.[78] Five copies of this Aramaic document have been identified. On the basis of the palaeographic evidence, the composition has been dated to the second century B.C.E., perhaps even the first half of that century—therefore quite probably before the settlement at Qumran. This fragmentary work recounts a dream vision in which two spirits do battle for Amram. If the text has been accurately reconstructed, each spirit has three names, Michael/Prince of Light/Melchizedek, Belial/ Prince of Darkness/Melchireša'. The complex multidimensional dualism would seem to have been developed at an early stage. The name Melchireša' also occurs in another fragmentary text 4Q280, 1-2, where he is the object of cursing.[79] Melchizedek is the central figure in 11QMelchizedek, where he is an angelic figure (*'elohim* in vs. 10) who takes vengeance on the lot of Belial.[80] The manuscript of 11QMelch dates from about the turn of the era and is a fragment of a larger composition. Although Melchireša' is not mentioned in the extant fragment, the full dualism of the earlier manuscripts is very probably presupposed. The variety of names and conceptions associated with these angelic figures shows that they were the objects of considerable speculation at Qumran.[81]

The dualism of Qumran has obvious continuity with elements of biblical tradition (e.g., the opposing angels in Zechariah 3 and Daniel 10) and more immediately with the demonology of *1 Enoch* and especially *Jubilees*. Yet there is a distinctly new development in the balanced dualism of the two angelic figures in such an indisputably early work as the *Testament of Amram*. The Persian coloring of this new development might be thought to favor the view that the Essenes or their Teacher came from the eastern Diaspora, but this is not a necessary conclusion.[82] Persian influence was possible even in the land of Israel.[83] The heightened dualism of the scrolls evidently reflects a polarization vis-à-vis the surrounding society beyond what was attested in the early Enoch literature or Daniel.

The metaphysical conflict of the two spirits does not necessarily connote a militant attitude on the part of the community. 1QS provides an explicit statement on this issue:

> To no man will I render the reward of evil,
> with goodness will I pursue each one,
> for judgment of all the living is with God. . . .
> As for the multitude of the men of the Pit,
> I will not lay hands on them till the Day of Vengeance. (1QS 10:17-19).

Presumably the directives of the *War Scroll* are intended for the Day of Vengeance. It is possible that the community felt that that day had arrived with the outbreak of the war against Rome. We know that the settlement was destroyed by force, but we may never be sure whether it was defended by the community or by some group of revolutionaries.[84] It is apparent that the imagery of cosmic warfare supported a pacifistic stance for most of the community's history. If indeed the members abandoned this stance in 66-68 c.e., in the belief that the Day of Vengeance had come, their fate must serve as another reminder of the harsh difference between apocalyptic imagery and military power.

ESCHATOLOGY IN THE HODAYOT

The adaptability of eschatological language to express more than one level of experience or expectation is most clearly visible in 1QH (*Hodayot*, Thanksgiving Hymns). As is widely recognized, these hymns use the eschatological language of resurrection and exaltation to express the present experience of the members of the community. So we read in 1QH 3:19-22:

> I thank Thee O Lord, for Thou hast released my soul from the grave,
> and from the abyss of Sheol Thou hast raised me up
> to an eternal height

> so that I can wander in the plain without limit,
> and so that I know that there is hope for him whom Thou hast formed
>   out of dust unto an eternal fellowship.
> And the perverted spirit Thou hast cleansed
>   from the great transgression
> to stand in the assembly with the hosts of the saints
> and to come into communion with the congregation
>   of the sons of heaven. [85]

This passage touches on one of the more vexed questions of the scrolls—whether they attest a belief in an afterlife. [86] No document that is likely to be the product of the Qumran community refers explicitly to resurrection. The reward of the righteous in the *Community Rule* (1QS) is couched in vague terms: "healing, great peace in a long life, multiplication of progeny, together with all everlasting blessings, endless joy in everlasting life and a crown of glory, together with a resplendent attire in eternal light." The fate of the wicked is more explicitly perdition in the fire of dark regions, at the hands of the destroying angels. Since the punishment of the wicked is clearly after death, we must assume that the "eternal life" of the righteous also extends beyond the grave. Josephus attributed to the Essenes a belief in immortality of the soul, and, although his formulation may have been tailored for a Hellenized audience, it seems probable that they held belief in afterlife which did not involve resurrection of the body. We have found such a belief already in *Jubilees* 23. [87]

The passage we have cited from 1QH 3 throws further light on this problem. The psalmist is already raised up to the "height" and enjoys the fellowship with the "saints" or angels. The *War Scroll* attests the idea that the holy angels will mingle with the community in the final battle (1QM 12:7-8). Therefore no one who is impure can go with the army (1QM 7:4-6). In 1QSa 2:3-11 no one who is smitten with any uncleanness can enter the assembly or hold office, for angels of holiness are with the congregation. Moreover, in the psalm that concludes 1QS we read that God "has caused them to inherit the lot of the Holy Ones. He has joined their assembly to the Sons of Heaven." The *Hodayot* too should be understood in this context. [88] The hymnist has been raised up from the dust because he has been admitted to the fellowship with the angels, by his membership in the eschatological community. The language of eternal life is used here primarily to express a depth experience in the present, although it is assumed that it will not be destroyed by death. [89] Similarly, the cosmological imagery is related to present experience. The hymnist can claim to have been resurrected from Sheol and to walk on the "everlasting heights." Such metaphorical use of language is attested already in the canonical Psalms, [90] but it acquires new realism in the heightened eschatological context of Qumran.

The "Messianic Woes"

The language of individual afterlife is not the only eschatological language used in a metaphorical sense in 1QH. The third column of the scroll contains two striking hymns which ostensibly refer to a more public eschatology, specifically the "messianic woes" and the destruction of the world by fire.

The first of these hymns extends from the beginning of the column (which is fragmentary) to line 18. The hymnist gives thanks for deliverance and proceeds to use a series of analogies for his previous distress:

> and they set the soul in affliction in the depths [of the sea],
> and like a besieged city [in the face of her enemies].
> And I am in distress, as a woman giving birth for the first time.

The latter analogy is then developed at length in lines 7–12. This passage is, in the words of Holm-Nielsen, "almost impossible to translate on account of the double meaning of the words."[91] Discussion has focused especially on lines 9–10:

> for in the breakers of death she giveth life to a man,
> and in the pangs of Sheol there goeth forth from the womb
>   of the pregnant one a
> wonderful counselor with his strength
> and a man child is brought forth from the birth canal.

Then in line 12 reference is made to one who is pregnant with *'p'h*, which is variously translated "wickedness" (Holm-Nielsen), "nought" (Mansoor),[92] or "asp/viper" (Dupont-Sommer)[93] The last is the most common biblical meaning of the word, but the ambiguity is undoubtedly intentional, as in line 18 one pregnant with *'wl* ("wickedness") is used in poetic parallelism with the spirits of *'p'h* ("nought" or "asp"). In any case this pregnant woman must suffer pain and terror:

> And the foundations of the wall shake as a ship upon the waters . . .
> and both they that dwell in the dust and they that go down to the sea
>   are terrified by the roar of the waters."

The imagery of sinking in the depths is continued and merges into a descent to the Sheol. Finally in line 18:

the doors of the pit close behind her that is pregnant with mischief
and the bars of eternity behind all the spirits of wickedness.[94]

Most commentators agree that the hymn falls into two sections, with the
division in line 12, where the second pregnant woman is introduced. Lines
7b-12a are completely taken up with the birth of a boy-child. The
pregnancy with the asp/wickedness does not occupy as much space, but it
provides the framework for lines 12b-18a. This section begins with the
travail of the one pregnant with the asp/wickedness and ends with her confinement in "the pit." The extensive storm imagery of lines 13-16 is framed
by these two references and only serves as supplementary elaboration of
this pregnancy. The hymn then is largely taken up with the contrast between a painful labor that issues in the birth of a *geber* ("man") and
another painful labor that culminates in imprisonment in Sheol.

The issue of the first pregnancy is described in line 10 as "a wonderful
counselor." The phrase is taken, of course, from Isa 9:5. In its original context it referred to a child who would sit on the throne of David, and it was
understood as a messianic prophecy in Christianity. Consequently, Dupont-
Sommer and others have assumed that a reference to the (a?) messiah is
intended here.[95] The majority of scholars deny that the passage envisages
a specific individual, but "there is tolerable agreement among them that
the background for lines 7-12 is a sketch of the Messianic woes, i.e. signs
and warnings of the dawn of the Messianic era."[96] Birth imagery is found
in an eschatological context in the New Testament and some Jewish apocalypses.[97] More significant, the fate of the woman pregnant with the asp/
wickedness in the second half of the hymn has clear eschatological connotations. She will be confined in Sheol with "all the spirits of the asp/
wickedness" (1QH 3:18). The destruction of the forces of wickedness is a
recurring feature of the eschatology of Qumran.[98] Since the outcome of the
evil pregnancy is clearly eschatological, parallelism suggests that the outcome of the good pregnancy is eschatological too. Accordingly, even if we
follow the majority of scholars, who reject the identification of the "wonderful counselor" as "the messiah," we must still recognize that the two
pregnancies are metaphorical sketches of the eschatological tribulation
and its outcome.

Yet the purpose of the hymn is not to prophesy the messianic age. Rather
it is a thanksgiving hymn, which describes the distress and deliverance of
the author.[99] The birth imagery is specifically introduced as an analogy in
line 7: "And I am in distress, as a woman giving birth for the first time."
It follows on two other analogies—the ship at sea and the besieged city,
which are not specifically eschatological. This consideration does not
remove the eschatological reference of the birth imagery. Rather, the

experience of the author is being illustrated at once by a double analogy: that of childbirth itself and that of the eschatological process evoked by the birth imagery. The purpose of the psalm is not to prophesy either the messiah or the messianic age. The eschatological reference serves as a metaphor for the psalmist's experience. It is inadequate, however, to say that it is "only a simile." The fact that eschatological language can be used in this way is highly significant. It presupposes the discernment of a pattern on several different levels. The distress of the righteous individual, which issues in deliverance, is like the pain of childbirth, which issues in the birth of a child and which in turn is analogous to the eschatological trials of the community, which issue in the messianic age. Conversely, the distress of the wicked is like a malignant labor, which in turn is analogous to eschatological disaster. The eschatological future is known by analogy with other patterns and can in turn serve as an analogy for other areas of experience. Eschatological language here presupposes and makes explicit a common pattern in present and future and so can be applied to the present situation, just as the language of eschatological war is applied in 1QS to the ongoing battle in human hearts.

THE DESTRUCTION BY FIRE

The second hymn in 1QH 3 extends from line 19 to line 36. In lines 19–23 the author gives thanks to God for elevating him from "the abyss of Sheol" to "an eternal height," although he is only "a creature of clay" who stands "within the border of ungodliness and with the vicious by lot." The hymn goes on to describe the tumults that surround "the soul of the poor." These include "the arrows of the pit" (line 27), "the period of wrath for all Belial" and the snares of death (line 28). Then follows a description of the eruption of the fiery floods of Belial, which devour "right down to the great deep" and "break through into the abyss" (lines 31–32), and finally the thundering of God and the "war of the heroes of heaven," which sweep the world "until the appointed consummation," which is for eternity (line 36).

The hymn is evidently giving thanks for deliverance already accomplished. Yet at least the last verse is indisputably eschatological and must refer to the future. In addition, the fiery flood of Belial would seem to be eschatological since it involves the destruction of the physical universe, and the motif has extensive parallels in Persian, Jewish, and Christian eschatology.[100] Translators and commentators disagree about how much of the hymn refers to the tumults experienced by the author in either present or past. There is general agreement that lines 25–28 refer to the actual experience of the author. Vermes translates the eruption of the floods of Belial (line 29) as future,[101] but it is difficult to draw a line between the "floods of Belial" and the "arrows of the pit" and the "period of wrath upon all

Belial," which precede that line.[102] Others translate by the past or present tenses for lines 29–33 and only use the future for the final consummation.[103]

The solution to this problem lies in the appreciation of the deliberate ambiguity of eschatological language which we have found throughout the Qumran documents. The primary reference here, as in 1QH 3:1–18, is clearly the deliverance of the individual, which is already realized. Both the nature of the deliverance (communion with the sons of heaven, line 22) and that from which the deliverance is required (the grave, Sheol) are expressed in eschatological language throughout. The tumults that surround the author in lines 25–28 are located in "the period of wrath upon all Belial," or the final period. Such language cannot be dismissed as "merely" metaphorical. It is certainly metaphorical, but it expresses the conviction of the author that the eschatological drama is already under way. If the "arrows of the pit" can refer to the present experience of the author, the "floods of Belial" can too. Even the war of the heroes of heaven, which clearly corresponds to that described in 1QM, may be conceived as already in progress.

The eschatological language of the hymn is not exhausted by, or coterminous with, the experience of the individual or his community. In fact, the author claims that he has already been raised to the eternal height. His victory is secure. Yet the eschatological tumult is certainly not finished. The deliverance of the individual from "the snares of the pit" (line 26) is only part of a wider process on the cosmic level. The afflictions that beset the individual are only part of a wider cosmic tumult that is due to the warring of Belial and the heavenly host. On the wider level that tumult is even thought to involve the destruction of the physical universe. Here again the underlying assumption is that there is a common pattern between human affairs and cosmic processes. Accordingly, cosmic language can be used metaphorically to express the state of the individual. The space in which the author of this hymn moves is the cosmic space of Sheol and the eternal height. The time in which he moves is the eschatological period of wrath against Belial. The pattern of future tumult and deliverance is already manifest in his own experience.

ESCHATOLOGICAL LANGUAGE

Two aspects of the scrolls are especially instructive for the nature of eschatological language. One is the plurality of future expectations that exist side by side. The second concerns the multidimensional ways in which the doctrines can be understood.

Although the "national, political, this-worldly" expectation of the messiahs is compatible with the ideas of cosmic war such as we find in

1QM, it undeniably reflects a different mode of eschatological thinking. The fiery destruction of the world in 1QH 3 is logically incompatible with the political this-worldly type of messianism. Accordingly, the expectations of the community should not be harmonized into a systematic body of doctrines. Rather, we must reckon with the persistence of diverse conceptions side by side in the same community.

In his study of this phenomenon Morton Smith concluded that the importance of eschatological doctrine for the sect had been exaggerated: "If a group had no single eschatological myth, it cannot have been organized as a community of believers in the myth it did not have. . . . If the variety of eschatological prediction is any evidence, eschatology was, for the members of these groups, a comparatively arbitrary and individual matter."[104] It is certainly true that Qumran did not have a systematic body of doctrine analogous to what later developed in Christianity. Smith seeks to explain the diversity of eschatological doctrines by assuming that different beliefs were held by different people. This position is difficult to maintain in view of the fact that diverse eschatological views, the ongoing war of the spirits and the expectation of the messiahs of Aaron and Israel, are preserved side by side in the *Community Rule*. The problem cannot be resolved by assigning the different ideas to different redactional stages. It is probably true that the discourse on the two spirits was composed separately from the passage that refers to the messiahs in 1QS 9, but the fact remains that they were combined and read as part of a single authoritative community rule for most of the history of the community. We cannot assume that either idea was ever ignored in favor of the other. Moreover, in CD the reference to Belial and the Prince of Lights occurs in the same unit as the allusion to the messianic "one who will teach righteousness at the end of days."[105] Concepts and formulations that were diverse from a tradition-historical point of view were nonetheless found to be compatible in the scrolls. Needless to say, this does not mean that all the eschatological motifs were developed at the same time or held with equal emphasis by all members of the community, but it does mean that the different types of eschatology cannot be seen as mutually exclusive and that we cannot posit either distinct groups or stages of the community on the basis of hypothetically "pure" eschatological beliefs.

This conclusion throws light on the nature and logic of eschatological belief at Qumran. In the well-known terminology of Ian Ramsey, the eschatological doctrines are "disclosure models" rather than "scale" or "picture models."[106] In picture modeling "a model is thought of as a replica, a copy picture . . . reproducing identically those properties common to model and original which, for the particular purpose in mind, are importantly relevant." If the eschatological doctrines of Qumran were understood as picture models, this would imply that the events predicted were expected to happen in precisely this way. In this case views that could not be reconciled with one another in detail must be presumed to have been held by different people. In contrast, "disclosure" or "analogue models" are "designed to reproduce as faithfully as possible the *structure* or web of relationship in an original." In this case differences in detail are not important, since the doctrines do not give exact literal descriptions of the future in any case. Instead, the emphasis is on "the structure or web of relationship"— the division of the world between two forces, symbolically called Light and Darkness and the conviction that Light will prevail.

The understanding of the eschatology of Qumran as "disclosure" or "analogue" modeling also throws light on the fact that doctrines can be understood on several different levels at once. The leadership of the messiahs of Aaron and Israel can be enacted by the present leaders of the community. The war of Light and Darkness is already raging in the hearts of humanity. The author of the *Hodayot* can claim to have already experienced the "messianic woes" and the "floods of Belial" and even the deliverance that follows them. The eschatological assertions of Qumran presuppose a coherence in the structure of the universe—past, present, and future. Their purpose is to disclose the structure or web of relationship that constitutes that coherence. Insights into the pattern of present experience can then be used to illuminate the future, and eschatological doctrines can disclose meaning in the present.

THE APOCALYPTICISM OF THE SCROLLS

The world view of the Qumran community has considerable affinities with the conceptual framework of the apocalypses. The world is mysterious and in need of revelation through the decoding of scriptures and the inspiration of the Teacher. The eschatological horizon is constantly in view, in the expectation of the messiahs and the cosmic war, and is even encountered already in the experience of the community. The affinity with the apocalypses is perhaps most noteworthy in the interest in the angelic world—an interest that was lacking in other eschatological writings such as the early sibyllines. To be sure, Qumran has its distinctive features. The mediator of revelation is not an angel but the Teacher, and the anticipation of eschatological salvation by fellowship with the angels is stronger in the *Hodayot* than in any apocalypse. Yet the understanding of the supernatural world and its significance for human affairs has closer analogies in the apocalypses than in any other strand of Judaism. It is not inappropriate, then, to refer to Qumran an an apocalyptic community or as an example of apocalypticism, although it cannot be taken as a typical setting for the production of apocalypses.

The significance of the scrolls for the study of apocalypticism lies in the fact that they show how cosmic and eschatological symbolism can be related to social organization. The cosmic dualism of light and darkness reflects the alienation of the community from the rest of Jewish society and its antagonistic attitude toward the Gentile powers. Yet the scrolls cannot be understood only in terms of rejection of the established order. They also affirm a positive counterstructure which is embodied in the organization of the community, in its hierarchical order, ritual practice, and distinctive calendar. Qumran does not fit the stereotype that apocalyptic or millennial groups are antistructural and antiritual,[107] but supports the view that apocalypticism retains the imprint of the particular tradition in which it develops.[108] In this case, the underlying tradition was priestly and hierarchical and closely related to what we find in *Jubilees,* and so, perhaps, to a strand of the Hasidim. The early apocalypses of both Enoch and Daniel were treasured at Qumran, but the community obviously drew on many other sources besides. Qumran provides no warrant for assuming that Jewish apocalypticism was a single unified phenomenon. It does, however, illustrate one setting where eschatological expectation and speculation about the angelic world played an integral part in the life of a community.

6
The Similitudes
of Enoch

THE ARAMAIC FRAGMENTS discovered at Qumran have thrown new light on much of the book of *Enoch*. In the case of the Similitudes (*1 Enoch* 37–71), however, no fragments have been found. J. T. Milik was thus led to conclude that the Similitudes are not a Jewish work at all but rather a late, third-century Christian composition.[1] This thesis has attracted considerable attention, since it involves a matter of central importance for New Testament studies as well as ancient Judaism: the figure of the "Son of Man," which plays a major role in the Similitudes. This document has been regarded as the principal evidence for Jewish speculation on a "Son of Man" figure in New Testament times. Its historical significance would be greatly altered if it were shown to be a later Christian product.

Milik's argument rests not only on the absence from Qumran but also on his theory that the Similitudes displaced the Book of Giants in an original Enochic pentateuch and on alleged parallels with Christian sections of the *Sibylline Oracles*. No aspect of this argument has withstood the test of criticism.[2] Absence from Qumran cannot prove that the Similitudes did not exist in this period. The Essene library did not include all the literature of the day, and the Similitudes may have been unacceptable in any case because of the near equality of the sun and moon in chap. 41, as opposed to the special treatment of the sun elsewhere in the scrolls.[3] There is no textual evidence that the Enochic books were ever regarded as a pentateuch. The parallels with the *Sibylline Oracles* are quite superficial. The overall genre is different, since the oracles lack the visionary aspect. The present form of the Similitudes, which explicitly identifies Enoch as the "Son of Man," must be Jewish. It is unlikely that a Jewish author would have accorded such a central role to a "Son of Man" figure after that expression had become established as a christological title. Indeed the Matthean "Son

142

of Man" passages (Matt 19:28 and 25:31), which refer to the "glorious throne," seem to depend on the Similitudes.[4] Consequently, a date prior to 70 C.E. is likely, and there is nothing in the Similitudes incompatible with this. The most specific historical allusions are the mention of the Parthians and Medes in 56:5-7 and a reference to hot springs in 67:5-13. The allusion to the Parthians is eschatological but is most plausibly dated after the invasion of Palestine by the Parthians in 40 B.C.E. The springs are said to serve the kings and the mighty but will change to become instruments of judgment. This passage is probably inspired by Herod's attempt to cure himself in the waters of Callirhoe, which is recorded by Josephus (*Antiquities* 17.6.5 §§171-73; *War* 1.33.5 §§657-58). The Similitudes, then, should be dated to the early or mid first century C.E.[5] Although the Ethiopic is the only extant text, it is probable that it derives from an Aramaic original.[6] The Similitudes fully belong in the discussion of ancient Jewish apocalypticism.

THE GENRE OF THE SIMILITUDES

The Similitudes of Enoch consist of three "parables" (chaps. 38-44, 45-57, and 58-69) and a double epilogue in chaps. 70 and 71.[7] Chapter 37 introduces the entire composition as a "vision of wisdom." The eschatological import of this wisdom is indicated by the observation that "the lot of eternal life has been given to me" (37:4).

Each parable is introduced by a chapter presenting the subject of the revelation proper. Chapter 38 begins with a question:

> When the community of the righteous appears, and the sinners are judged for their sins and are driven from the face of the dry ground, and when the Righteous One appears before the chosen righteous whose works are weighed by the Lord of Spirits, and (when) light appears to the righteous and chosen who dwell on the dry ground, where (will be) the dwelling of the sinners, and where the resting-place of those who have denied the Lord of Spirits? It would have been better for them if they had not been born.[8]

What is at issue, then, is the eschatological resting-place on the day of judgment. The judgment is also the occasion when "the secrets of righteousness" are revealed. These secrets evidently concern the final destiny of both righteous and wicked. The chapter sounds another characteristic note of the Similitudes when it adds that "the mighty kings" will be destroyed and those who inhabit the earth will not be mighty and exalted.

The revelation proper begins with the ascent of Enoch to "the end of heaven." There he sees "the dwelling of the righteous and the resting-places of the holy" with the angels and the holy ones. He then sees "a thousand thousands and ten thousand times ten thousand" who stand before the Lord of Spirits (40:1) and the four archangels, who are identified by Enoch's angelic guide. In chap. 41 he is shown all the secrets of heaven. Once again, the resting-places of the holy are first on the list, but the secrets include also the cosmological mysteries of lightning and thunder, sun and moon, etc. When Enoch inquires about the flashes of lightning and the stars of heaven, he is told: "Their likeness has the Lord of Spirits shown to you; these are the names of the righteous who dwell on the dry ground and believe in the name of the Lord of Spirits for ever and ever" (43:4). Although the exact nature of the correspondence is less than clear, it is evident that there is some analogy between the order of the heavens and the righteous on earth.

The first parable is interrupted by a brief wisdom poem, which is an inversion of the great hymn in Sirach 24. In Sirach, wisdom sought a resting-place and found it in Jerusalem, and was identified with "the book of the law of the Lord." In *1 Enoch* 41 wisdom found no place where she could dwell, so she returned to heaven and took her seat with the angels. The earth was given over to iniquity. Although this poem seems intrusive in its present context, it fits quite well with the thought of the Similitudes. Wisdom is not to be found on earth but is with the angels in heaven. It can only be obtained by special revelation such as is given to Enoch by his angelic guide in the course of his ascent. This passage illustrates nicely the fundamental difference between the wisdom tradition and the apocalypses. Both find wisdom in the order of the universe, but for the apocalyptist this wisdom is hidden and is obscured by iniquity on earth.[9]

The second parable is "about those who deny the name of the dwelling of the holy ones and the Lord of Spirits." These, we are told, will neither ascend to heaven nor come on earth. More specifically, this parable concerns the judgment day when the Chosen One will sit on his throne of glory.

The parable proper presupposes Enoch's ascent and begins directly with his vision of "one who had a head of days" and another "whose face had the appearance of a man." Enoch's dialogue with the angelic guide here mainly concerns that "Son of Man" and the day of judgment. It is significant that "wisdom has been poured out like water" before him and is no longer withdrawn as in chap. 41. Enoch learns the future destiny of righteous and wicked (chaps. 50 and 51) and also sees cosmological secrets (chap. 52) which "serve the authority of his messiah" and the places and instruments of judgment (chaps. 53–57). The places of judgment are built into the structure of the universe and are already prepared. They are not presented as a matter of future hope, but of present knowledge.

The third parable is said in chap. 58 to be about the righteous and the chosen, and their destiny. The revelation begins with the cosmological secrets of thunder, lightning, etc. Chapter 60 has a brief vision of the Head of Days, which is introduced as a separate vision, and then reverts to the cosmological mysteries. This chapter has been thought to be a fragment of the Book of Noah.[10] Chapters 61–64 are devoted to the "Son of Man" figure and the judgment. Chapters 65–67 appear to be a fragment of the Book of Noah dealing with the flood and may have been part of a larger corpus of Enoch literature, since Enoch figures as Noah's grandfather.[11] It is related to its present context by the theme of judgment insofar as the flood provides an analogy for the final destruction. Chapters 68–69 deal with the judgment of the fallen angels. The double epilogue in chaps. 70–71 concludes the book with the final assumption of Enoch.

The three parables of Enoch are evidently complementary, in the manner of the visions of Daniel. The epilogue provides an appropriate conclusion, but the main themes of the day of judgment and the destiny of the righteous are prominent from the start. The revelations are parables or similitudes insofar as they involve a complex set of analogies: between the fate of the righteous and that of the wicked, the holy on earth and the holy ones in heaven, the mysterious order of the cosmos and the lot of the righteous.[12] The macrogenre is clearly apocalypse. Enoch receives his revelations by visions in the course of an ascent, and they are explained by his angelic guide. The revelations concern the transcendent world of the heavens and the impending judgment of humanity. Although the frequent allusions to "the kings and the mighty" indicate a political interest, there is no review of history such as we find in the "historical" apocalypses.[13] As in all the Jewish apocalypses that describe heavenly ascents, there is a mystical tendency in the emphasis on revealed wisdom.

THE RIGHTEOUS IN THE SIMILITUDES

It is clear from the introductory chapters—38, 45, and 58—that the major focus of the Similitudes is on the destiny of "the righteous and the chosen" and their wicked counterparts. The final destiny of both parties is emphatically clear. The righteous will enjoy their heavenly resting-places with the holy angels (41:2; 51:4) and will also dwell on a transformed earth (45:5). The wicked will be punished and swallowed up in Sheol.

In contrast, statements about the earthly career of the righteous are frustratingly vague.[14] The term "righteous," which is used interchangeably with "chosen" and "holy," is used as a quasi-technical term or even title for a community.[15] There are, however, a few specific references. In 43:4 we read of "the names of the righteous who dwell on the dry ground and believe in the name of the Lord of Spirits for ever and ever." Chapter 47 refers to the "blood of the righteous," thereby implying that they are persecuted. In 48:6 the righteous "have hated and rejected this world of iniquity, and all its works and its ways they have hated in the name of the Lord of Spirits, for in his name they are saved." The picture of the righteous ones can be filled out from the more frequent descriptions of their opponents, "those who commit sin and evil" (45:5). They are "the kings and the powerful" (46:4; cf. 38:4; 48:8; 53:5; 54:2; 62:9; 63:1). They are also the ones "who have denied the name of the Lord of Spirits" (38:2; cf. 41:2; 45:1). These two characteristics are related. They deny the name of the Lord of Spirits because "their power rests on their riches, and their faith is in the gods which they have made with their hands" (46:7) and their "hope has been on *the scepter of* our kingdom and of our glory" (63:7). The issue that divides the righteous and the wicked is belief in the heavenly world of the Lord of Spirits and the Son of Man, and in the judgment where they will prevail. Those who lack such a belief put their trust in such power as is available in the present. Those who enjoy power in the present, the kings and the mighty, are especially prone to such an attitude. Conversely, those who are powerless and more likely to "hate and reject this world of iniquity." Yet powerlessness in itself is no virtue and does not constitute righteousness. Righteousness is rather an attitude of rejecting this world and having faith in the Lord of Spirits and the Son of Man. Faith here involves both belief in the existence of the Lord of Spirits and the Son of Man and trust and dependence on them for salvation. We should note that the Similitudes do not explicitly refer to keeping the law or distinguish between Jew and Gentile. It is probably true that the law is presupposed, and that the "kings and the powerful" who trust in the gods they themselves have made are Gentile rulers, but the opposition is not formulated in terms of Jew and Gentile. It is probable that "righteous" refers to a much narrower group than the Jewish people.

The faith of the righteous entails wisdom and knowledge. This in itself is not surprising since righteousness and wisdom go hand in hand not only in Old Testament wisdom but also in the mythology of the ancient Near East. In the Jewish tradition wisdom had come to be identified with the law of Moses (Sir 24:23) and was said to have made its dwelling in Israel (Sir 24:8). This identification is not apparent in the Similitudes. Indeed, the wisdom poem in *1 Enoch* 42 is in direct contradiction to Sirach 24. Instead, wisdom is only accessible by special revelation. It is said to abound in the presence of God (48:1; 49:1). The spirit of wisdom dwells in the Chosen One who stands before the Lord of Spirits (49:3). This wisdom is not readily available. Righteousness and faith involve secrets that are known only by revelation. This revelation is never related to the Mosaic covenant. Most obviously it is given to and through Enoch himself ("until now there has not been given by the Lord of Spirits such insight as I have received in accordance with my insight" (37:4). The Similitudes themselves are the revelation of the wisdom disclosed to Enoch in his heavenly journey, in which he sees "all the secrets of heaven" including the judgment (41:1). Yet the revelation of the Similitudes presupposes an antecedent revelation of the "name" of the Son of Man and expects a further definitive revelation in the future. In 48:7 we are told that the wisdom of the Lord of Spirits has revealed the Son of Man to the holy and righteous (cf. 62:7) and in 69:26 the righteous rejoice "because the name of that Son of Man had been revealed to them." The Son of Man or his name is then a fundamental object of revelation, but he in turn "will reveal all the treasures of that which is secret" (46:3) and "judge the things that are secret" (49:4). The final and definitive revelation of the Son of Man is still in the future, on the day of judgment, and that is when he will judge the things that are secret. For the present, faith in "that Son of Man" provides assurance that there will indeed be a judgment over which he will preside. This faith presumably undergirds righteous actions, but it also seems to be constitutive of righteousness in itself, since it involves not only belief but also the attitude of trust, in contrast to the self-sufficiency of the wicked.

"THAT SON OF MAN"

The Similitudes, then, are exceptional among the Jewish apocalypses in focusing attention on a single figure, who is designated as the "Chosen One" or "that Son of Man," or even "messiah" (48:10; 52:4). Since early Christianity also focuses on a single figure who is often called "Son of Man" this individual in the Similitudes acquires considerable historical interest and has given rise to an enormous literature.[16]

The "Son of Man" figure first appears in chap. 46 in the second parable. Enoch sees "one who had a head of days," whose head was white like wool, and with him "another, whose face had the appearance of a man and his face (was) full of grace, like one of the holy angels." The accompanying angel explains: "This is the Son of Man who has righteousness, and with whom righteousness dwells; he will reveal all the treasures of that which is secret."

The manner in which he is introduced does not presuppose that "Son of Man" is a well-known title: Enoch sees a figure who had "the appearance of a man," and this figure is subsequently referred to as "that Son of Man."[17] The expression "Son of Man" then is a periphrastic way of referring to the figure with "the appearance of a man" in 46:3. The inference that "Son of Man" "would naturally be read as the equivalent of 'man'"[18] is not warranted, however, since it neglects some important considerations. First, a figure with the appearance of a man is quite commonly found to be an angel in apocalyptic literature.[19] Whether the figure is in fact a man depends on whether he should be identified as Enoch throughout the Similitudes, a problem to which we shall return below. Second, the expression "Son of Man" is an allusion to Daniel 7 (especially in the context of the vision of the head of days in chap. 46). Therefore, whenever the expression "that Son of Man" is repeated it is not simply equivalent to "the figure you saw" but also implies that this figure carries the eschatological associations of Daniel 7. Although the Similitudes do not assume that "Son of Man" is a well-known title, the expression serves to establish an identity that is more than just "a human figure."

The identity of this "Son of Man" figure does not depend entirely on its association with Daniel. The "Son of Man who has righteousness" cannot be distinguished from the "Righteous One" of 38:2 and 53:6.[20] It is also generally agreed that "the Chosen One," who appears in all three parables, is the same being, since he exercises the same functions as the "Son of Man," and the two expressions are interchanged in such a way that the identification is not in doubt.[21] Both the Righteous One and the Chosen One are used in association with the broader categories of "the righteous" and "the chosen" and these are also described as "the holy" (e.g., 48:1, 4). These terms have several layers of reference. Besides the holy on earth there are "the holy ones who dwell in the heavens" (47:2)—primarily the angelic host but also transformed human righteous ones after their death, since we are told that they "all will become angels in heaven" (51:4) and they have their "dwellings with the angels and their resting-places with the holy ones" (39:5). When "the chosen will begin to dwell with the chosen" (61:4), the human, earthly, chosen ones will begin to dwell with the heavenly. In short, the human community of the elect and the righteous stands in very close association with the angelic world and will ultimately be merged with it. The righteous, elect "Son of Man" figure is directly related to both the human and the heavenly righteous.[22] The association does not lie only in "the fact that the son of man figure and the elect and righteous have in common certain basic qualities, those of election and righteousness."[23] His entire function is defined in relation to the human righteous ones: "He will be a staff to the righteous and the holy, that they may lean on him and not fall" (48:4); "the wisdom of the Lord of Spirits has revealed him to the holy and the righteous, for he has kept safe the lot of the righteous" (48:5), and after the judgment "with that Son of Man will they dwell and eat and lie down and rise up for ever and ever" (62:14). His function as eschatological revealer and judge is to vindicate the righteous and condemn their enemies.

This close connection between the individual Son of Man and the community of the righteous has led some scholars to invoke the allegedly Hebrew conception of corporate personality.[24] This idea has rightly been criticized insofar as it implies "psychical unity" and rests on outdated anthropological theories that have been widely discredited.[25] There is no room for doubt that the Similitudes present the "Son of Man" as an individual figure distinct from the community. However, the communal dimension of the figure does not stand or fall with corporate personality. Mowinckel put the matter well: "Representative unity and a corporate conception of the leader as the bearer of the whole, and of the individual as a type of the race, is not the same as literal and actual identity. The fact that in the cult a person represents the whole, or in a symbolic sense *is* the whole, means that there is an intimate community of destiny between them. . . ."[26] The relation of the king to his people illlustrates the point. The unity involved in the Similitudes is evidently closer to Mowinckel's "representative unity" than to corporate personality. Yet the relation of the king to his people is not the closest analogy we can find. Throughout the parables the Son of Man or Chosen One is located in the heavenly sphere in the presence of the Lord of Spirits: "For from the beginning the Son of Man was hidden and the Most High kept him in the presence of his power and revealed him (only) to the chosen" (62:7, cf. 48:6). As Sjöberg has remarked, he is not a man, at least not in the usual sense of the word, but is rather a heavenly being.[27] A closer analogy is found with the patron deities of nations in Near Eastern mythology. These deities have a representative unity with their peoples, although they are definitely distinguished from them. While "the gods of Hamath and Arpad" (Isa 36:19) cannot be conceived of apart from the nations they represent, there is no doubt that any divinity was assumed to have greater power than its people and to be able to act independently over against them. The heavenly counterparts of nations played an important part in apocalyptic literature, most notably in Daniel 10, where the angelic "princes" of Persia and Greece do battle with Michael, "the prince of your people." We have argued above that the "one like a son of man" in Daniel 7 should be understood in this sense, as the heavenly counterpart of the faithful Jews. The Similitudes differ from Daniel insofar as the human community is not identified in national terms but as the "righteous" or the "chosen." Correspondingly, its heavenly counterpart is not identified as Michael, the patron of Israel, (who appears independently as one of the archangels) but as "the Son of Man who has righteousness" or the "Chosen One." The difference in terminology is at least potentially significant and may suggest that the community which produced the Similitudes did not find its basic identity in membership of the Jewish people but was sectarian in character. Yet the correspondence between "the Chosen One" and the community of the chosen is analogous to that between Michael and Israel or any other mythological counterpart of a group or nation.

There is a parallelism of action, or "structural homologue"[28] between the earthly and heavenly counterparts. George Nickelsburg has noted the similarity between the Similitudes and Daniel in this respect. In Daniel "the son of man stands parallel to the (people of) saints (of the Most High). His exaltation means their exaltation."[29] Similarly in *1 Enoch* the manifestation of the "Son of Man" figure entails the triumph of the righteous. Nickelsburg has further argued that both the Similitudes and Wisdom 1-5 reflect a common exegetical tradition based on Isaiah 52-53.[30] In Isaiah and Wisdom a single figure, the servant and the righteous man, suffers, dies (at least in Wisdom; the interpretation of Isaiah is disputed), and is exalted. In the Similitudes the Son of Man stands parallel to the persecuted community and is finally exalted, but there is no suggestion that he suffers or dies. Yet the parallels with Isaiah 53 are significant. In Isaiah and Wisdom the true nature and destiny of the servant and the righteous man are hidden until the time of the judgment and cause consternation when they are revealed . In *1 Enoch* the Son of Man is hidden until the judgment and also causes panic on his appearance. The hiddenness of the Son of Man corresponds to the sufferings of the righteous community and the hidden character of their destiny. The structural homologue between the Son of Man and the community is thus complete. Although he does not share their suffering, the pattern of hiddenness and revelation is common to both. The fact that he is preserved from their sufferings makes him a figure of pure power and glory and an ideal embodiment of the hopes of the persecuted righteous. The efficaciousness of the "Son of Man" figure requires that he be conceived as other than the community, since he must possess the power and exaltation which they lack.

In short, the Son of Man is not a personification of the righteous community, but is conceived, in mythological fashion, as its heavenly *Doppelgänger*. Now it is characteristic of mythological thinking that such a *Doppelgänger* is conceived to be *more* real and permanent than its earthly counterpart and prior to it in the order of being.[31] From a modern critical perspective, the reverse is true. It "is a question of men before it is a question of angels."[32] The human community is the datum of our experience and knowledge. The heavenly counterpart is posited on the basis of this datum. While the Son of Man is conceived of as a real being, he symbolizes the destiny of the righteous community both in its present hiddenness and future manifestation.[33]

THE IDENTIFICATION WITH ENOCH

Up to this point we have not considered the disputed question of the precise identification of the Son of Man. The question arises because of two passages in the epilogues. The first, 70:1, is a disputed reading. The editions of Charles and Knibb read that Enoch's name was lifted up "to the presence of that Son of Man *and* to the presence of the Lord of Spirits." However, a few manuscripts—namely, U, V, and W—support a different reading: "the name of that son of man was raised aloft . . . to the Lord of Spirits."[34] The second passage is 71:14, where an angel tells Enoch: "You are the Son of Man who was born to righteousness. . . ." The problem, then, is that throughout the Similitudes Enoch has observed "that Son of Man" with no indication that he is seeing himself. Then in 71:14 (and possibly in 70:1) he is identified with the figure in his visions. The solution of Charles was to emend 71:14 to read "this is the Son of Man . . ." and change "you" to "him" in the following verses.[35] This procedure has no basis in the text and is clearly unacceptable. Three possible solutions deserve serious consideration.

First, "Son of Man" in 71:14 may not have the technical reference ("that Son of Man") but may be used as a common noun ("that man who").[36] According to this interpretation Enoch is not identified with "that Son of Man" and there is no contradiction between chaps. 70 and 71. A parallel to this usage is found in *1 Enoch* 60:10, where Enoch is directly called "Son of Man" "after the manner of Ezekiel,"[37] with no eschatological implications; but this passage may be part of a Noachic fragment, presumably from a different author. Against this theory, however, 71:16 ("all . . . will walk according to your way . . . with you will be their dwelling and with you their lot") strongly suggests an identification with the "Son of Man" of 48:7, and 71:14 corresponds closely to 46:3. Also the phrase "Son of Man" is used throughout the Similitudes (apart from the Noachic 60:10) with specific reference to a single figure. A distinction in 71:14 strains probability and must be considered unlikely.

The second possible solution might seem at first glance to be the most straightforward: the identification with Enoch may be intended throughout.[38] Chapter 71 might then be viewed as the climax of the revelation, disclosing that the "name revealed to the elect" (69:26) is the name of Enoch himself.[39] However, the "name" is not necessarily a title or a proper name, but the person himself—as is clearly shown in 70:1 where Enoch's name is lifted up to heaven.[40] Moreover, there are serious problems with the view that the identification with Enoch was intended throughout.

First, there is the disputed reading in 70:1 where most manuscripts show a clear distinction between Enoch and the Son of Man. On purely textual grounds this reading is better than that of the three manuscripts (U, V, and W) which imply an identification. The disagreement of the manuscripts requires us to suppose that some copyists emended the reading of 70:1. If the majority reading is original, then it would appear that U, V, and W were changed to conform to 71:14. If the reading in U is original,[41] then the other copyists presumably changed the text to distinguish Enoch from the Son of Man. In that case, however, we are at a loss as to why they did not also change 71:14, but introduced a contradiction into the text. In short, the reading of U is more easily explained as a scribal alteration. Accordingly, it seems more plausible that the majority reading is original and therefore that Enoch was distinguished from the "Son of Man" in 70:1. Second, there is no parallel in the apocalyptic literature for a visionary who fails to recognize himself in his visions.[42] Yet Enoch does not identify himself with "that Son of Man" in the "parables." Third, there is a problem connected with the alleged preexistence of the Son of Man in *1 Enoch* 48.[43] In 48:2 his name was named even before the sun and the constellations were created, and in 48:6 he was chosen and hidden before the world was created. He is known only by special revelation to the chosen ones and is revealed to others only in the eschatological judgment. There is no suggestion that he was in any sense revealed in the "historical" life of Enoch.

There is no doubt that Enoch was eventually identified with the "Son of Man," and this tradition is later developed in the figure of Metatron in *3 Enoch*.[44] In view of the problems we have considered, especially the textual evidence in chap. 70, it would seem that this identification was not presupposed in the Similitudes but was introduced as a secondary stage.

The third possible solution is that chap. 71 is a redactional addition to the Similitudes.[45] This view is not an ad hoc solution to the "Son of Man" problem but arises independently from literary considerations. Chapters 70 and 71 constitute a double epilogue to the Similitudes. Each tells how Enoch was carried up to the heavens.[46] Redundancy and duplication are not in themselves surprising in a work such as the Similitudes, but we usually find such redundancy in the visions, not in the narrative framework. Accordingly, the repetition here strongly suggests the hand of a redactor. Of course this argument is strengthened if we follow the majority reading at 70:1, which makes a clear distinction between Enoch and the Son of Man in contradiction to 71:14.

The view that chap. 71 is redactional explains why other passages stand in tension with that chapter and allows us to recover the original sense of the Similitudes.[47] The question remains why the identification was eventually made.[48] In fact, the identification could claim some basis in the original text. Enoch was in any case preeminent among the righteous ones and shared to some degree the Son of Man's role as revealer. The figure of Enoch was widely used as a paradigm of righteousness. It was the destiny of all the righteous to be with "that Son of Man" in the heavenly resting-places (62:14). Enoch had already attained that destiny and so was distinguished from other humans. Accordingly, his identification with the "Son of Man" was not as drastic an innovation as it might at first seem.

We can only hypothesize what stimulus may have occasioned the identification of Enoch with "that Son of Man." One obvious possibility is that the identification was made in response to the Christian appropriation of "Son of Man" as a title for Jesus. The identification would then deny the christological use of the title and affirm that Enoch, sage of the heavenly mysteries, was the model to be followed, rather than Christ. Enoch was believed to have made the transition from earth to heaven, just as Christians believed Jesus had, and Enoch could accordingly be used as a Jewish answer to Christianity.

THE FUNCTION OF THE SIMILITUDES

The Similitudes of Enoch are designed to reassure the righteous that their destiny is secure in the hands of "that Son of Man." Their representative lives in heaven and their resting-places are prepared. What they must do is believe and trust. The authority of Enoch and of his visions provides a basis for belief. The Similitudes do not appear to envisage any acute historical crisis. They can apply to any situation where the righteous feel oppressed by the kings and the mighty. In the first century c.e., they could apply to any Jews who resented the rule of the pagan Romans or the impious Herods. The Similitudes offered to the powerless the assurance of a special destiny guaranteed by a heavenly patron. The heavenly world would furnish the respect and dignity denied them in the present.

We may suspect that the matrix of the Similitudes was somewhat more specific than this. The quasi-technical terminology of "righteous" and "chosen" suggests that "the community of the righteous" (38:1) was an actual community and not just a general reference to righteous people. The terminology of "righteous" and "chosen" is drawn from the earlier Enoch books (e.g., the Apocalypse of Weeks). Greenfield and Stone have noted some terminological resemblances to the Qumran scrolls—for example, "spirits" for angels and the term "lot" (*1 Enoch* 48:2).[49] In view of the absence of the Similitudes from Qumran, we may safely conclude that they were not composed there. In view of the popularity of the other sections of *1 Enoch* at Qumran, and of the near equality of sun and moon in chap. 41, we should hesitate to ascribe them to the group that composed the earlier Enoch writings. In any case there is no independent evidence that an "Enoch group" remained in existence from the third century down to the first century C.E. It is sufficient that the authors of the Similitudes were well versed in the earlier Enoch books and adapted some of their conceptions and terminology. Nonetheless it is quite possible that the Similitudes originated in a closed circle somewhat analogous to Qumran. The quasi-technical terminology and the distinctive faith in "that Son of Man" support the idea that the authors of the Similitudes belonged to a group apart.

RELATION TO THE NEW TESTAMENT

The historical significance of the Similitudes lies primarily in their attestation of speculation on a "Son of Man" figure outside of Christianity. The Similitudes did not significantly influence the New Testament in this matter. The belief that Jesus would come as Son of Man on the clouds of heaven can be adequately explained as an adaptation of Daniel 7 in conjunction with other Old Testament texts without reference to the Similitudes. Only in two Matthaean passages, 19:28 and 25:31, where the Son of Man sits on his glorious throne (cf. *1 Enoch* 61–62) is Enochic influence probable, and this is distinctly a secondary development. The Similitudes do, however, show that an interpretation and application of Daniel 7 similar to what we find in the New Testament had some currency in Judaism in this period. Scholarly debate has focused too narrowly on the question whether "Son of Man" was a title in Judaism. As we have seen in the Qumran scrolls, titular usage for supernatural figures was quite fluid. More important is the fact that several documents accord a preeminent place to an angelic figure—Michael in Daniel and 1QM, Melchizedek in 11QMelch, the Angel of Truth in 1QS.[50] "That Son of Man" in the Similitudes must be ranked with these figures although he is distinct from, and above, the archangels. It is also noteworthy that the "Son of Man" figure in the Similitudes is identified with the messiah.[51] The Similitudes thus pave the way for understanding the messiah as a supernatural figure, as we will find in the later Jewish apocalypses. It is apparent that Jewish conceptions of savior figures in this period were variable, but the Similitudes illustrate the *kind* of speculation that was also at work in the New Testament development of christological titles.

It is also significant that the Similitudes place primary emphasis on faith in this heavenly Son of Man, and in the heavenly realities in general, rather than on practice of the law as the means to salvation. We should not, of course, exaggerate the analogy with Paul. There is no polemic here against the law, and the implications of faith are certainly altered when focused on the death and resurrection of Jesus. Yet there is a limited analogy that should not be ignored. Not all of Judaism can be classified as "covenantal nomism." Faith in apocalyptic mysteries, which has a central role here, was also an important factor in early Christianity.

7
After the Fall:
4 Ezra, 2 Baruch, and
the Apocalypse of Abraham

No EXTANT JEWISH APOCALYPSE can be associated with the Jewish revolt against Rome which broke out in 66 C.E. Josephus claims that some alleged revelations contributed to Jewish unrest. After his account of the Sicarii, he refers to "another body of villains, with purer hands but more impious intentions, who no less than the assassins ruined the peace of the city. Deceivers and impostors, under the pretense of divine inspiration fostering revolutionary changes, they persuaded the multitude to act like madmen and led them out into the desert under the belief that God would there give them tokens of deliverance. Against them Felix, regarding this as but the preliminary to insurrection, sent a body of cavalry and heavy-armed infantry, and put a large number to the sword" (*War* 2.13.4 §§258–60). This episode recalls the story of Taxo in the *Testament of Moses*, the martyrs in 1 Macc 2:29–38 and even the general attitude of the book of Daniel. There is no evidence, however, that the "impostors" to whom Josephus refers in this passage gave literary expression to their hopes, and we do not know how far these hopes were apocalyptic in nature. Again, Josephus claims that "what more than all else incited them to the war was an ambiguous oracle, likewise found in their sacred scriptures, to the effect that at that time one from their country would become ruler of the world" (*War* 6.5.4 §312). Josephus claimed that the oracle referred not to a Jewish leader but to Vespasian. We do not know what scriptural passage Josephus had in mind. The "sacred scriptures" may be conceived broadly here to include

155

such documents as the *Sibylline Oracles*.[1] The hope involved was not necessarily apocalyptic in any sense. Indeed, there is no evidence that apocalyptic expectations played any significant part in the Jewish revolt.

In contrast, we have several major apocalypses from the period after the revolt: 4 Ezra, *2 Baruch*, and the *Apocalypse of Abraham*, all of which are likely to have been composed in the land of Israel, and *3 Baruch*, which is more probably a product of the Diaspora. Unlike Daniel or the Animal Apocalypse these works were not composed in the throes of the conflict. In all cases some time is likely to have elapsed after the fall of the temple. The underlying questions of all these works, however, are shaped in large part by the catastrophe of 70 C.E. They may, accordingly, be viewed as one cluster of Jewish responses to that national tragedy.[2] The most engaging, profound, and problematic of these works is surely 4 Ezra, which ranks as one of the greatest of the apocalypses.

4 EZRA

4 Ezra (2 Esdras 3–14)[3] is preserved in Latin and various other ancient versions including Armenian, Syrian, and Georgian.[4] There is general agreement that the original language was Hebrew.[5] There is also a consensus that the book was written in Palestine about the end of the first century C.E. The apocalypse begins with the statement: "In the thirtieth year after the overthrow of the city I was in Babylon" (3:1) but neither the date nor the place can be taken as evidence of the actual provenance. The figure thirty years is taken from Ezek 1:1. The location in Babylon is prompted by the fictive association with the fall of the first temple, and also by Ezekiel (although it has on occasion been thought to imply that the book was composed in Rome). Most attempts to date 4 Ezra have been based on the vision in chaps. 11–12 of an eagle with twelve wings and three heads. The eagle is the Roman Empire. It is probable that the three heads represent the Flavians—Vespasian, Titus, and Domitian—and possible that the twelve wings are the emperors from Caesar to Domitian.[6] This interpretation points to a date in the last decade of the first century, and the rounded figure of thirty years in the superscription is compatible with this. In view of the content of the book there is no doubt that 4 Ezra was written in the period after the fall of Jerusalem, whatever the precise date.

UNITY AND STRUCTURE

The literary unity of 4 Ezra was the subject of a classic debate at the end of the nineteenth century between R. Kabisch and H. Gunkel.[7] Kabisch, writing in 1889 and using the source-critical methods then in vogue argued that the book contained five separate sources from five separate authors, which were then combined by a redactor. Gunkel, writing in 1900, recognized that there are indeed inconsistencies in the text but argued that these may reflect diverse traditions on which the author drew rather than distinct documentary sources. Gunkel's view has prevailed in subsequent research,[8] although the source-critical approach has been perpetuated in the English-speaking world through the work of G. H. Box and R. H. Charles.[9] Box distinguished (1) S, a Salathiel apocalypse that contained the bulk of chaps. 3-10; (2) E, an Ezra apocalypse from which the signs of the end in 4:52-5:13 and 6:13-29 are extracts; (3) the eagle vision; (4) the Son of Man vision; (5) E2, containing the bulk of chap. 14; and, finally, a redactor who connected the whole and made minor insertions. Box found strong evidence for the use of an independent source in the very first verse, where the visionary is identifed as "I Salathiel, who am also Ezra." Salathiel (Hebrew Shealtiel) was the father of Zerubbabel (according to Ezra 3:2; 5:2; Neh 12:1). Why his name should be used here is a mystery. Box held that "the only adequate explanation is that an editor or compiler is using an independent writing in which the seer who is the recipient of the revelations that follow spoke in the name of Salathiel."[10] The revelation would here be transferred to the more authoritative figure of Ezra. However, it is odd that no other mention of Salathiel survived, if he was the recipient of the revelations in chaps. 3-10. Some other explanations may be suggested. Ezra was a highly authoritative figure in Judaism, but in this book he is the spokesman for a very skeptical position. It is posssible that an editor wished to suggest that the visionary was not *the* Ezra but rather the lesser figure Salathiel, whose name was chosen because he did live during the exile. It is also possible that an editor was aware of the chronological difficulty of placing Ezra thirty years after the fall of Jerusalem and sought to resolve the problem by identifying the visionary with Salathiel. In either case, the identification could result from editorial intervention and need not reflect an independent documentary source.

Even source critics like Kabisch and Box recognized that 4 Ezra, in its present form, consists of seven units, which are commonly called "visions" although that label is not appropriate in all cases.[11] These units are (1) 3:1-5:19; (2) 5:20-6:34; (3) 6:35-9:25; (4) 9:26-10:59; (5) 10:60-12:51; (6) 13:1-58; (7) 14:1-48. The first three are dialogues between Ezra and the angel Uriel. At the end of the first and second, Ezra fasts for seven days in accordance with the angel's command. After the third he is bidden to wait seven days without fasting, but eating the flower of the field. The fourth unit consists of the vision of Zion, at first as a woman, then transformed as a city. The vision is explained by the angel, who then tells Ezra to "remain here tomorrow night." On the second night Ezra has the vision of the eagle, which is followed by an interpretation. At the end of this unit Ezra remains in the field for seven days eating the flowers. The dream vision of the "man from the sea" follows with its interpretation. After this he waits three days and then he encounters the voice from the bush.

Within the final, seventh unit there is another intermission of a day (14:27–36), when Ezra addresses the people and engages the scribes. Then he withdraws again to the field and is inspired to dictate ninety-four books. In this case, however, the intermission is not simply a void. Ezra's activity during the day is recorded and the entire chapter is a continuous narrative. Accordingly, most scholars have recognized that the intermission does not indicate a new unit.[12] Its main purpose is to allow Ezra a summary parting message to the people while leaving the reception of the inspired books in the climactic final position.

A sevenfold structure is also found in 2 Baruch and in the New Testament book of Revelation.[13] The main objections to the originality of this structure in 4 Ezra have concerned the eagle vision (10:60–12:51) and the so-called Son of Man vision (more properly the "man from the sea," chap. 13). These chapters have often been regarded as redundant, and this impression has been bolstered by formal considerations.[14] The interlude before the eagle vision is only one night, not seven days, and the visions are introduced directly, without any introductory prayer by Ezra. Yet we have seen from Daniel and the Similitudes of Enoch that redundancy is a well-attested compositional device in apocalypses. Minor variations, such as the interval of one day instead of seven, do not necessarily indicate separate sources either. Such variations occur throughout the book—for example, Enoch fasts after the first two episodes but eats flowers after the third.[15] More important, all critics agree that chap. 10 is a turning point in the book. We should expect some formal variations in the following chapters. The omission of Ezra's complaints in chaps. 11–13 is not due to a different hand but to the shifting emphasis of the book. The inclusion of these visions is necessary to fill out the sevenfold structure but also to provide balance over against the skeptical probings of Ezra in the earlier chapters.[16] The final unit in chap. 14 provides an epilogue to the entire composition. While chaps. 11–13 undoubtedly contain traditional material, there is no good reason to deny their authenticity in 4 Ezra.

The macrostructure of 4 Ezra is clearly an apocalypse. Ezra is the pseudonymous seer, who receives revelation through the mediation of the angel Uriel, about the transcendent world which is to come. Yet within this framework the author fashions a highly original and distinctive work. The first three units, 3:1–5:19; 5:20–6:34 and 6:35–9:25 are not properly visions, but are dialogues between Ezra and the angel. The dialogue was used as a medium of revelation in Daniel 10–12. The originality of 4 Ezra lies in the extent of the dialogue, but also in its skeptical character. In a manner reminiscent of Job, 4 Ezra presses the question of the justice of God and at first is hesitant to accept apocalyptic revelations of a transcendent world. Then, in the fourth unit, 9:26–10:59, there is a sudden reversal and Ezra comes to share the angel's point of view. This acceptance is consolidated in the eagle and "man from the sea" visions. At the end Ezra himself becomes mediator of revelation for the rest of the people.

The central problem of interpretation in 4 Ezra undoubtedly concerns the transition of Ezra from skeptic to believer. This problem is basic to our understanding of the purpose and the coherence of the book. Scholars have held widely different opinions on this issue. On the one hand, some have held that the skeptical questions of Ezra in the dialogues are put forward only so that they can be definitively refuted by the angel. Ezra, then, is the mouthpiece for an erroneous line of thought. He possibly represents some group or movement that the author opposes, possibly a point of view that had not found clear social expression.[17] On the other hand, some have held that Ezra articulates the author's position and that his complaints are never really answered. Ezra's role reversal in chap. 10 is seen as ironic,[18] or the author is said to have "produced a masterful presentation of his doubts behind a respectable curtain of concern for Israel."[19] Still others, following the pioneering work of Gunkel, have seen the tensions of the book as evidence of an inner struggle[20] or sought an interpretation in which the authenticity of the questions and the acceptance of the final revelation are held together in a conversion experience of Ezra.[21] Since the skeptical probings are attributed to the same Ezra who is authenticated as mediator of revelation in the final chapter, his doubts can scarcely be attributed to an opposition party.[22] The kind of interpretation associated with Gunkel has the advantage of respecting the unity of the central figure throughout. The apocalyptic revelations of chaps. 11–13 must be seen as the culmination of a movement that begins with the probings of chap. 3.

The Dialogues

4 Ezra is more explicit than most apocalypses about the problem besetting the visionary: "I was perturbed . . . because I visualized the ruin of Zion and the affluence of those who lived in Babylon." These reflections are not an immediate response to the catastrophe of 70 c.e., but rather contemplate the enduring state of affairs that resulted from it. In comparing the fate of Zion with that of Babylon, Ezra moves beyond the specific historical crisis to the general problem of theodicy or the justice of God. The events of 70 c.e. are the catalyst for the broader question. Of course the standard apocalyptic device of pseudonymity already serves to put the problem in a wider perspective. Ostensibly, the occasion of Ezra's perplexity is

the catastrophe of 586 B.C.E. and the resulting exile. The defeat by Rome is only a reenactment of one of the major paradigms of Jewish history.

The opening prayer of Ezra also serves to relate the present dilemma to the universal human situation. Ezra recites the outline of history, beginning with Adam. This passage is quite different from the reviews of history that are presented in other apocalypses in the guise of prophecy. It is also different from the traditional Deuteronomic recitation of salvation history.[23] The emphasis is not on salvation but on failure. Ezra recognizes that in each generation some remnant was spared. This theme had been used in Enoch's Apocalypse of Weeks to build the expectation of a final deliverance for the chosen few. Ezra, in contrast, emphasizes that even the remnants attain no lasting salvation: "For the first Adam, laden with an evil inclination, transgressed and was overcome; so did all those who issued from him" (3:21). If the law was in the heart of the people, so was the "root of evil," and so the chosen people eventually came to ruin. Two fundamental problems emerge already in this opening prayer. One is the "evil inclination," which is present in human nature from the beginning and poses the question of God's justice toward humanity at large. The second is the relative justice of Israel's fate: "Does Babylon really act any better than Zion?" (3:31). This question is not a new one, but it is pursued in 4 Ezra with unusual intensity. The fate of Israel puts the whole system of the Mosaic covenant in doubt: "When did the inhabitants of the earth not sin before you? Or what nation has so well executed your commandments? You will find exceptional individuals who have kept your commandments, but nations you will not find" (3:35-36). If only "exceptional individuals" can keep the commandments, then membership of a covenant people becomes irrelevant. This pessimistic conclusion is borne out by the actual destruction of Zion.

The angel's reply is reminiscent of God's reply to Job from the whirlwind. It consists of a list of impossible questions which emphasize how little Ezra understands: "Weigh for me the weight of fire, measure for me the measure of the wind, or recover for me the day that is past" (4:5). Yet these are said to be things of this world with which Ezra has been associated. The angel pointedly remarks that he is not asking about the exits out of hell or the ways of paradise, since Ezra might have answered that he has neither descended into the abyss nor ascended to heaven. These, of course, are precisely the accomplishments of apocalyptic visionaries such as Enoch. The point here is that Ezra cannot hope to make sense of the world by ordinary human wisdom, even on the premises of the Deuteronomic covenant. Apocalyptic revelation is necessary, and that is what the angel will eventually provide.

Ezra reformulates his question, with a tenacity surpassing that of Job:

> Pray tell me, O Lord, why has the faculty of perception been given to
> me? For I did not mean to inquire about the ways above, but rather
> about those things we experience daily:
>> Why Israel is subjected to abuse by the nations . . .
>> The law of our fathers rendered ineffective . . .
>> For we leave this world like grasshoppers
>> Our life is like a vapor
>> And we are unworthy of receiving mercy. (4:22–24)

The angel's reply is indirect. No answer is given to the question, Why?
Instead Ezra is told: "If you continue, you will see, and if you go on living,
you will often marvel—because the age is speedily coming to an end; for
it cannot bear the things promised to the righteous. . . ." The mystery persists why this age is as it is. We are not told why the grain of evil was sown
in the heart of Adam. We cannot proceed faster than the Most High; and,
although we are assured that God knows best, we cannot ultimately comprehend his ways. At this point Ezra is distracted from probing the question of justice by curiosity about the end that is to come. He is assured that
the time which has passed is greater than that which is left, and he is told
some signs that will precede the end. He is also promised the revelation of
"things greater than these" after seven days. The effect is bewilderment and
amazement. Ezra's initial questions have not been answered, but his attention has been diverted from the distress of the present to the prospect of
the world to come.

The main substance of the angel's reply is that this age is passing away.
This point will be elaborated much more explicitly, in the third dialogue.
The way of the Lord still encompasses both ages.[24] There is no question
here of an ultimate dualism. Yet the emphasis is on the discontinuity between this age and the world to come. There is no smooth evolution from
this age to the next.

Ezra's problem has been suppressed at the end of the first dialogue, but
it has not gone away. The second dialogue does little more than recapitu-
late the first. Ezra's prayer provides a shorter historical review than his
earlier one and focuses more directly on the problem of Zion: "Why have
you dispersed your only one among the many?" (5:28). Again the angel
begins by contrasting Ezra's limited comprehension with the unlimited, if
unfathomable, understanding of the creator. Does Ezra love Israel more
than God does? Again there is a brief bombardment with impossible questions: "Count for me those not yet come, collect for me the spattered
drops . . ." (5:36). Ezra is told flatly that he will not be able to discover the
judgment of God or the purpose of his love for his people.

The angel not only frustrates Ezra's initial question; he also diverts his attention to the future. The creation is already old and in decline (5:48–55). Moreover, the demise of this world had been planned from the beginning. All is securely under divine control. Again, the dialogue concludes with the recitation of signs of the end and a promise of further revelations. This time the angel's purpose is explicit: "Believe, do not fear, and do not be overanxious to speculate uselessly about former times, that you may not be taken by surprise in the last times" (6:33–34).

We can begin at this point to appreciate the purpose of the repetition. The angel is not engaged in rational argumentation but in the psychological process of calming fear and building trust. For this purpose the repetition is crucial, as the fears are gradually eroded by expression and the trust accumulates through multiple reassurances.

The third dialogue not only recapitulates the other two but enlarges and deepens the discussion. Ezra begins by rehearsing the works of creation. The point of this recital is made explicit in 6:55–56: "I have spoken about all these things before you, Lord, because you said that you created the firstborn world for us. As for the rest of the nations sprung from Adam, you declared them to be as nothing, like spittle, and you have likened their profusion to drippings from a bucket. . . . So if the world was created for us, why do we not enjoy possession of the heritage of our world?" Ezra here gives voice to the basic dilemma of the covenantal tradition.

The angel's reply affirms that "I did make the world for their sakes" but subtly changes the presuppositions of the traditional theology. The heir can only claim his inheritance if he traverses the danger set before him. The basis of salvation is individual merit, not membership of a covenant people. Accordingly, the focus shifts from the specific destiny of Israel to the more general problem of human inability to satisfy the law. The angel's insistence that Ezra should "think about what is to come, rather than what now is" (7:16) is disregarded for the moment so that this question may be pursued.

Ezra complains about the fate of the wicked, since indeed the bulk of humanity seems to fall into this category (7:48). The angel's reply is harsh: "You are not a judge superior to God, nor more discriminating than the Most High. Let the many who exist perish rather than that the law of God . . . be slighted" (7:19–20). This pronouncement is buttressed not with a rationale or explanation but with an extended eschatological scenario. That which God will bring about requires no further justification.

The scenario is of considerable interest, since it is the most explicit formulation of the eschatology presumed throughout 4 Ezra. First, the signs will come, then "the hidden city" (presumably the heavenly Jerusalem) and the messiah will be revealed.[25] The messiah will reign for four hundred years but will then die. After seven days of primordial silence the resurrection will follow. The reign of the messiah is included at the end of this age, as a transitional phase, but the age to come is separated from this one by a gulf of seven days "just as it was at the very beginning." 4 Ezra is heir to a longer tradition of eschatological speculation than were Daniel or the Enoch apocalypses. Here the expectation of national restoration under a messiah is integrated with the more typical apocalyptic hope of retribution beyond death in a far more thorough manner than was the case in any earlier document. The three-stage scenario, which distinguishes the reign of the messiah from the world to come, is compatible with all the formulations of 4 Ezra, although it is often difficult to be sure which stage the author has in mind when he speaks of the "end."[26] The fundamental point, however, is that "the Most High made not one world, but two" (7:50). The other world is that beyond the resurrection and the judgment, although the reign of the messiah might be regarded as a limited anticipation of it. The belief in another world, beyond this one, is fundamental to all the apocalypses in some form. Both worlds are, of course, within the design of the same God, but they are sharply separated from each other, nonetheless.

The judgment that follows the resurrection is severe: "Then the end will come, and compassion will vanish, pity will cease and forbearance will be withdrawn. Only judgment will remain . . ." (7:33). There will be no intercession for others thereafter (7:102-15). The severity results from 4 Ezra's generally grim view of the world, where pity is not much in evidence at any stage. It is not required by the apocalyptic expectation of a final judgment, which could accommodate a far more merciful God, as we will find in the *Testament of Abraham*. Yet this severity is in itself the most persistent problem that besets Ezra, for "the world to come will bring joy to the few, but torment to the many" (7:47). The angel counters that just as gold is precious because it is rare, so the value of the righteous is also enhanced by their scarcity. Moreoever, he suggests that Ezra "must not get entangled with scorners nor reckon yourself with those who are tormented. For indeed you have a treasure of works stored up with the Most High" (7:77). Once more Ezra is distracted from his questioning by a detailed account of what happens after death (7:78-101).

Ezra, however, is reluctant to distinguish himself from sinful humanity: "O Adam what have you done? Although you (alone) sinned, the fall was not yours alone but ours too, who descended from you" (7:117-18). When he concedes that God knows best about the totality of mankind, he still appeals for mercy on Israel. The angel commends him for his humility in not reckoning himself with the just (8:49), but is still uncompromising. Ezra is bidden to ask no further questions about the multitude of those who are lost, who have only themselves to blame. Instead he is to concern himself with the salvation of the just and is again instructed in the signs of the end. He is scarcely persuaded as yet. His last statement in the dialogues is a simple assertion: "I said before, say now, and will say hereafter: more numerous are the lost than the saved as the tide is greater than a drop" (8:15–16). This statement does not quite reject the angel's consolation, but it is a rueful reminder of the real limitations of the salvation to come.

The dialogues conclude with a forward pointer. Ezra is to wait seven days without fasting but go into a field of flowers and eat only the flowers. The double change, in diet and location, mark the transition to the visions of chaps. 10–14.

THE VISIONS

The fourth section of 4 Ezra, or first vision, is generally recognized as the turning point of the book. Ezra begins, in a manner similar to the other dialogues, to complain about the destruction of Israel. In this case, however, he is distracted by a vision of a woman who is grieving for the death of her only son. Ezra suddenly assumes the role of comforter, although his tone is rather severe. He scolds the woman for being obsessed with her individual problem, while "Zion the mother of us all" has suffered a much greater bereavement, and the earth has greatest grief of all. He concludes with the advice: "Therefore keep your grief to yourself and bear gallantly your calamities, for if you accept as right the verdict of God, you will get back your son in his time and be highly extolled among women" (10:16–17). When she refuses, Ezra insists: "Permit yourself to be persuaded because of the calamity of Zion," but while he is speaking she is transformed into a city with massive foundations. Then Uriel, the angel, appears and explains to Ezra that the woman was Zion and that God had shown him the glory of (the future, restored) Jerusalem because of his wholehearted grief over her ruin.

This encounter marks the end of Ezra's complaints against God. From this point on his transformation is complete. He readily acquiesces in the remaining revelations and at the end becomes himself a mediator of revelation to others. The fact of this transformation is obvious enough. The reason for it is less immediately apparent. We cannot agree with the view that Ezra's advice is "an ironic answer to the woman, an answer that Ezra cannot accept for himself."[27] Ezra's acceptance of the answer is confirmed in all the remaining sections of the book. Those who speak of a "conversion" or "experiential solution" are on the right track, but how does this conversion come about? The crucial element is the reversal of Ezra's role when he meets the woman.[28] Now that he is cast in the role of comforter he gets a new perspective on the grief of an individual. We might compare the technique of Nathan in his famous parable. There David is induced to pass judgment before he knows that he is judging himself. The allegorical presentation of the case obscures the king's personal interest and allows him to view it with detachment. Similarly, the allegorical dress of Zion deceives Ezra so that he does not at first realize that the advice he gives applies to himself too. He tells the woman to let herself be persuaded because of the calamity of Zion, but the logic of his argument is that we cannot see our problems in perspective and so must resign ourselves before the providence of God. This, of course, is what the angel has been telling Ezra all along. He is able to see the justification of this argument when it is applied to another more readily than when it was addressed to himself.

Ezra's conversion is now consolidated by two dream visions, which clearly show the influence of Daniel 7. In the first, "I saw an eagle coming up out of the sea; it had twelve feathered wings and three heads" (11:1). The vision continues with a complex allegory of wings and winglets, which defies precise identification, but the eagle is obviously Rome, and the three heads, as noted above, should most probably be identified with Vespasian, Titus, and Domitian. Then a raging lion comes out of the forest to denounce the eagle: "The Most High declares to you: Are you not the only one of the four beasts left that I appointed to hold sway over my world that through them the end of my times might come?" (11:39). The accusations are primarily concerned with injustice and oppression and conclude with the promise: "Thus the whole earth will be relieved and delivered from your power; then it can hope for justice and the compasssion of him who made it" (11:46).

The dependence on Daniel is explicit in the interpretation: "The eagle you observed coming up out of the sea is the fourth kingdom that appeared in a vision to Daniel your brother, but it was not interpreted to him in the same way I now interpret to you" (12:11-12). Besides the clear application to Rome, Ezra diverges from Daniel in the major role assigned to the lion, "the anointed one whom the Most High has reserved till the end of days, who will arise from the seed of David" (12:32). The interpretation informs us that the messiah's role is not only to accuse but also to destroy. Then "the remnant of my people he will set free with compassion and grant them joy until the end, the day of judgment about which I spoke to you at the beginning" (12:34).

The eagle vision may be understood as a reinterpretation of the fourth beast of Daniel 7, and the vision that follows in 4 Ezra relates to the "one like a son of man" in that chapter. In 4 Ezra 13 the wind "brought up out of the depths of the sea something resembling a man and that man was flying with the clouds of heaven." In Daniel, and in the eagle vision, the sea was the source from which the beasts arose. Here the sea connotes the depths of mystery ("Just as no one can search out or perceive what may be in the depths of the sea, so no one on earth will be able to see my son or those who are with him except in the time of his day" [13:51]). The description of this figure departs radically from Daniel. There is no reference here to the "holy ones of the Most High." In part, his appearance is modeled on old theophanic traditions of the divine warrior: all who hear his voice melt like wax before the fire.[29] The mountain he carves out for himself recalls the stone hewn from the mountain in Daniel 2. The assault of the multitude recalls the traditional motif of the attack of the nations on Mount Zion. The manner in which he slays his enemies with the breath of his mouth is paralleled in Revelation 19 ("the sword of his mouth") and evidently reflects apocalyptic traditions that were current at the end of the first century. In the interpretation the "man" is explicitly identified as the messiah.[30] He will gather the ten lost tribes. His functions are the same as in the eagle vision: he will berate the peoples for their impiety and destroy their host but protect the people who survive.

The technique of these visions is familiar from our earlier discussion of Daniel 7.[31] The allegorical dreams provide perspective on the state of the Jews under Roman rule at the end of the first century. The allusions to Daniel suggest that Rome is acting out an ancient, mythic paradigm, in this case the paradigm articulated in Daniel 7. In fact the details of both visions diverge widely from that of Daniel, whose vision serves as a point of departure in both cases, but is never interpreted systematically. In part the divergence results from new historical data—hence the introduction of the eagle, the symbol of Rome. In greater part it results from the fusion of different eschatological traditions, specifically from the introduction of the motifs associated with the Davidic messiah, who played no part in Daniel.[32]

In both visions there are indications that the author is working with traditional material, for which he has supplied new interpretations. Since both have a point of departure in Daniel 7, we should expect that the author would have combined them in a single vision if he were working de novo. There is also some unevenness in the way in which the interpretation follows the vision, especially in chap. 13—for example, the sea, which figures at the beginning of the vision, is not explained until the end.[33] More important than the question of sources, however, is the manner in which the material has been put together by the author. The visions form a complementary pair. The eagle vision is very obviously rooted in the traditional hope for a Davidic messiah. Its culmination is the removal of the most specific enemy of Judaism at the time, the Roman Empire. Only here does 4 Ezra show deep concern over oppression and social injustice.[34] The vision of the "man from the sea" draws on a different complex of traditions, which is associated in modern scholarship with the "Son of Man." Here the enemy is universal—"all the peoples." In the earlier tradition there was a clear-cut distinction between the hope for salvation by an angel (e.g., Michael in Daniel) and by a human messiah, although we have seen that both conceptions were maintained at Qumran, and the "Son of Man" figure in the Similitudes of Enoch was also called messiah. In 4 Ezra the "one like a man" is definitely the messiah, and we know from chap. 7 that he is human and will die. Yet he also embodies many of the traits of the heavenly savior. He rises mysteriously from the sea and is apparently preexistent ("whom the Most High has kept for many ages through whom to deliver his creation" [13:26; compare 7:28]). His appearance is accompanied by the traditional signs of a theophany. His powers are supernatural, and he represents far more than a restoration of the Davidic kingdom. In short, the messiah has not simply displaced the expectation of a heavenly savior. The two strands of tradition have been fused so that both have been transformed.

How far do these visions respond to the original complaints of Ezra? They promise that the humiliation of Israel will not last forever and that the balance over against the other nations will be set right. The emphasis on the coming of the messiah tends to highlight the aspect of national fulfillment and to obscure the problem raised by Ezra, that so few even of the Jews will be saved. Yet the visions do not at all contradict the severe stance of the angel in the dialogues. Even here only a remnant of the people will be saved (12:34). The interpretations do not address the question whether any non-Jews will be saved. The legend of the lost tribes in chap. 13 promises that the messiah will collect a "peaceful host," but even this legend offers only limited hope for the Jews with whom Ezra was acquainted. On the whole the two visions reinforce the position of the angel in the dialogues. By ignoring the difficulties raised earlier by Ezra, they urge us to think positively about what is to come, rather than about what now is.

THE EPILOGUE

The final chapter constitutes an epilogue to the revelations, which presupposes that conviction has already been attained. Ezra is cast as the new Moses, summoned by God from the bush. This is the only clear instance where God speaks directly to Ezra.[35] The purpose of the divine speech is not to add to the revelation that has been given (the status of world history is briefly summarized in 14:9-12) but to commission Ezra to "caution your people, console their humble ones, teach their wise ones" (14:13). The analogy with Moses becomes more explicit when Ezra is inspired to dictate to his scribes for forty days. This is necessary because the Torah has been burned (14:21). Yet Ezra's task is not simply to restore the books of Moses, and he cannot be understood as a prophet of the Mosaic law.[36] First, he is directly inspired (after drinking a firelike liquid). His authority then is not subject to that of Moses. In fact since the law of Moses is presumed to be burned, Ezra now becomes an ultimate authority on divine revelation. Second, he dictates a total of ninety-four books. Twenty-four of these are released to the people and presumably correspond to the Hebrew Bible. There are seventy more, however, which are reserved for the wise men. The secret revelations given to Ezra throughout 4 Ezra are representative of this further wisdom. Hence the brunt of Ezra's exhortation to the people is to renounce mortal life and hasten to get out of these times, and look to the judgment after death (14:14, 35). As in Daniel and Enoch, the wisdom of the wise consists not in their knowledge of the Mosaic law but in the apocalyptic wisdom that comes from additional revelation.[37] The final chapter then claims the highest authority for Ezra. His revelation endorses the Mosaic law, but its main purpose is to provide the further revelation which is necessary to make sense of human experience. We can appreciate why the author had to violate chronology to place his meditation on the fall of Jerusalem on the lips of a figure who could bear such weighty authority.

THE TECHNIQUE OF 4 EZRA

The commissioning of Ezra in the final chapter sets the seal on his acceptance of the ultimate justice of God's judgment. His final message to the people ("control your inclination . . . for judgment comes after death") may be regarded as a summary of his message. This summary, however, by no means adequately represents the impact of the book. Approximately half the work has been devoted to the skeptical questions of the dialogue. As in the Book of the Watchers and Daniel 7 the apocalypse deepens our perception of the problem before we can proceed to the solution. The probing questions of Ezra have a cathartic effect. They bring to expression the fears and frustrations of a sensitive and perceptive Jew in the wake of the catastrophe of 70 C.E. The fact that no real answer to these questions is forthcoming ("you will be unable to discover my judgment" [5:40]) sets the stage for the eschatological revelation. When Ezra finally acquiesces in this revelation, it is not because he has been given a persuasive argument but because of pastoral necessity. Ezra realizes when he is cast in the role of comforter that we must let ourselves be persuaded (10:20). We believe because we need to believe. The belief is consolidated not by new arguments but by repetition of traditional symbols. If our problems cannot be solved we must look away from them and contemplate what is positive. It is probable that the story of Ezra represents the author's own spiritual journey. As a literary work the book stands as a guide to the perplexed. By identifying with Ezra, the reader can acknowledge the dilemmas of history, but come to experience the "apocalyptic cure"[38] by turning his attention to the transcendent perspective provided by the angel and the dream visions.

Ezra is a reluctant apocalyptist. He accepts the apocalyptic revelation only because of necessity. His initial disposition is far from Enochic speculation ("I did not mean to inquire about the ways above" [4:23]). His (frustrated) expectations are focused rather on the Deuteronomic covenant and the election of Israel. 4 Ezra does not deny that covenant but can only salvage it by buttressing it with further revelations and by reconceiving the judgment on a strict basis of individual merits, after death.

Because of the Deuteronomic presuppositions of the early questions, 4 Ezra has often been regarded as a Pharisaic apocalypse.[39] This characterization receives some support from analogies with the rabbinic writings in such matters as the "evil inclination," the distinction between this world and the world to come, and the signs of the end.[40] Yet 4 Ezra's conceptions are generally atypical of rabbinic literature. The difference is apparent in the sharpness of the break between this world and the world to come.[41] It is also apparent in the pessimistic attitude to the judgment, which sees most of humanity as helpless before the evil inclination and allows little if any place for atonement or divine mercy.[42] The perception of human inability to satisfy the law is closer to Paul's teaching in Romans than to the typical attitudes of the rabbis. This is not to deny that 4 Ezra falls within the spectrum of Jewish opinion at the end of the first century C.E. Parallels can be found for such pessimism,[43] and the Judaism of Jamnia was remarkably tolerant of diversity.[44] There is no reason to regard 4 Ezra as sectarian in any sense.[45]

If 4 Ezra is exceptional in its pessimism about human performance, its attitude cannot fairly be described as "legalistic perfectionism."[46] We do not know what level of legalistic performance was regarded as necessary: at least a few, such as Ezra, could meet the standard. The pessimism of the book springs not so much from its lofty standards as from historical experience. If the destruction of Jerusalem represented the judgment of God, that judgment is indeed severe. Moreover, most of the Gentiles could not be said to fulfill the law—even on a lenient interpretation. The anguish of the author comes in part from a concern for those outside the covenant. Even within his own people Ezra is reluctant to distinguish himself from the wicked. If God, as portrayed in this book, seems to lack compassion, the same cannot be said of the author. His sympathy with fallen human nature and perception of the real limitations of any hope for salvation give this book a humane spirit, which sets it apart from most other apocalypses.

2 BARUCH

2 Baruch is closely related to 4 Ezra to such a degree that some form of interdependence must be posited. The text is preserved in a Syriac manuscript that was translated from Greek but most probably derived from a Hebrew original.[47] There can be little doubt that it was composed in the period between the two Jewish revolts. As in 4 Ezra, the destruction at the hands of the Babylonians serves as an allegory for the fall of 70 C.E. More precise indications of date are difficult to find. B. Violet argued that the earthquake in 70:8 must be that which ravaged Antioch in 115 C.E., but in fact it may be merely a stereotypical eschatological sign and not a historical reference at all.[48] The opening verse of the apocalypse refers to the twenty-fifth year of Jeconiah (Jehoiakin) as the occasion of the destruction. This date makes no historical sense. Jehoiakin was taken into exile in the first year of his reign in 597, when he was eighteen years old. The temple was destroyed in 587/86. The figure twenty-five is apparently taken from Ezek 40:1 ("in the twenty-fifth year of our exile"). It may also be an approximate indication of the actual date of composition (i.e., about 95 C.E.)[49] However, the figure of twenty-five years obviously bears some relation to the thirty years given at the beginning of 4 Ezra and must be understood in the context of the overall relations between the two apocalypses. For the present, we may take it that *2 Baruch* was roughly contemporary with 4 Ezra. We will return to the question of priority after we have considered *2 Baruch* in some detail.

STRUCTURE AND UNITY

Like 4 Ezra, *2 Baruch* is usually divided into seven sections, although there is far less consensus about their precise delimitation.[50] Two indicators are especially important.[51] On four occasions Baruch is said to fast for seven days (9:1–2; 12:5; 21:1; 47:1–2).[52] On three occasions he addresses the people (31:1–34:1; 44:1–46:7; 77:1–26). If we allow that each of these indicators marks the end of a unit (the address in 44:1–46:7 is reinforced by the fast in 47:1–2) and that the final letter (78:1 to the end) is a further unit, we arrive at a sevenfold division: (1) 1:1–9:2; (2) 10:1–12:5; (3) 13:1–20:6; (4) 21:1–34:1; (5) 35:1–47:2; (6) 48:1–77:26; (7) 78:1 to the end. This structure is by no means a simple replica of 4 Ezra, but there are some similarities. The first three units are devoted to developing the problem addressed by the apocalypse. Each is terminated by a seven-day fast. These are followed by an extensive eschatological prophecy in the fourth section and then by two allegorical visions in the fifth and sixth units. The final section has the character of an epilogue. Unlike 4 Ezra, Baruch never presses skeptical questions, and so this apocalypse has neither the tension nor the dramatic conversion process of 4 Ezra. It does, however, have a clear movement, from the distress of the early chapters to the consolation of the visions.[53] The contrast between the brevity of the first three units and the length of the subsequent revelations is significant for the emphasis of the book. In this regard the lengthy cloud and water vision (sixth unit), which with its attendant dialogue occupies more than one-third of the work, must be regarded as the climactic revelation.[54]

As in the case of 4 Ezra, there has been extensive debate over the unity of 2 *Baruch*. R. H. Charles distinguished no fewer than six separate sources:[55] three passages that deal with the messiah (27:1–30:1; 36–40 and 53–74) designated A^1, A^2 and A^3. Chapter 85 constituted B^3, and the remaining narrative sections were divided between the "optimistic" B^1 and "pessimistic" B^2. No subsequent scholars have endorsed this dissection in full, but the quest for sources has not been abandoned.

There is no doubt that 2 *Baruch* draws on diverse traditional material.[56] There are some apparent contradictions in detail,[57] but they are not beyond dispute. So 32:2–3 ("after a little time the building of Zion will be shaken in order that it may be built again") has usually been taken to imply a date before the destruction of the temple and therefore before the situation described in chap. 1. It is possible, however, that the shaking is not destructive but results in the rebuilding of Zion—compare Hag 2:6–7, where God will shake the nations to fill the temple treasury. Statements that only those who are in the land will be protected (29:2; cf. 71:1) appear to contradict the promise of the return of the exiles (78:7), but the return could be envisaged before the final crisis so that the exiles are by then in the land. According to 13:3 and 25:1 Baruch will be preserved until the end of times, but several other passages refer to his impending death (43:2; 44:2; 46:7; 78:5; 84:1). Here again the contradiction may be only apparent, since Baruch could be preserved after death, and indeed this is the only way in which he could be thought to have been preserved at the time 2 *Baruch* was written. These examples may suffice to illustrate the slippery nature of the supposed contradictions.

The basic argument for distinguishing sources in 2 *Baruch* does not rest on these matters of detail but on the alleged tension between two kinds of eschatology, one optimistic and oriented toward national restoration and the other pessimistic, looking for the end of this world and a judgment beyond. These two strands of tradition were indeed distinct in origin, but we have seen that they were woven together in the dream-visions of 4 Ezra. The issue in 2 *Baruch* is whether the diverse traditions were successfully assimilated or whether the author felt obliged to contradict some of the traditions that he incorporated.

The tension in eschatological conceptions has been alleged in the treatment of the temple and the messiah. In chap. 4 God tells Baruch that there is a heavenly temple that will be revealed in the end-time. In chap. 6, however, the temple vessels are hidden, so that they may be restored when Jerusalem is delivered. The final letter gives a different reason for hiding the temple vessels, which does not imply restoration. Should we conclude that the author is not interested in the rebuilding of the temple? Perhaps, but this is not to say that he is contradicting his sources. We must bear in mind that there are two destructions of the temple involved. The first, by the Babylonians, was a matter of history. It was followed by a restoration. 2 Baruch acknowledges this fact by the use of traditional legends about the temple vessels,[58] and the restoration has some typological implications for the eschatological time. The destruction that more immediately concerned the author, although it is veiled behind the typology, was that of 70 C.E. There is no indication that the author expected the second temple to be rebuilt again. Therefore the heavenly Jerusalem and temple are ultimately more important for the author's own time. Strictly speaking, there is no contradiction in the expectation of 2 Baruch. We should bear in mind, however, that an apocalypse does not aspire to formulate doctrine in a consistent way, but to suggest the future hope by means of symbols. Both the legends pertaining to the temple vessels and the traditional idea of a heavenly Jerusalem could play a part in suggesting that the temple would endure in some form.

In the case of the messiah, there is not even an apparent contradiction. The objection here is that he receives no attention in Baruch's addresses to the people. We should not conclude, however, that "the author is not interested in the Anointed One. He happens to be present in his sources . . ." Still less is the author "correcting" the traditional hope of national restoration.[59] The message of the work cannot be extracted only from the direct addresses without regard to the revelations, which form the underpinning of those speeches. The correlation between the apocalyptic framework and the specific message of the book is a crucial issue in the interpretation of 2 Baruch, which throws much light on the relation of this work to 4 Ezra and indeed on the entire apocalyptic genre.

The Opening Narrative

The opening scene of 2 Baruch (1:1-9:2) is not set in the exile, as in 4 Ezra, but before the destruction. Baruch is given advance warning of what is to happen and is also given an explanation for it. The southern tribes are to be punished for their sins, just as the northern ones were, but they will only be removed from God's favor *for a time*. Baruch is also assured that the efficacy of himself and those who are like him is in no way impaired. They must retire from Jerusalem before it can fall. When Baruch protests that he would rather die than see the destruction of Zion, the Lord assures him that the destruction is temporary, and moreover reveals that the present edifice is not the temple that was prepared before creation. There is a heavenly temple preserved with God, just as paradise is. The destruction of the earthly temple, then, is not as great a catastrophe as it might seem. When Baruch complains of the humiliation involved in destruction at the hands of Gentiles, he is assured that "the enemy will not overthrow Zion." He is then allowed to witness four angels who burn down the walls of Jerusalem. Before they do this, however, the temple vessels are hidden in the earth "so that strangers may not get possession of them," for Jerusalem will again be delivered.

This narrative opening precludes from the start the kind of anguished questioning we find in 4 Ezra. The destruction of Jerusalem is still a calamity, and the humiliation at the hands of the Gentiles is real. The brief second section of *2 Baruch* (10:1-12:5) is taken up completely with a powerful lament, which shows that the grief is profound and that the destruction is taken very seriously. Yet even at the end of his lament Baruch can tell Babylon that this state of affairs will not last and that the divine wrath will be aroused against her. God's ultimate providential care for Israel is not in doubt. The righteous are spared, the vessels protected; and even the city walls escape the indignity of violation by the Gentiles. Baruch is allowed insight into the heavenly world and into God's plan, which puts the problem in perspective from the outset. This perspective will be enlarged and confirmed by the eschatological revelations.

THE DIALOGUE IN SECTION 3

The opening unit includes dialogue between Baruch and the Lord within the narrative. In the third section (13:1-20:6), the dialogue predominates. This is the section in which Baruch comes closest to the probing questions of 4 Ezra, but there are some characteristic differences. The dialogue begins with God's reply to Baruch's lamentation. Baruch is appointed as an eschatological witness against the nations. Israel is chastised so that it may ultimately be saved, whereas the Gentiles, who are allowed to run their course, are headed for final destruction. This argument was widespread in Judaism in the Hellenistic and Roman periods (e.g., Wis 12:20-22; 2 Macc 7:18-19).

Baruch raises two objections. First, a judgment on the nations at some future time does not provide retribution for the preceding generations. Second, Zion should have been pardoned for the deeds of the righteous, not condemned for the offenses of the sinners. Even here Baruch readily admits his inability to comprehend the way of God, in terms reminiscent of the angel's replies to Ezra. He also points to the nucleus of the solution: "The righteous justly hope for the end, and without fear depart from this habitation, because they have with thee a store of works preserved in treasuries" (14:12). He adds: "Woe to us who are now shamefully treated and at that time look forward to evils." He includes himself with the wicked, presumably because of the judgment on his generation, although he has already been clearly set apart in the opening narrative.

God's reply underlines the importance of the world to come. Since the righteous can hope for salvation beyond death, the retribution does not only apply to the last generation. Years in this world are of little account (compare Wis 3:1-19). In effect, the Most High has made not one world but two (4 Ezra 7:50). Baruch, however, does not emphasize the discontinuity. The judgment after death is the fulfillment of the Deuteronomic law, and sinners are guilty because they know the law (compare Rom 7:7-12). If many have sinned, while only a few kept the law, this is a matter of human responsibility. We must infer that the true Israel, which is heir to the promises, consists of those who keep the law.

The problem of Zion is more apparent than real, as might have been inferred from the passage on the heavenly temple in chap. 6. Here we are told that God has taken away Zion so that he may "more speedily visit the world in its season." Presumably, that visitation will entail the revelation of the true Zion. Again, the promises of the covenant will be fulfilled but on a different level from what we might have expected. Like Ezra, Baruch is told not to worry about the past and to look to the future, but in this case the future may be said to offer a satisfactory fulfillment to a much greater degree.

THE VISIONS

2 Baruch involves no great reversal of roles or sudden conversion such as we found in 4 Ezra 10. Yet the fourth section (21:1-34:1) is a transitional unit. Up to this point, there had been no extensive eschatological revelation. It is introduced here as a vision (22:1), but the vision is not described. Instead we have a dialogue between Baruch and a heavenly voice, which is presumably the voice of God. The episode concludes not with a fast, as in the first three units, but with an address to the people.

The unit begins with a prayer of Baruch, which does not question the justice of God but asks that its manifestation be hastened. The voice replies that the number of those to be born must be completed, although in fact the time of redemption is near. This assurance leads naturally to the signs of the judgment. The time of tribulation will be divided into twelve woes. These are of a highly general nature, the "wars, famine and pestilence" typical of the prophecies of doom in the Hebrew Bible and the *Sibylline*

Oracles. Then the messiah will begin to be revealed. *2 Baruch* presupposes an eschatological scenario similar to 4 Ezra. After a period of time (unspecified here) the messiah will "return in glory." This presumably corresponds to the death of the messiah in 4 Ezra, although it is characteristically put in a more positive way.[60] The resurrection and judgment follow. Baruch draws the moral of the revelation for the people: "We should not be distressed so much over the evil that has now come as over that which is still to be" (32:5). Revelation of the future puts the present in perspective. Yet the law will protect those who practice it. Observance of the law gains greater urgency in view of the coming judgment.

The fifth section (35:1–47:2) presents the first allegorical vision, which follows a very brief lamentation by Baruch. The vision itself parallels the more elaborate eagle vision in 4 Ezra. In this case, the cedar is the last remnant of the forest of wickedness. Over against the cedar stands the vine. A fountain from under the vine submerges the forest, and the vine rebukes the cedar. The vision itself has no allusion to Daniel 7, but the interpretation claims that the forest symbolizes a sequence of four kingdoms. Since this symbolism is not apparent, we may suspect that the vision was not composed for its present context. Both the vine and the fountain are referred to the reign of the messiah. The analogy with the eagle vision lies in the prominence of the messiah and his role in rebuking the Gentile power. The reign of the messiah clearly belongs to this age rather than to the world to come: "His principate will stand for ever, until the world of corruption is at an end . . ." (40:3).

2 Baruch goes beyond 4 Ezra in clarifying the composition of the people who will benefit from the messiah. The criterion is not ethnicity but observance of the law. Proselytes are included, apostates are not.[61] *2 Baruch* envisages fulfillment of the covenantal promises, but in the process the covenantal people must be redefined. Conversion to Judaism is still a prerequisite for salvation, but the promises do not apply to all Jews. In view of this insistence on individual performance, it is only natural that Baruch should warn the people: "If ye endure and persevere in His fear and do not forget His law, the times shall change over you for good, and ye shall see the consolation of Zion" (44:7).

The climactic revelation of the book comes in the long sixth section, which runs from chap. 48 to chap. 77. Baruch begins with a long prayer for mercy, concluding with an affirmation: "In Thee do we trust, for lo! Thy law is with us, and we know that we shall not fail so long as we keep Thy statutes" (48:22). God responds "from thy words I will answer thee" by affirming that judgment is in accordance with the law. Mercy, then, only applies to those who convert and obey. Baruch laments: "O Adam what hast thou done to all those who are born from thee" (48:42), in a rare expression of sympathy for sinful humanity, but even here he does not dispute the justice of God. Instead he goes on to ask about the form of the afterlife. He is told that the earth will restore as it received, but both just and wicked will then be transformed. The righteous will be made like unto the angels and equal to the stars (51:10). This coming judgment puts human values in perspective: "For what then have those who were on earth exchanged their soul?" (51:15).

This dialogue addresses the question of individual retribution. It is complemented by a vision that explains the order of history by an allegory of a cloud that rains alternately black and white waters.[62] Even before this vision is explained, Baruch praises God "who revealest to those who fear Thee what is prepared for them" (54:4). He goes on to assert that "justly do they perish who have not loved Thy law" (54:14) and that "Adam is therefore not the cause, save only of his own soul, but each of us has been the Adam of his own soul" (54:19). This passage is significant in two respects. The lament in 48:43 ("O Adam what has thou done . . .") rings hollow in retrospect. On the other hand, the affirmation of individual responsibility is an important modifier for the cloud and waters vision. Although the sequence of history is predetermined, the choice of the individual is not.[63]

The interpretation of the vision, by the angel Ramiel, serves a number of functions. Like historical reviews in other apocalypses, it shows that the course of history is measured out, even from the beginning. History is an aspect of the cosmos. It also shows that the greater number of periods has passed. The end is relatively near. Baruch himself is located under the eleventh (black) waters. The twelfth period, however, is not the last, but refers to the restoration after the exile. This in turn will be followed by a dark period, which presumably includes the time of the real author. Finally, the messianic age, symbolized by the lightning of the vision, will come. The postexilic period, then, is a kind of epilogue to history which does not merit a special number.

The vision not only addresses the duration of history. It also discerns a pattern, in which light and darkness alternate. This pattern is reminiscent of the Deuteronomic history, but the transition from one period to the next is not ascribed to human agency in any way. Instead, it is determined from above. The pattern, however, places the darkness of the present in perspective. This period must eventually yield to brighter times, even to the lightning of the messiah. The interpretation ends with a description of the transformed world in the messianic age, but this must be understood as the prelude to the resurrection.

Baruch's final address to the people repeats a familiar message. If you observe the law, you will be protected. The catastrophe that has happened is a punishment for transgression. God is merciful, but his mercy is evidently contingent on obedience. This remains true in the final letter. If God "judge us not according to the multitude of His mercies, woe unto all of us who are born" (84:11). Even here there is no forgiveness for unreformed sinners, but 2 *Baruch* evidently envisages a greater role for mercy than does 4 Ezra.

THE LETTER

The final section (78:1 to the end) consists of Baruch's letter to the nine and one-half tribes. Baruch recapitulates the fall of Jerusalem, noting that the enemy was not allowed to destroy the walls. He states that God "showed me visions, that I should not again endure anguish, and He made known to me the mystery of the times" (81:4). These revelations are not repeated here, but they are nonetheless important. They are the basis for Baruch's confidence that the power of the Gentiles will pass like vapor and that this age is coming to an end. In the meantime "we have nothing now save the Mighty One and His law" (85:3). The main emphasis of the letter falls on the need for observance. "If therefore we direct and dispose our hearts we shall receive everything that we lost, and much better things than we lost by many times" (85:4). The urgency of this advice derives from the fact that

> the youth of the world is past,
> and the strength of the creation already exhausted
> and the advent of the times is very short. (85:10)

History, in short, is the limited time of decision.

COVENANTAL THEOLOGY

The central message of 2 *Baruch* is quite clearly the need to observe the law. The eschatological revelations are clearly subordinated to this end. The religion of the book has been described as "covenantal nomism," since salvation depends on the mercy of God in forgiving those within the covenant people who are basically obedient.[64] The dependence on Deuteronomy is explicit at several points (e.g., 19:1; 84:1-6). We should note, however, that the traditional Deuteronomic covenant undergoes some revision here. First, it must be buttressed by the apocalyptic revelations that Baruch receives. Second, the covenantal people is not constituted simply by the Jewish people, but by those who observe the law, with the inclusion of proselytes and the exclusion of apostates. Finally, the promised salvation finds its fulfillment not in this world but in the world to come. Salvation lies not only in the future of the covenant people but also in the destiny of the individual. As in all the apocalypses, salvation is salvation *out of* this world. 2 *Baruch* can say, like Paul, that "if there were this life only, which belongs to all men, nothing could be more bitter than this" (21:13, cf. 1 Cor 15:19). Yet even in an age of dark waters Baruch is never deprived of "the Mighty One and his law."[65] Accordingly, there is significant continuity from this world to the next.

Even more obviously than 4 Ezra, 2 *Baruch* is related to the rabbinic Judaism of the day. In chap. 2, Baruch and Jeremiah are bidden to withdraw from Jerusalem before its fall. There is an obvious analogy with the escape of Yohanan ben Zakkai during the siege by the Romans. Like the sages, 2 *Baruch* attempts to reconstitute Jewish life around the Torah, when the temple is no more. The ideas of the book have been compared with the teachings of Joshua ben Hananiah (especially in its positive attitude toward proselytes)[66] and Akiba.[67] The messianic expectation of the book fits well with the ideas of these sages: speculation is discouraged, but the expectation still plays a significant part.[68] The ideas of 2 *Baruch* fall well within the mainstream of rabbinic Judaism and there is no reason whatever to ascribe the work to a sect or conventicle. The book shows a strong concern for the welfare of the community at large, which extends also to the Diaspora. Unlike 4 Ezra it does not suggest that special revelations should be reserved for the wise among the people. The theme of leadership plays a prominent role. The fear of the people in the face of Baruch's impending death is similar to Baruch's own distress regarding the destruction of Jerusalem.[69] He assures them that "there shall not be wanting to Israel a wise man, nor a son of the law to the race of Jacob" (46:4). The sage plays a crucial role as mediator between God and the community.

The most striking affinities of 2 *Baruch* are undoubtedly those with 4 Ezra. Charles listed some sixty-six passages that show correspondences.[70] The affinities involve the total conception of the two works. Both are apocalypses of the "historical" type, which make extensive use of dialogue as a revelatory form. Both show a sevenfold structure and use seven-day fasts as one of the division markers. In both cases the problem is articulated in the earlier units, and there are allegorical visions in the fifth and sixth episodes. The final section involves a writing, in each book. Both books take the destruction of Jerusalem as their point of departure and use the Babylonian crisis as an allegory for 70 C.E. Both consider questions of theodicy and ultimately appeal to very similar eschatological scenarios, which distinguish this age from the world to come and locate the reign of the messiah in the conclusion of this age.

Within the framework of these affinities there are also significant differences. Ezra converses with an angel, until the final chapter. Baruch usually converses with God; the angel Ramiel is only introduced to interpret the cloud and waters vision. 2 *Baruch* has no real equivalent of the impassioned dialogue between Ezra and Uriel in 4 Ezra 3–9 or of the reversal of Ezra's role in chap. 10. On the other hand, 4 Ezra has nothing to correspond to the narrative about the fall of the temple in 2 *Baruch*. The revelation given to Ezra in chap. 14, which is in large part reserved for the wise among the people, is very different from Baruch's letter to the exiled tribes.

The most significant differences, however, lie in the respective attitudes of Ezra and Baruch. Ezra is driven by skeptical questioning and never acknowledges that his questions have been adequately answered. Baruch has special knowledge of what really happened to Jerusalem, from the very outset. Although the lament in 2 *Baruch* 10–11 displays real grief, Baruch's distress is not nearly so profound as that of Ezra, and he shows little resistance to the explanations he is given. Underlying the different degrees of distress are different theological presuppositions. Baruch's concern is focused much more narrowly on the people of Israel than is the case in 4 Ezra. He also shows far less sympathy for sinners. In 2 *Baruch* the lament "O Adam what hast thou done" (48:42), which directly echoes 4 Ezra 7:118, is canceled by an assertion that each of us is the Adam of his own soul (54:19). Baruch affirms in a way that Ezra never does that "justly do they perish who have not loved Thy law" (54:14). On the other hand, 2 *Baruch* is generally the more optimistic book. While 4 Ezra gives the impression that scarcely anyone can fulfill the law, 2 *Baruch* says that "others not a few have been righteous" (20:11), emphasizes free will rather than the evil inclination, and leaves some room for divine mercy toward those who repent, including proselytes. Although the sharpest differences are apparent between Baruch and Ezra's speeches in the dialogues, even the revelations of Uriel do not correspond exactly to the theology of 2 *Baruch*, since they endorse Ezra's pessimistic view of the judgment. Besides, we have seen that Ezra's complaints in the dialogues must be viewed as an integral part of the work.[71]

In view of the numerous points of contact between the two apocalypses, it is difficult to avoid the impression that one is deliberately taking issue with the other, although it need not have been written exclusively as a response. Scholars have differed on the question of priority. Recently Bogaert has suggested that the figures given in the superscriptions (twenty-five years in 2 *Baruch* and thirty in 4 Ezra) reflect the approximate number of years after the fall of Jerusalem in each case.[72] It is possible, however, that 2 *Baruch* used the lower figure deliberately to claim greater antiquity than 4 Ezra. Most critics have been impressed by 4 Ezra's greater "spontaneity."[73] Indeed it is easier to see why 2 *Baruch* should have responded to 4 Ezra than vice versa. Ezra might well be thought to have given too much weight to skepticism and not to have been sufficiently decisive in affirming divine justice. 2 *Baruch* then provides its own account of what happened in the fall of Jerusalem and leaves no doubt about the adequacy of the law. The case for the priority of 4 Ezra is not fully conclusive, but the balance of probability inclines in that direction.

This is not to deny that 2 *Baruch* has its own integrity as an apocalypse. The primary purpose of the work is not to engage in polemics but to lay a sure foundation for trust in God and obedience to the law. The apocalyptic revelations are combined with the assertions and exhortations of Baruch to this end. The apocalypse works primarily by positive thinking and by repeated assertions of the efficacy of the law. It gives little scope to the expression of fears and doubts. For this reason it lacks the emotional power of 4 Ezra, but it was surely more acceptable to the scribal leaders, and probably to most of the people.

Taken together, 4 Ezra and 2 *Baruch* throw some interesting light on the nature of the apocalyptic genre. Both share a common framework, which posits a need for special supernatural revelation, over and above what was given in the Torah, and both base their hope of salvation on the belief that there is another world, and life, beyond this one. In both books this framework serves not only to console but also to add urgency to present decisions. Within this framework, however, there is room for substantial disagreement on significant theological issues, such as the degree of human responsibility and the extent of those who will be saved. The genre, in short, does not entail a consistent doctrine. Rather it provides an imaginative view of the world, usually expressed in traditional symbols, within which there is room for a variety of theological doctrines, even in apocalypses which address a common problem, like the fall of the temple. Both 2 *Baruch* and 4 Ezra draw heavily on theological traditions that are far closer to the rabbinic material than was the case in the books of Enoch. Perhaps for this reason they show little interest in speculation about the heavenly world. They are also averse to calculations about the time of the end. They illustrate well the way in which the genre could be brought to bear on existential and historical problems and the flexibility with which it could incorporate diverse theological traditions.

THE APOCALYPSE OF ABRAHAM

A very different theological tradition is represented in the third apocalypse from this period, the *Apocalypse of Abraham*.[74] The work is preserved in Slavonic, which was most probably translated from Greek, but there are clear signs that the original was in Hebrew or Aramaic.[75] The land of Israel is accordingly the most probable place of composition. The approximate date is indicated by the fact that the destruction of the temple is the main event to which reference is made. The book belongs to the same general period as 4 Ezra and *2 Baruch* and shares some of their concerns about theodicy. In place of the Deuteronomic tradition, which informs these books, however, the mystical tendency of the early Enoch books is taken up here. The *Apocalypse of Abraham* is exceptional among the Jewish apocalypses in combining the motif of the heavenly journey with the review and periodization of history, characteristic of the "historical" apocalypses.

The book falls naturally into two parts. Chapters 1–8 recount the story of Abraham's conversion from idolatry. Chapters 9–32 constitute the apocalypse proper. The apocalypse, however, clearly presupposes the legend and refers back to it at several points (e.g., Jaoel is identified as the one who destroyed Terah's house, in chap. 10; God cites the example of Terah as an illlustration of free will in chap. 26). In addition, the voice that calls to Abraham in chap. 8 anticipates the heavenly voice in chap. 9. Both parts have clear points of departure in the biblical text. The legend explains why Abraham was told to go forth from his father's house (Genesis 12). The apocalypse is woven around the story of Abraham's sacrifice in Genesis 15[76] (with an allusion to Genesis 22 insofar as the sacrifice is located on a high mountain).

The theme of Abraham's conversion was a popular one in postbiblical Jewish literature. It was treated already in *Jubilees* 11 and in Josephus (*Antiquities* 1.7.1 §154) and Philo (*De Abrahamo* 15). Closer parallels to the *Apocalypse of Abraham* are found in the midrashim.[77] Here it is the occasion for a parody of idol worship, which was also a popular theme.[78] In its present context the story serves two purposes. It defines the religion of Abraham as the rejection of idolatry, and it suggests that idolators are ultimately doomed to destruction as Terah is in chap. 8.

The apocalypse proper is developed through several well-defined stages.[79]

Chapters 9–12 state the command to sacrifice, with the promise that "I will show thee the ages which have been created . . . and what shall come to pass in them" (chap. 9). They also introduce Jaoel, as Abraham's angelic guide.

Chapters 13–14 recount the actual sacrifice and the attempt of Azazel to divert Abraham.

Then in chap. 15 the angel takes Abraham up to heaven on the wing of a pigeon. There he assists Abraham in uttering the celestial song (chap. 17). This is followed by a vision of the divine throne (chap. 18). Abraham is bidden to count the stars which are beneath him in the fifth heaven, and the promise of innumerable descendants follows (chap. 20).

In chap. 21 Abraham is shown a "picture" in which all creation is reflected and humanity is divided into two parties, on the right side and on the left. God explains that those on the right are the chosen people, those on the left the Gentiles.

In chap. 23 he is told to look again at the picture and consider the story of the fall so that he may know how it will be for his seed at the end of the age. Here the focus is on the role of Azazel, who is said to have power over those that will do evil.

In chap. 24 he is bidden to look again at the picture. This time he is shown the sequence of history, beginning with Adam. This is in effect a catalogue of sins: impurity, theft, unlawful desire. The culminating sin is idolatry: "I saw there the likeness of the idol of jealousy, having the likeness of woodwork such as my father was wont to make." The "idol of jealousy" recalls Ezekiel 8, where the practice of idolatry in the temple is given as the reason for its destruction. Here too the idol is associated with the temple. God's idea of the temple and the priesthood is contrasted with the way in which the people anger him by idolatry and slaughter. When Abraham asks why this is so he is referred to the example of Terah, to show that it is a matter of human free will.

In chap. 27 Abraham looks again at the picture and sees how the Gentiles, from the left side, run through four entrances and plunder the temple. He is told that this will happen "on account of thy seed who anger me by reason of the statue which thou sawest, and on account of the human slaughter in the picture." The righteous, in contrast, are rewarded with "righteous-dealing rulers." The four "entrances" represent periods of one hundred years or an hour of the age. This ungodly age is divided into twelve hours, but "before the Age of the righteous beginneth to grow, my judgment shall come upon the lawless heathen through the people of thy seed." Ten plagues will come upon the heathen, but the "righteous men of thy seed" will be restored in the temple. They "shall destroy those who have destroyed them and shall insult those who have insulted them."

In chap. 30 Abraham is returned to earth but complains that "what my soul longed to understand in my heart I do not understand." God interprets this as the ten plagues, which he then outlines, in a manner similar to the signs of the end in 2 Baruch 27. Chapter 31 completes the eschatological scenario. The Elect One will come to gather the Jews from the nations. Those who have insulted them will not only be burned but also will be food for the fire of Hades. The apocalypse concludes with the biblical prediction of the exile in Egypt (Gen 15:14).

THE UNDERLYING QUESTIONS

Although both parts of the *Apocalypse of Abraham* are attached to elements in the biblical story, the text is not generated by exegetical concerns. The problem addressed is not that of the meaning of the texts in

Genesis but that of the prominence of evil in the world, especially in the form of idolatry. A corollary of this question is the special role of Abraham and his descendants, the people who reject idolatry. These questions are ultimately brought into focus by the destruction of the temple. The *Apocalypse of Abraham*, like 4 Ezra, may be said to contain a response to the destruction of the temple, but its primary concern is with broader issues of universal significance.

The questions of evil and the special role of the chosen people are not formulated by Abraham at the outset, as they were by Ezra. They emerge in the course of a narrative that gives a comprehensive account of the world and its history. This account is given through supernatural revelation. The voice of God in chap. 9 bases the revelation of the ages and "what is reserved" on the knowledge of the God, who was before the ages and created the light of the world.

Abraham is not brought immediately into the presence of God. Instead, the angel Jaoel is sent "in the likeness of a man" (compare the angelophany in Daniel 10). The name is evidently a substitute for Yahweh, or Yahweh El, and Jaoel is said to be "a power in virtue of the ineffable Name that is dwelling in me." His heavenly functions include restraining both the Cherubim and Leviathan, and teaching the celestial song. He and Michael are appointed to be with the descendants of Abraham. In all, Jaoel bears striking resemblance to Metatron in Hekalot literature. Metatron is "the little Yahweh" (*3 Enoch* 12), whose name is like the name of God himself (*b. Sanhedrin* 38b).[80] The *Apocalypse of Abraham* is evidently heir to a tradition of mystical speculation that goes beyond that associated with the archangel Michael or with the "Son of Man" in the Similitudes of Enoch.

A second major supernatural figure is introduced in the figure of Azazel, in chap. 13. Azazel is depicted as a fallen angel, whose heavenly garments are given to Abraham. He is associated with the fires of the netherworld in chap. 14 and again in chap. 31. We have already seen how Azazel was identified as the leader of the fallen angels in the Book of the Watchers (where the name was originally 'Aśa'el). He plays a more obvious role in human history than does Jaoel.

Abraham's vision of the divine throne draws heavily on Ezekiel and stands directly in the tradition of Merkavah speculation.[81] Unlike *2 Enoch* or *3 Baruch*, Abraham is not said to ascend through the heavens one by one but is placed directly in the seventh heaven. From this vantage point he is allowed to view the expanses which are under the firmament and to verify the first principle of cosmology, which is made explicit in chap. 19: there is no other God but the one he has sought.

The picture of the world which is introduced in chap. 21 exemplifies in an exceptionally clear way the combination of cosmology and history which is always implied in the apocalyptic world view. The course of history and its consummation are built into the structure of creation from the beginning. Both the heavens and the ages of the world are displayed in orderly numbers which reflect the providential control of God. On the spatial axis, Abraham notes both the paradise of the righteous (the Garden of Eden) and the abyss and its torments. The historical axis is divided into twelve hours, a form of periodization that is also found in 2 *Baruch's* vision of the cloud and waters and probably derives ultimately from Persian sources.[82] The period of oppression by the Gentiles is specified as four "hours" of a hundred years each—a reflection of the four kingdoms of Daniel, which were also reflected in 2 *Baruch* and 4 Ezra. The destruction of the temple must be presumed to take place at the end of the four hours, and so at the end of the age. The periodization of history serves its usual purpose of showing that the course of events is predetermined and that the end is near.

Not only are cosmos and history divided in an orderly way; so also is humanity. The picture reveals a great multitude, half on the right and half on the left, representing the chosen people and the Gentiles respectively. The symmetrical division suggests a dualistic view of the world. The nature and extent of this dualism constitute the most controversial problem in the *Apocalypse of Abraham.* In two passages, in chaps. 20 and 22, Azazel appears to be in partnership with God, specifically sharing the heritage of the chosen people. In the case of chap. 22, the reference to Azazel is omitted in one manuscript and seems to be added as a gloss in another. Rubinkiewicz concludes that both this passage and that in chap. 20 have been interpolated by a Bogomil scribe.[83] This suggestion finds support in chap. 29, where the disputed expression "with Azazel" occurs in a passage that is definitely interpolated. An explicit statement that Azazel shares in the heritage of the chosen people would be extraordinary in a Jewish text but has some basis in the original apocalypse. Indeed Abraham's question about the status of Azazel at the end of chap. 20 provides an admirable occasion for the exposition of the world which follows. Some part of the chosen people is in any case supposed to be sinful and so to be under the dominion of Azazel. The entire conception may be compared with the doctrine of the two spirits at Qumran.[84] The ultimate supremacy of God is not in doubt. The role of Azazel is carefully delimited in the discussion of the fall in chap. 23: "They who will to do evil . . . over them I gave him power." Abraham's further question, about why God "willed to effect that evil should be desired in the hearts of men" is never directly answered. The review of history that follows establishes the undeniable fact of human sinfulness, and the example of Terah affirms that it is a matter of free choice.

The *Apocalypse of Abraham* does not provide a satisfactory explanation of the origin of evil, any more than 4 Ezra did. The solution lies in the future, in the promise of retribution. Some retribution is provided already in this age, in the punishment of Israelite sin by the destruction of the temple. At this point, however, the second underlying problem of the book emerges: What is the ultimate role of the chosen people descended from Abraham? The answer to this question can be given only in eschatological terms. We must presume that the chastisement involved in the destruction of the temple leaves a purified remnant, although this is not explicitly stated.

The eschatological expectations of this apocalypse are confused by a strange insertion in chap. 29 about a man "from the left side of the heathen" who is insulted and beaten by those on the right side but is worshiped "by the heathen with Azazel." This passage must be taken as a reference to Christ, although the suggestion that he is worshiped by Azazel is unorthodox and reflects a sectarian, Bogomil viewpoint.[85] The eschatology of the Jewish work can be seen in chap. 31, where the Elect One comes to gather the exiles. A passage at the end of chap. 29 says that the righteous will be gathered to the place "which thou sawest devastated" and will be established through sacrifices. This passage is obviously Jewish and envisages a restoration of the temple. There is no reference to resurrection, but the mockers will be food for the fire of Hades, and the righteous had been seen in the Garden of Eden in chap. 21. The eschatological scenario remains elliptic, but it is apparent that both individual retribution after death and the future restoration of the nation are envisaged. The hope of humanity lies beyond the present world, or beyond the present age.

The *Apocalypse of Abraham* resolves its underlying problems by placing them in the context of a construction of the world which embraces both cosmology and history. The origin of evil is only partially explained by the role of Azazel. Ultimately, sin is attributed to free human choice. The election of Abraham is not finally explained either. The problem here is not the cause of the election (which lies in the free choice of God) but how it can be maintained, given the prevalence of idolatry even within the chosen people. This problem, like the problem of evil itself, can be resolved only by the eschatological finale. The book can scarcely be said to provide a rational argument to show that this solution is satisfactory, but that is not its purpose. It proposes a view of the world on the authority of Abraham and his heavenly visions and acquires force from its use of biblical and traditional allusions. The imaginative achievement of such a synthesis of history and cosmology is considerable. The frank recognition of human sinfulness and affirmation of free will enhance its credibility. The total effect enables the reader to set the problems of the present in perspective against the grand design of creation, and thereby be reassured and acquire a basis for action.

The more specific messages of the *Apocalypse of Abraham* are difficult to discern. The focal point of history is the destruction of the temple. The *Apocalypse of Abraham* attributes this calamity to the sins of the Jews, without the misgivings of 4 Ezra over the disproportion of the punishment. In chaps. 25 and 27 the sins are discussed with greater specificity, but both passages are enigmatic. In chap. 25, God's ideal of the temple is used as a foil against which his anger with the people should be understood. Cultic defilement would seem to be implied,[86] and this is corroborated by an allusion to Ezekiel 8 ("the idol of jealousy"). There is also a cryptic reference to a man slaughtering. In chap. 27 God's anger is caused by the "statue" (which apparently signifies idolatry) and murder in the temple. The temple has evidently been defiled, and some criticism of the priesthood may be inferred. The slaughter and murder most probably refer to the murders and assassinations in the inner-Jewish struggles at the time of the revolt against Rome (compare *Sib. Or.* 4:118). The blame for the defilement may fall on the Zealots no less than on the priesthood. Unfortunately the text is too unclear to permit firm conclusions.

Although the violence of 66–70 c.e. is apparently condemned, the apocalypse is not ultimately pacifistic. In the eschatological age the righteous "shall destroy those who have destroyed them and shall insult those who have insulted them" (chap. 29) and God will burn with fire those who have insulted them and ruled them in this age (chap. 31). Can we discern here an attitude that "may have contributed to the atmosphere which precipitated the revolt of Bar Kokhba"?[87] Perhaps, but a qualification is in order. The violence is envisaged as eschatological. The apocalypse does not advocate rebellion against Rome until the end of the age. Whether it could be used to sanction recourse to arms would depend on whether the messianic age was thought to have arrived—as indeed Akiba thought in the case of Bar Kokhba. The attitude of the *Apocalypse of Abraham* may be somewhat similar to the Qumran *War Scroll* in this respect.

The main clues to the provenance of the apocalypse lie in its references to the temple. On the one hand there is concern over cultic defilement and the hope for restoration of righteous sacrifices. On the other hand, the defilement of the temple may imply a critique of the priesthood. The author *may* have belonged to a group that was priestly in character but alienated from the priesthood of the first century. Both the mystical tendencies and the dualism of the apocalypse find some parallels in the Qumran scrolls, but the *Apocalypse of Abraham* takes a clearer stand on the question of free will. The evidence is scarcely sufficient to warrant the proposal of Box that the author was an Essene.[88] It is in any case uncertain how far the Essenes maintained a separate identity after 70 c.e. It is true, however, that the *Apocalypse of Abraham* represents a different strand of Judaism from what we found in 4 Ezra and in 2 *Baruch*.

8
Apocalyptic Literature from the Diaspora in the Roman Period

Two CLUSTERS OF TEXTS from the Hellenistic Diaspora are relevant to the discussion of apocalypticism. On the one hand, the *Sibylline Oracles* bear obvious resemblances to the "historical" apocalypses. On the other hand, the actual apocalypses of the Diaspora all involve heavenly journeys and incline to the mystical end of the apocalyptic spectrum.

THE SIBYLLINES

We have already seen some of the affinities between the *Sibyllines* and the historical apocalypses in the case of *Sib. Or.* 3. These affinities became more pronounced in the Roman period when additions to *Sib. Or.* 3 reflect in their predictions of catastrophe and their heightened mythological imagery the growing alienation of Egyptian Judaism. This tradition is carried further in *Sib. Or.* 5. A different Sibylline tradition is represented in *Sib. Or.* 1 and 2 and *Sib. Or.* 4. In these books the analogy with apocalyptic eschatology (of the historical type) is more complete. They attest an elaborate periodization of history, culminating in the resurrection and the judgment of the dead. The *Sibyllines* are of course always presented as oracles, the direct inspired speech of the sibyl. The manner of revelation remains clearly distinct from that of the apocalypses.

SIB. OR. 5
The tradition of anti-Roman polemic developed in the additions to *Sib. Or.* 3 is continued in *Sib. Or.* 5. This is a composite work, consisting of six

substantial oracles. The four central oracles (52–110; 111–78; 179–285; 286–434) show a common pattern:[1] (1) oracles against various nations (mainly Egypt in the first and third oracles, various Asiatic countries in the second and fourth); (2) the return of Nero as an eschatological adversary; (3) the advent of a savior figure; (4) a destruction, usually by fire (the manner is not specified in 52–110). These four oracles were composed after the destruction of Jerusalem in 70 C.E. but before the great Diaspora revolt in 115–17 C.E. The concluding oracle of the book (435–531) was most probably written after the Diaspora revolt. The latest oracle in the book is found in vss. 1–51, a survey of history from Alexander to Hadrian (or, if vs. 51 is original, to Marcus Aurelius), which refers to the emperors by the numbers represented by their initials. This oracle is very different in spirit from the rest of the book and is closer to the pro-Roman sibylline tradition which is found in *Sib. Or.* 11–14.

The bulk of *Sib. Or.* 5 is taken up with prophecies of doom against various nations. Egypt is the main subject in two of the oracles, and is denounced for idolatry (81–85) and for persecution of the Jews (68–69). These oracles arise naturally enough from the Jewish experience in Egypt. There are also prophecies of doom against the Gauls (200–205) and Ethiopians (206–13), with whom the Jews had no significant contact. The principal enemy, however, is Rome, which is denounced as an "effeminate and unjust, evil city, ill-fated above all" (162–78). Like Babylon, Rome has said "I alone am" (compare Isa 47:8; Rev 18:7). Accordingly, she will be cast down to the nether regions of Hades. Rome is condemned for immorality (adultery and homosexuality, 5:166; 386–393) and for arrogance, but the wrath of the sibyl is aroused for more immediate reasons. In 5:155–61 it is said that a great star will burn "the deep sea and Babylon itself and the land of Italy, because of which many holy faithful Hebrews and a true people perished." "Babylon" here is a code name for Rome, as in the book of Revelation, and presupposes the analogy between the destructions of 586 B.C.E. and 70 C.E. The great sin of Rome is the destruction of the temple. In 5:398–413 the sibyl utters what is perhaps the most powerful lament for the second temple: "When I saw the second temple cast headlong, soaked in fire by an impious hand, the ever-flourishing, watchful temple of God, made by holy people and hoped by their soul and body to be always imperishable. . . . But now a certain insignificant and impious king has gone up, cast it down and left it in ruins. . . ." *Sib. Or.* 5 reacts to the fall of the temple not by pondering divine justice (like 4 Ezra) or seeking to fill the gap it left in religious life (like 2 *Baruch*) but by venting its outrage against the heathen power that was responsible.

The sibyl's hatred of Rome also finds expression in the role of Nero as eschatological adversary. At the time of his death there was a widespread belief that Nero had escaped to the Parthians, with whom he had long had friendly relations, and would return leading a Parthian host.[2] This belief was fueled by the appearance of an impostor shortly after Nero's death, and another some twenty years later. The popular belief was given an eschatological cast in *Sib. Or.* 4 and 5 and also in *Sib. Or.* 3:63-74, which refers to Nero as "Beliar" who would come from the line of Augustus.[3] Originally Nero was not thought to have died. Subsequently the belief arose that he would return from the dead—*Nero redivivus.* This belief is reflected in the book of Revelation in the beast who had "a mortal wound" on one of its heads but was healed (chap. 13) and who "was and is not and is to ascend from the bottomless pit" (chap. 17). In Revelation this figure is representative of Roman power and is deliberately fashioned as an Antichrist.[4] *Nero redivivus* continued to play a part in the later sibyllina (*Sib. Or.* 8:68-72; 139-69) and in the Antichrist legend of the Middles Ages.[5]

Sib. Or. 5 makes extensive use of the Nero legend. *Sib. Or.* 5:137-54 describes "a great king of great Rome" who is clearly identified as Nero by his theatrical ambitions and the murder of his mother. He is said to flee from "Babylon" (Rome) and take refuge with the Persians, or Parthians. The destruction of the temple is still attributed to him. In *Sib. Or.* 5:214-27 he is clearly identified by a reference to the cutting of the isthmus of Corinth. In 5:361-70 he is identified as a "matricide" who will come in the last time to destroy every land and conquer all, including "the one because of whom he himself perished" (presumably Rome).[6] In view of his association with the Persians and his eschatological role, he must also be identified with the "Persian" who will come "like hail" in vss. 93-97.[7] The charges against Nero are the same as the charges against Rome: he is morally evil, he claimed to be God (vss. 34, 140) and he is responsible for the destruction of the temple.

The four central oracles of the book look beyond the evils of the present order and beyond the return of Nero to the advent of a savior figure. In 108-9 he is "a certain king sent from God" to defeat "the Persian" when the latter attempts to destroy the city of the blessed ones." This formulation is compatible with traditional messianic expectations but also recalls a similar expectation in the *Oracle of Hystaspes.*[8] In vss. 414 and 256 the savior appears as a heavenly figure who comes from the expanses of heaven, or "from the sky." In the oracle in 111-78 the function of the savior is exercised by "a great star," which burns the sea and Babylon (158-59). Stars were frequently associated with the advent of savior figures in the Hellenistic world.[9] In the Jewish tradition stars were identified with angels.[10] Moreover, astral imagery had messianic connotations because of Balaam's oracle.[11] Hence the leader of the revolt against Rome in 132 c.e. was called Bar Kokhba, son of the star. *Sib. Or.* 5 reflects the merging of traditions.

Whether the savior figure is expected to be a Davidic king is not clear; this is never said of him. It is apparent, however, that he has a strongly supernatural character, as indeed the messiah also has in 4 Ezra. Unlike *Sib. Or.* 3, which based its hopes on the Ptolemaic house, *Sib. Or.* 5 has to look for a savior from beyond this world.

The oracles in 179–285 and 286–434 conclude with prophecies of the restoration of Jerusalem. In 247–85 the focus is a broad one, on "delightful Judea," but Jerusalem will be surrounded by a great wall as far as Joppa. The Gentiles will be converted to revere the law (265) and the earth will be transformed. In 420–27 "the city which God desired" is made more brilliant than the stars, equipped with a holy temple and an immense tower touching the clouds and visible to all. In both cases the restoration is this-worldly and conforms to the messianic oracles of Isaiah rather than to apocalyptic eschatology. The focus of eschatological hope on Jerusalem is remarkable in a document of the Diaspora. For most of the history of the Diaspora, the exiled Jews had been content to seek their future in the land of their residence. In the great revolt of 115–17 C.E., however, there are indications that the rebels aspired to bring about the end of the Diaspora and to return to Jerusalem.[12] It is also noteworthy that *Sib. Or.* 5:484–88 exultingly prophesies the destruction of Isis and Sarapis. The temple of Sarapis in Alexandria was one of the most conspicuous casualties of the revolt, and the rebel Jews were noted for their hostility to the pagan cults. *Sib. Or.* 5, more than any other document we have, is likely to reflect the attitude of those who joined in the great and tragic uprising.

Despite its hopes for a savior figure and for the restoration of Jerusalem, *Sib. Or.* 5 is predominantly a pessimistic book. The motif of destruction by fire is found in three of the central oracles. In 155–61 the great star will destroy the whole earth and burn the deep sea and "Babylon." The sea here may echo the ancient mythological tradition in which Yamm or Sea is the embodiment of chaos, the enemy of life and fertility. The advent of the savior figure in 256 is followed by a shower of blazing fire from heaven. Again in 414–33 the savior destroys every city with fire and burns the nations of evildoers. This motif has biblical roots and also has parallels in Persian eschatology.[13] It marks a negative conclusion to the present age and stresses the discontinuity with the state of salvation which is to come.

The pessimism of *Sib. Or.* 5 is most readily obvious in the final oracle. The sibyl prophesies the destruction of Isis and Sarapis (484–88) and then goes on to envisage the conversion of Egypt and the building of a temple to the true God. Even this eschatological temple will not last, however, but will be destroyed by the "Ethiopians." The Ethiopians were traditional enemies of Egypt. Ethiopia was also associated with Gog and Magog in *Sib. Or.* 3:319–20 and may serve here as a general reference for eschatological adversaries. It is indicative of the general xenophobia of *Sib. Or.* 5 that such a remote people is accorded a key destructive role in the final scenario.

The book concludes with a battle of the stars, which ends when heaven casts them all to earth.[14] The earth is set ablaze and the sky remains starless. The closing note of the book, then, is a bleak one of cosmic desolation. It is an apt expression of the world view of Egyptian Judaism after the failure of the great revolt.

The eschatological oracles of *Sib. Or.* 5 frame an ethical message, which is found in the condemnations of the nations for idolatry (vss. 75-85, 278-80, 353-56, 403-5, 495-96) and sexual immorality, especially homosexuality (386-93, 495-96).[15] The dominant emphasis of the book, however, is not ethical but political. The main function of the sibyl is to articulate Jewish anger against the nations in general and Rome in particular. This anger is generated in part by social oppression[16] but chiefly by the humiliation of the destruction of the temple and the arrogance of Rome in posturing as God. *Sib. Or.* 5 is quite probably representative of the feelings of Jews who joined in the revolt in the time of Trajan. We should note that apocalyptic literature was not usually inclined to foment rebellion, but *Sib. Or.* 5 differs from the apocalypses in significant respects, over and beyond the manner of revelation. Despite the propensity for mythological imagery and the supernatural character of the savior figure, *Sib. Or.* 5 does not envisage salvation beyond this world. There is no judgment of the dead, either of the individual soul or of a resurrected humanity in the endtime. Consequently, the outcome of political struggles such as the revolt against Rome is far more crucial for the sibyl than for an apocalyptist like *2 Baruch.*

The tradition of sibylline protest against Rome survived the revolt and was taken up again in a collection of oracles now preserved in *Sib. Or.* 8 and composed in the time of Marcus Aurelius. These later oracles indict Rome on grounds that are predominantly social. The later development of Jewish sibyllines in Egypt, however, was mainly pro-Roman. Books 12-14 continue a tradition initiated in *Sib. Or.* 11, which was probably composed in the first century in Alexandria. These oracles string together brief comments on the reigns of the successive emperors. They have minimal eschatological interest and show little analogy to the apocalypses.[17]

Sib. Or. 1 and 2

Two sibylline books from the first century c.e. were not composed in Egypt. These are the Jewish substratum of *Sib. Or.* 1 and 2, and *Sib. Or.* 4. These oracles share an elaborate periodization of history and an expectation of resurrection and judgment of the dead.

It is generally recognized that the first two books of the standard Sibylline collection constitute an original unit, structured by a division of history into ten generations.[18] The first seven generations are preserved without interpolation in *Sib. Or.* 1:1–323. At this point the sequence is disrupted by an interpolation concerning the career of Christ. When the sequence is resumed in 2:15 we are confronted already with the tenth generation, so the eighth and ninth have been lost. The remainder of *Sib. Or.* 2 (vss. 34–347) deals with eschatological crises and the judgment of the dead. There are some clear Christian passages, but the full extent of the Christian redaction is uncertain. Verses 154–76, which culminate in the universal rule of the Hebrews, "as of old," are definitely Jewish. The resurrection in 2:214–37, which is strongly physical in character and recalls Ezekiel 37, is also probably Jewish.

Because of the complications introduced by the Christian redaction, little can be said about the provenance and purpose of the Jewish oracle. There are indications that the place of composition was Phrygia, the first land to emerge after the flood, where Ararat is located. Since the destruction of Jerusalem is mentioned only in a Christian redactional passage (1:393–96) the Jewish oracle was probably composed before then.[19] In view of the loss of the eighth and ninth generations any conclusions on the date and purpose of the Jewish oracle can only be tentative.

The most interesting analogy with the apocalyptic literature lies in the division of history into ten generations followed by a resurrection. The tenfold periodization was found in the Apocalypse of Weeks and in 11QMelchizedek, but it is unlikely that the sibyl derived it from other Jewish sources. Such a schematization is presupposed in several sibylline oracles including the Cumean sibyl of Virgil's *Fourth Eclogue*. The roots of the conception most probably lie in the Persian division of world history into millennia, which also involved a belief in resurrection.[20] In *Sib. Or.* 1 and 2 the periodization is found in a particularly elaborate form. It embraces all of history from creation to the final judgment. The first five generations end with the flood, the second five with destruction by fire, in accordance with the notion of the Great Year.[21] We have seen that the motif of destruction by fire was prominent in *Sib. Or.* 5 even when the full periodization of history was not developed.

In the present form of *Sib. Or.* 1 and 2 the overview of history provides a framework for ethical teaching. The schematization of history builds the impression that the impending destruction is inevitable. The imminence of the judgment provides an occasion for presenting crucial ethical values. So Noah is presented as preaching to his contemporaries before the flood (1:150–70; 174–98). The sins mentioned are commonplace–violence, deceit, adultery, etc. Because of the Christian redaction it is not clear whether humanity is given a similar warning in the tenth generation. It is also possible that the Jewish oracle had a stronger political thrust than is now apparent.

SIB. OR. 4

Sib. Or. 4 also shows evidence of redactional layers. In this case the final product is still distinctly Jewish. The original oracle is structured by a division of history into ten generations and four kingdoms (vss. 49–101). The overview begins after the flood. The Assyrians rule for six generations, the Medes for two, and the Persians for one. The tenth generation and the fourth kingdom coincide in the Macedonian empire. We should expect this climactic kingdom to be followed by the eschatological finale, but instead the account is prolonged to refer to the Romans (102–51). Rome is not integrated into the numerical sequence, but neither is it a final, definitive kingdom. We must assume that the passage on Rome was added to update the oracle. The original oracle may have included the final section on the conflagration, resurrection, and judgment (173–92), in a manner analogous to *Sib. Or.* 1 and 2. Since Macedonia is the last kingdom in the sequence, that oracle was presumably written before the rise of Rome. There is no clear evidence to show whether the author was Jewish. The decline of history explicit in the schema implies that Macedonia is the nadir of history and that its demise is imminent (compare the use of the four-kingdom schema in Daniel 2). The original oracle, then, may be considered a document of Near Eastern resistance to Hellenism.[22]

The passage on Rome in vss. 102–51 extends the view of history through the destruction of the Jerusalem temple. Unlike *Sib. Or.* 5, this oracle expresses no outrage but suggests that it is a punishment for the folly and impiety of the Jews. The legend of Nero's return, which plays such a prominent part in *Sib. Or.* 5, serves here to introduce the eschatological time. The sibyl sounds the familiar sibylline theme that Rome will pay back its plunder to Asia. The oracle then has an aspect of anti-Roman polemic.

The major emphasis of the oracle, however, falls not on the political element but on the plea for conversion, and specifically on the demand that "wretched mortals" should "wash your whole bodies in perennial rivers" (165). If this and the more general ethical demands are not obeyed, "there will be fire throughout the whole world" (173). The oracle is exceptional in making the destruction conditional on human obedience or disobedience. Both the periodization of history and the concluding prophecy of resurrection seem to imply that the course of events is set, and this may well have been the view of the original oracle. In any case *Sib. Or.* 4 provides a good illustration of the use of periodization and eschatological expectation to throw ethical demands into high relief and add urgency to the demand for obedience.

The demand for baptism in the face of the impending judgment is perhaps the most striking aspect of *Sib. Or.* 4. The most obvious analogies are found in the New Testament account of John the Baptist and again in early Christianity in Acts 2. *Sib. Or.* 4 shows no sign of Christian authorship and has been thought to derive from a Jewish baptist movement in the Jordan valley.[23] Its date is indicated by a reference to the eruption of Vesuvius (79 C.E.), which is taken as an eschatological sign in vs. 130.

The theology of *Sib. Or.* 4 can be filled out from the opening passage in vss. 6–39. These verses stress the transcendence of the invisible God. In addition to the usual polemic against idolatry and immorality, the sibyl insists that God does not have a temple of stone but an invisible one in heaven. She goes on to praise those who reject all temples, altars, and animal sacrifices. In the light of this passage the sibyl's lack of outrage over the destruction of the temple is intelligible. Like Stephen and the Hellenists in Acts, this sibyl attached little value to the earthly temple. We find here another position in the spectrum of Jewish responses to the fall of the temple, different at once from the apocalypses of 4 Ezra and *2 Baruch* and from the Egyptian sibylline tradition of *Sib. Or.* 5.

THE APOCALYPSES

The *Sibylline Oracles* can be called "apocalyptic" only in an extended sense of the term. The actual apocalypses that have survived from the Diaspora are quite different in character. None of them contains a review of history, but all involve heavenly ascents. Three major Diaspora apocalypses have survived, *2 Enoch* (Slavonic), the *Testament of Abraham*, and *3 Baruch*.[24]

The *Apocalypse of Zephaniah* may well derive from Egyptian Judaism, too, but it has survived only in a quotation in Clement (*Stromateis* 5.11.77) and in a brief fragment in Sahidic.[25] A more extensive apocalyptic fragment in Akhmimic has also been thought to belong to the *Apocalypse of Zephaniah*, but the visionary's name is never mentioned.[26] The quotation in Clement tells how Zephaniah was lifted up to the fifth heaven and saw there angels who were called "lords." The Sahidic fragment describes a vision of the underworld and the torments of sinners. The Akhmimic fragment begins with a tour over the visionary's city. The greater part of the apocalypse is concerned with the netherworld and the punishment of the damned. The visionary prays to be delivered but is shown the catalogue of his sins before he is told that he is written in the book of life. Throughout he is in dialogue with an angel. He witnesses the recording angels of good and evil, and when he prays the angel Eremiel comes to deliver him. He is also allowed to witness the angels at prayer. At the end he is told of the coming "Day of the Lord" when heaven and earth will be destroyed. None of the fragments shows any elements that are indisputably Christian, although the visions of the netherworld find their closest analogies in the Christian apocalypses of Peter and Paul.[27] In the Coptic fragments, the dominant concern for individual salvation is reflected in the visionary's anxiety for deliverance from the netherworld. The Akhmimic text spells out its ethical message in the sins attributed to the visionary—mainly neglect of social obligations to the sick, widows, etc. It is apparent, however, that both fragments do not merely exhort but achieve a considerable emotional effect through the tour of otherworldly regions. Because of the fragmentary state of the apocalypse, basic questions of date, provenance, and interpretation remain uncertain. We cannot even be sure that the quotation in Clement and the Coptic fragments belong to the same work.

2 ENOCH

2 Enoch (Slavonic) is the most elaborate of the Diaspora apocalypses. Despite the contention of J. T. Milik that it is a late, Christian work of the ninth or tenth century,[28] there is a general consensus that it is Jewish and no later than the first century, because of the importance attached to animal sacrifice.[29] The work has survived in two Slavonic recensions, of which the shorter is the more original.[30] This shorter recension contains no clear Christian elements.[31] The original language was most probably Greek.[32] Egypt is the most likely place of composition in view of allusions to Egyptian mythology and affinities with Philo and other Diaspora writings.[33]

The structure of *2 Enoch* has been said to correspond to major blocks of material in *1 Enoch*.[34] Enoch's ascent and commission (chaps. 3–37)[35] would be the counterpart of *1 Enoch* 12–36; his return to earth and instructions (chaps. 38–66), of *1 Enoch* 81, 91–105; and the story of Melchizedek's birth, of *1 Enoch* 106–7 (the birth of Noah). The correspondences, however are quite loose. The ascent in *2 Enoch* is structured by the sequence of seven heavens, which was not suggested in the older work. The instructions in *2 Enoch* are divided into three distinct exhortations: the first in 39–55 summarizes the revelation and draws the morals; the second is Enoch's parting testament to Methusalem and his brothers (58–63); the third is a farewell address to the multitude assembled to see him (65–66). The story of Melchizedek is a formally distinct unit and is widely thought to be of different origin.[36] The debt to *1 Enoch* lies mainly in the tradition that Enoch had ascended to the heavens and returned to instruct his sons. Although occasional details (e.g., the reference to the Watchers in chap. 18) reflect the earlier books, both the cosmology and the ethical message of *2 Enoch* are largely independent of *1 Enoch*.

At the beginning of the book Enoch is "in great trouble, weeping with my eyes" and asleep on his couch, when "two very big men," obviously angels, come to escort him to the heavens. In the course of the ascent two kinds of material are emphasized: cosmological and eschatological. The cosmological emphasis is dominant in the first, fourth, and sixth heavens. In the first, Enoch sees the angels who govern the stars and the elements; in the fourth, the movements of the sun and moon and regulation of time; and in the sixth, the seven angels who supervise the order of the world. The second, third, and fifth heavens reveal eschatological rewards and punishments. The second heaven contains the place of punishment of the rebellious angels. The third contains paradise, which is both the original Garden of Eden and the place prepared for the just. This heaven also contains, in the north, the place of punishment for sinners. In the fifth heaven Enoch meets the Watchers, who are mourning the fall of their fellow angels. He tells how he has seen their place of punishment and urges the Watchers to persevere in the service of God. Finally, in the seventh heaven Enoch enters the heavenly court, is anointed with sweet oil, given new garments, and transformed to an angel-like state. Then the angel Vreveil (Uriel?) dictates to Enoch "all things in heaven and earth and sea, the courses and dwellings of all the elements, the seasons of the years, the courses and mutations of the days, and the commandments and teachings" (chap. 23). Enoch writes them all down in 360 books. Then God himself tells him how he created the world. The account is very different from that of Genesis. "All creation" which God wished to create is contained in a stone in the belly of "the very great Adoil," and the foundation of creation is brought forth by another mythical monster Arouchaz. Enoch is then given thirty days to transmit what he has learned to his children.

The purpose of Enoch's revelation is stated by God in chaps. 33–35 (Vaillant, chap. 12). His writings are to survive the impending flood, which will come upon humanity because of idolatry, injustice, and fornication. They will be the means of salvation for humanity after the flood. The instructions of Enoch to his sons and the assembled multitude have their basis in the cosmology and eschatology revealed in the course of his ascent. In content, they are remarkably humanistic: they are mainly concerned with such matters as clothing the naked and feeding the hungry. There are warnings against idolatry, but the most striking theme is the insistence that whoever offends "the face of a man" offends the face of God (44:1; compare 52:6; 60:1). This ethic is grounded in creation: God made man in his own likeness (44:1). Likewise Enoch reminds Methusalem and his brothers of the relation between man and beast established at creation, but this in turn is linked directly to the judgment, when even the souls of the animals will accuse mankind (chap. 58). The sin of idolatry is shown by Enoch's experience of the sole authority of God in the heavens and the fact that all the heavenly hosts acknowledge his supremacy (33:7). Yet the appeal to the order of creation is balanced throughout by an appeal to the coming judgment. When Enoch returns to earth he begins by summarizing the mysteries he has learned (39-55). The account of the secrets of nature culminates in the assertion that "before man was, a judgment place was prepared for him" (49:2), and the moral instructions, complete with blessings and curses, are given in the light of that assertion for "all this will be laid bare in the weighing scales and on the books on the day of the great judgment" (52:15). Similarly, in the course of the ascent, the places of reward and punishment in the third heaven provide the occasion for lists of virtues and vices. Cosmology and eschatology, then, are complementary factors which support the ethical message of the book. Indeed, eschatology is built in to the cosmology of 2 *Enoch*, since provision for the judgment is an integral part of creation from the beginning.

Unlike many of the apocalypses we have reviewed, 2 *Enoch* does not appear to have been written in the context of any great historical crisis. We are not told why Enoch is weeping and grieving in the opening chapter. We may infer from the words attributed to God in chaps. 33-35 that the underlying problem is the sinful conduct of humanity, which will provoke the flood.[37] The threat of the flood, of course, pertains to the time of the pseudepigraphical visionary Enoch, but it carries the implication of another judgment now to come. The problem, however, is no more specific than human sinfulness, the prevalence of idolatry and injustice. 2 *Enoch*, then, has the character of a reflection on the human situation in general. As such it constitutes a kind of wisdom book.

The wisdom of Enoch is apocalyptic wisdom, which posits a supernatural revelation not normally accessible to humanity. It shares with the Jewish wisdom tradition the conviction that right conduct depends on right understanding. For right understanding, however, it is necessary to go beyond the bounds of normal human experience to discover the order of creation, the geography of the heavens and the nature of the final judgment. This revelation not only transcends the scope of traditional, proverbial wisdom. It also bypasses the Mosaic covenant. Enoch goes to the source of creation. No account is taken of a special history of Israel. It is noteworthy too that the moral exhortations do not mention the peculiarly Jewish laws such as circumcision or dietary regulations. The broadly humanistic insistence on justice and dignity conforms rather to the common ethic of Hellenistic Judaism and is distinguished as Jewish only by its prohibition of idolatry and its reliance on the authority of the Jewish sage Enoch.

In view of the general nature of the instructions of Enoch it seems very unlikely that this work is the product of a conventicle or closed circle. The only element that suggests the practice of a special group is the peculiar requirement that the four legs of a sacrificial animal be tied together. Since this practice is contrary to the usage in the Mishnah, it has been thought to be "the accepted rite of a sect, which repudiated the sacrificial customs prevailing in Jerusalem."[38] The practice was common in Egypt, however, and the author of 2 *Enoch* may have assumed it in ignorance rather than repudiation of the custom in Jerusalem. In any case, 2 *Enoch* makes no attempt to promote membership in a distinct group.

The purpose of 2 *Enoch* is primarily hortatory. The illocutionary function of consolation, which is prominent in 4 Ezra and 2 *Baruch,* recedes here. Yet the impact of the book cannot be adequately appreciated if it is reduced to the ethical teaching. The ethics of 2 *Enoch* acquire their authority, ultimately "from the mouth of the Lord" (39:2). Yet the persuasive force of the apocalypse does not rely, as prophecy often does, on "the word of the Lord." It derives from the total view of the universe, guaranteed by the experience of Enoch— "this have my eyes seen from the beginning even to the end" (40:8). It is important that the places of judgment, reward, and punishment are already prepared and in existence, and are the potential objects of mystical experience such as Enoch's.[39] The eschatology is primarily concerned with the fate of the individual after death, but it also provides for a general judgment with cosmic effects. The individual cannot be divorced from society or from the cosmos. The synoptic view of cosmic order and of the place of the individual within it provides the basis for persuasion and also for consolation in the face of whatever distress may be encountered in the present time.

As in all the apocalypses, the conception of cosmic order in 2 *Enoch* involves a sharp division between the present world of normal human experience and the "other" transcendent world revealed to Enoch. Here the division is primarily in spatial terms, although the temporal dimension is also present in the expectation of the coming judgment. The persuasiveness of the book depends on the acceptance of, or belief in, the reality of the transcendent world. Faith, in the sense of insight into the heavenly world, is the underpinning of present action.

3 BARUCH

Unlike 2 *Enoch,* 3 *Baruch* takes its point of departure from a specific problem: Baruch is weeping over the captivity of Jerusalem. The analogy of situations strongly suggests that the real date of composition was after 70 c.e. Egyptian provenance is suggested primarily by the affinities with other products of Diaspora Judaism.[40] Some verses in chaps. 4 and 11–15 are clearly Christian, but the secondary character of the Christian redaction is obvious in chap. 4. The inserted verses give the vine a positive connotation, but the chapter still concludes by asserting that nothing good comes through it.

As in *2 Enoch*, an angel comes to escort Baruch through the heavens. In this case only five heavens are mentioned. It is uncertain whether this number is original or is an abbreviation of the more usual seven.[41] It is apparent that *3 Baruch* does not regard the fifth heaven as the highest, but this is as high as the visionary goes. The first two heavens are occupied respectively by those who built the tower of strife against God and those who gave counsel to build the tower. Both now have hybrid animal forms ("faces of oxen, horns of stags, feet of goats," etc.) The third heaven is the most complex. There Baruch sees a dragon which devours the bodies of the wicked, and Hades in the form of a monster which drinks from the sea. (In 5:1-3, Hades is simply the belly of the dragon.)[42] He also sees the vine, "the plant which led Adam astray" and hears of its sinful effects. He sees how the phoenix shields the world from the rays of the sun, and how the sun is defiled by witnessing the sins of humanity and must be purified every day. Finally, he sees the movements of the moon. The fourth heaven is occupied by a multitude of birds which sing the praise of the Lord. These are generally thought to represent the souls of the righteous.[43] The gate to the fifth heaven is closed, until Michael opens it to receive the prayers of men. Michael takes the merits of humanity in baskets up to God in a higher heaven. He returns with rewards for the meritorious and a stern insistence that those who have no merits fail through their own fault. Baruch is then returned to earth.

3 Baruch contains no testament or farewell address to serve as the vehicle for its hortatory message. That message is conveyed in the course of the revelations especially by the lists of vices; those associated with the vine and those which defile the sun in chap. 4, and those reported by the angels in chap. 13. Most of the sins are commonplace—murder, adultery, etc.— but the special blame attached to the vine gives the book an ascetic accent. The hortatory aspect of the book derives from the fact that those who sin "are surrendering themselves to eternal fire" (4:16). The moral, that one should do otherwise, is clearly implied.

In *3 Baruch*, however, the illocutionary function of consolation has a clearer role than in *2 Enoch* and predominates over the exhortation. Baruch is initially grieving over the fall of Jerusalem at the hands of the Gentiles: "Lord, why did you set your vineyard on fire, and lay it waste?" The angel's response to his distress is remarkable: "Understand, O man greatly beloved, and do not trouble yourself so greatly over the destruction of Jerusalem. . . . Come and I will show you the mysteries of God." The mysteries of God are the five heavens through which Baruch is then guided. The heavenly tour does not so much answer Baruch's questions as distract from them by placing the problems in the broader perspective of the structure of the entire universe. This process has been described as an "apocalyptic cure."[44] The grief of the Jew after the destruction of 70 C.E. is given fictional expression in the story of Baruch. Both author and reader can then imaginatively identify with Baruch in his ascent through the heavens. The wonders of "the mysteries of God" allay the original grief and fear, and so at the end we are caught up with Baruch in glorifying God. The problem is resolved in a manner similar to what we have seen in 4 Ezra, not by rational argument but by concentration on wonderful revelations.

Three elements in the revelations respond directly to Baruch's original grief. First, he witnesses the punishment of the builders of the tower—that is, the Babylonians. Presumably these find their counterparts in the Romans. It is noteworthy, however, that they are not said to be punished for destroying Jerusalem but for cruelty in imposing the labor of brick making, even on a woman in the hour of childbirth,[45] and for attempting to discover the nature of heaven. We may see here an indictment of Rome for arrogance and oppression, but this is not in itself the cause of the fall of Jerusalem.

Second, the vine is singled out as the tree that led Adam astray. In chap. 1, however, Israel, or Jerusalem, is the vineyard of God. If the symbolism is used consistently, the implications are stunning.[46] If no good comes through the vine, no good can come through the vineyard either. This would amount to a definitive rejection of Jerusalem, unparalleled in Jewish literature, which might, however, be seen as the culmination of a tendency in Diaspora Judaism.[47] There is no explicit allusion to Jerusalem (or the vineyard) in the discussion of the vine in chap. 4, and so we cannot be certain of the implication, but this interpretation of the symbolism would throw much light on the angel's advice not to trouble oneself about the salvation of Jerusalem. There is certainly no hint of a restoration of Jerusalem in 3 Baruch, and in this regard it differs sharply from 4 Ezra and 2 Baruch.

The third passage that bears on Baruch's opening question is found in chap. 16. Michael reports the pronouncement of God on those who had no merits: "Be not sad of countenance and weep not, nor let the sons of men alone. But since they angered me in their works, go and make them envious and angry and provoked against a people that is no people, a people that has no understanding. Further, besides these, send for the caterpillar and the unwinged locust, and the mildew. . . . For they did not hearken to my voice, nor did they observe my commandments. . . ."[48] The covenantal overtones of this passage are obvious; 16:2 is "a paraphrase, verging on a quotation of the LXX of Deuteronomy 32:21."[49] The people of whom the

Jews are now envious and against whom they are angry—chiefly the Romans—are a people that is no people and has no understanding. Yet this slighting of the Gentiles involves no absolution for Jerusalem. The Jews are provoked in this way because they as a people had no merits to present to God (although the righteousness of individuals like Baruch is surely presumed). The covenant has been broken and there is no hint that it will be restored. Instead it is replaced with a system of individual rewards and punishments. This position might be seen as the logical culmination of the kind of analysis advanced by Ezra in 4 Ezra 3–9. In this context the salvation of Jerusalem is of little significance.

The resolution of Baruch's distress depends on the reality of the heavenly world disclosed in the visions. *3 Baruch* does not even seem to envisage a public general judgment as 2 Enoch did. The individualized judgment of the dead is presented as the solution to the public historical crisis of the fall of Jerusalem. The eschatology, in turn, is integrated into a total view of the universe, the credibility of which is enhanced by the wealth of cosmological detail. The system of judgment is not merely future but is already in operation. Human conduct and historical crises must be related to an understanding of the cosmic order, but this understanding in turn depends on supernatural revelations and so in effect becomes a matter of belief or of imagination about a transcendent world.

THE TESTAMENT OF ABRAHAM

The final apocalypse of the Hellenistic Diaspora is the *Testament of Abraham*. [50] In this case the generic classification is disputed. [51] Abraham's heavenly journey is only one episode in the story of his death and is narrated in the third person (so the work is not strictly pseudepigraphical). Yet the apocalypse proper is not merely a subordinate element but provides the crucial revelation on which the story turns. What is important here is not so much to decide whether the *Testament of Abraham* should be labeled an "apocalypse" as to understand how Abraham's ascent and vision of the judgment function in the context of the whole narrative. In no case can the work be said to be a "testament." Indeed Abraham conspicuously fails to make a testament. [52]

The *Testament of Abraham* is preserved in two recensions. While both may go back to a common original, the longer form (Recension A) provides the more coherent outline of the story. [53] The original language was most probably Greek. [54] Egyptian provenance is supported by parallels in Egyptian mythology (e.g., the weighing of the souls) and in Egyptian Jewish literature (e.g., the *Testament of Job*). [55] The date is usually put in the first century C.E. on the basis of parallels to other Hellenistic Jewish writings, but clear evidence is lacking.

The *Testament of Abraham* takes as its point of departure the end of Abraham's life, when the archangel Michael is sent to announce his death. The opening chapters illustrate the virtue of Abraham, so that Michael "cannot pronounce the mention of death to that righteous man, for I have not seen his like upon the earth—merciful, hospitable, just, truthful, pious, refraining from any evil action" (chap. 4). Yet when Abraham learns Michael's identity and mission he refuses to go with him but requests to see "the whole of the inhabited world and all the creations" while still in the body (chap. 9). He is then taken in the cherubim chariot and shown the whole world, and he is then brought to the gate of heaven to witness the judgment. Yet when he is returned to earth in chap. 15 he still refuses to go. Then Death is sent to him in disguise (chap. 16). Abraham still refuses to go and asks for further revelations—this time the true nature of Death and all his metamorphoses. Finally Death has to take Abraham by deceit, by inducing him to kiss his hand. The angels convey his soul to heaven. There is evident parallelism between the mission of Michael and the heavenly tour, on the one hand, and the mission of Death and his revelations, on the other.[56]

The most striking feature of the *Testament of Abraham* is the patriarch's reluctance to die. His refusal to obey the divine command in this regard, despite protestations of his loyalty (e.g., chap. 9), not only constitutes "a veritable parody on the biblical and traditional Abraham"[57] but also is highly ironic in view of Michael's admiration of his righteousness. The point of this irony is related to the underlying problem of the work, which is that "the common inexorable bitter cup of death" (chap. 1) comes upon all, including Abraham. If Abraham stands apart from the rest of humankind by his righteousness, he at least shares the instinctive human denial of death. He becomes then a figure with whom we can identify, so that by following through his (fictional) experience we can experience an "apocalyptic cure" for the fear of death.

For those who believe in a judgment of the dead the fear of death is often bound up with fear of the judgment, as Epicurus already knew. Consequently, the revelations to Abraham in the course of his ascent bear directly on the judgment. This motif is introduced already in the overview of the earth. When Abraham sees thieves and fornicators he prays that they be destroyed on the spot, and so they are. God is moved to bid Michael turn the chariot back: "For behold, Abraham has not sinned and he has no mercy upon the sinners. I, in contrast, made the world, and I do not wish to destroy any one of them but I await the death of the sinner, until he turns and lives" (chap. 10). Then at the first gate of heaven Abraham sees the grief of Adam "mourning over the destruction of the wicked, for the lost are many but the saved are few" (chap. 11). The judgment itself is a fearsome spectacle.[58] Angels with fiery whips drive hordes of souls to destruction. Abel, son of Adam, presides over the judgment[59] "looking like the sun, like a son of God," with recording angels on the right and on the left. Other angels weigh the souls in the balance and test them in fire. Abraham is told that this is only the first judgment. A second by the twelve tribes of Israel and a third by God himself will follow.

The catalysis in this revelation comes when a soul is found whose sins and righteous deeds are equally balanced. Abraham is moved to ask what it needs to be saved. He asks the angel to join him in prayer and the soul is saved. Abraham now repents of having had sinners destroyed during his tour. Most important, he recognizes that his previous zeal was sinful and prays for forgiveness.[60] He is forgiven and the sinners are restored to life. Abraham is informed that God does not requite in death those whom he destroyed living on the earth.

The tour on the chariot, then, is not a mere diversion, even though it does not persuade Abraham to yield up his soul. It puts the judgment of the dead in a new perspective. The number of the saved is still slight in proportion to the damned, as in 4 Ezra. The severity of the judgment is modified, however, by a number of considerations. First, intercession is possible. Abraham's prayer can supply the deficiency of a soul. (This was explicitly denied in 4 Ezra.) Second, God, as creator, has mercy on sinners and is less severe than a righteous human being like Abraham. He does not further punish those who have been destroyed on earth. We may add that Abraham is found to be a sinner after all, since his excessive zeal is offensive to God.

The revelations of the judgment scene also put the revelation of Death in perspective. Abraham sinned by destruction of life. Death boasts that he is "the destroyer of the world" and devastates the world for seven ages (symbolized by seven dragons' heads).[61] In all, there are seventy-two deaths, only one of which is the just death in its fitting hour. Yet, if God has mercy on those who die prematurely, the victory of Death is hollow. Consequently, Death, for all his hideous appearance, is no longer so terrible.

Of course the human fear of death persists. Some seven thousand servants die at the very sight of Death (they are later revived), and Abraham faints. Abraham continues to the end in his refusal to die. Yet the understanding provided by the revelation should mitigate the fear of death. Finally, the peaceful removal of Abraham's soul by the angels provides the concluding paradigm for those who follow in his footsteps.

The illocutionary function of the *Testament of Abraham* is primarily consolation. Ordinary mortals who fear death are reassured that this is only human—even Abraham was reluctant to go. Yet, if the fear is based on the judgment, there is more hope than we may have thought; and even

Abraham was not without sin. The book also has a hortatory message, which is implied in the experience of Abraham. Mercy, rather than severity, is pleasing to God. The apocalyptic ascent of Abraham to the place of judgment provides the crucial underpinning for both the consolation and the exhortation.

The *Testament of Abraham* differs from 2 *Enoch* and 3 *Baruch* in its lack of attention to cosmological detail. There is no sequence of numbered heavens here. Yet the scene of the judgment at the first gate of heaven is extremely important. The *Testament of Abraham* speaks only of the judgment of individuals, not of a general judgment which is to come. Belief in the judgment after death and in its present ongoing reality is a presupposition of the book that provides the context for the consolation and exhortation conveyed.

It is apparent that the technique of the *Testament of Abraham* is very similar to that of 3 *Baruch*. In both cases we can speak of an "apocalyptic cure" although the underlying problems are different—in 3 *Baruch* the fate of Jerusalem, in the *Testament of Abraham* the fear of death. Like 3 *Baruch* and 2 *Enoch*, the *Testament of Abraham* is remarkably tolerant and humane in its ethics, and there is no evidence whatever that it was produced by a sect or conventicle.[62] The open and tolerant atmosphere, coupled with irony and even humor, is quite different from the stereotypes of apocalypticism and indeed marks an extreme on the spectrum of apocalyptic writings. The lack of dualism and imminent expectation or eschatological fervor should not be taken to deny that the *Testament of Abraham* is apocalyptic in any sense. The importance of this work for the genre is that it shows how the common apocalyptic motifs of the heavenly journey and judgment scene can be used in the service of diverse viewpoints. The apocalyptic framework is not itself tied to a particular ideology. It rather constitutes the premises of argument, within which disagreement is still possible on specific matters, such as the possibility of intercession or the severity of the judgment. Belief in a transcendent world and judgment of the dead most often served to separate the sheep from the goats or sons of light from sons of darkness, but it was not necessarily so. The *Testament of Abraham* shows that these beliefs could also serve to enhance the sense of human solidarity, so that even the righteous Abraham is in need of mercy and has to submit to the common fate of death.

Epilogue:
The Legacy of
Jewish Apocalypticism

WE HAVE SEEN THAT the Jewish apocalypses were not produced by a single "apocalyptic movement" but constituted a genre that could be utilized by different groups in various situations. This genre was characterized by a conventional manner of revelation, through heavenly journeys or visions, mediated by an angel to a pseudonymous seer. It also involved a conceptual framework which assumed that this life was bounded by the heavenly world of the angels and by the prospect of eschatological judgment. The genre does not involve doctrinal consistency. The conceptual framework is a symbolic structure that can be given expression through different theological traditions and with varying emphases on the pattern of history or the cosmology of the heavenly regions. The apocalyptic revelation provides a comprehensive view of the world, which then provides the basis for exhortation or consolation. The problems to which these revelations are addressed vary in kind. An apocalypse can provide support in the face of persecution (e.g., Daniel); reassurance in the face of culture shock (possibly the Book of the Watchers) or social powerlessness (the Similitudes of Enoch); reorientation in the wake of historical trauma (2 Baruch, 3 Baruch), consolation for the dismal fate of humanity (4 Ezra) or comfort for the inevitability of death (the Testament of Abraham). The constant factor is that the problem is put in perspective by the otherworldly revelation of a transcendent world and eschatological judgment.

It should be apparent that there is only limited overlap between the Jewish apocalyptic literature and anthropological descriptions of millenarian movements.[1] Five traits of such movements have been singled out:

205

the promise of heaven on earth soon, the overthrow or reversal of the present social order, a terrific release of emotional energy, a brief life span of the movement, and the central role of a prophetic or charismatic leader.[2] "Heaven on earth" is only occasionally an accurate description of apocalyptic expectation and the apocalypses scarcely ever provide evidence of a charismatic leader. Hope for the imminent transformation of the social order is generally typical of the historical type of apocalypse, but even these can be taken to represent a movement only in a few cases (e.g., the early Enoch books, Daniel), and then we lack the independent evidence that would enable us to fill out the description of the presumed movement. The major apocalyptic movements from the period under consideration were the Qumran community and early Christianity. Neither was characterized by the production of apocalypses, but both shared in different degrees the apocalyptic world view.

THE SURVIVAL OF THE GENRE

Mention of Christianity brings us to the question of the legacy of Jewish apocalypticism. Despite frequent assertions to the contrary, the genre did not die out at the end of the first century C.E. It is poorly attested in rabbinic Judaism,[3] but various aspects of the tradition flourished in the Hekalot literature[4] and in messianic and eschatological expectation.[5] In Christianity, the genre proliferated, from the second century on.[6] Here again we may distinguish the "horizontal" eschatological concerns associated with the "pursuit of the millennium" in the Middle Ages and the "vertical" visionary literature which attained a literary afterlife through its adaptation in Dante's *Divine Comedy*.[7]

The main historical importance of Jewish apocalypticism, however, does not lie in the survival of the genre or in its influence on medieval Christianity. It lies rather in its role in the very origins of the Christian religion which has dominated the Western world for two millennia.

We return here to Ernst Käsemann's claim that apocalypticism is the mother of Christian theology. At the outset, some qualification is in order. Many other factors went into the making of Christianity, not least the charismatic personality of Jesus of Nazareth. Since Christianity in its earliest phase (pre-70 C.E.) did not produce apocalypses, it can be called an apocalyptic movement only in an extended sense, insofar as it shares the apocalyptic world view. The kind of movement that we find in early Christianity is not in any case a typical matrix for the apocalyptic genre. What is at issue in Käsemann's thesis is the degree to which the admittedly distinctive Christian movement was shaped by the view of the world which was most fully articulated in the apocalypses. While apocalypticism was not the only contributing factor, it was surely one crucial ingredient in the formation of the new religion. We cannot attempt a full analysis of the apocalyptic dimension of early Christianity here, but can only indicate some focal areas.

CHRISTIAN ORIGINS

The importance of apocalypticism for Christian origins centers on the most basic of all Christian beliefs, the resurrection of Jesus from the dead. The resurrection was never viewed as an isolated miracle but rather as a revelatory event that provided a new perspective on life and history. The new perspective could be articulated in various ways and in time was found to be compatible with various theological and philosophical systems. In the earliest stages of Christianity, however, the context in which the understanding of the resurrection developed was distinctly apocalyptic. This point can be illustrated by considering two major witnesses to early Christianity, the letters of Paul and the "Son of Man" passages in the Synoptic Gospels. In both illustrations, the major affinities of the New Testament are with the "historical" apocalypses of Daniel's type rather than with the otherworldly journeys of Enoch.

PAUL

The earliest discussion we have of the resurrection is provided by Paul in 1 Corinthians 15. His argument is striking, since he makes no mention of an empty tomb. Rather, he mentions the apparitions of Jesus to the apostles, to more than five hundred brethern at one time, and to Paul himself. Yet even the visions are not regarded as conclusive proof, for "if there is no resurrection of the dead, then Christ has not been raised" (1 Cor 15:13). An empty tomb or visions can be explained in various ways and cannot convince anyone who denies a priori that resurrection is possible. For Paul, the resurrection of Jesus is not an isolated event. It is not enough to believe that God could raise a privileged individual as he had taken Elijah up to heaven according to the Old Testament. Rather, Christ is the first fruits of those who have fallen asleep, and his resurrection is as fateful for humanity as the sin of Adam had been. In short, Paul argues that the resurrection of Jesus must be understood in the context of a general resurrection and presupposes a full scenario such as we find in the historical apocalypses.[8] Since one person has already been raised the rest cannot be far behind. The end is at hand. The urgency of this belief is apparent in 1 Cor 15:51–52: "Lo! I tell you a mystery. We shall not all sleep but we shall all be changed, in a moment, in the twinkling of an eye, at the last trumpet.

For the trumpet will sound, and the dead will be raised imperishable, and we shall be changed."

Paul's eschatological revelation is not given in the form of an apocalypse, but it is declared to be a *mystery*. The terminology is reminiscent of Qumran.[9] Paul presents himself as a "steward of the mysteries" (1 Cor 4:1). The mysteries are not only eschatological; they embrace the full plan of God which has hitherto been hidden: "Yet among the mature we do impart wisdom, although it is not a wisdom of this age or of the rulers of this age who are doomed to pass away. But we impart a secret and hidden wisdom of God, which God decreed before the ages for our glorification. None of the rulers of this age understood this. . . ." This wisdom is imparted not by men but by the spirit. The precise manner of revelation is not described in 1 Corinthians but in 2 Corinthians 12 Paul can boast of visions and revelations of the Lord: "I know a man in Christ who fourteen years ago was caught up to the third heaven—whether in the body or out of the body I do not know, God knows. And I know that this man was caught up into Paradise . . . and he heard things that cannot be told, which man may not utter." It would seem that Paul's revelatory experience embraced some of the media that we have found to be typical of the apocalypses.

The crucial element in Paul's revelation is the affirmation of another world and life, beyond this one: "If for this life only we have hoped in Christ, we are of all men most to be pitied" (1 Cor 15:18). Undoubtedly Paul felt, at least in the earlier part of his career, that this world would pass *soon*, even in his own lifetime. The most explicit assertion is found in 1 Thess 4:15-17: "we who are alive, who are left until the coming of the Lord, shall not precede those who have fallen asleep. For the Lord himself will descend from heaven with a cry of command, with the archangel's call, and with the sound of the trumpet of God. And the dead in Christ will rise first; then we who are alive, who are left, shall be caught up together with them in the clouds to meet the Lord in the air. . . ." That such imminent expectation was rampant in early Christianity can be seen from such passages as 2 Thessalonians 2 or Mark 13, which warn against premature eschatological excitement.

The lively sense that this world is passing away underlies much of Paul's practical theology. So he writes to the Corinthians: "I mean, brethren, the appointed time has grown very short, from now on let those who have wives live as though they had none, and those who mourn as though they were not mourning, and those who rejoice as though they were not rejoicing, and those who buy as though they had no goods, and those who deal with the world as though they had no dealings with it. For the form of this world is passing away" (1 Cor 7:29-31). Paul's advice on such matters as marriage and slavery is largely determined by this perspective.[10]

Even more basic, the apocalyptic perspective determined Paul's under-standing of salvation. The death of Jesus showed that salvation must be sought beyond this life in resurrection. The way to salvation was hence-forth to be like Christ: "Do you not know that all of us who have been baptized into Christ Jesus were baptized into his death? We were buried therefore with him by baptism into death, so that as Christ was raised from the dead by the glory of the Father, we too might walk in newness of life. For if we have been united with him in a death like his, we shall certainly be united with him in a resurrection like his" (Rom 6:3–5). In Daniel, the martyrs who lose their lives in this world are precisely those who shine like the stars in resurrection. The example of Jesus has evidently far greater force for Paul and becomes a normative example for Christians so that the death and resurrection of Jesus becomes an allegory for the pattern of Christian life. The new event of Jesus' death holds a central place in Paul's theol gy, but its significance is viewed in an apocalyptic context, insofar as it points the way to the resurrection.

THE SON OF MAN

The belief in the resurrection of Jesus led the early Christians to the con-viction that the end was at hand. It also led to new ideas of who Jesus was. The followers of Jesus searched the scriptures in the days after the cruci-fixion for anything that would make sense of the death of their leader. The messianic passages of the Old Testament must now be read in a new light, and the key was provided by the apocalyptic hope of resurrection.[11] Daniel had made sense of the death of the righteous martyrs by affirming that they would be resurrected. Now the shocking death of Jesus could be explained in the same way and the explanation found confirmation in the visions of the disciples. Jesus was not regarded as just another martyr, but as the messiah; and so the early Christians sought support for their beliefs in the prophecies of the Old Testament. The process is exemplified in Acts 2. There Psalm 16 ("For thou wilt not abandon my soul to Hades nor let thy holy one see corruption") is read in a novel way as a prophecy of the resur-rection of the messiah. Again, Psalm 110 ("The Lord said to my lord, sit at my right hand") is taken to mean that the messiah is exalted to the right hand of God in heaven. The exegetical method here is similar to that prac-ticed in the Qumran commentaries and shows no regard for the original historical context of the prophecies. Given the belief that Jesus was exalted to heaven it was inevitable that he would also be identified with the "one like a son of man" of Daniel. The sequence of associations is apparent in Stephen's vision in Acts 7: "Behold I see the heavens opened and the Son of Man standing at the right hand of God." In several passages in the

Synoptic Gospels the emphasis is on the future coming of Jesus as "Son of Man" on the clouds of heaven.

It is possible that Jesus used the expression "son of man" to refer to himself, as a circumlocution for "I" (e.g., "the son of man has nowhere to lay his head"),[12] but the belief that he would come again as Son of Man on the clouds of heaven presupposes both the resurrection and the ascension. Only when Jesus had gone up to heaven did it make sense to expect that he would come on the clouds. The expectation of the Son of Man was not only a belief that the end was coming. As in Daniel, the figure on the clouds is the vindicator of those who are buffeted in the present: "They will deliver you up to councils and you will be beaten in synagogues, . . . you will be hated by all for my name's sake . . . but in those days, after that tribulation, the sun will be darkened . . . and then they will see the Son of Man coming in clouds with great power and glory. And then he will send out the angels, and gather his elect from the four winds, from the ends of the earth to the winds of heaven" (Mark 13). In Matthew 25 the Son of Man sits on his throne of glory and presides over the final judgment. The assignment of judgment to the Son of Man marks a development over Daniel 7, but is paralleled in (and probably influenced by) the Similitudes of Enoch.

The identification of Jesus with the "Son of Man" in Daniel serves nicely to illustrate the blend of apocalyptic tradition and new experience that went into the formation of Christianity. In Daniel, the "one like a son of man" was a heavenly figure, most probably the archangel Michael. In Mark he is also a heavenly figure, but he has a different history, since he is identified with the man from Nazareth who was crucified. Jesus is a role model for the persecuted Christians in a way that Michael could never be for their Jewish ancestors.[13] Yet the Son of Man in Mark 13 comes in power and glory. He is not only a model for the Christians, but he is also the heavenly power that ensures their final triumph.

These few comments on Paul and the Son of Man passages may serve to indicate that apocalypticism is not a peripheral matter in the New Testament but bears on our understanding of the fundamentals of Christian faith. An adequate discussion of this issue would require no less than a full analysis of Christian origins. Here it must suffice to say that Käsemann's thesis, exaggerated though it be, cannot be lightly dismissed by Christian theology.

THE BOOK OF REVELATION

Even a cursory glance at early Christian apocalypticism such as this would be incomplete without some discussion of the book of Revelation. This is, of course, the book from which the genre apocalypse takes its name, and it is, as far as we now know, the first book that was explicitly presented as an *apokalypsis* (1:1). Whether or not this term was intended as a genre label, the revelation is characterized in a way that underlines its affinity with the Jewish apocalypses: it is mediated to John by an angel and concerns "what must soon take place." The content of Revelation is in fact focused on the eschatological scenario that culminates in the end of this world and the judgment of the dead. It also includes visions of the divine throne and elaborate mythological imagery reminiscent of Daniel. It is, in short, a full-blown apocalypse by the definition accepted in this study.

Nonetheless, one encounters occasional attempts to dispute "whether the Apocalypse is an apocalypse"[14] or at least to minimize its apocalyptic character and present it instead as a work of Christian prophecy.[15] Two aspects of Revelation have been especially controversial: first, the book is presented as a circular letter to the seven churches; and, second, it is not pseudonymous.

The epistolary formula in 1:4 ("John to the seven churches in Asia: Grace to you and peace . . .") underlines the hortatory character of Revelation, a point that is reinforced by the messages to the seven churches and by the command at the end not to seal up the book (22:10). All of this bears on the purpose of Revelation and the manner of its circulation. It does not at all clarify the internal literary structure of the book or its conceptual structure. (It is significant that the epistolary introduction comes *after* the work has been introduced as an apocalypse.) Moreover, we have found that the Jewish apocalypses commonly had a hortatory purpose and were intended for circulation, by whatever means. In this respect the contrast between Daniel, who is commanded to seal his book (12:4), and John, who is forbidden to do so, is more apparent then real. Daniel intends that the revelation be made public in the time of Antiochus Epiphanes (i.e., in the time of the real author). The apparent secrecy of sealing the book is an offshoot of the pseudonymity of Daniel and serves to explain why his book had not been in general circulation.[16]

Pseudonymity was a constant feature of the Jewish apocalypses. Since John is presumably the author's real name, Revelation is anomalous in this respect. The significance of this deviation is proportional to the importance of pseudepigraphy within the genre. Here it must be said that pseudepigraphy was basically a way of lending authority to a text, although it had other ramifications besides. It was not the sole basis for authority. A book like 4 Ezra claimed its authority primarily on the basis of the revelation given by the angel—and even, to a lesser degree, on the words of God himself. That the supposed recipient of this revelation was the venerable Ezra added to the authority. The need for such a pseudonym in a Jewish context has often been related to the decline of prophecy, at least to the diminished respect for prophecy in the postexilic period.[17] There was undoubtedly a renewal of prophecy in the eschatological fervor of early Christianity. Yet John does not speak directly in the name of the Lord. In all but the matter of pseudonymity he adheres to the apocalyptic manner of revelation—mediation by an angel, visions, even a brief suggestion of a heavenly ascent in 4:1. John referred to his work as "prophecy" (1:3; compare 22:7, 10) but evidently saw no tension between this designation and "apocalypse" (1:1). Prophecy is a very broad category, which could embrace the Jewish apocalypses and diverse oracular material. In literary form the closest parallels to Revelation are provided by the other apocalypses. The absence of pseudonymity is a very limited departure from the conventions of the genre, which has little bearing on the conceptual structure of the work.

Underlying the scholarly disputes about the genre of Revelation is the theological question whether Christian faith entailed a significant transformation of the genre as it had developed in Judaism. The answer to this question does not depend on a specific issue like pseudonymity but on the overall structure of Revelation.

After the prefatory letters to the seven churches, the revelations are associated with two heavenly scrolls.[18] The first is the scroll with seven seals which is opened by the Lamb. The opening of the seven seals is accompanied by a series of seven visions. The seven seals are followed by seven trumpets, accompanied by plagues and catastrophes. Then in chap. 10 the second scroll is introduced—a little scroll open in the hand of the angel. This scroll heralds a series of revelations that reflect more clearly the social and political context of the apocalypse. First there is an unnumbered series of visions, then the sequence of seven bowls, and finally another series of unnumbered visions, culminating in the new heaven and new earth of chap. 21. The successive series of visions, both those associated with the seals, trumpets, and bowls and the unnumbered series, display an eschatological pattern of crisis, including persecution, judgment and salvation. The concluding chapters provide by far the most elaborate account of the judgment and salvation and constitute a grand finale for the eschatological drama. Revelation envisages a complex scenario that weaves together different strands of Jewish eschatological tradition. First Satan is confined for a thousand years, while the martyrs return to life and reign with Christ. Then Satan is released for a final assault on the saints, but he, Death, Hades, and all the damned are thrown into the lake of fire. The general resurrection and judgment are followed by the revelation of the new heaven and new earth.

Throughout these revelations the heavenly backdrop of the earthly actions is kept constantly in view. The scroll with the seven seals is introduced in a vision of the divine throne and heavenly court. The supernatural dimension is perhaps most obvious in chap. 12, where the dragon, or Satan, is thrown from heaven by the Archangel Michael. The force of evil on earth, which for John is embodied in the Roman Empire, is represented by mythological allusions to beasts in chap. 13, which draw on the imagery of Daniel. It is clear that the beasts derive their power from the dragon. Angels play a prominent role throughout. Before the resurrection, the souls of the martyrs are kept "under the altar" in heaven, waiting for the Lord to "judge and avenge our blood on those who dwell upon the earth" (6:10).

Revelation, then, shares the typical apocalyptic view of the world as the arena of angels and demonic powers in the present and subject to a definitive eschatological judgment. The problem addressed by Revelation, the present sovereignty of Rome, is put in perspective by this view of the world. Christ is the firstborn of the dead, and his death and resurrection are held to inaugurate the eschatological era. Consequently, history is foreshortened in Revelation. There is no extended review of history in the guise of prophecy, such as we had in Daniel.[19] Interest is focused on the period between the death of Jesus and the end. Yet the contrast with an apocalypse such as Daniel should not be exaggerated. The eschatological age which has begun is the age of eschatological woes, as can be seen clearly in chap. 12. It is not a period of proleptic fulfillment but corresponds rather to the reign of the fourth beast in Daniel. The tension between present and future results from the contrast between the *vision* of the future and the experience of the present. In this respect Revelation is no different from Daniel or the Similitudes of Enoch (which also lacks the extended "prophecies" of past history).[20]

The distinctively Christian character of Revelation derives not from its view of history but from the central role of Jesus Christ. Even here the transformation of the genre is not as great as we might expect. Christ combines the roles of revealer (in part) and of heavenly warrior and judge, but these roles are conceived in accordance with Jewish tradition. The portrayal of Christ as the rider whose robe is dipped in blood and who rules the nations with a rod of iron (Revelation 19) is not based on the stories or deeds of Jesus of Nazareth but on traditional portrayals of the divine warrior or of the messiah.[21] The manner in which Jesus assumes roles that had been defined in Jewish contexts is clear in Revelation 12: Michael and his angels fight the dragon and throw him down from heaven, but the victory is ascribed to Christ.[22] The substitution of Christ for Michael does have significant implications, however. The death and exaltation of Jesus is now the means by which the dragon is cast down and provides a paradigmatic model for Christians. They too can defeat the dragon if they are "washed in the blood of the lamb" and are prepared to lay down their lives. Consequently, the martyrs are the ones who are raised to reign with Christ in the first resurrection. The example of Jesus makes it possible for his followers to relinquish the world, even their own lives, in the hope of

ultimate exaltation. Detachment from this world, in the hope of the glory
that is above or is to come, is a common characteristic of the Jewish apocalypses. Revelation is especially reminiscent of Daniel, where the *maśkîlîm*
who submit to death in the persecution are singled out to shine like the
stars in the resurrection. The difference in Revelation is that the impulse
to martyrdom, and to the rejection of this world, is intensified by the
example of Jesus, who achieved his victory by his crucifixion.[23] The impact
of Christ then is to intensify an element that was already present in the
Jewish genre.

Our remarks on Revelation, as on the New Testament in general, are intended only to indicate the degree to which Jewish apocalypticism shaped
the presuppositions of early Christianity. Too often New Testament
scholars use a caricature of the Jewish apocalyptic literature as a foil to
display supposedly distinctive features of Christianity. The distinctiveness
is usually diminished when the comparative material is understood in its
own right. A study of Christian apocalypticism fully informed by the study
of the apocalyptic genre remains an urgent *desideratum*.

THEOLOGICAL IMPLICATIONS

For Christian theology, at least, the contemporary relevance of the genre
emerges most clearly when we appreciate its influence on the foundational
writings of Christianity. The most obvious implication of the study of the
genre concerns the nature of apocalyptic language. Paul's scenario for the
rapture in 1 Thessalonians and the multiple formulations of cosmic
destruction in Revelation are *tours de force* of the imagination just as much
as Enoch's heavenly journey. No one would now regard the visions of
Enoch as accurate descriptions of a world above the sky or reliable predictions of a time to come. The very multiplicity of apocalyptic visions, even
within a single book like Revelation, should prevent us from taking any one
of them in a simple and absolute way.

The language of the apocalypses is not descriptive, referential news-
paper language, but the *expressive* language of poetry, which uses symbols
and imagery to articulate a sense or feeling about the world. Their abiding
value does not lie in the pseudoinformation they provide about cosmology
or future history, but in their affirmation of a transcendent world. Even
if the physical universe were to endure forever, there is no doubt that the
social and cultural worlds we inhabit are constantly crumbling. Christianity
inherited from the Jewish apocalypses a way of affirming transcendent
values, those things we should affirm even when the world around us col-
lapses. Beyond the thresholds of life and of this world we can only see as
in a glass darkly. The apocalyptic revelations are symbolic attempts to

penetrate the darkness, which provide ways of imagining the unknown, not factual knowledge. The value of these imaginative ventures cannot be assessed by a correspondence theory of truth, but only by evaluating the actions and attitudes which they supported. The measure of Daniel's visions is not whether Antiochus died or the resurrection followed in the manner predicted, but whether the *maśkîlîm* did well to lay down their lives in adherence to their faith.

Apocalyptic language is not only expressive; it also has a pragmatic aspect. We have seen that apocalypses typically exhort and console. They do not take the stance of a neutral observer, but take and urge a very definite point of view. In the words of 4 Ezra, we are asked to let ourselves be persuaded. Accordingly, apocalyptic language is *commissive* in character: it commits us to a view of the world for the sake of the actions and attitudes that are entailed. This aspect of apocalyptic language has not been adequately appreciated by theologians. The apocalyptic literature does not lend itself easily to the ontological and objectivist concerns of systematic theology. It is far more congenial to the pragmatic tendency of liberation theology, which is not engaged in the pursuit of objective truth but in the dynamics of motivation and the exercise of political power.[24]

There are, of course, enormous differences between the view of the world advanced in the apocalypses and that of any modern liberationist. The apocalypses often address the issues of political and social liberation, but they conspicuously lack a program for effective action. While the Maccabees took up arms against Antiochus Epiphanes, the "action" of the *maśkîlîm* in Daniel was to instruct the masses and wait for the victory of Michael. In the wake of the destruction of Jerusalem, 4 Ezra and 3 *Baruch* divert their attention to the mysteries of God. The visionaries were seldom revolutionaries. Their strong sense that human affairs are controlled by higher powers usually limited the scope of human initiative. The apocalyptic revolution is a revolution in the imagination. It entails a challenge to view the world in a way that is radically different from the common perception. The revolutionary potential of such imagination should not be underestimated, as it can foster dissatisfaction with the present and generate visions of what might be. The legacy of the apocalypses includes a powerful rhetoric for denouncing the deficiencies of this world.[25] It also includes the conviction that the world as now constituted is not the end. Most of all it entails an appreciation of the great resource that lies in the human imagination to construct a symbolic world where the integrity of values can be maintained in the face of social and political powerlessness and even of the threat of death.

Abbreviations

AB	Anchor Bible
ANET	*Ancient Near Eastern Texts Relating to the Old Testament,* edited by J. B. Pritchard. 3d ed. Princeton: Princeton University Press, 1969.
ANRW	*Aufstieg und Niedergang der römischen Welt,* edited by W. Haase and H. Temporini. Berlin: de Gruyter.
APOT	*The Apocrypha and Pseudepigrapha of the Old Testament,* edited by R. H. Charles. 2 vols. Oxford: Clarendon, 1913.
AUSS	*Andrews University Seminary Studies*
BA	*Biblical Archaeologist*
BASOR	*Bulletin of the American Schools of Oriental Research*
Bib	*Biblica*
BJRL	*Bulletin of the John Rylands University Library of Manchester*
BR	*Biblical Research*
BZ	*Biblische Zeitschrift*
BZNW	Beihefte zur ZNW
CBA	Catholic Biblical Association of America
CBQ	*Catholic Biblical Quarterly*
CBQMS	Catholic Biblical Quarterly Monograph Series
EJ	*Encyclopedia Judaica*
FOTL	The Forms of Old Testament Literature
HDR	Harvard Dissertations in Religion
HR	*History of Religions*
HSM	Harvard Semitic Monographs
HTR	*Harvard Theological Review*
HTS	Harvard Theological Studies
HUCA	*Hebrew Union College Annual*
IDBSup	*The Interpreter's Dictionary of the Bible: Supplementary Volume,* edited by Keith Crim et al. Nashville: Abingdon, 1976.

IEJ	*Israel Exploration Journal*
Int	*Interpretation*
JAAR	*Journal of the American Academy of Religion*
JBL	*Journal of Biblical Literature*
JCS	*Journal of Cuneiform Studies*
JJS	*Journal of Jewish Studies*
JNES	*Journal of Near Eastern Studies*
JSHRZ	Jüdische Schriften aus hellenistisch-römischer Zeit
JSJ	*Journal for the Study of Judaism*
JSNT	*Journal for the Study of the New Testament*
JSOT	*Journal for the Study of the Old Testament*
JSOTSup	Journal for the Study of the Old Testament—Supplement Series
JSS	*Journal of Semitic Studies*
JTC	*Journal for Theology and the Church*
JTS	*Journal of Theological Studies*
LCL	Loeb Classical Library
LXX	Septuagint
MT	Masoretic Text
NTS	*New Testament Studies*
OTM	Old Testament Message
OTS	*Oudtestamentische Studien*
PVTG	Pseudepigrapha Veteris Testamenti Graece
RB	*Revue biblique*
RHR	*Revue de l'histoire des religions*
RelStudRev	*Religious Studies Review*
RQ	*Revue de Qumrân*
RSR	*Recherches des science religieuse*
SBLDS	Society of Biblical Literature Dissertation Series
SBLMS	Society of Biblical Literature Monograph Series
SBT	Studies in Biblical Theology
SVTP	Studia in Veteris Testamenti Pseudepigrapha
TDNT	*Theological Dictionary of the New Testament.* 10 vols. Grand Rapids: Eerdmans, 1964–76.
TLZ	*Theologische Literaturzeitung*
VT	*Vetus Testamentum*
VTSup	Vetus Testamentum Supplements
ZAW	*Zeitschrift für die alttestamentliche Wissenschaft*
ZNW	*Zeitschrift für die neutestamentliche Wissenschaft*
ZThK	*Zeitschrift für Theologie und Kirche*

Notes

Chapter 1: The Apocalyptic Genre

1. E. Käsemann, "The Beginnings of Christian Theology," *JTC* 6 (1969) 40.
2. K. Koch, *Ratlos vor der Apokalyptik*. English trans. *The Rediscovery of Apocalyptic*.
3. G. Ebeling, "The Ground of Christian Theology," *JTC* 6 (1969) 51.
4. M. E. Stone, "Lists of Revealed Things in the Apocalyptic Literature," in *Magnalia Dei: The Mighty Acts of God*, ed. F. M. Cross et al., 439-43; P. D. Hanson, "Apocalypse, Genre," "Apocalypticism,"*IDBSup*, 27-34. See the comments of M. A. Knibb, "Prophecy and the emergence of the Jewish apocalypses," in *Israel's Prophetic Tradition: Essays in Honour of Peter Ackroyd*, ed. R. Coggins et al., 160-61. Knibb, like Stone, prefers a twofold distinction between the apocalypses and apocalyptic eschatology.
5. F. Lücke, *Versuch einer vollständigen Einleitung in die Offenbarung Johannis und in die gesamte apokalyptische Literatur*. For the early discussions of apocalyptic literature see J. M. Schmidt, *Die jüdische Apokalyptik*, and P. D. Hanson, "Prolegomena to the Study of Jewish Apocalyptic," in *Magnalia Dei*, 389-413. A sampling of the older (and some recent) literature can be found in *Apokalyptik*, ed. K. Koch and J. M. Schmidt. More recent essays are collected in *Visionaries and Their Apocalypses*, ed. P. D. Hanson. Much of the relevant literature can be found in J. H. Charlesworth, ed., *The Old Testament Pseudepigrapha*.
6. M. Smith, "On the History of *Apokalyptō* and *Apokalypsis*," in *Apocalypticism in the Mediterranean World and the Near East*, ed. D. Hellholm, 9-20.
7. *The Cologne Mani Codex: "Concerning the Origin of his Body,"* trans. R. Cameron and A. J. Dewey, 47-62 (pp. 36-48). The codex dates from the late fourth or early fifth century C.E.
8. A. Fowler, "The Life and Death of Literary Forms," *New Literary History* 2 (1971) 199-216. The metaphor of life and death suggests too organic a view of forms and genres, but the insight into phases of development remains valid.
9. *Apocalypse: The Morphology of a Genre*, ed. J. J. Collins.
10. Analysis of the Christian material in *Semeia* 14 was contributed by A. Yarbro Collins, the Gnostic material by F. T. Fallon, the Greco-Roman material by H. W. Attridge and the rabbinic Jewish material by A. J. Saldarini.
11. G. von Rad argued that "apocalyptic" is not a single genre but rather a *mixtum compositum* of smaller forms (*Theologie des Alten Testaments*, 2:330). It is true that any apocalypse contains several subsidiary forms—visions, prayers, exhortations, etc. This fact cannot preclude the presence of a generic framework that holds these elements together. In the case of a composite work like Daniel we can still claim that the apocalypse is the

dominant form of the book. For discussion of the constituent forms see J. J. Collins, *Daniel, with an Introduction to the Apocalyptic Literature.*

12. This list may be regarded as a refinement of the more diverse characteristics of the apocalyptic writings presented and discussed by D. S. Russell, *The Method and Message of Jewish Apocalyptic,* 104–39.

13. In this respect it also differs from the "family resemblance" approach advocated by J. G. Gammie, "The Classification, Stages of Growth and Changing Intentions in the Book of Daniel," *JBL* 95 (1976) 192–93. Gammie is correct in insisting that a broader corpus of related literature is relevant to the discussion.

14. A few Christian apocalypses, most notably Revelation and Hermas, are not pseudonymous.

15. L. Hartman, "Survey of the Problem of Apocalyptic Genre," in *Apocalypticism,* ed. D. Hellholm, 329–43; D. Hellholm, *Das Visionenbuch des Hermas als Apokalypse,* 14–95; M. Gerhart, "Generic Studies: Their Renewed Importance in Religious and Literary Interpretation," *JAAR* 45 (1977) 309–25.

16. E. D. Hirsch, Jr., *Validity in Interpretation,* 68–102.

17. E. P. Sanders, "The Genre of Palestinian Jewish Apocalypses," in *Apocalypticism,* ed. D. Hellholm, 447–59.

18. M. E. Stone, "Lists of Revealed Things"; idem, *Scriptures, Sects and Visions;* I. Gruenwald, *Apocalyptic and Merkavah Mysticism;* C. Rowland, *The Open Heaven.*

19. See the remarks of B. McGinn on the later Christian use of apocalyptic rhetoric in support of the empire and papacy (*Visions of the End,* 33–36).

20. Rowland, *The Open Heaven;* J. Carmignac, "Qu'est-ce que l'Apocalyptique? Son emploi à Qumrân," *RQ* 10 (1979) 3–33; H. Stegemann, "Die Bedeutung der Qumranfunde für die Erforschung der Apokalyptik," in *Apocalypticism,* ed. D. Hellholm, 495–530.

21. Compare Rowland, *The Open Heaven,* 14: "To speak of apocalyptic, therefore, is to concentrate on the theme of the direct communication of the heavenly mysteries in all their diversity." Rowland later (p. 50) posits a threefold structure of legends, visions, and admonitions, but neither the legends nor the admonitions are consistent features of the genre.

22. Rowland, *The Open Heaven,* 29, 71. J. Carmignac argues that the term "eschatology" is too diffuse to be of any service ("Les Dangers de l'Eschatologie," *NTS* 17 [1971] 365–90).

23. J. J. Collins, "Apocalyptic Eschatology as the Transcendence of Death," *CBQ* 36 (1974) 21–43.

24. Rowland, *The Open Heaven,* 29–37, 71.

25. Koch, *The Rediscovery of Apocalyptic,* 28–33.

26. Stone, "Lists of Revealed Things," 440, 443.

27. Hanson, *IDBSup,* 30.

28. For elaboration of the following section see my forthcoming essay, "The Apocalyptic Literature in Recent Scholarly Study," in *Early Judaism and Its Modern Interpreters,* ed. R. A. Kraft and G. W. E. Nickelsburg.

29. In addition to his monumental *Apocrypha and Pseudepigrapha of the Old Testament,* Charles published editions of *1 Enoch, Ascension of Isaiah, 2 Baruch, Jubilees, Testaments of the Twelve Patriarchs, Assumption of Moses,* and (with W. R. Morfill) *2 Enoch.*

30. Cited by J. Barr, "Jewish Apocalyptic in Recent Scholarly Study," *BJRL* 58 (1975) 32 (from the *Dictionary of National Biography* [1931–1940] 170).

31. Cited by Barr, "Jewish Apocalyptic," 31.

32. Ibid.

33. H. H. Rowley, *The Relevance of Apocalyptic;* D. S. Russell, *Method and Message.*

34. Barr, "Jewish Apocalyptic," 32.

35. Preface to A. Lacocque, *The Book of Daniel,* xxii–xxiii.

36. N. Perrin, "Eschatology and Hermeneutics: Reflections on Method in the Interpretation of the New Testament," *JBL* 93 (1974) 3–14. See my critique, "The Symbolism of Transcendence in Jewish Apocalyptic," *BR* 19 (1974) 5–22.

37. H. Gunkel, *Schöpfung und Chaos in Urzeit und Endzeit;* idem, "Das vierte Buch Esra," *Die Apokryphen und Pseudepigraphen des Alten Testaments,* ed. E. Kautzsch, 2:331–401. See

J. M. Schmidt, *Die jüdische Apokalyptik*, 195-204; Hanson, "Prolegomena," 393-96.

38. On the various nonreferential aspects of biblical language see G. B. Caird, *The Language and Imagery of the Bible.*

39. L. Hartman, *Asking for a Meaning: A Study of 1 Enoch 1-5*, 22.

40. J. W. Rogerson, *Myth in Old Testament Interpretation.*

41. Hooke, "The Myth and Ritual Pattern in Jewish and Christian Apocalyptic," *The Labyrinth*, 213-33; Bentzen, *Daniel*; Mowinckel, *He That Cometh.*

42. Hanson, "Jewish Apocalyptic against its Near Eastern Environment," *RB* 78 (1971) 31-58; Cross, "New Directions in the Study of Apocalyptic," *JTC* 6 (1969) 157-65.

43. For elaboration of the following see my essay "Apocalyptic Genre and Mythic Allusions in Daniel," *JSOT* 21 (1981) 83-100.

44. F. M. Cross, *Canaanite Myth and Hebrew Epic.*

45. For example, W. Bousset, *Die Religion des Judentums im späthellenistischen Zeitalter.*

46. Von Rad, *Theologie*, 2:315-30. A connection between wisdom and the apocalyptic literature was proposed as early as 1857 by L. Noack.

47. H.-P. Müller, "Mantische Weisheit und Apokalyptik," in *Congress Volume: Uppsala 1971*, VTSup 22, 268-93; J. J. Collins, *The Apocalyptic Vision of the Book of Daniel*, 67-88; J. VanderKam, *Enoch and the Growth of an Apocalyptic Tradition*, chap. 3. Note also the critique of von Rad by P. von der Osten-Sacken, *Die Apokalyptik in ihrem Verhältnis zu Prophetie und Weisheit.*

48. M. Hengel, *Judaism and Hellenism*, 1:210-18.

49. J. J. Collins, "Cosmos and Salvation: Jewish Wisdom and Apocalyptic in the Hellenistic Age," *HR* 17 (1977) 121-42.

50. Rowland, *The Open Heaven*, 205-8.

51. Koch, *The Rediscovery of Apocalyptic*, 21.

52. R. Knierim, "Old Testament Form Criticism Reconsidered," *Int* 27 (1973) 441.

53. Ibid., 438. Knierim suggests that "myth" may be considered such a genre.

54. Ibid., 464.

55. P. Vielhauer, "Apocalypses and Related Subjects," in *New Testament Apocrypha*, ed. E. Hennecke and W. Schneemelcher, 2:598.

56. Ibid.

57. Hartman, "Survey"; Hellholm, *Das Visionenbuch*, 1:52-58. The term is taken from J. L. Austin, *How to do Things with Words*, 98-108.

58. P. D. Hanson, *The Dawn of Apocalyptic.*

59. Hanson, *IDBSup*, 33.

60. H. Gese, "Anfang und Ende der Apokalyptik dargestellt am Sacharjabuch," *ZThK* 70 (1973) 20-49; R. North, "Prophecy to Apocalyptic via Zechariah," in *Congress Volume: Uppsala 1971*, VTSup 22, 47-71. The visions lack the transcendent eschatology of the apocalypses.

61. M. A. Knibb regards Zechariah 1-8 as an apocalypse but admits that its form is inchoate ("Prophecy and the emergence of the Jewish apocalypses," 175). His claim that the visions express an eschatology, however, requires a very broad definition of that term.

62. For a different view see L. Greenspoon, "The Origin of the Idea of Resurrection," in *Traditions in Transformation*, ed. B. Halpern and J. Levenson, 247-321.

63. For contrasting assessments of Isaiah 24-27 see W. R. Millar, *Isaiah 24-27 and the Origin of Apocalyptic*; and J. Vermeylen, *Du prophète Isaïe à l'Apocalyptique*, 1:349-81.

64. J. T. Milik, *The Books of Enoch*, 5-7. Milik (p. 31) further argues that these Enochic books are presupposed in Genesis, but his arguments have been widely rejected.

65. Ibid., 36-37. On Enoch's association with Galilee see G. W. E. Nickelsburg, "Enoch, Levi and Peter: Recipients of Revelation in Upper Galilee," *JBL* 100 (1981) 575-600.

66. Milik, *Books of Enoch*, 13-18, 29-30. P. Grelot, "La géographie mythique d'Hénoch dans les apocryphes et dans la Bible: Son origine et signification," *RSR* 46 (1958) 5-26 and 181-210; Stone, *Scriptures, Sects and Visions*, 39; and most recently VanderKam, *Enoch.*

67. Above, n. 47.

68. VanderKam, *Enoch*, chap. 3: "However similar Mesopotamian divination and Jewish apocalypticism may be in some respects, they certainly have not produced comparable literature."

69. A. K. Grayson and W. G. Lambert, "Akkadian Prophecies," *JCS* 18 (1964) 7–30; W. W. Hallo, "Akkadian Apocalypses," *IEJ* 16 (1966) 231–42. Hallo's designation "apocalypses" has been generally rejected. For sober evaluations see W. G. Lambert, *The Background of Jewish Apocalyptic*; S. A. Kaufman, "Prediction, Prophecy and Apocalypse in the Light of New Akkadian Texts," in *Proceedings of the Sixth World Congress of Jewish Studies, 1973*, ed. A. Shinan, 221–28; VanderKam, *Enoch*, chap. 3.

70. A. K. Grayson, *Babylonian Historical-Literary Texts*, 6.

71. Ibid., 21; Lambert, *The Background of Jewish Apocalyptic*, 13.

72. VanderKam notes that dream reports about otherworldly travel also fall within the province of divination, but he adds that these are generally of consequence only to the dreamer himself (*Enoch*, chap. 3).

73. For a review of the subject, with extensive bibliography, see G. Widengren, "Leitende Ideen und Quellen der iranischen Apokalyptik," in *Apocalypticism*, ed. D. Hellholm, 77–162; A. Hultgård, "Das Judentum in der hellenistisch-römischen Zeit und die iranische Religion— ein religionsgeschichtliches Problem," *ANRW* 19/1, ed. W. Haase, 512–90; and with a different interpretation H. G. Kippenberg, "Die Geschichte der Mittelpersischen Apokalyptischen Traditionen," *Studia Iranica* 7 (1978) 49–80.

74. See J. Tavadia, *Die Mittelpersische Sprache und Literatur der Zarathustrier;* M. Boyce, "Middle Persian Literature," in *Handbuch der Orientalistik*, vol. 4/1, 31–66.

75. B. T. Anklesaria, *Zand-ī Vohuman Yasn*. See G. Widengren, "Iran and Israel in Parthian Times with Special Regard to the Ethiopic Book of Enoch," in *Religious Syncretism in Antiquity*, ed. B. Pearson, 115; Hultgård, "Das Judentum," 525–26.

76. Kippenberg argues that the schema of twelve thousand years was derived from the Babylonian zodiac and cannot be earlier than the fourth century B.C.E. ("Die Geschichte," 53).

77. J. G. Griffiths, *Plutarch's De Iside et Osiride*, 193.

78. Diogenes Laertius *Proem* 6–9. Hultgård, "Das Judentum," 543.

79. J. R. Hinnells, "The Zoroastrian Doctrine of Salvation in the Roman World: A Study of the Oracle of Hystaspes," in *Man and His Salvation: Studies in Memory of S. G. F. Brandon*, ed. E. J. Sharpe and J. R. Hinnells, 125–48.

80. Kippenberg, "Die Geschichte," 74.

81. Hinnells, "The Zoroastrian Doctrine of Salvation," 145–46. The Persian character of the oracle was established by H. Windisch, *Die Orakel des Hystaspes*. See also C. Colpe, "Der Begriff 'Menschensohn' und die Methode der Erforschung messianischer Prototypen," *Kairos* 12 (1970) 81–112.

82. Hultgård, "Das Judentum," 524–48; Widengren, "Iran and Israel," 110–24.

83. M. Haug and E. W. West, *The Book of Arda Viraf*.

84. Hultgård, "Das Judentum," 527–28; Widengren, "Iran and Israel," 126–27.

85. For further material see Collins, "The Persian Apocalypses," *Semeia* 14 (1979) 207–17.

86. See the classic study of J. Bidez and F. Cumont, *Les Mages Hellénisés*.

87. D. Flusser, "The four empires in the Fourth Sibyl and in the Book of Daniel," *Israel Oriental Studies* 2 (1972) 148–75.

88. F. Cumont, *Astrology and Religion among the Greeks and Romans*, 3–21. On the Chaldeans see Diodorus Siculus 2.29–31; Philo *Mig. Abr.* 32 (178–81); *Quis Heres* 20 (96–99).

89. For elaboration of the following see my articles "Cosmos and Salvation," and "Jewish Apocalyptic against its Hellenistic Near Eastern Environment," *BASOR* 220 (1975) 27–36.

90. Attridge, "Greek and Latin Apocalypses," *Semeia* 14 (1979) 162–67; Hengel, *Judaism and Hellenism*, 1:210–17. On the motif in general see C. Colpe, "Die Himmelsreise der Seele ausserhalb und innerhalb der Gnosis," in *Le Origini dello Gnosticismo*, ed. U. Bianchi, 429–47. For Greek parallels on the afterlife, heaven, and the netherworld see T. F. Glasson, *Greek Influence on Jewish Eschatology*.

91. On this material see H. D. Betz, "The Problem of Apocalyptic Genre in Greek and Hellenistic Literature: The Case of the Oracle of Trophonius," in *Apocalypticism*, ed. D. Hellholm, 577-97.

92. Attridge, "Greek and Latin Apocalypses," 168-70; Hengel, *Judaism and Hellenism*, 1:181-202.

93. A. W. Mair, *Callimachus, Lycophron and Aratus.* The poem is Alexandrian and dates to either the third or the early second century B.C.E.

94. C. C. McCown, "Hebrew and Egyptian Apocalyptic Literature," *HTR* 18 (1925) 357-411. On the earlier material see J. Assmann, "Königsdogma und Heilserwartung. Politische und kultische kaosbeschreibungen in altägyptischen Texten," in *Apocalypticism*, ed. D. Hellholm, 345-77.

95. F. Daumas, "Littérature prophétique et exégétique égyptienne et commentaires esséniens," in *À la rencontre de Dieu: Mémorial Albert Gelin*, ed. A. Barucq, 203-21.

96. On *Bocchoris* and the *Potter's Oracle* see L. Koenen, "The Prophecies of a Potter: A Prophecy of World Renewal Becomes an Apocalypse," in *Proceedings of the Twelfth International Congress of Papyrology*, ed. D. H. Samuel, 249-54; F. Dunand, "L'Oracle du Potier et la formation de l'apocalyptique en Egypte," *L'Apocalyptique*, 39-67.

97. So Koenen, "The Prophecies of a Potter."

98. See further J. Z. Smith, "Wisdom and Apocalyptic," in *Religious Syncretism in Antiquity*, ed. B. Pearson, 136-37.

99. J. Z. Smith, "Native Cults in the Hellenistic Period," *HR* 11 (1971) 236-49.

100. For exploratory studies see R. R. Wilson, "This World—and the World to Come," *Encounter* 38 (1977) 117-24; J. G. Gager, *Kingdom and Community: The Social World of Early Christianity.*

101. Compare R. R. Wilson, "From Prophecy to Apocalyptic: Reflections on the Shape of Israelite Religion," *Semeia* 21 (1981) 79-95. Contrast C. Münchow, *Ethik und Eschatologie*, 143-48.

102. W. Schmithals, *The Apocalyptic Movement* (the original German title was *Die Apokalyptik: Einführung und Deutung*).

103. Wilson claims that apocalyptic groups arise in situations of deprivation ("From Prophecy to Apocalyptic," 84-85).

104. G. W. E. Nickelsburg, "Social Aspects of Palestinian Jewish Apocalypticism," in *Apocalypticism*, ed. D. Hellholm, 639-52.

105. J. Z. Smith, "Wisdom and Apocalyptic," 140.

106. Von Rad, *Theologie*, 2:316.

107. M. Stone, "Apocalyptic—Vision or Hallucination," *Milla wa-Milla* 14 (1974) 47-56; Rowland, *The Open Heaven*, 214-47; S. Niditch, "The Visionary," in *Ideal Figures in Ancient Judaism*, ed. G. W. E. Nickelsburg and J. J. Collins, 153-79.

108. B. M. Metzger, "Literary Forgeries and Canonical Pseudepigrapha," *JBL* 91 (1972) 3-24.

109. Charles, *APOT*, 2:ix.

110. Hanson, *The Dawn of Apocalyptic*, 252.

111. See further my discussion in *The Apocalyptic Vision of the Book of Daniel*, 67-74.

112. Rowland, *The Open Heaven*, 243; J. Lindblom, *Prophecy in Ancient Israel.* D. S. Russell appealed to the supposedly Hebrew notions of corporate personality and contemporaneity to suggest a quasi-mystical identification with the pseudonymous hero (*Method and Message*, 132-39).

113. M. Eliade, *Shamanism: Archaic Techniques of Ecstasy*, 266; R. R. Wilson, *Prophecy and Society in Ancient Israel*, 54-56.

114. D. Hellholm, "The Problem of Apocalyptic Genre and the Apocalypse of John," in *Society of Biblical Literature 1982 Seminar Papers*, ed. K. H. Richards, 168. Hellholm would accept the emended version as a "paradigmatic" definition. He is primarily concerned with developing a "syntagmatic" approach, but its significance cannot be assessed until publication of the second volume of his dissertation.

115. Compare *Semeia* 14, pp. 9, 12. On the hortatory function of the apocalypses see further Münchow, *Ethik und Eschatologie*. An exception is found in *Testament of Levi* 3–5, where the primary purpose is to lend authority to the priesthood of Levi.

Chapter 2: The Early Enoch Literature

1. R. H. Charles, *APOT*, 2:168–70; also *The Book of Enoch*. This is one of the few instances in which Charles's division of an apocalyptic book has stood the test of time.

2. Text and translation: M. A. Knibb, *The Ethiopic Book of Enoch*. See also the textual information provided by E. Isaac, "1 Enoch," in *The Old Testament Pseudepigrapha*, ed. J. H. Charlesworth, 1:6, 10–12.

3. M. Black, *Apocalypsis Henochi Graece*. Extracts from the Greek and Latin literature were known before the discovery of the Ethiopic text.

4. J. T. Milik, *Books of Enoch*, 4. On the Book of the Giants that was preserved and adapted in Manichaeism, see Milik, *Books of Enoch*, 298–339. Milik's conclusions on the late date of the Similitudes will be discussed in a later chapter.

5. So D. Dimant, "The Biography of Enoch and the Books of Enoch," *VT* 33 (1983) 14–29.

6. *Books of Enoch*, 7. On the identification of the fragments see J. VanderKam, *Enoch*, chap. 4.

7. See M. E. Stone, "The Book of Enoch and Judaism in the Third Century, B.C.E.," *CBQ* 40 (1978) 479–92; idem, *Scriptures, Sects and Visions*, 31.

8. So RSV, but see VanderKam, who argues that *'ĕlōhîm* ("God") should be translated "angels" (*Enoch*, chap. 2). Compare Dimant, "Biography of Enoch," 21.

9. For the following compare VanderKam, *Enoch*, chap. 2; P. Grelot, "La Légende d'Hénoch dans les apocryphes et dans la Bible: Son origine et signification," *RSR* 46 (1958) 5–26, 181–210. Less reliable is H. Ludin Jansen, *Die Henochgestalt*.

10. G. Widengren, *The Ascension of the Apostle and the Heavenly Book*, 7–8; W. G. Lambert, "Enmeduranki and Related Matters," *JCS* 21 (1967) 126–38; VanderKam, *Enoch*, chap. 2.

11. R. Borger, "Die Beschwörungsserie Bīt Mēseri und die Himmelfahrt Henochs," *JNES* 33 (1974) 183–96.

12. *ANET*, 95.

13. Ibid.

14. M. Braun, *History and Romance*; J. J. Collins, *Between Athens and Jerusalem: Jewish Identity in the Helenistic Diaspora*, chap. 1.

15. Ps.-Eupolemus *PE* 9.17.2–9.

16. For bibliography and much of the following discussion see my article "The Apocalyptic Technique: Setting and Function in the Book of the Watchers," *CBQ* 44 (1982) 91–111; also G. W. E. Nickelsburg, "The Books of Enoch in Recent Research," *RelStudRev* 7 (1981) 210–17.

17. J. VanderKam, "Enoch Traditions in Jubilees and other Second-Century Sources," in *Society of Biblical Literature 1978 Seminar Papers*, ed. P. J. Achtemeier, 1:235, despite the demurral of Dimant, "Biography of Enoch," 23.

18. Milik, *Books of Enoch*, 25.

19. On the theophanic tradition and its mythical allusions see F. M. Cross, *Canaanite Myth and Hebrew Epic*, 100–105.

20. L. Hartman, *Asking for a Meaning*. Compare the thesis of E. P. Sanders that *1 Enoch* shares the pattern of "covenantal nomism" (*Paul and Palestinian Judaism*). C. Münchow recognizes that the law is placed in a wider context in *1 Enoch* (*Ethik und Eschatologie*, 39–40).

21. G. W. E. Nickelsburg, "Apocalyptic and Myth in 1 Enoch 6–11," *JBL* 96 (1977) 383–405; P. D. Hanson, "Rebellion in Heaven, Azazel and Euhemeristic Heroes in 1 Enoch 6–11," *JBL* 96 (1977) 195–233. The name 'Aśa'el is original in the Aramaic and presupposed by the Greek. The Ethiopic has Asael in 6:7 but Azazel elsewhere. The name Azazel is found in the

fragmentary "pesher on Azazel and the angels" (4Q180) at Qumran. See Milik, *Books of Enoch*, 248–52.

22. D. W. Suter, "Fallen Angel, Fallen Priest: The Problem of Family Purity in 1 Enoch 6–16," *HUCA* 50 (1979) 115–35.

23. Nickelsburg, *Jewish Literature between the Bible and the Mishnah*, 54; idem, "Enoch, Levi and Peter: Recipients of Revelation in Upper Galilee," *JBL* 100 (1981) 586–87.

24. 4QTLevi^a 8.3.6–7 is cited by Milik as the earliest allusion to the Book of the Watchers (*Books of Enoch*, 23–24). The context of the fragment is *Testament of Levi* 14. It refers to an accusation by Enoch, which presumably corresponds to his accusation against the Watchers and which is applied to the sons of Levi. The manuscript dates from the second century. In *Testament of Levi* 14:1 (Greek), Levi tells his sons that he has "learnt from the writing of Enoch that in the end ye will transgress against the Lord" and emphasizes sexual sins and marriage with Gentiles. The reference to the Watchers in CD 2:16 is not explicitly applied to the priesthood.

25. So, independently, J.-C. Picard, "Observations sur l'Apocalypse grecque de Baruch," *Semitica* 20 (1970) 87–90; J. G. Gager, *Kingdom and Community*, 54–55. See C. Lévi-Strauss, *Structural Anthropology*, 186–205.

26. For a succinct formulation of Lévi-Strauss's theory see E. Leach, "Lévi-Strauss in the Garden of Eden: An Examination of Some Recent Developments in the Analysis of Myth," in *Claude Lévi-Strauss: The Anthropologist as Hero*, ed. E. Nelson Hayes and Tanya Hayes, 51.

27. 1 Enoch 16:3. The Greek is corrupt here and reads "a mystery which was from God."

28. H. D. Betz, "On the Problem of the Religio-Historical Understanding of Apocalypticism," *JTC* 6 (1969) 146–54. Betz discusses parallels from the *Kore Kosmu* and the Pseudo-Clementine homilies.

29. I. Gruenwald, *Apocalyptic and Merkavah Mysticism*, 36; C. Rowland, "The Visions of God in Apocalyptic Literature," *JSJ* 10 (1979) 137–54.

30. For the biblical precedents and later elaborations see Gruenwald, *Apocalyptic and Merkavah Mysticism*, 29–72.

31. C. Rowland, *The Open Heaven*, 255.

32. Ibid., 124–26.

33. Milik, *Books of Enoch*, 25. This contention is supported by the apparent finality of 19:3: "And I Enoch alone saw the sight, the ends of everything; and no man has seen what I have seen."

34. Originally four compartments were envisaged. See the detailed treatment by M.-T. Wacker, *Weltordnung und Gericht: Studien zu 1 Henoch 22*.

35. Ibid., 132–233.

36. C. A. Newsom, "The Development of 1 Enoch 6–19; Cosmology and Judgment," *CBQ* 42 (1980) 310–29.

37. Widengren, *Ascension of the Apostle*, 10. The association of power and wisdom in the biblical tradition is especially conspicuous in Second Isaiah and Daniel 2–6, both of which have a Babylonian setting. On the heavenly tablets see further S. Paul, "Heavenly Tablets and the Book of Life," *Journal of the Ancient Near Eastern Society of Columbia University* 5 (1973) 345–53.

38. Milik, *Books of Enoch*, 19.

39. O. Neugebauer, *The Astronomical Chapters of the Ethiopic Book of Enoch (72–82): With Additional Notes on the Aramaic Fragments by M. Black*; also VanderKam, *Enoch*, chap. 2.

40. For example, R. T. Beckwith, "The Earliest Enoch Literature and its Calendar: Marks of their Origin, Date and Motivation," *RQ* 10 (1981) 365–403.

41. J. VanderKam, "The 364-Day Calendar in the Enochic Literature," *Society of Biblical Literature 1983 Seminar Papers*, ed. K. H. Richards.

42. VanderKam argues strongly that chap. 80, like 81, is a secondary addition, since the disruptions come before the new creation and so contradict 72:1 (*Enoch*, chap. 2). This is possible, but scarcely necessary, since it requires an unduly rigid consistency. We should note,

however, that chap. 80 is not attested at Qumran. If the Astronomical Book circulated without chaps. 80 and 81 it would lack the eschatological interest that is constitutive of an apocalypse.

43. Charles, *APOT*, 2:171. F. Dexinger, *Henochs Zehnwochenapokalypse und offene Probleme der Apokalyptikforschung*, 102.

44. M. Black, "The Apocalypse of Weeks in the Light of 4QEn^g," *VT* 28 (1978) 464-69.

45. *APOT*, 2:171.

46. So VanderKam, *Enoch*, chap. 6 and, more tentatively, Nickelsburg, *Jewish Literature*, 150. The theme of testifying is found also in chap. 81.

47. *Books of Enoch*, 248-51. See further P. J. Kobelski, *Melchizedek and Melchireša*, 49-51.

48. G. W. E. Nickelsburg, "The Apocalyptic Message of 1 Enoch 92-105," *CBQ* 39 (1977) 313-15.

49. On the basis of this passage VanderKam (*Enoch*, chap. 6) questions the appropriateness of the usual designation "10-week apocalypse," but the significant course of history is concentrated in the ten weeks.

50. Black, "The Apocalypse of Weeks in the Light of 4QEn^g," *VT* 28 (1978) 464-69.

51. On the social message of the Epistle see Nickelsburg, *Jewish Literature*, 145-51; idem, "Riches, the Rich and God's Judgment in 1 Enoch 92-105 and the Gospel According to Luke," *NTS* 25 (1979) 324-44. On the background of the period see M. Hengel, *Judaism and Hellenism*, 1:6-57.

52. Milik, *Books of Enoch*, 49.

53. Ibid., 49-51.

54. Ibid., 53. Note, however, that *Jubilees* combines a version of the Watchers story with a doctrine of the earthly origin of sin.

55. For the important links between the Epistle and the Wisdom of Solomon see Nickelsburg, *Resurrection, Immortality and Eternal Life in Intertestamental Judaism*, 112-30; L. Ruppert, *Der leidende Gerechte*, 70-105.

56. Charles, *APOT*, 2:170-71; Milik, *Books of Enoch*, 44; Nickelsburg, *Jewish Literature*, 93. See also D. Dimant, "History according to the Vision of the Animals (Ethiopic Enoch 85-90)," *Mhqry yrwšlym bmhšbt yśr'l* 2 (1982) 18-37 (in Hebrew).

57. For other examples of such transformation see J. H. Charlesworth, "The Portrayal of the Righteous as an Angel," in *Ideal Figures in Ancient Judaism*, ed. G. W. E. Nickelsburg and J. J. Collins, 135-47.

58. *APOT*, 2:255.

59. So LXX, supported by evidence from Qumran. The MT reads "sons of Israel." See P. W. Skehan, "A Fragment of the 'Song of Moses' (Deut 32) from Qumran," *BASOR* 136 (1954) 12-15.

60. See further VanderKam, *Enoch*, chap. 6.

61. Charles, *APOT*, 2:257; Milik, *Books of Enoch*, 43. See 2 Macc 4:33-35 and Dan 9:26.

62. Milik, *Books of Enoch*, 44; 2 Macc 11:6-12.

63. For a study of the terminology with special attention to parallels from Qumran, see Dexinger, *Henochs Zehnwochenapokalypse*, 164-77.

64. This point is emphasized by S. B. Reid, "1 Enoch: The Rising Elite of the Apocalyptic Movement," in *Society of Biblical Literature 1983 Seminar Papers*, ed. K. H. Richards.

65. G. W. E. Nickelsburg, "The Epistle of Enoch and the Qumran Literature," *JJS* 33 (1982) 333-48.

66. Hanson, "Rebellion in Heaven," 226.

67. The identification with Azazel is already made in a fragmentary Hebrew text from Qumran which speaks of Azazel and the angels (Milik, *Books of Enoch*, 251).

68. For example, M. D. Herr, "The Calendar," in *The Jewish People in the First Century*, ed. S. Safrai and M. Stern, 834-64.

69. J. VanderKam, "The Origin, Character and Early History of the 364-Day Calendar: A Reassessment of Jaubert's Hypotheses," *CBQ* 41 (1979) 390-411; idem, "2 Maccabees 6, 7a and Calendrical Change in Jerusalem," *JSJ* 12 (1981) 1-23. A. Jaubert held that the solar

calendar was official in the postexilic period but that lunar modifications had been introduced by the time of Ben Sira (*The Date of the Last Supper*).

70. P. R. Davies argues that the decrees of Antiochus suppressed the Jewish festivals and introduced pagan ones, which had no bearing on the Jewish cultic calendar (cf. 2 Macc 6:6) ("Calendrical Change and Qumran Origins: An Assessment of VanderKam's Theory," *CBQ* 45 [1983] 80–89).

71. Jaubert's argument for the official use of the solar calendar depends on implications in the priestly writings of the Old Testament, but this evidence does not necessarily bear on the official calendar of the third or second century. It has been disputed, moreover, by J. Baumgarten, "The Calendar in the Book of Jubilees and the Bible," in *Studies in Qumran Law*, 101–14. On the other hand, the apparent evidence for a lunar calendar in the Hebrew text of Sir 43:6–7 is not decisive either. The ancient versions say only that the sign for a festival is derived from the moon—possibly referring to the new moon. See further VanderKam, "The Origin, Character and Early History of the 364-Day Calendar," 409.

72. VanderKam, "The 364-Day Calendar in the Enochic Literature," in *Society of Biblical Literature 1983 Seminar Papers*, ed. K. H. Richards.

73. Trans. G. Vermes, *The Dead Sea Scrolls in English*, 97.

74. P. R. Davies, *The Damascus Covenant: An Interpretation of the "Damascus Document,"* 61–63.

75. Ibid., 83. Despite his dogmatic assertion that "the plain meaning of the text" refers to an exilic generation and not to another, more recent generation, Davies later admits that a sixth-century date is not required (p. 202), thereby undercutting his whole attempt to attach a chronological value to CD 3:12–13.

76. So also M. A. Knibb, "Exile in the Damascus Document," *JSOT* 25 (1983) 109–10.

77. Compare also *Testament of Moses* 4:8, but the interpretation is disputed.

78. See further M. A. Knibb, "The Exile in the Literature of the Intertestamental Period," *Heythrop Journal* 17 (1976) 253–72.

79. So especially J. Murphy-O'Connor, "The Essenes and their History," *RB* 81 (1974) 215–44, followed now by Davies.

80. Davies, *Damascus Covenant.*

81. So Davies.

82. So Murphy-O'Connor.

83. See the discussion of Knibb, who responds to the objection against the absolute use of *šûb* to indicate repentance ("Exile in the Damascus Document," 105–7).

84. In CD 7:19, "The star is the Interpreter of the Interpreter of the Law who will come to Damascus," the reference is again to the location of the community. Even Murphy-O'Connor allows that Damascus refers to Qumran in this case ("The Essenes and their History," 221–22). It remains unclear, however, why the expression "the land of the north" (CD 7:14) should be used, since it is not very appropriate for either Babylon or Qumran. Presumably it is synonymous with Damascus, as a place of exile.

85. Hengel, *Judaism and Hellenism*, 1:97.

86. J. J. Collins, *The Apocalyptic Vision of the Book of Daniel*, 201–5; G. W. E. Nickelsburg, "Social Aspects of Palestinian Jewish Apocalypticism," in *Apocalypticism*, ed. D. Hellholm, 639–52; P. R. Davies, "Hasidim in the Maccabean Period," *JJS* 28 (1977) 127–40.

87. V. Tcherikover, *Hellenistic Civilization and the Jews*, 197–203.

88. Ibid., 197.

89. J. P. Thorndike ("The Apocalypse of Weeks and the Qumran Sect," *RQ* 3 [1961] 163–84) argues that the Apocalypse of Weeks is a veiled history of the Qumran sect, but her position has been widely rejected.

90. VanderKam, "Enoch Traditions," 229–45.

91. There are also differences between the various Enochic books. According to the Animal Apocalypse (89:6) the offspring of the Watchers perish in the flood. *1 Enoch* 98:4–5 insists that sin has not been sent upon the earth, but humans created it. Both points implicitly contradict the Book of the Watchers.

92. See further M. Testuz, *Les Idées Religieuses du Livre des Jubilés*, 101–19; Nickelsburg, *Jewish Literature*, 73–80.

93. In the Ethiopic text Moses is sometimes said to write the book, sometimes the angel, but the confusion may be a problem of translation. VanderKam argues that in the original Hebrew Moses alone wrote down what the angel dictated ("The Putative Author of the Book of Jubilees," *JSS* 26 [1981] 209–17).

94. R. H. Charles, *The Book of Jubilees or the Little Genesis*, 25; VanderKam, *Textual and Historical Studies in the Book of Jubilees*, 262–63.

95. The tradition that the law was given by angels is found in the New Testament (Acts 7:53; Gal 3:19; Heb 2:2).

96. It is interesting to note that the *Testament (Assumption) of Moses* picks up where *Jubilees* leaves off. The title "Testament of Moses" precedes a quotation from *Jubilees* in the Catena of Nicephorus (Charles, *APOT*, 2:2). A connection between the two works is possible, but very hypothetical.

97. Nickelsburg, *Resurrection*, 31–33; G. L. Davenport, *The Eschatology of the Book of Jubilees*, 32–46.

98. Testuz, *Les Idées Religieuses*, 75–92; VanderKam, *Textual and Historical Studies*, 265–67.

99. Charles, *APOT*, 2:2. The title "Apocalypse of Moses" is more commonly applied to a variant of the *Life of Adam and Eve* (Nickelsburg, *Jewish Literature*, 253–56).

100. Testuz, *Les Idées Religieuses*, 12.

101. Compare Rowland, *The Open Heaven*, 51–52.

102. VanderKam, *Textual and Historical Studies*, 217–24.

103. Ibid., 258–80; Testuz, *Les Idées Religieuses*, 179–95; K. Berger, *Das Buch der Jubiläen*, 295–98.

104. VanderKam, *Textual and Historical Studies*, 283. Compare Testuz, *Les Idées Religieuses*, 33; A. Jaubert, *La notion d'alliance dans le Judaisme*, 93–94, 115, 475.

105. The Qumran fragments require a date prior to 100 B.C.E. Nickelsburg prefers a date about 168 since *Jubilees* 23 contains no allusion to Antiochus Epiphanes (*Jewish Literature*, 77; compare J. A. Goldstein, "Jewish Acceptance and Rejection of Hellenism," in *Jewish and Christian Self-Definition*, ed. E. P. Sanders, A. I. Baumgarten, and A. Mendelson, 2:64–87). B. Z. Wacholder also argues for a date before the revolt (*The Dawn of Qumran*, 41–42). Berger argues for a date between 145 and 140 (*Das Buch der Jubiläen*, 300). Davenport distinguishes three stages: the body of the work is dated prior to the Maccabean revolt; 1:4b–26, part of 1:29, 23:14–31, and 50:5 are dated to 166–160; 1:27–28 and a few other verses were added later (*Eschatology*). The reasons for this division are not compelling.

Chapter 3: Daniel

1. For a bibliographic survey see K. Koch, *Das Buch Daniel*.

2. For a recent formulation of the conservative arguments see G. F. Hasel, "The Book of Daniel: Evidences Relating to Persons and Chronology," *AUSS* 19 (1981) 37–49; idem, "The Book of Daniel and Matters of Language: Evidences Relating to Names, Words, and the Aramaic Language," *AUSS* 19 (1981) 211–25.

3. See the classic discussion by H. H. Rowley, *Darius the Mede and the Four World Empires;* also L. F. Hartman and A. A. DiLella, *The Book of Daniel*, 46–54.

4. J. J. Collins, *The Apocalyptic Vision of the Book of Daniel*, 46–48; A. Lacocque, *The Book of Daniel*, 74–75; Hartman and DiLella, *The Book of Daniel*, 178–80.

5. For example, Hasel argues that since Cyrus did not assume the title "King of Babylon" for about nine months, this is evidence for Darius as a historical person. In fact, it provides no evidence whatever for Darius. Hasel also construes a fragmentary Babylonian text to imply a lapse into madness by Nebuchadnezzar.

6. J. Day, "The Daniel of Ugarit and Ezekiel and the Hero of the Book of Daniel," *VT* 30 (1980) 174–84. The name Dânêl is given to an angelic figure in *1 Enoch* 6:7 and 69:2.

7. P. M. Casey, "Porphyry and the Origin of the Book of Daniel," *JTS* 27 (1976) 15–33.

8. There is, however, an ongoing tradition of conservative scholarship that holds to the exilic date, for example, J. G. Baldwin, *Daniel: An Introduction and Commentary.*

9. D. W. Gooding is, to my knowledge, unique in holding that chaps. 1–5 and 6–12 constitute two symmetrical halves ("The Literary Structure of the Book of Daniel and its Implications," *Tyndale Bulletin* 32 [1981] 43–79).

10. J. T. Milik, "'Prière de Nabonide' et autres écrits d'un cycle de Daniel," *RB* 63 (1956) 407–15; R. Meyer, *Das Gebet des Nabonid.*

11. Milik ("'Prière de Nabonide'") also published an Apocalypse of Pseudo-Daniel (4QpsDan), which he dates about 100 B.C.E. and which involves a court setting and a prophecy of history. This work may be modeled on the canonical Daniel or may be derived independently from the Daniel tradition.

12. The main defender of a Maccabean date for the whole book was H. H. Rowley, "The Unity of the Book of Daniel," in *The Servant of the Lord and Other Essays on the Old Testament,* 237–68.

13. So, recently, Hartman and DiLella, *The Book of Daniel,* 14–15.

14. See further, Collins, *Apocalyptic Vision,* 11–19.

15. A. Lenglet, "La structure littéraire de Daniel 2–7," *Bib* 53 (1972) 169–90.

16. For fuller treatment see Collins, *Apocalyptic Vision,* 27–65; idem, *Daniel, 1 & 2 Maccabees,* 20–68; J. A. Montgomery, *The Book of Daniel,* 113–281. P. R. Davies argues for a closer relationship between the tales and the visions ("Eschatology in the Book of Daniel," *JSOT* 17 [1980] 33–53). See my response in "Apocalyptic Genre and Mythic Allusions in Daniel," *JSOT* 21 (1981) 83–100.

17. S. Niditch and R. Doran, "The Success Story of the Wise Courtier: A Formal Approach," *JBL* 96 (1977) 179–93.

18. Compare Deutero-Isaiah, which carries on a recurring polemic against Chaldean wise men. See Collins, *Apocalyptic Vision,* 44–45; P. von der Osten-Sacken, *Die Apokalyptik in ihrem Verhältnis zu Prophetie und Weisheit,* 18–27; J. G. Gammie, "On the Intention and Sources of Daniel I–VI," *VT* 31 (1981) 282–92.

19. W. Lee Humphreys nuances his conclusion differently ("A Life-Style for the Diaspora: A Study of the Tales of Esther and Daniel," *JBL* 92 [1973] 211–23).

20. A. L. Oppenheim, *The Interpretation of Dreams in the Ancient Near East.*

21. E. L. Ehrlich, *Der Traum im Alten Testament;* A. Resch, *Der Traum im Heilsplan Gottes.*

22. H.-P. Müller, "Mantische Weisheit und Apokalyptik," in *Congress Volume: Uppsala 1971,* VTSup 22, 268–93. Note the critique of dreams in Sir 31:1–8 (34:1–8); also 40:5–7.

23. So Niditch and Doran, "Success Story," 192.

24. In Hesiod the iron generation is the fifth. The fourth generation is not associated with a metal.

25. D. Flusser, "The four empires in the Fourth Sibyl and in the Book of Daniel," *Israel Oriental Studies* 2 (1972) 167. Flusser's article provides the fullest treatment of the four kingdoms.

26. J. W. Swain, "The Theory of the Four Monarchies: Opposition History under the Roman Empire," *Classical Philology* 35 (1940) 1–21.

27. J. J. Collins, "The Place of the Fourth Sibyl in the Development of the Jewish Sibyllina," *JJS* 25 (1974) 365–80.

28. On Near Eastern resistance to Hellenism see the colorful, but not always reliable, account of S. K. Eddy, *The King is Dead.*

29. G. Widengren, "Iran and Israel in Parthian Times, with Special Regard to the Ethiopic Book of Enoch," in *Religious Syncretism in Antiquity,* ed. B. A. Pearson, 91–92; Eddy, *The King is Dead,* 19. Also such older scholars as R. Reitzenstein and F. Cumont. Chapter 3 of the *Bahman Yasht* has a variant of this vision with seven branches instead of four. M. Boyce suggests that the sevenfold schema developed under Babylonian influence and chap. 1 is more purely Iranian ("Middle Persian Literature," in *Handbuch der Orientalistik,* 4/1:49).

30. E. Bickermann, *Four Strange Books of the Bible*, 62–63; P. R. Davies, "Daniel Chapter Two," *JTS* 27 (1976) 392–401.

31. So Collins, *Apocalyptic Vision*, 36–43.

32. Dan 2:38, which is certainly Jewish, echoes Jer 27:6, where God declares that he has given Nebuchadnezzar the beasts of the field to serve him, but this is far from presenting his reign as a golden age. Jewish perceptions of Nebuchadnezzar in the Hellenistic period are reflected in the book of Judith.

33. Collins, *Apocalyptic Vision*, 41; Eddy, *The King is Dead*, 125–27.

34. A. K. Grayson, *Babylonian Historical-Literary Texts*, 14–15.

35. G. F. Hasel, "The Four World Empires of Daniel 2 Against Its Near Eastern Environment," *JSOT* 12 (1979) 17–30.

36. Grayson, *Babylonian Historical-Literary Texts*, 17.

37. Grayson cites *Sib. Or.* 3:381–87 as another possible Babylonian oracle, but this is doubtful (*Babylonian Historical-Literary Texts*, 18).

38. Hasel argues that there was no fixed schema and that Daniel 2 is in some respects closer to the *Dynastic Prophecy* than to the other four kingdom passages ("Four World Empires"). However, while the schema Assyria–Media–Persia was not universal, it was widespread; and it can explain the inclusion of Media in Daniel, whereas the Babylonian prophecy cannot. Grayson sees the closest parallels in Daniel not in Daniel 2 but in 8:23–25 and 11:3–45 (*Babylonian Historical-Literary Texts*, 21). So also W. G. Lambert, *The Background of Jewish Apocalyptic*.

39. S. A. Kaufman, "Prediction, Prophecy and Apocalypse in the Light of New Akkadian Texts," in *Proceedings of the Sixth World Congress of Jewish Studies, 1973*, ed. A. Shinan, 224. The "prophecy" is *ex eventu* down to this point. The "son" in question is apparently Nebuchadnezzar's son Amel-Marduk. His dynasty was in fact short-lived. See further P. Höffken, "Heilszeitherrscherwartung im babylonischen Raum," *Die Welt des Orients* 9 (1977) 57–71.

40. For contrasting interpretations of the conflict see, on the one hand, V. Tcherikover (*Hellenistic Civilization and the Jews*, 191–203) and M. Hengel (*Judaism and Hellenism*, 1:267–314), who argue that the fighting first broke out among the Jews, and on the other hand F. Millar ("The Background to the Maccabean Revolution: Reflections on Martin Hengel's 'Judaism and Hellenism,'" *JJS* 29 [1978] 1–21) and J. A. Goldstein (*1 Maccabees*, 104–60), who argue that Antiochus initiated it.

41. On the development of the apocalyptic vision see K. Koch, "Vom profetischen zum apokalyptischen Visionsbericht," in *Apocalypticism*, ed. D. Hellholm, 413–46. See further S. Niditch, *The Symbolic Vision in Biblical Tradition*.

42. Persian influence is chronologically possible but remains uncertain in both Zechariah and Daniel. H. S. Kvanig claims to have identified an Akkadian background for Daniel 7, but the parallels are very tenuous ("An Akkadian Vision as Background for Daniel 7," *Studia Theologica* 35 [1981] 85–89).

43. See further Collins, *Apocalyptic Vision*, 96–97.

44. F. M. Cross, *Canaanite Myth and Hebrew Epic*, 112–20. Note also J. Day, "The Old Testament Utilisation of Language and Imagery Having Parallels in the Baal Mythology of the Ugaritic Texts" (diss., Cambridge, 1977).

45. So Hartman and DiLella, *The Book of Daniel*, 211.

46. A. J. Ferch objects that "the sea and beasts are interpreted as the earth and four kings or kingdoms, not as chaos symbols" ("Daniel 7 and Ugarit: A Reconsideration," *JBL* 99 [1980] 75–86). This is to confuse different levels of meaning, as if one were to say that an object is not red but a box. See my critique of Ferch in "Apocalyptic Genre and Mythic Allusions in Daniel," 91–94.

47. J. A. Emerton, "The Origin of the Son of Man Imagery," *JTS* 9 (1958) 225–42: "The act of coming with clouds suggests a theophany of Yahweh himself. If Dan vii 13 does not refer to a divine being, then it is the only exception out of about seventy passages in the OT" (231–32).

48. For the following see Cross, *Canaanite Myth and Hebrew Epic,* 112–20 (on Baal); 13–43 (on El); Collins, *Apocalyptic Vision,* 100–101.

49. Cross, *Canaanite Myth and Hebrew Epic,* 16; M. Pope, *El in the Ugaritic Texts,* 32.

50. For a summary and development of the distinction of separate sources in Daniel 7 on form-critical grounds see R. Kearns, *Vorfragen zur Christologie II,* 3–51. See my critique of this approach in *Apocalyptic Vision,* 127–32.

51. For a review of possible mythological backgrounds and defense of the Canaanite hypothesis see C. Colpe, "Ho huios tou anthrōpou," *TDNT,* 8:408–20. Kearns gives the Canaanite hypothesis a new twist insofar as he holds that the expression usually translated "son of man" (*bar 'nāšā'*) is a corrupted form of an old Semitic term *bnš,* which was used as an epithet of Baal (*Vorfragen zur Christologie*).

52. The arguments of Ferch against the relevance of the Ugaritic parallels depend heavily on a demand for complete reproduction (despite a disclaimer, "Daniel 7 and Ugarit," 86). So he repeatedly emphasizes that Daniel has no parallel to Mot, although no scholar has claimed otherwise.

53. Recent defenders of this position include Hartman and DiLella, *The Book of Daniel,* 85–102; P. M. Casey, *Son of Man,* 7–50; N. W. Porteous, *Daniel,* 192. These scholars also deny the mythological allusions in Daniel 7. For the term "steno-symbol" applied to Daniel see N. Perrin, "Eschatology and Hermeneutics: Reflections on Method in the Interpretation of the New Testament," *JBL* 93 (1974) 11.

54. For example, G. R. Beasley-Murray, "The Interpretation of Daniel 7," *CBQ* 45 (1983) 44–58.

55. Collins, *Apocalyptic Vision,* 123–52 (with older bibliography). Other recent supporters of the angelic interpretation include Lacocque, *The Book of Daniel,* 133; R. Hammer, *The Book of Daniel,* 79; Rowland, *The Open Heaven,* 178–82.

56. Casey (*Son of Man,* 51–70) argues that the corporate interpretation was the original one in the Syriac tradition, but his earliest witness is Porphyry. Evidence for the corporate interpretation in rabbinic literature is rare and late.

57. The evidence has been laid out several times: C. W. Brekelmans, "The Saints of the Most High and their Kingdom," *OTS* 14 (1965) 305–29; L. Dequeker, "The 'Saints of the Most High' in Qumran and Daniel," *OTS* 18 (1973) 133–62; G. F. Hasel, "The Identity of the 'Saints of the Most High' in Daniel 7," *Bib* 56 (1975) 173–92. The judgments of these scholars on the interpretation of the evidence differ and must be evaluated with caution.

58. The expression "holy people" (*'am qodeš,* 12:7) cannot be regarded as an equivalent linguistic expression to "holy ones" (contra Casey, *Son of Man,* 44–45).

59. Some proponents of the angelic interpretation, such as M. Noth ("The Holy Ones of the Most High," in *The Laws in the Pentateuch and Other Essays,* 215–28) and Dequeker ("The 'Saints of the Most High'") resort to interpolation theories to explain these verses. This procedure is neither justified nor necessary.

60. The parallel passage in the interpretation of the dream is textually corrupt, but it may also be read as an assault on the angelic host; see Collins, *Apocalyptic Vision,* 139.

61. P. D. Miller, *The Divine Warrior in Early Israel,* 21–23, 66–69.

62. So DiLella objects that "Daniel 7 would then have virtually no meaning or relevance for the addressees of the book" (Hartman and DiLella, *The Book of Daniel,* 91; compare Casey, *Son of Man,* 44). If so, the explicit triumph of Michael in Daniel 12 would be equally meaningless.

63. Lacocque, *The Book of Daniel,* 131: "It is a question of men before it is a question of angels."

64. Contra Casey, who takes it as "the people consisting of the holy ones" (*Son of Man,* 41).

65. So also U. B. Müller, *Messias und Menschensohn in jüdischen Apokalypsen und in der Offenbarung des Johannes,* 28; Rowland, *The Open Heaven,* 181.

66. See further B. Lindars, "Re-enter the Apocalyptic Son of Man," *NTS* 22 (1975–76) 52–72.

67. For example, Hartman and DiLella, *The Book of Daniel,* 11–14; Casey, *Son of Man,* 9–10; also B. Hasslberger, *Hoffnung in der Bedrängnis,* 411.

68. E. Leach, "Genesis as Myth," in *Myth and Cosmos*, ed. J. Middleton, 1-13.

69. For discussion see Collins, *Apocalyptic Vision*, 106-8, 138-41; Lacocque, *The Book of Daniel*, 167-73.

70. A. Lacocque, "The Liturgical Prayer in Daniel 9," *HUCA* 47 (1976) 119-42; O. H. Steck, *Israel und das gewaltsame Geschick der Propheten*, 110-36.

71. B. W. Jones, "The Prayer in Daniel IX," *VT* 18 (1968) 488-93.

72. For the term see G. W. Buchanan, *The Consequences of the Covenant*, 9-17.

73. For different nuances as to whether Daniel thinks in terms of an "end" or "goal" of history, contrast M. Noth ("The Understanding of History in Old Testament Apocalyptic," in *The Laws in the Pentateuch*, 194-214) with K. Koch, "Spätisraelitisches Geschichtsdenken am Beispiel des Buches Daniel," *Historische Zeitschrift* 193 (1961) 1-32.

74. See Rowland, *The Open Heaven*, 98-101.

75. M. Eliade, *The Myth of the Eternal Return*, 3-4.

76. See, for example, Hartman and DiLella, *The Book of Daniel*, 286-305. For Babylonian parallels to this kind of prophecy see Lambert, *The Background of Jewish Apocalyptic*.

77. R. J. Clifford, "History and Myth in Daniel 10-12," *BASOR* 220 (1975) 23-26.

78. Hengel, *Judaism and Hellenism*, 1:175-80; O. Plöger, *Theocracy and Eschatology*, 22-25; and most recent commentators.

79. G. W. E. Nickelsburg, *Resurrection, Immortality and Eternal Life*, 11-27.

80. L. Hartman, "The Function of Some So-Called Apocalyptic Timetables," *NTS* 22 (1976) 1-14. It is noteworthy that despite the passage of time Josephus could still affirm that Daniel not only prophesied future things but also fixed the time at which they would come to pass (*Antiquities* 10.11.7 §267).

81. This is not to suggest that Daniel depends directly on *1 Enoch*, but only to note that Daniel did not invent the genre.

Chapter 4: Related Genres: Oracles and Testaments

1. For the following see J. J. Collins, *The Sibylline Oracles of Egyptian Judaism*, 1-19.

2. See H. Cancik, "Libri Fatales, Römische Offenbarungsliteratur und Geschichtstheologie," in *Apocalypticism*, ed. D. Hellholm, 549-76.

3. One of the surviving Roman sibylline oracles deals with the birth of an androgyne. See further Livy 42.2.6; Tibullus 2.5.67-74.

4. D. Flusser, "The four empires in the Fourth Sibyl and in the Book of Daniel," *Israel Oriental Studies* 2 (1972) 163-65.

5. Dionysius of Halicarnassus 4.62.6.

6. The most complete collection of the fragmentary pagan sibyllina is still to be found in C. Alexandre, *Excursus ad Sibyllina*.

7. See Strabo 17.1.43(814) for a flurry of oracular activity in connection with Alexander the Great. In general, see S. K. Eddy, *The King is Dead*; H. Fuchs, *Der geistige Widerstand gegen Rom in der antiken Welt*.

8. Suetonius *Augustus* 31.1.

9. F. Dunand, "L'Oracle du Potier et la formation de l'apocalyptique en Egypte," in *L'Apocalyptique*, 39-67.

10. J. R. Hinnells, "The Zoroastrian Doctrine of Salvation in the Roman World: A Study of the Oracle of Hystaspes," in *Man and His Salvation*, ed. E. J. Sharpe and J. R. Hinnells, 125-48.

11. The anomalous numbering arises from the nature of the manuscript tradition. The two main collections are numbered 1-8 and 9-14, but books 9 and 10 merely repeat material from the first collection, and so they are omitted in the standard editions. See my introductions to, translations of, and notes for all twelve books in *The Old Testament Pseudepigrapha*, ed. J. H. Charlesworth, 1:317-472.

12. For details see Collins, *Sibylline Oracles*, 21–33. The classic treatment is that of J. Geffcken, *Komposition und Entstehungszeit der Oracula Sibyllina* V. Nikiprowetzky defends the unity of the book with only minor exceptions (*La Troisième Sibylle*).

13. A. Kurfess, "Christian Sibyllines," in *New Testament Apocrypha*, ed. E. Hennecke and W. Schneemelcher, 2:707.

14. The term is derived from Euhemerus of Messene, who published an anthropological theory of the gods about 300 B.C.E. He held that the gods were originally great kings and benefactors of humanity.

15. The fourth and combined first and second books of *Sibylline Oracles* are structured around a sequence of ten kingdoms. Compare the tenfold schematization of history in the Apocalypse of Weeks.

16. Collins, *Sibylline Oracles*, 37.

17. There is a general consensus on this point. The only dissenter is Nikiprowetzky, who identifies the seventh king somewhat paradoxically as Cleopatra VII (*La Troisième Sibylle*, 215).

18. P. Fraser, *Ptolemaic Alexandria*, 1:709–13, 2:989–99. The Jewish temple at Leontopolis was built in Philometor's reign. Josephus claims that Philometor's entire army was under the command of two Jews, Onias and Dositheus (*Against Apion* 2.49). The Jewish philosopher Aristobulus allegedly dedicated his book to Philometor (Clement *Stromateis* 1.150.1).

19. Macedonia was divided after the battle of Pydna in 168 B.C.E. and was made a Roman province in 147 B.C.E.

20. Polybius 31.20 and 18. Fraser, *Ptolemaic Alexandria*, 1:120, 2:214.

21. For example, H. C. Lanchester, "The Sibylline Oracles," *APOT*, 2:389.

22. Collins, *Sibylline Oracles*, 29. Other notorious invaders were Cambyses and Artaxerxes Ochus.

23. Philometor was only three or four years old when he came to the throne, and he was still a youth when Antiochus invaded.

24. So, recently, A. Momigliano, "La Portata Storica dei Vaticini sul Settimo Re nel Terzo Libro degli Oracoli Sibillini," in *Forma Futuri*, 1077–84. Isa 41:2, 25 is often invoked in this connection, but there the connotation "east" is quite explicit (from the sunrise).

25. Collins, *Sibylline Oracles*, 40–43. See also *Between Athens and Jerusalem*, chap. 2, for a critique of Momigliano's position.

26. J. Nolland ("Sib Or 3. 265–94, An Early Maccabean Messianic Oracle," *JTS* 30 [1979] 158–67) argues that the typology points to a Davidic messiah, but the king who played the crucial role in the restoration in the sixth century was the pagan king Cyrus.

27. See especially V. Tcherikover, *Hellenistic Civilization and the Jews*, 39–89.

28. This is the phrase of E. P. Sanders, *Paul and Palestinian Judaism*.

29. See Collins, *Between Athens and Jerusalem*, chap. 4.

30. Ibid., chap. 2.

31. Momigliano ("La Portata Storica," 1081) finds an allusion to the rebellion in lines 194–95 ("and then the race of the great God will again be strong"), but the reference here is to a future revival.

32. M. Delcor, "Le Temple d'Onias en Egypte," *RB* 75 (1968) 188–205.

33. Tcherikover, *Hellenistic Civilization*, 280.

34. Collins, *Sibylline Oracles*, 51.

35. P. Vielhauer, "Apocalypses and Related Subjects," in *New Testament Apocrypha*, ed. E. Hennecke and W. Schneemelcher, 2:600.

36. Collins, *Sibylline Oracles*, 57–64; W. W. Tarn, "Alexander Helios and the Golden Age," *JRS* 22 (1932) 135–48.

37. See my introduction to *Sib. Or.* 11 in *Old Testament Pseudepigrapha*, ed. J. H. Charlesworth, 1:430–433; A. Kurfess, *Sibyllinische Weissagungen*, 333–41.

38. E. von Nordheim argues for a more complex definition, including a pattern of historical retrospective, ethical exhortation, and prediction of the future, a pattern typical of the *Testaments of the Twelve Patriarchs* (*Die Lehre der Alten, I*).

39. Compare also the last words of Joshua (Joshua 23-24), Samuel (1 Samuel 12), David (1 Kgs 2:1-9; 1 Chronicles 28-29). Von Nordheim promises a full discussion of the background of the genre in *Die Lehre der Alten, II.*

40. M. Küchler, *Früjüdische Weisheitstraditionen*, 415-19; E. Lohmeyer, *Diatheke*, 32-35.

41. The so-called *Testament of Abraham* is not a testament at all (see chap. 8 below). The *Testament of Solomon* is Christian in its present form and bears only a superficial resemblance to the testamentary form. See the overview of the corpus in von Nordheim, *Die Lehre der Alten, I.*

42. The basic edition, translation, and commentary are still those of R. H. Charles, *The Assumption of Moses;* see also his treatment in *APOT*, 2:407-24. The identification was based on 1:14, which corresponds to a quotation from the *Assumption of Moses* by Gelasius (*Hist. Eccl.* 2.17.17).

43. Both a *Testament* and an *Assumption* are mentioned in the *Stichometry* of Nicephorus and other lists. The *Assumption* referred to a dispute between Michael and the devil, which is alluded to already in the New Testament in Jude, verse 9. The allusion is not identified in Jude but is specified in Clement, Origen, and Gelasius.

44. J. J. Collins, "The Date and Provenance of the Testament of Moses," in *Studies on the Testament of Moses*, ed. G. W. E. Nickelsburg, 19-20.

45. G. W. E. Nickelsburg, "An Antiochan Date for the Testament of Moses," in *Studies on the Testament of Moses*, ed. G. W. E. Nickelsburg, 33-37.

46. Charles, *Assumption*, 28-30.

47. J. Licht, "Taxo, or the Apocalyptic Doctrine of Vengeance," *JJS* 12 (1961) 95-103.

48. So Nickelsburg, *Jewish Literature*, 80-83. For the arguments see *Studies on the Testament of Moses*, ed. G. W. E. Nickelsburg, 15-43. For literary evidence of the redaction see A. Yarbro Collins, "Composition and Redaction of the Testament of Moses 10," *HTR* 69 (1976) 179-86. A number of scholars still date the whole document to the first century C.E., for example, E. Brandenburger, *Himmelfahrt Moses*, 59-60. See also J. Priest, "Testament of Moses," in *The Old Testament Pseudepigrapha*, ed. J. H. Charlesworth, 1:921.

49. D. J. Harrington, "Interpreting Israel's History: The Testament of Moses as a Rewriting of Deut 31-34," in *Studies on the Testament of Moses*, ed. G. W. E. Nickelsburg, 59-68.

50. Charles (*Assumption of Moses*, 14) identifies this figure as Daniel, but for no good reason. If the figure can be specified at all he was presumably a leader of the postexilic community, possibly the high priest.

51. The name Taxo (Greek *taxōn*) has been correlated with the Hebrew *mĕhôqēq* (S. Mowinckel, "The Hebrew Equivalent of Taxo in Ass. Mos. IX," in *Congress Volume: Copenhagen 1953*, VTSup 1, 88-96). It means "orderer" and may be roughly equivalent to "one who is over them."

52. Compare the theophany in *1 Enoch* 1.

53. On the revised *Testament of Moses* see Nickelsburg, *Jewish Literature*, 212-14.

54. Collins, "Date and Provenance," 28-29.

55. W. R. Farmer, *Maccabees, Zealots and Josephus*, 125-58.

56. Collins, *Apocalyptic Vision*, 215-18.

57. Several scholars have ascribed the *Testament* to the Qumran sect. For a defense of this view see E.-M. Laperrousaz, "Le Testament de Moïse," *Semitica* 19 (1970).

58. For example, Charles, *Assumption of Moses*, 15.

59. D. R. Schwartz, "The Tribes of As. Mos. 4:7-9," *JBL* 99 (1980) 217-23.

60. H. D. Slingerland, *The Testaments of the Twelve Patriarchs.*

61. M. de Jonge, *The Testaments of the Twelve Patriarchs: A Study of their Text.*

62. M. de Jonge, ed., *Studies on the Testaments of the Twelve Patriarchs.*

63. J. Becker, *Die Testamente der zwölf Patriarchen;* idem, *Untersuchungen zur Entstehungsgeschichte der Testamente der zwölf Patriarchen;* A. Hultgård, *L'Eschatologie des Testaments des Douze Patriarches, I;* H. C. Kee, "The Testaments of the Twelve Patriarchs," in *The Old Testament Pseudepigrapha*, ed. J. H. Charlesworth, 1:775-828.

64. The main proponents of this view are A. Dupont-Sommer, *Nouveaux aperçus sur les manuscrits de la Mer Morte;* M. Philonenko, *Les Interpolations chrétiennes des Testaments*

des Douze Patriarches et les manuscrits de Qoumrân. Note also the view of D. Flusser, who finds here a fusion of the Essene and Pharisaic outlooks ("The Testaments of the Twelve Patriarchs," *EJ* 13 [1971] 184–86).

65. The issues have been complicated by uncertainties about the text of the *Testaments*. At least there is now a consensus that the Christian elements cannot be removed by textual criticism. For the Greek text see M. de Jonge, *The Testaments of the Twelve Patriarchs. A Critical Edition of the Greek Text.*

66. De Jonge, *The Testaments: A Study of Their Text*, 71.

67. This document was published by M. Gaster, "The Hebrew Text of One of the Testaments of the Twelve Patriarchs," in *Proceedings of the Society of Biblical Archeology* (1893–94), 33–49, 109–17. For a recent study see T. Korteweg, "The meaning of Naphtali's visions," in *Studies on the Testaments*, ed. M. de Jonge, 261–90.

68. A translation of these fragments and the Hebrew *Testament of Naphtali* can be found in Charles, *APOT*, 2:361–67.

69. J. T. Milik, "Le Testament de Lévi en araméen: fragment de la grotte 4 de Qumrân," *RB* 62 (1955) 398–406. On the Aramaic Levi see J. C. Greenfield and M. E. Stone, "Remarks on the Aramaic Testament of Levi from the Cairo Geniza (Planches XIII– XIV)," *RB* 86 (1979) 214–30.

70. M. de Jonge, "Notes on Testament of Levi II–VII," in *Studies on the Testaments*, ed. M. de Jonge, 256.

71. Ibid., 251–58. Note the important fragment published by Milik (*Books of Enoch*, 23–24), which has its context in *Testament of Levi* 14.

72. Nickelsburg, *Jewish Literature*, 234. Fragments of the testaments of Judah, Joseph, and Benjamin have also been identified from Qumran, but they are very scanty and less than certain. See J. T. Milik, "Écrits préesséniens de Qumrân: d'Hénoch à Amram," in *Qumrân*, ed. M. Delcor, 91–106.

73. Becker, *Die Testamente*, 23–27; H. W. Hollander, *Joseph as an Ethical Model in the Testaments of the Twelve Patriarchs*, 92.

74. For a detailed analysis see von Nordheim, *Die Lehre der Alten, I*, 89–107.

75. M. de Jonge, *The Testaments: A Study of their Text*, 83–86.

76. See especially K. Baltzer, *The Covenant Formulary*.

77. *T. Issachar* 6; *T. Levi* 10, 14–15, 16; *T. Judah* 23; *T. Zebulun* 9:5–7; *T. Dan* 5:4, 8–9; *T. Naphtali* 4; *T. Asher* 7; *T. Benjamin* 9:1–2.

78. So Küchler, *Frühjüdische Weisheitstraditionen*, 415–545; von Nordheim, *Die Lehre der Alten, I*, 11.

79. *T. Simeon* 5:4; *T. Levi* 10:5; 14:1; 16:1; *T. Judah* 18:1; *T. Zebulun* 3:4; *T. Dan* 5:6; *T. Naphtali* 4:1; *T. Benjamin* 9:1; 10:6. The reference in *T. Zebulun* is to the "law of Enoch." This is surely an error. A number of manuscripts more plausibly read the "law of Moses."

80. For example, in *Testament of Levi* 16:1 Levi claims to have read in the book of *Enoch* that his descendants will err for seventy weeks. The clearest allusion to seventy weeks (of years) is in Daniel's reinterpretation of Jeremiah, but compare the seventy shepherds in the Animal Apocalypse and the schema of weeks in the Apocalypse of Weeks. In *Testament of Levi* 17 the seventy weeks are understood as seven jubilees, thereby corresponding to the first seven weeks in the Apocalypse of Weeks.

81. Milik, *Books of Enoch*, 23–24.

82. Nickelsburg, *Jewish Literature*, 236; idem, "Enoch, Levi and Peter: Recipients of Revelation in Upper Galilee," *JBL* 100 (1981) 575–600.

83. The textual tradition on these chapters is confused. See Charles, *APOT*, 2:304–6; de Jonge, *The Testaments: A Critical Edition*, 24–29.

84. A possible Christian reference is found in 2:11: "through you and Judah, the Lord will be seen among men, saving among them the whole race of men."

85. Charles, *APOT*, 2:289–90.

86. See J. J. Collins, "The Epic of Theodotus and the Hellenism of the Hasmoneans," *HTR* 73 (1980) 91–104.

87. In *Jub.* 30:18 Levi is chosen as priest after his zealous action against Schechem, after

the manner of Phineas in Numbers 25. In *Testament of Levi* 6 the appointment to priesthood comes first. In *Jubilees* the main point of the story is a polemic against intermarriage with the Gentiles.

88. Greenfield and Stone, "Remarks," 219. The Aramaic apocryphon seems to presuppose a calendar similar to that of Qumran and the Enoch literature.

89. Compare also Hermas, *Mandates*. See J.-P. Audet, "Affinités littéraires et doctrinales du 'Manuel de Discipline,'" *RB* 59 (1952) 219–38; 60 (1953) 41–82.

90. The term "messiah" is not actually used in the *Testaments*. I use it to refer to an eschatological savior figure who is human rather than angelic.

91. De Jonge, *The Testaments: A Study of their Text*, 86–89.

92. Hultgård, *L'Eschatologie*, 1:64–68.

93. Greenfield and Stone, "Remarks," 219.

94. Hultgård, *L'Eschatologie*, 1:268–90. Also his "The Ideal 'Levite,' the Davidic Messiah, and the Saviour Priest in the Testaments of the Twelve Patriarchs," in *Ideal Figures in Ancient Judaism*, ed. G. W. E. Nickelsburg and J. J. Collins, 93–110. Hultgård believes that the Jewish origin of the *Testaments* can be established.

95. Hultgård, *L'Eschatologie*, 1:68.

96. *T. Judah* 25; *T. Benjamin* 10:6–10; *T. Zebulun* 10:1–4; *T. Simeon* 6:7. Afterlife is also implied in *T. Levi* 18:10–14.

97. Hultgård, *L'Eschatologie*, 1:69.

98. The blessing on Judah in *Jub.* 31:18–20 is thought by Hultgård to imply a Davidic messiah (*L'Eschatologie*, 1:71–72). For surveys see J. H. Charlesworth, "The Concept of Messiah in the Pseudepigrapha," *ANRW* 19/2, 188–218; E. Schürer, *The History of the Jewish People in the Age of Jesus Christ*, rev. G. Vermes, F. Millar, and M. Black, 2:488–554. Schürer regards the "king from the sun" in *Sib. Or.* 3:652 as a Jewish messiah.

99. G. B. Gray, "The Psalms of Solomon" in Charles, *APOT*, 2:630; Nickelsburg, *Jewish Literature*, 212; J. Schüpphaus, *Die Psalmen Salomos*, 127–37.

100. Nickelsburg, *Jewish Literature*, 208. On the portrait of the messiah see further G. L. Davenport, "The 'Anointed of the Lord' in Psalms of Solomon 17," in *Ideal Figures*, ed. Nickelsburg and Collins, 67–92.

Chapter 5: Qumran

1. F. M. Cross, *The Ancient Library of Qumran*, 76–78.

2. H. Stegemann, "Die Bedeutung der Qumranfunde für die Erforschung der Apokalyptik," in *Apocalypticism*, ed. D. Hellholm, 495–530. Stegemann regards the *Temple Scroll* as a pre-Qumran document of the third or fourth century. B. A. Levine argues that it belongs in the same category as *Enoch* and *Jubilees* ("The Temple Scroll: Aspects of its Historical Provenance and Literary Character," *BASOR* 233 [1978] 5–23). Its sectarian character is defended by Y. Yadin, *The Temple Scroll*; idem, "Le Rouleau du Temple," in *Qumrân*, ed. M. Delcor, 115–19; J. Milgrom, "The Temple Scroll," *BA* 41 (1978) 105–20. Most recently B. Z. Wacholder has argued that the scroll is the "Qumranic Torah," the constitution of the sect, authored by the Teacher of Righteousness, before the foundation of the Qumran community (*The Dawn of Qumran*). Stegemann also assigns the *War Scroll* to the gray area, since it may be pre-Qumran in part.

3. Stegemann also puts the *Visions of Amram* and the *Angelic Liturgy* in this category ("Die Bedeutung"). Mention should also be made of 4QPsDan and the reported "Apocalypse of Ten Jubilees" (Milik, *Books of Enoch*, 254). See further Collins, "The Jewish Apocalypses," *Semeia* 14 (1979) 48–49; J. Carmignac, "Qu'est que l'Apocalyptique? Son emploi à Qumrân," *RQ* 10 (1979–81) 3–33.

4. Cross, *Ancient Library*, 70–106; G. Vermes, *The Dead Sea Scrolls: Qumran in Perspective*, 116–30.

5. R. de Vaux, *Archaeology and the Dead Sea Scrolls*; Cross, *Ancient Library*, 51–70; Vermes, *The Dead Sea Scrolls: Qumran in Perspective*, 29–39.

6. For a recent overview see Vermes, *The Dead Sea Scrolls: Qumran in Perspective*, 142–56. For a reconstruction see H. Stegemann, *Die Entstehung der Qumrangemeinde*.

7. Jonathan was the first to assume the high priesthood in 152, but the tenure was formalized when Simon was inaugurated ten years later. Jonathan is identified as the Wicked Priest by Vermes (*The Dead Sea Scrolls: Qumran in Perspective*, 151) and many others. The arguments for Simon are presented by Cross (*Ancient Library*, 109–60).

8. J. Murphy-O'Connor, "The Essenes and their History," *RB* 81 (1974) 215–44; idem, "The Essenes in Palestine," *BA* 40 (1977) 100–124.

9. For a list of suggested identifications see Vermes, *The Dead Sea Scrolls: Qumran in Perspective*, 160.

10. Wacholder's book, *The Dawn of Qumran*, appeared after the completion of this manuscript. His thesis is intriguing, but many of his arguments appear quite tenuous.

11. For a convenient tabulation see A. Mertens, *Das Buch Daniel im Lichte der Texte vom Toten Meer*.

12. De Vaux, *Archaeology*, 22–23. J. H. Charlesworth considers the possibility that Qumran was burned by the Parthians around 40 B.C.E. ("The Origin and Subsequent History of the Authors of the Dead Sea Scrolls: Four Transitional Phases among the Qumran Essenes," *RQ* 10 [1979–81] 226).

13. Charlesworth, "Origin and Subsequent History," 230–31. The evidence for later Essenism is very tentative.

14. Primarily Pliny *Natural History* 5.15; Josephus *War* 2.8.2-13 §§119–61; *Antiquities* 13.5.9 §§172–73 and 18.1.5 §§18–22; and Philo *Quod omnis probus liber sit* 12–13 and *Hypothetica* 11.1-18. Philo's *De Vita Contemplativa* describes the Therapeutae, a related but apparently different sect. For the patristic material see A. Adam and C. Burchard, *Antike Berichte über die Essener*.

15. Vermes, *The Dead Sea Scrolls: Qumran in Perspective*, 87.

16. *Antiquities* 18.1.5. §§18–19. The precise meaning of this passage is much disputed. It may mean that the Essenes sacrificed separately, by different rites, rather than that they completely abstained. Compare the equally obscure passage in CD 6:11-20.

17. Hippolytus and Josephus appear to have drawn on a common source. See M. Smith, "The Description of the Essenes in Josephus and the Philosophoumena," *HUCA* 29 (1958) 273-313.

18. Josephus (*War* 2.8.7 §§137–42) posits an initial stage of one year followed by another stage of two years. In 1QS 6 there is an initial examination followed by two stages of one year each. The two accounts are not necessarily at variance, if we assume that Josephus's first year is prior to the initial examination.

19. Vermes, *The Dead Sea Scrolls: Qumran in Perspective*, 87–115.

20. See M. Black, *The Scrolls and Christian Origins*, 34.

21. This is certainly true of the document as it now stands, not only in cols. 19 and 20, which refer to the Teacher of Righteousness, but also in col. 1:11. P. R. Davies regards this reference as secondary (*Damascus Covenant*, 175, 200). This conclusion is necessitated not by anything in the text but by his theory that the original document antedates the Teacher. His point that "if this reference is original it certainly cannot indicate the same figure" is again necessitated only by his theory.

22. Vermes, *The Dead Sea Scrolls: Qumran in Perspective*, 106-9.

23. Josephus's claim that he had made trial of all three Jewish sects, Sadducees, Pharisees, and Essenes, before his nineteenth year, cannot be taken seriously (*Life* 2 §§10-11).

24. The few skeletons of women and children that have been found at Qumran can be explained if the settlement at Qumran was the scene of the renewal of the covenant for all the sect (Vermes, *The Dead Sea Scrolls: Qumran in Perspective*, 108-9).

25. On the legal material see L. H. Schiffmann, *The Halakhah at Qumran*; J. M. Baumgarten, *Studies in Qumran Law*.

26. Cross, *Ancient Library*, 121.

27. J. T. Milik, *Ten Years of Discovery in the Wilderness of Judaea*, 87; G. Jeremias, *Der*

Lehrer der Gerechtigkeit, 168–77. See the objections of B. P. Kittel, *The Hymns of Qumran*, 9–10.

28. Y. Yadin argued for a Roman date, mainly on the basis of cols. 2–7, which are largely independent of the rest of the work (*The Scroll of the War of the Sons of Light against the Sons of Darkness*, 246). P. R. Davies maintains a Maccabean date for cols. 2–9 and argues for a complex history of composition, culminating in the Roman era (*1QM, The War Scroll from Qumran*). Other scholars regard the framework, cols. 1, 15–19, as the oldest section, and indeed as one of the oldest sectarian documents. So. L. Rost, "Zum Buch der Kriege der Söhne des Lichts gegen die Söhne der Finsternis," *TLZ* 80 (1955) 206; P. von der Osten-Sacken, *Gott und Belial*; J. J. Collins, "The Mythology of Holy War in Daniel and the Qumran War Scroll," *VT* 25 (1975) 610–11.

29. Wacholder argues that the *pesher* on Habakkuk is pre-Maccabean, while the *pesher* on Nahum is later (*The Dawn of Qumran*, 192).

30. A blatant example is Davies's excision of the reference to the Teacher of Righteousness in CD 1 (above, n. 21).

31. Davies distinguishes in three columns of the *War Scroll* (1QM 10–12) no fewer than nine "individual elements, whose origins, purposes and theology would seem to be rather diverse" (*1QM*, 92). He attaches great importance to the lack of specifically dualistic terminology in many "individual elements," even where these are only a few verses in length and are not incompatible with an underlying dualism.

32. The excellent form-critical analysis of 1QS by J. Pouilly (*La Règle de la Communauté de Qumrân: Son Evolution Littéraire*), based on the work of Murphy-O'Connor, does not warrant the evolutionary theory he proposes.

33. A rare example is found in the fragment of an earlier recension of the *War Scroll* published by C. H. Hunzinger, "Fragmente einer älteren Fassung des Buches Milḥamā aus Höhle 4 von Qumran," *ZAW* 69 (1957) 131–51. This fragment, which parallels 1QM 14:4b–16, appears less sectarian in its terminology (e.g., it reads "for his people" instead of "for the remnant of your people"). Unfortunately the fragment is too brief to support any broader thesis about the genesis of the *War Scroll*.

34. R. E. Brown, *The Semitic Background of the term "Mystery" in the New Testament*; C. Rowland, *The Open Heaven*, 113–20.

35. P. Schulz, *Der Autoritätsanspruch des Lehrers der Gerechtigkeit in Qumran*; D. Patte, *Early Jewish Hermeneutic in Palestine*, 211–31.

36. M. P. Horgan, *Pesharim: Qumran Interpretations of Biblical Books*; O. Betz, *Offenbarung und Schriftforschung in der Qumransekte*.

37. On the analogy with midrashim compare W. H. Brownlee, *The Midrash Pesher of Habakkuk*. G. Brooke ("Qumran Pesher: Towards the Redefinition of a Genre," *RQ* 10 [1979–81] 483–503) regards pesher as a subtype of midrash.

38. On the covenantal theology of Qumran see E. P. Sanders, *Paul and Palestinian Judaism*, 233–328.

39. For the following see my article, "Patterns of Eschatology at Qumran," in *Traditions in Transformation*, ed. B. Halpern and J. D. Levenson, 351–75.

40. S. Mowinckel, *He That Cometh*, 281.

41. See especially A. S. van der Woude, *Die messianischen Vorstellungen der Gemeinde von Qumran*.

42. CD 12:23–13:1; 14:19; 19:11. CD 20:1 refers to a messiah from Aaron and from Israel. Note also the prophecy of the star and the scepter in 7:18–20. In CD 2:12 and 6:1 the word Messiah is used with reference to the prophets. See K. G. Kuhn, "The Two Messiahs of Aaron and Israel," in *The Scrolls and the New Testament*, ed. K. Stendahl, 54–64.

43. L. Ginzberg, *An Unknown Jewish Sect*, 209–56. J. Starcky argued that CD represents a distinct stage, when the two messiahs were merged into one ("Les quatres étapes du messianisme à Qumrân," *RB* 70 [1963] 481–505). So also A. Caquot, "Le messianisme qumrânien," in *Qumrân*, ed. M. Delcor, 231–47. For a critique see R. E. Brown, "J. Starcky's Theory of Qumran Messianic Development," *CBQ* 28 (1966) 51–57.

44. Balaam's oracle is also cited in CD 7:18-20, where the star and scepter appear to refer to two distinct individuals (in the *Testimonia* both refer to the kingly messiah), and in 1QM 11:6.

45. See van der Woude, *Die messianischen Vorstellungen*, 29.

46. S. Talmon, "Typen der Messiaserwartung un die Zeitenwende," in *Probleme biblischer Theologie*, ed. H. W. Wolff, 571-88. Compare J. Carmignac, "La future intervention de Dieu selon la pensée de Qumrân," in *Qumrân*, ed. M. Delcor, 219-29.

47. Talmon, "Typen der Messiaserwartung," 583.

48. Two other possible instances of messianic activity should be noted. In CD 14:19 Rabin translates: "until there shall arise the Messiah of Aaron and Israel and he will make conciliation for their trespass . . ." (C. Rabin, *The Zadokite Documents*, 70). However, the passage is very fragmentary, and the verb for "make conciliation" *ykpr* could also be read as a *pual*, with "their trespass" as subject, so "their trespass will be covered over." Second, in 1QM the chief priest may possibly be viewed as a priestly messiah, but he is not the agent of the military victory, which rests with God and Michael.

49. See the succinct summary of this material by G. Vermes, *The Dead Sea Scrolls in English*, 18-25. For other aspects of the community's organization see his *The Dead Sea Scrolls: Qumran in Perspective*, 87-109.

50. 1QSa probably presupposes 1QS. See van der Woude, *Die messianischen Vorstellungen*, 97. 1QSa provides for a community with women and children.

51. 1QSa 2:11. Trans. Cross, reading *ywlyk* ("sends") for *ywlyd* ("causes to be born") (*Ancient Library*, 87-88). The text is fragmentary.

52. The word *hkwhn*, the priest, is restored but is not disputed.

53. Cross, *Ancient Library*, 90.

54. The phrase here is *yôrê haṣṣedeq*, while it usually appears as *môrê haṣṣedeq* or *mwrh ṣdq*.

55. Cross, *Ancient Library*, 227-28.

56. *Mwrh hyhyd*. Possibly the phrase should be read as *mwrh hyḥd* ("the teacher of the community").

57. *Mwrh ṣdq*. CD 20:28 refers to the same individual simply as *mwrh* (teacher).

58. Davies, *Damascus Covenant*, 123-25.

59. Even on Davies's hypothesis CD 6:11 would have to be reinterpreted after the death of the Teacher to refer to a second Teacher of Righteousness, who was still future. But the hypothesis of the earlier stage is then superfluous and gratuitous. The view of J. Allegro, A. Dupont Sommer and others that the resurrection of the Teacher is envisaged has been thoroughly refuted. See van der Woude, *Die messianischen Vorstellungen*, 71-72.

60. See van der Woude, *Die messianischen Vorstellungen*, 67-74.

61. Davies takes the star as a historical figure but the scepter as eschatological (*Damascus Covenant*, 147). Such a separation of the two figures is hard to justify and seems to be required by Davies's theory rather than by the text. This passage appears to be secondary in its present context.

62. The phrase in 1QS 6 is *dôrēš battôrâ*. Vermes has proposed that this figure should be identified with the *měbaqqēr* (*The Dead Sea Scrolls in English*, 22), but this now seems to me questionable. In 1QS 6 the interpreter is distinguished from the priest, but in the eschatological passages in *Florilegium* and CD 7 he is distinguished from the Davidic messiah and from the prince of the congregation. Whether the function of interpreting the law was necessarily identified with a particular office is uncertain.

63. Mention should be made of two other texts that have possible, but doubtful, messianic connotations. 4QMess ar predicts the birth of one who is called "the Elect of God" and who has been variously identified as the messiah or as Noah. In 4QPsDan A[a] the titles "Son of God" and "Son of the Most High" appear, but the referent is obscure. J. T. Milik, the editor, suggests that it is a Seleucid king. "Restorative" eschatology is also relevant to other aspects of the scrolls—for example, the ideal temple in the *Temple Scroll*.

64. Mowinckel, *He That Cometh*, 282.

65. Trans. Yadin, *The Scroll of the War*, 316.

66. So Talmon, "Typen," 586–87. Starcky also assigns 1QM to a late phase of the sect ("Les quatres étapes").

67. Von der Osten-Sacken, *Gott und Belial,* 28–41, 116–23.

68. Above, n. 28.

69. Von der Osten-Sacken, *Gott und Belial,* 73–87.

70. The name Belial is probably to be associated with the netherworld, possibly with the Canaanite god Mot. See N. J. Tromp, *Primitive Conceptions on Death and the Nether World,* 125.

71. G. W. Buchanan, *The Consequences of the Covenant,* 9–17.

72. Collins, "The Mythology of Holy War," 604–9. Compare the account of Persian religion in Plutarch *On Isis and Osiris* 46–47.

73. K. G. Kuhn, "Die Sektenschrift und die iranische Religion," *ZThK* 49 (1952) 293–316. On the general question of Persian influence on the scrolls see S. Shaked, "Qumran and Iran. Further Considerations," *Israel Oriental Studies* 2 (1972) 433–46; R. N. Frye, "Qumran and Iran," in *Christianity, Judaism and Other Greco-Roman Cults,* ed. J. Neusner, 3:167–74; P. J. Kobelski, *Melchizedek and Melchireša',* 84–98.

74. Yadin, *The Scroll of the War,* 21–25.

75. Vermes, *The Dead Sea Scrolls: Qumran in Perspective,* 52. Davies suggests that the king of the Kittim may be a Roman consul, but there is no parallel for such an identification (*1QM,* 89).

76. P. Wernberg-Møller, "A Reconsideration of the Two Spirits in the Rule of the Community (1QSerek III,13–IV,26)," *RQ* 3 (1961) 413–41.

77. So H. W. Huppenbauer speaks of the dualisms in the Qumran texts (*Der Mensch zwischen zwei Welten*).

78. J. T. Milik, "4QVisions de 'Amram et une citation d'Origene," *RB* 79 (1972) 77–97; Kobelski, *Melchizedek,* 24–36.

79. Milik, "Milkî-ṣedeq et Milkî-reša' dans les anciens écrits juifs et chrétiens," *JJS* 23 (1972) 95–144; Kobelski, *Melchizedek,* 37–48.

80. A. S. van der Woude, "Melchizedek als himmlische Erlösergestalt in den neuge-fundenen eschatologischen Midraschim aus Qumran Höhle XI," *OTS* 14 (1965) 354–73; M. de Jonge and A. S. van der Woude, "11QMelchizedek and the New Testament," *NTS* 12 (1965–66) 301–26; Kobelski, *Melchizedek,* 3–23.

81. Interest in the angelic world at Qumran is also attested in the so-called *Angelic Liturgy* (J. Strugnell, "An Angelic Liturgy at Qumran—4Q Serek Šîrôt 'Ôlat Haššabbat," in *Congress Volume: Oxford 1959,* VTSup 7, 318–45).

82. Kobelski, *Melchizedek,* 85.

83. Compare Wacholder (*The Dawn of Qumran,* 212–18) on Persian influence in the Hellenistic period.

84. Milik, *Ten Years,* 54–55. Josephus (*War* 2.8.10 §§152–53) claims that the Essenes exhibited great bravery under torture by the Romans.

85. Trans. S. Holm-Nielsen, *Hodayot: Psalms from Qumran,* 64. Compare 1QH 11:3–14.

86. For a review of opinions and discussion of the evidence see G. W. E. Nickelsburg, *Resurrection, Immortality and Eternal Life,* 144–69.

87. *War* 2.8.11 §154; *Antiquities* 18.1.2–6 §18. Hippolytus also attributes to them the belief that the flesh will arise and be immortal (*Refutatio omnium haeresium* 9.27). See Nickelsburg, *Resurrection,* 167–68.

88. See especially H. W. Kuhn, *Enderwartung und gegenwärtiges Heil.*

89. Compare the idea of eternal life in the Wisdom of Solomon and in the Gospel of John (e.g., John 5:24).

90. C. Barth, *Die Errettung vom Tode in den individuellen Klage- und Dankliedern des Alten Testaments,* 117, 145, 152.

91. Holm-Nielsen, *Hodayot,* 53. Some examples of the ambiguities: *ḥbl* means "pain," especially with childbirth, but it can also mean "bond," "snare" and be associated with Sheol (e.g., 1QH 3:9); *mšbrym* can be understood as "breakers" or "birth canal"; *bkwr* may be from

the root *bkr* ("firstborn"), but it can also be understood as *kwr* ("furnace") with the preposition *b*.

92. M. Mansoor, *The Thanksgiving Hymns*, 114.

93. A. Dupont-Sommer, *The Essene Writings from Qumran*, 208; idem, "La mère de l'Aspic dans un hymne de Qoumrân," *RHR* 147 (1955) 174–88.

94. So Holm-Nielsen, *Hodayot*. The word translated "mischief" is '*wl* and "wickedness" is '*p'h* (which could be "asp/viper").

95. Dupont-Sommer, "La mère de l'Aspic," 174–88. See further M. Delcor, *Les Hymnes de Qumrân*, 120–21.

96. Holm-Nielsen, *Hodayot*, 61. So also van der Woude, *Die messianischen Vorstellungen*, 156.

97. The most frequently discussed parallel is Revelation 12. See A. Yarbro Collins, *The Combat Myth in the Book of Revelation*, 67–69, 92.

98. 1QM 1:5, 15; 1QS 4:12–13, 19; *Book of the Mysteries* 5 (Dupont-Sommer, *Essene Writings*, 327). See van der Woude, *Die messianischen Vorstellungen*, 156.

99. S. Mowinckel, "Some Remarks on Hodayoth 39:5–20," *JBL* 75 (1956) 265–76.

100. H. Ringgren, "Der Weltbrand in den Hodajot," in *Bibel und Qumran*, ed. S. Wagner, 177–82.

101. Vermes, *The Dead Sea Scrolls in English* 159. The use of tenses in the hymn is confusing since it vacillates between imperfects with waw consecutive and simple imperfects.

102. Holm-Nielsen translates the phrase *qṣ ḥrwn lkwl bly'l* as "the moment of anger upon all corruption." However, *bly'l* occurs in "the floods of Belial" in the following line and the juxtaposition is surely deliberate. "All Belial" should be understood as "all the forces of Belial." *Qṣ ḥrwn* very probably implies a pun on *qṣ 'ḥrwn*, "the last age.'"

103. Holm-Nielsen uses the present tense down to line 36b; Delcor and Mansoor vacillate between past and present tense; and Kittel uses the present tense throughout (*The Hymns*).

104. M. Smith, "What is implied by the Variety of Messianic Figures?" *JBL* 78 (1959) 66–72.

105. Davies defines the unit as 5:17–6:11a (*Damascus Covenant*, 119).

106. I. T. Ramsey, *Models and Mystery*, 1–21.

107. S. R. Isenberg and D. E. Owen, "Bodies, Natural and Contrived: The Work of Mary Douglas," *RelStudRev* 3 (1977) 1–16.

108. R. R. Wilson, "From Prophecy to Apocalyptic: Reflections on the Shape of Israelite Religion," *Semeia* 21 (1981) 79–95.

Chapter 6: The Similitudes of Enoch

1. Milik, *Books of Enoch*, 89–98.

2. For a review of the literature see D. W. Suter, "Weighed in the Balance: The Similitudes of Enoch in Recent Discussion," *RelStudRev* 7 (1981) 217–21.

3. See J. C. Greenfield and M. E. Stone ("The Enochic Pentateuch and the Date of the Similitudes," *HTR* 70 [1977] 51–65), who attribute this insight to David Flusser.

4. J. Theisohn, *Der auserwählte Richter*, 149–82.

5. So also Greenfield and Stone on different grounds; D. W. Suter, *Tradition and Composition in the Parables of Enoch*, 32. M. A. Knibb ("The Date of the Parables of Enoch: A Critical Review," *NTS* 25 [1979] 345–59) prefers a date in the period 70–135 C.E. (after the destruction of Qumran). J. H. Charlesworth ("The SNTS Pseudepigrapha Seminars at Tübingen and Paris on the Books of Enoch," *NTS* 25 [1979] 315–23) reports that M. Black, who formerly shared Milik's views, now sees the Similitudes as Jewish and post-Christian, from about 100 C.E.

6. N. Schmidt, "The Original Language of the Parables of Enoch," in *Old Testament and Semitic Studies in Memory of W. R. Harper*, 2:329–49; E. Ullendorff, "An Aramaic 'Vorlage' of the Ethiopic Text of Enoch?" in *Ethiopia and the Bible*, 31–62.

7. See the outline by M. D. Hooker, *The Son of Man in Mark*, 36–37.

8. Quotations follow the translation of M. A. Knibb, *The Ethiopic Book of Enoch.*

9. J. J. Collins, "Cosmos and Salvation: Jewish Wisdom and Apocalyptic in the Hellenistic Age," *HR* 17 (1977) 140.

10. Charles, *APOT*, 2:168.

11. Another Noachic passage can be found in 54:7–55:2; also sometimes assigned to this source is 67:1–69:25. A major Noachic passage is found in *1 Enoch* 106–8.

12. D. W. Suter, "Māšāl in the Similitudes of Enoch," *JBL* 100 (1981) 193–212. Enoch is also said to utter a parable in *1 Enoch* 1:3.

13. Collins, "The Jewish Apocalypses," *Semeia* 14 (1979) 39. The Similitudes are assigned to Type 2B.

14. For the following see Collins, "The Heavenly Representative. The 'Son of Man' in the Similitudes of Enoch," in *Ideal Figures in Ancient Judaism*, ed. G. W. E. Nickelsburg and J. J. Collins, 111–33.

15. D. Hill, "Dikaioi as a Quasi-Technical Term," *NTS* 11 (1965) 296–302.

16. For bibliography see C. Colpe, "Ho huios tou anthrōpou," *TDNT*, 8:423–27; U. B. Müller, *Messias und Menschensohn in jüdischen Apokalypsen und in der Offenbarung Johannes*, 36–60; P. M. Casey, "The Use of Term 'Son of Man' in the Similitudes of Enoch," *JSJ* 7 (1976) 11–29; idem, *Son of Man: The Interpretation and Influence of Daniel 7*, 99–112.

17. On the Ethiopic terminology see Casey, "The Use of Term 'Son of Man,'" 14–18; idem, *Son of Man*, 100–102.

18. Casey, "The Use of Term 'Son of Man,'" 23.

19. For example, Dan 8:15; 9:21; 10:5; 12:6.

20. Some manuscripts read "righteousness" instead of Righteous One at 38:2.

21. Hooker, *The Son of Man in Mark*, 38–40.

22. U. B. Müller, *Messias und Menschensohn*, 45.

23. So Casey, "The Use of Term 'Son of Man,'" 13.

24. For example, T. W. Manson, "The Son of Man in Daniel, Enoch and the Gospels," in *Studies in the Gospels and Epistles*, 123–45; D. S. Russell, *The Method and Message of Jewish Apocalyptic*, 350–52.

25. J. W. Rogerson, "The Hebrew Conception of Corporate Personality—A Re-examination," *JTS* 21 (1970) 1–16.

26. S. Mowinckel, *He That Cometh*, 381. Mowinckel's discussion is flawed by his reliance on a theory of primordial man and *anima generalis* which cannot be maintained.

27. E. Sjöberg, *Der Menschensohn im Äthiopischen Henochbuch*, 50. This remains true despite the use of Old Testament motifs and passages associated with the royal, Davidic messiah (Theisohn, *Der Auserwählte Richter*, 53–59) and the fact that he is called messiah (48:10).

28. For the phrase see G. Theissen (*Sociology of Early Palestinian Christianity*, 121), who uses it with reference to the Son of Man in the New Testament.

29. G. W. E. Nickelsburg, *Resurrection, Immortality and Eternal Life*, 77.

30. Ibid., 70–78. The influence of the Isaianic servant songs has also been noted by J. Jeremias, "Pais theou," *TDNT*, 5:687–88; U. B. Müller, *Messias und Menschensohn*, 38–39; and Theisohn, *Der Auserwählte Richter*, 114–26.

31. See M. Eliade, *The Myth of the Eternal Return*, 3–6.

32. A. Lacocque, *The Book of Daniel*, 131.

33. Compare the remarks of Theissen (*Sociology*, 101) on the function of the Son of Man in the New Testament.

34. Casey, "The Use of Term 'Son of Man,'" 25–26. The reading in V is slightly different from that in U and W.

35. Charles, *APOT*, 2:237.

36. Mowinckel, *He That Cometh*, 443. This view should be distinguished from D. S. Russell's theory of a "Son of Man idea," which is flawed by its reliance on the notion of corporate personality (*Method and Message*, 352).

37. Charles, *The Book of Enoch*, 156.

38. So Hooker, Casey, and A. Caquot ("Remarques sur les chap. 70 et 71 du livre éthiopien d'Hénoch," in *Apocalypses et Théologie de l'Espérance*, ed. H. Monloubou, 111-12).

39. Hooker, *The Son of Man in Mark*, 41-42.

40. U. B. Müller, *Messias und Menschensohn*, 59. So also Manson, "The Son of Man," 136.

41. So Casey, who appeals to "considerations of intrinsic probability" (*Son of Man*, 105).

42. Caquot ("Remarques," 121) points to the vision of Levi in the *Testament of Levi*, but Levi recognizes himself throughout.

43. Sjöberg, *Der Menschensohn*, 83-101; Mowinckel, *He That Cometh*, 370-73. Manson questions whether preexistence is really implied except as a project in the mind of God ("The Son of Man," 136).

44. On Metatron see I. Gruenwald, *Apocalyptic and Merkavah Mysticism*, 181-208.

45. U. B. Müller, *Messias und Menschensohn*, 54-59; Colpe, "Ho huios tou anthrōpou," *TDNT*, 8:426.

46. In fact there are three statements of the translation of Enoch: 70:1-2; 71:1 and 71:5. U. B. Müller defines the addition as 71:5-17.

47. M. Black recognized the tension between chap. 71 and the main body of the Similitudes but suggested that 70-71 is the older stratum, because of its similarity to the elevation of Enoch in *1 Enoch* 14 ("The Eschatology of the Similitudes of Enoch," *JTS* 3 [1952] 8). Against this theory is the fact that the Similitudes do not otherwise betray the identification of the "Son of Man" with Enoch.

48. Hooker, *The Son of Man in Mark*, 42.

49. Greenfield and Stone, "The Enochic Pentateuch," 56-57.

50. B. Lindars, "Re-Enter the Apocalyptic Son of Man," *NTS* 22 (1975-76) 52-72; P. J. Kobelski, *Melchizedek and Melchireša*, 130-37. See also Rowland (*The Open Heaven*, 94-113) on the idea of an exalted angel.

51. *1 Enoch* 48:10. See Theisohn, *Der auserwählte Richter*, 53-59.

Chapter 7: After the Fall:
4 Ezra, 2 Baruch, and the Apocalypse of Abraham

1. Variants of this oracle are found in Tacitus *Histories* 2.13 and Suetonius *Vespasian* 4. In Tacitus, the oracle says that "the east would become strong," a motif that recalls *Sib. Or.* 3:350-80, or even the *Oracle of Hystaspes* (Lactantius *Divine Institutions* 7.15.11).

2. Another range of responses is preserved in the rabbinic literature. See A. J. Saldarini, "Varieties of Rabbinic Responses to the Destruction of the Temple," in *Society of Biblical Literature 1982 Seminar Papers*, ed. K. H. Richards, 437-58.

3. The nomenclature of the Ezra books is confusing: 1 Ezra = the canonical book of Ezra; 2 Ezra = the book of Nehemiah; 3 Ezra = 1 Esdras (Jewish apocryphon); 4 Ezra = 2 Esdras 3-14; 5 Ezra = 2 Esdras 1-2 (Christian); 6 Ezra = 2 Esdras 15-16 (Christian). There is also a Christian *Apocalypse of Ezra* in Greek.

4. B. Violet, *Die Ezra-Apokalypse, I: Die Ueberlieferung;* M. E. Stone, *The Armenian Version of IV Ezra*.

5. On the questions of date, provenance, and language see J. M. Myers, *I and II Esdras*, 113-19, 129-31; J. Schreiner, *Das 4. Buch Esra*, 291-306.

6. Myers, *I and II Esdras*, 299-302.

7. R. Kabisch, *Das vierte Buch Esra auf seine Quellen untersucht;* H. Gunkel, "Das vierte Buch Esra," in *Die Apokryphen und Pseudepigraphen des alten Testaments*, ed. E. Kautzsch, 2:331-401.

8. For the history of scholarship see A. L. Thompson, *Responsibility for Evil in the Theodicy of IV Ezra*, 85-120; E. Brandenburger, *Die Verborgenheit Gottes im Weltgeschehen*, 22-57.

9. G. H. Box, *The Ezra Apocalypse;* idem, "IV Ezra," *APOT*, 2:542-624; R. H. Charles, *A Critical History of the Doctrine of a Future Life*, 283-97.

10. Box, "IV Ezra," 549. This problem must be seen in the wider context of other identifications of Ezra that were current in Jewish tradition. See R. A. Kraft, "'Ezra' Materials in Judaism and Christianity," *ANRW* 19/2, 119–36.

11. So already G. Volkmar, *Das vierte Buch Esra.*

12. The general consensus on this point has been challenged by W. Harnisch, who argues that chap. 14 should be viewed as two distinct units ("Der Prophet als Widerpart und Zeuge der Offenbarung. Erwägungen zur Interdependenz von Form und Sache im IV Buch Esra," in *Apocalypticism*, ed. D. Hellholm, 461–93).

13. A. Yarbro Collins, *The Combat Myth in the Book of Revelation*, 5–55.

14. So, recently, Harnisch, "Der Prophet als Widerpart"; W. Harrelson, "Ezra among the wicked in 2 Esdras 3–10," in *The Divine Helmsman*, ed. J. L. Crenshaw and S. Sandmel, 21–39.

15. Brandenburger, *Die Verborgenheit Gottes*, 107.

16. See further E. Breech, "These Fragments I have Shored against my Ruins: The Form and Function of 4 Ezra," *JBL* 92 (1973) 267–74.

17. E. Brandenburger, *Adam und Christus*, 27–36; idem, *Die Verborgenheit Gottes*, 42–51; W. Harnisch, *Verhängnis und Verheissung der Geschichte*, 60–67 and passim. Harnisch goes further than Brandenburger in identifying the skeptical viewpoint with a group.

18. So Harrelson, "Ezra among the wicked."

19. Thompson, *Responsibility for Evil*, 269.

20. Gunkel sees the book as a record of the author's inner struggle ("Das vierte Buch Esra," 340). So also C. G. Montefiore, *IV Ezra. A Study in the Development of Universalism;* M. Knibb, *The Second Book of Esdras*, 109.

21. So M. E. Stone, "Reactions to Destructions of the Second Temple: Theology, Perception and Conversion," *JSJ* 12 (1981) 195–204. P. Hayman concludes that "overwhelming religious experience can dissolve any kind of intellectual doubt" ("The Problem of Pseudonymity in the Ezra Apocalypse," *JSJ* 6 [1975] 47–56). Compare Thompson, *Responsibility for Evil*, 340–42.

22. Compare Hayman, "The Problem of Pseudonymity," 50.

23. See P. G. R. de Villiers, "Understanding the Way of God: Form, Function and Message of the Historical Review in 4 Ezra 3:4–27,"in *Society of Biblical Literature 1981 Seminar Papers*, ed. K. H. Richards, 357–78.

24. K. Koch, "Esras erste Vision. Weltzeiten und Weg des Höchsten," *BZ* 22 (1978) 46–75.

25. The Latin "filius meus Jesus" is obviously a Christian emendation. There is general agreement that the original read "my messiah." It is also apparent, in the light of the versions, that "filius" translates the Greek *pais*, which in turn reflects the Hebrew *'abdî*, "my servant." See U. B. Müller, *Messias und Menschensohn*, 90.

26. M. E. Stone argues that "the end" refers to "the crucial turning point of the eschatological process" and refers in some cases to the advent of the messiah, in other cases to the transition from this world to the next" ("Coherence and Inconsistency in the Apocalypses: The Case of 'The End' in 4 Ezra," *JBL* 102 [1983] 229–43). Against this view P. Schäfer argues that the three-stage schema is presupposed throughout and that the messiah belongs to this age, before the end ("Die Lehre von den zwei Welten im 4. Buch Esra und in der tannaitischen Literatur," in *Studien zur Geschichte und Theologie des Rabbinischen Judentums*, 244–91).

27. Harrelson, "Ezra among the wicked," 36. Harrelson argues that the vision of Zion transformed shows that the narrow logic of sin and punishment is revoked, but nothing else in 4 Ezra substantiates this optimism.

28. See especially W. Harnisch, "Die Ironie der Offenbarung: Exegetische Erwägungen zur Zionsvision im 4. Buch Esra," in *Society of Biblical Literature 1981 Seminar Papers*, ed. K. H. Richards, 79–104.

29. Compare Pss 46:6; 68:2; 97:5; Mic 1:4; *1 Enoch* 1:6.

30. Latin "my son" most probably reflects an original "my servant." See above, n. 25.

31. See also A. Lacocque, "The Vision of the Eagle in 4 Esdras, A Rereading of Daniel 7

in the First Century C.E.," in *Society of Biblical Literature 1981 Seminar Papers*, ed. K. H. Richards, 237–58.

32. U. B. Müller, *Messias und Menschensohn*, 83–134.

33. M. E. Stone, "The Concept of the Messiah in IV Ezra," in *Religions in Antiquity: Essays in Memory of E. R. Goodenough*, ed. J. Neusner, 295–312. See also Stone's dissertation, "Features of the Eschatology of IV Ezra."

34. For the denunciation of Rome compare especially Revelation 17–18 and *Sib. Or.* 8:1–216.

35. In the eagle and "man from the sea" visions Uriel is not mentioned but is probably the implied speaker. Ezra's prayers are addressed to God, but that was also the case in the opening dialogues, where the angel is clearly the respondent. Some manuscripts add a reference to the angel at 12:10 (see Myers, *I and II Esdras*, 292).

36. Contra Harnisch, "Der Prophet als Widerpart."

37. Compare U. Luck, "Das Weltverständnis in der jüdischen Apokalyptik. Dargestellt am Äthiopischen Henoch und am 4 Esra," *ZThK* 73 (1976) 283–305.

38. The phrase of J. C. Picard, apropos of 3 Baruch.

39. For example, Harnisch, *Verhängnis und Verheissung*, 327.

40. G. F. Moore, *Judaism in the First Centuries of the Christian Era*, 1:479–93 (on the evil inclination); 2:321–95 (on messianism and eschatology).

41. Schäfer, "Die Lehre von den zwei Welten," in *Studien zur Geschichte und Theologie des Rabbinischen Judentums*, 290–91.

42. See especially E. P. Sanders, *Paul and Palestinian Judaism*, 409–18.

43. F. Rosenthal (*Vier Apokryphische Bücher aus der Zeit und Schule R. Akibas*, 39–71) argued for a special affinity between 4 Ezra and the teaching of Eliezer ben Hyrcanus in such matters as the severity of the judgment (*'Arakin* 17a) and the exclusion of the Gentiles from salvation (*Tosefta Sanhedrin* 13).

44. S. J. D. Cohen, "Yavneh Revisited: Pharisees, Rabbis and the End of Jewish Sectarianism," in *Society of Biblical Literature 1982 Seminar Papers*, ed. K. H. Richards, 45–61.

45. Contra H. C. Kee, "'The Man' in Fourth Ezra: Growth of a Tradition," in *Society of Biblical Literature 1981 Seminar Papers*, ed. K. H. Richards, 199–208. In this connection it should be noted that the sharp antithesis between rabbinic and apocalyptic religion posited by D. Rössler (*Gesetz und Geschichte*) has been widely discredited.

46. Sanders, *Paul and Palestinian Judaism*, 409.

47. A. F. J. Klijn, *Die syrische Baruch-Apokalypse*, 107–11. The letter in chaps. 78–87 is more extensively preserved. A few verses from chaps. 12–14 are also preserved in Greek.

48. B. Violet, *Die Apokalypsen des Esra und des Baruch in deutscher Gestalt*, XCII.

49. P. Bogaert, *Apocalypse de Baruch*, 287–95. Bogaert's suggestion that the apocalypse was prompted by persecution under Domitian is gratuitous. The earliest citation is in the *Epistle of Barnabas*.

50. Ibid., 58–67. Much of the disagreement concerns the assigning of the transitional verses.

51. A. F. J. Klijn, "The Sources and the Redaction of the Syriac Apocalypse of Baruch," *JSJ* 1 (1970) 68.

52. In 5:7 Baruch fasts "until the evening," but the fast does not disrupt the continuity of the narrative.

53. G. Sayler, "2 Baruch. A Story of Grief and Consolation," in *Society of Biblical Literature 1982 Seminar Papers*, ed. K. H. Richards, 485–500.

54. Bogaert (*Apocalypse*, 61), following Violet and Schürer, feels obliged to cut this unit after chap. 52, although he admits the lack of a formal indicator.

55. R. H. Charles, *The Apocalypse of Baruch*; idem, "II Baruch," *APOT*, 2:470–526. Before Charles similar analyses were proposed by R. Kabisch and E. de Faye.

56. The affinities between Pseudo-Philo, 4 Ezra, and 2 *Baruch* are significant in this regard. See Bogaert, *Apocalypse*, 242–58.

57. Klijn, *Die syrische Baruch-Apokalypse*, 111.

58. This material is paralleled in *Pesiqta Rabbati* (Bogaert, *Apocalypse*, 222–41) and also in the *Paralipomena of Jeremiah* (Bogaert, *Apocalypse*, 177–221; G. W. E. Nickelsburg, "Narrative Traditions in the Paraleipomena of Jeremiah and 2 Baruch," *CBQ* 35 [1973] 60–68).

59. Klijn, "The Sources and the Redaction," 69–76. See also his introduction, "2 Baruch," in *The Old Testament Pseudepigrapha*, ed. J. H. Charlesworth, 1:615–620.

60. U. B. Müller sees a Christian interpolation here (*Messias und Menschensohn*, 142–44).

61. This is the most probable interpretation of an unclear text; see Bogaert, *Apocalypse*, 75–78.

62. On this vision see A. B. Kolenkow, "An Introduction to II Baruch 53, 56–74: Structure and Substance."

63. On determinism in *2 Baruch* and *4 Ezra* see Harnisch, *Verhängnis und Verheissung*, 249–67.

64. E. P. Sanders, "The Covenant as a Soteriological Category and the Nature of Salvation in Palestinian and Hellenistic Judaism," in *Jews, Greeks and Christians: Studies in Honor of W. D. Davies*, ed. R. Hamerton-Kelly and R. Scroggs, 11–44.

65. Accordingly, Klijn ("The Sources and the Redaction," 72) disputes Harnisch's assertion that this is a time of the absence of God. Yet Harnisch's view has some basis too, since there is at least an absence of salvation in the present.

66. Bogaert, *Apocalypse*, 443–44.

67. Rosenthal, *Vier Apokryphische Bücher*, 72–103. Akiba was said to have comforted his colleagues after the destruction by emphasizing that restoration as well as destruction had been prophesied (*Sifre Deut* 4:3).

68. For the views of the sages see E. E. Urbach, *The Sages*, 1:667–92. Akiba eventually endorsed Bar Kokhba as messiah.

69. Sayler, "2 Baruch."

70. Charles, *The Apocalypse of Baruch*, 170–71. See also A. B. Kolenkow, "The Fall of the Temple and the Coming of the End," in *Society of Biblical Literature 1982 Seminar Papers*, ed. K. H. Richards, 243–50.

71. Harnisch tends to exaggerate the similarity between the two books, since he identifies the viewpoint of 4 Ezra with that of the angel (*Verhängnis und Verheissung*).

72. Bogaert, *Apocalypse*, 287–88.

73. Violet, *Die Apokalypsen des Esra und des Baruch*, LXXXI–XC.

74. N. Bonwetsch, *Apokalypse Abrahams*; G. H. Box, with J. I. Landsman, *The Apocalypse of Abraham*; B. Philonenko-Sayar and M. Philonenko, *L'Apocalypse d'Abraham*. This apocalypse was not included in the collections of Charles and Kautzsch but is included in P. Riessler, *Altjüdisches Schrifttum ausserhalb der Bibel*, 13–39; and J. H. Charlesworth, *Old Testament Pseudepigrapha*, where the treatment is by R. Rubinkiewicz and H. G. Lunt.

75. For example, the names of the idols Merumath and Barisat. See Box, *The Apocalypse*, XV. On the text see E. Turdeanu, "L'Apocalypse d'Abraham en Slave," in *Apocryphes Slaves et Roumains de l'Ancien Testament*, 173–200.

76. The tradition of Abraham's ascent is found in 4 Ezra 3:13–14; 2 Baruch 4:5; Pseudo-Philo's *Biblical Antiquities* 18:5 and *Testament of Abraham*.

77. *Bereshith Rabba* 38:19 (on Gen 11:28), *Tanna debe Eliyaha* 2:25. See Box, *The Apocalypse*, 88–94.

78. Compare the story of Bel and the Dragon. The biblical prototype of idol parodies is Isa 44:9–20.

79. A detailed analysis of the structure is provided by R. Rubinkiewicz, "La vision de l'histoire dans l'Apocalypse d'Abraham," *ANRW* 19/2, 1:137–51, based on his dissertation, "L'Apocalypse d'Abraham (en slave)."

80. See further G. Scholem, *Major Trends in Jewish Mysticism*, 67–70; I. Gruenwald, *Apocalyptic and Merkavah Mysticism*, 54–55; C. Rowland, *The Open Heaven*, 101–3.

81. Gruenwald, *Apocalyptic and Merkavah Mysticism*, 55–57; Rowland, *The Open Heaven*, 86–87.

82. Compare the division of history into twelve thousand years in the *Bundahišn*.

83. Rubinkiewicz, "La vision de l'histoire," 139–41. Rubinkiewicz also identifies other possible glosses. The Bogomils were a heretical sect in the Balkan peninsula between the tenth and the fourteenth century. See Turdeanu, *Apocryphes Slaves*, 1–17. Rubinkiewicz's view is rejected by Philonenko and Philonenko-Sayar (*L'Apocalypse d'Abraham*, 24), who admit interpolations only in 29:2b–11 and in 17:8–10, which was composed in Greek.

84. Compare Philonenko, *L'Apocalypse d'Abraham*, 32.

85. J. Licht, "Abraham, Apocalypse of," *EJ* 2:126–27.

86. G. W. E. Nickelsburg, *Jewish Literature between the Bible and the Mishnah*, 298.

87. So J. R. Mueller, "The Apocalypse of Abraham and the Destruction of the Second Jewish Temple," in *Society of Biblical Literature 1982 Seminar Papers*, ed. K. H. Richards, 342–49.

88. Box, *The Apocalypse*, xxi–xxiv. So now also Philonenko, *L'Apocalypse d'Abraham*, 34.

Chapter 8: Apocalyptic Literature
from the Diaspora in the Roman Period

1. J. J. Collins, *The Sibylline Oracles of Egyptian Judaism*, 57–64.

2. Ibid., 80–87; Tacitus *Histories* 2.8; Suetonius *Nero* 57; Dio Chrysostom *Orations* 21.10.

3. Belial is also said to come in the likeness of Nero ("a lawless king, the slayer of his mother") in *Ascension of Isaiah* 4:1.

4. A. Yarbro Collins, *The Combat Myth in the Book of Revelation*, 174–90.

5. B. McGinn, *Visions of the End*, 23 and passim. On the Antichrist see the classic work of W. Bousset, *The Antichrist Legend*.

6. The notion that Nero would return to conquer Rome is common in the later tradition.

7. Nero had been hailed as an emanation of Mithras by the Parthian Tiridates, whom he enthroned as king of Armenia.

8. Lactantius *Divine Institutions* 7.17: God will "send from heaven a great king."

9. Collins, *Sibylline Oracles*, 90. Comets marked the births of Alexander, Augustus, Mithridates, and of course Jesus.

10. Judg 5:20; Job 38:7. Compare *1 Enoch* 104:2–6. In Rev 22:16 Jesus is referred to as the morning star.

11. Num 24:17. Compare CD 7:18–20; 4QTestimonia and *Testament of Judah* 24:1.

12. J. J. Collins, *Between Athens and Jerusalem*, chap. 3. See also M. Hengel, "Messianische Hoffnung und politischer 'Radikalismus' in der 'jüdisch-hellenistischen Diaspora,'" in *Apocalypticism*, ed. D. Hellholm, 653–84.

13. R. Mayer, *Die biblische Vorstellung vom Weltbrand*.

14. This motif is found also in *Sib. Or.* 2:200–201; 5:207–13; 2 Pet 3:12. Compare Seneca *Consolatio ad Marciam* 26.6; *Thyestes* 844–74; *Nat. Quaest.* 3.29.1; and Nonnus *Dionysiaca* 38.347–409. The idea is related to the Stoic concept of *ekpyrōsis*.

15. On the ethics of the sibyl see Collins, *Between Athens and Jerusalem*, chap. 4.

16. *Sib. Or.* 5:416–17: the savior figure will restore the wealth to the good.

17. See my introductions to the later sibylline books in *Old Testament Pseudepigrapha*, ed. J. H. Charlesworth, 430–68.

18. J. Geffcken, *Komposition und Entstehungszeit der Oracula Sibyllina*, 47–53.

19. A. Kurfess, "Oracula Sibyllina I/II," *ZNW* 40 (1941) 151–65. Geffcken maintained a later, third-century date.

20. D. Flusser, "The four empires in the Fourth Sibyl and in the Book of Daniel," *Israel Oriental Studies* 2 (1972) 148–75.

21. Collins, *Sibylline Oracles*, 101–2. The doctrine of two world cycles is implicit in Hesiod and explicit in Heraclitus and Plato (*Politicus* 273 b–c). See also Josephus *Antiquities* 1.2.3 §§70–71; *Life of Adam and Eve* 49; I. Chaine, "Cosmogonie aquatique et conflagration finale d'après la secunda Petri," *RB* 46 (1937) 207–16.

22. J. J. Collins, "The Place of the Fourth Sibyl in the Development of the Jewish Sibyllina," *JJS* 25 (1974) 365-80.

23. J. Thomas, *Le Mouvement Baptiste en Palestine et Syrie*, 46-60. Although *Sib. Or.* 4 is clearly Jewish, it bears noteworthy resemblances to Ebionite and Elcasaite Christian sectarian teachings.

24. J. J. Collins, "The Genre Apocalypse in Hellenistic Judaism," in *Apocalypticism*, ed. D. Hellholm, 531-48.

25. G. Steindorff, *Die Apokalypse des Elias, eine unbekannte Apokalypse und Bruchstücke der Sophonias-Apokalypse*.

26. The fragments are combined in P. Riessler, *Altjüdisches Schrifttum ausserhalb der Bibel*, 168-77. See now O. S. Wintermute, "Apocalypse of Zephaniah," in *The Old Testament Pseudepigrapha*, ed. J. H. Charlesworth, 1:497-515.

27. The motif also had a background in Greek and Roman literature. See the classic discussion of A. Dieterich, *Nekyia. Beiträge zur Erklärung der neuentdeckten Petrusapokalypse*. M. Himmelfarb emphasizes the affinities with Jewish apocalypses such as the Book of the Watchers (*Tours of Hell*, 41-67).

28. J. T. Milik, *Books of Enoch*, 107-16. His main argument concerns the use of a late Greek word *syrmaiographa*, but a single term cannot determine the date of the whole document.

29. For the arguments see J. C. Greenfield, "Prolegomenon," in H. Odeberg, *3 Enoch or the Hebrew Book of Enoch*, XVIII-XX; U. Fischer, *Eschatologie und Jenseitserwartung im Hellenistischen Diasporajudentum*, 38-41. There is a probable reference to *2 Enoch* in Origen *De Principiis* 1.3.2.

30. A. Vaillant, *Le Livre des Secrets d'Hénoch, texte slave et traduction francaise;* R. H. Charles and W. R. Morfill presuppose the priority of the longer recension (*The Book of the Secrets of Enoch*). F. Andersen argues that neither recension can be accepted simply as the original ("2 Enoch," in *The Old Testament Pseudepigrapha*, ed. J. H. Charlesworth, 1:92-94).

31. Fischer, *Eschatologie*, 39-41. Vaillant regarded the short recension as Judeo-Christian.

32. A. Rubinstein, "Observations on the Slavonic Book of Enoch," *JJS* 13 (1962) 1-21.

33. R. H. Charles, "The Book of the Secrets of Enoch," *APOT*, 2:426; M. Philonenko, "La cosmologie du 'livre des secrets d'Hénoch,'" *Religions en Egypte Hellénistique et Romaine*, 109-16; Fischer, *Eschatologie*, 40.

34. G. W. E. Nickelsburg, *Jewish Literature*, 185.

35. The chapter divisions given here are those of Charles, in *APOT*. In Vaillant's numbering the ascent is described in chaps. 3-9.

36. Fischer, *Eschatologie*, 40.

37. Vaillant, *Le Livre des Secrets*, 3. Compare *1 Enoch* 83.

38. S. Pines, "Eschatology and the Concept of Time in the Slavonic Book of Enoch," in *Types of Redemption*, ed. R. J. Z. Werblowski and J. C. Bleeker, 75. Compare *m. Tamid* 4:1.

39. On the mysticism of *2 Enoch*, see I. Gruenwald, *Apocalyptic and Merkavah Mysticism*, 47-51; Rowland, *The Open Heaven*, 85.

40. J. C. Picard, *Apocalypsis Baruchi Graece*, 77-78; Fischer, *Eschatologie*, 75. The main affinities are with *2 Enoch* and the *Testament of Abraham*.

41. Origen *De Principiis* 2.3.6 refers to a book of Baruch which treats of seven heavens, and this is usually assumed to be *3 Baruch*. Picard denies that *3 Baruch* ever referred to more than five (*Apocalypsis*). See now H. E. Gaylord, Jr., "3 Baruch," in *The Old Testament Pseudepigrapha*, ed. J. H. Charlesworth, 1:655-56.

42. On the relation between Hades and the dragon see Fischer, *Eschatologie*, 80-82.

43. H. M. Hughes, "3 Baruch or The Greek Apocalypse of Baruch," *APOT*, 2:539. Compare *Sanhedrin* 92b.

44. J. C. Picard, "Observations sur l'Apocalypse grecque de Baruch. I: Cadre historique et efficacité symbolique," *Semitica* 20 (1970) 77-103, with reference to Lévi-Strauss's discussion of the "shamanistic cure."

45. The brick making recalls the labors of the Israelites in Egypt.

46. Picard, "Observations," 101-2.

47. Collins, *Between Athens and Jerusalem*, chap. 6.

48. Trans. Hughes, *APOT*, 2:541.

49. Nickelsburg, *Jewish Literature*, 302.

50. For text and translation see M. E. Stone, *The Testament of Abraham*.

51. E. Janssen, *Testament Abrahams*, 196.

52. A. B. Kolenkow, "The Genre Testament and the Testament of Abraham," in *Studies on the Testament of Abraham*, ed. G. W. E. Nickelsburg, 139-52.

53. G. W. E. Nickelsburg, "Structure and Message in the Testament of Abraham," in *Studies on the Testament of Abraham*, 92.

54. M. Delcor, *Le Testament d'Abraham*, 34; Janssen, *Testament Abrahams*, 198-99. N. Turner, who once defended a Hebrew Original of recension B ("The Testament of Abraham: A Study of the Original Language, Place of Origin, Authorship and Relevance") has now abandoned this view. See E. P. Sanders, "The Testaments of the Three Patriarchs," in *The Old Testament Pseudepigrapha*, ed. J. H. Charlesworth, 1:873-74.

55. Delcor, *Le Testament*, 67 68; Janssen, *Testament Abrahams*, 199-201. F. Schmidt argued that B was the prior recension and that it was composed in Palestine ("Le Testament d'Abraham: Introduction, édition de la recension courte, traduction et notes"). See Nickelsburg, *Studies on the Testament of Abraham*, 15-16.

56. Nickelsburg, *Jewish Literature*, 249-50.

57. Ibid., 251.

58. For Jewish Greek and Egyptian parallels to various motifs in the judgment scene see G. W. E. Nickelsburg, "Eschatology in the Testament of Abraham: A Study of the Judgment Scenes in the Two Recensions," in *Studies on the Testament of Abraham*, 23-64.

59. It should be noted that "Son of Adam" would be equivalent to "son of man" in Hebrew. On this judgment scene see Rowland, *The Open Heaven*, 107-9.

60. Kolenkow, "The Genre Testament," 142.

61. This is the only hint of a periodization of history in the *Testament of Abraham*. Compare the beast with seven heads in Revelation 17, but the idea of a seven-headed beast is ancient (e.g., the Ugaritic Shilyat of seven heads).

62. Delcor ascribes the *Testament of Abraham* to the Therapeutae (*Le Testament*, 73). The view that the book is Christian, which was current at the turn of the century, has long been abandoned.

Epilogue: The Legacy of Jewish Apocalypticism

1. For example, K. Burridge, *New Heaven, New Earth*; B. Wilson, *Magic and the Millennium*.

2. J. G. Gager, *Kingdom and Community: The Social World of Early Christianity*, 21, building on I. C. Jarvie, *The Revolution in Anthropology*, 51.

3. A. J. Saldarini, "Apocalypses and 'Apocalyptic' in Rabbinic Literature and Mysticism," *Semeia* 14 (1979) 187-205.

4. I. Gruenwald, *Apocalyptic and Merkavah Mysticism*.

5. G. W. Buchanan, *Revelation and Redemption*.

6. A. Yarbro Collins, "The Early Christian Apocalypses," *Semeia* 14 (1979) 61-121.

7. B. McGinn, *Visions of the End*; idem, *Apocalyptic Spirituality*. The genre was developed in a distinctive way in Gnosticism; see F. T. Fallon, "The Gnostic Apocalypses," *Semeia* 14 (1979) 123-58.

8. For recent discussions of Pauline apocalypticism see J. C. Beker, *Paul the Apostle*; W. A. Meeks, "Social Functions of Apocalyptic Language in Pauline Christianity," in *Apocalypticism*, ed. D. Hellholm, 685-703; H.-H. Schade, *Apocalyptische Christologie bei Paulus*.

9. R. E. Brown, *The Semitic Background of the term "Mystery" in the New Testament*.

10. On the correlation between eschatology and community see further Meeks, "Social Functions." Compare Acts 2, where the communal existence of the early Christians follows directly from the expectation of the end.

11. See N. Perrin, *A Modern Pilgrimage in New Testament Christology*, especially 10-22.

12. For recent discussions of this problem see M. Casey, *Son of Man: The Interpretation and Influence of Daniel 7*, 224-39; G. Vermes, "The Son of Man Debate," *JSNT* 1 (1978) 19-32; J. A. Fitzmyer, "Another View of the 'Son of Man' Debate," *JSNT* 4 (1979) 58-68.

13. See especially G. Theissen, *Sociology of Early Palestinian Christianity*, 24-30.

14. For example, J. Kallas, "The Apocalypse—An Apocalyptic Book?" *JBL* 86 (1967) 69-80.

15. For example, E. S. Fiorenza, "The Phenomenon of Early Christian Apocalyptic," in *Apocalypticism*, ed. D. Hellholm, 295-316.

16. J. J. Collins, "Pseudonymity, Historical Reviews and the Genre of the Revelation of John," *CBQ* 39 (1977) 329-43.

17. For example, R. H. Charles, *APOT*, 2:ix.

18. For the literary structure of Revelation see A. Yarbro Collins, *The Combat Myth in the Book of Revelation*, 5-55; idem, *The Apocalypse*, xii-xiv.

19. Note, however, the seven heads of the beast in Rev 17:9-12, which represent the reigns of seven kings. See Collins, "Pseudonymity," 338-40.

20. The manner of revelation in the Similitudes is rather similar to Revelation: predominantly visions, but with a brief reference to an ascent.

21. Compare Isaiah 63; Ps 2:9; 4 Ezra 13:8-11.

22. It is probable that a Jewish source is incorporated in Revelation 12. See A. Yarbro Collins, *Combat Myth*, 101-45.

23. See further A. Yarbro Collins, "The Political Perspective of the Revelation to John," *JBL* 96 (1977) 241-56. For a full discussion of the social setting and function see now her *Crisis and Catharsis. The Power of the Apocalypse*.

24. On the genre of liberation theology see C. H. Strain, "Ideology and Alienation: Theses on the Interpretation and Evaluation of Theologies of Liberation," *JAAR* 45 (1977) 473-90.

25. See, for example, the theological interpretation of Revelation by J. Ellul, *Apocalypse. The Book of Revelation*.

Bibliography

Adam, A., and C. Burchard. *Antike Berichte über die Essener*. 2d ed. Berlin: de Gruyter, 1972.

Alexandre, C. *Excursus ad Sibyllina*. Paris: Didot, 1856.

Andersen, F. "2 Enoch." In *The Old Testament Pseudepigrapha*, edited by J. H. Charlesworth, 1:91–221. Garden City, NY: Doubleday, 1983.

Anklesaria, B. T. *Zand-ī Vohuman Yasn*. Bombay: Camay Oriental Institute, 1967.

Assmann, J. "Königsdogma und Heilserwartung: Politische und kultische kaosbeschreibungen in altägyptischen Texten." In *Apocalypticism*, edited by D. Hellholm, 345–77. Tübingen: Mohr (Siebeck), 1983.

Attridge, H. W. "Greek and Latin Apocalypses," *Semeia* 14 (1979) 159–86.

Audet, J.-P. "Affinités littéraires et doctrinales du 'Manuel de Discipline.'" *RB* 59 (1952) 219–38; 60 (1953) 41–82.

Austin, J. L. *How to Do Things with Words*. 2d ed. Cambridge, MA: Harvard University Press, 1975.

Baldwin, J. G. *Daniel: An Introduction and Commentary*. Tyndale Old Testament Commentaries. Downers Grove, IL: InterVarsity, 1978.

Baltzer, K. *The Covenant Formulary*. Philadelphia: Fortress, 1971.

Barr, J. "Jewish Apocalyptic in Recent Scholarly Study." *BJRL* 58 (1975) 9–35.

Barth, C. *Die Errettung vom Tode in den individuellen Klage- und Dankliedern des Alten Testaments*. Zollikon: Evangelisches Verlag, 1947.

Baumgarten, J. M. "The Calendar in the Book of Jubilees and the Bible." In *Studies in Qumran Law*, 101–14. Leiden: Brill, 1977.

Beasley-Murray, G. R. "The Interpretation of Daniel 7." *CBQ* 45 (1983) 44–58.

Becker, J. *Die Testamente der zwölf Patriarchen*. JSHRZ 3/1. Gütersloh: Mohn, 1974, 1980.

———. *Untersuchungen zur Entstehungsgeschichte der Testamente der zwölf Patriarchen*. Leiden: Brill, 1970.

Beckwith, R. T. "The Earliest Enoch Literature and its Calendar: Marks of their Origin, Date and Motivation." *RQ* 10 (1981) 365-403.

Beker, J. C. *Paul the Apostle.* Philadelphia: Fortress, 1980.

Bentzen, A. *Daniel.* 2d ed. Tübingen: Mohr (Siebeck), 1952.

Berger, K. *Das Buch der Jubiläen.* JSHRZ 2/3. Gütersloh: Mohn, 1981.

Betz, H. D. "On the Problem of the Religio-Historical Understanding of Apocalypticism." *JTC* 6 (1969) 146-54.

————. "The Problem of Apocalyptic Genre in Greek and Hellenistic Literature: The Case of the Oracle of Trophonius." In *Apocalypticism*, edited by D. Hellholm, 577-97. Tübingen: Mohr (Siebeck), 1983.

Betz, O. *Offenbarung und Schriftforschung in der Qumransekte.* Tübingen: Mohr (Siebeck), 1960.

Bickermann, E. *Four Strange Books of the Bible.* New York: Schocken, 1967.

Bidez, J., and F. Cumont. *Les Mages Hellénisés.* 2 vols. Paris: Les Belles Lettres, 1938.

Black, M. *Apocalypsis Henochi Graece.* PVTG 3. Leiden: Brill, 1970.

————. "The Apocalypse of Weeks in the Light of 4QEn^g." *VT* 28 (1978) 464-69.

————. "The Eschatology of the Similitudes of Enoch." *JTS* 3 (1952) 1-10.

————. *The Scrolls and Christian Origins.* New York: Scribner, 1961.

Bogaert, P. *Apocalypse de Baruch.* 2 vols. Paris: Cerf, 1969.

Bonwetsch, N. *Apokalypse Abrahams.* Leipzig: Deichert, 1897.

Borger, R. "Die Beschwörungsserie Bīt Mēseri und die Himmelfahrt Henochs." *JNES* 33 (1974) 183-96.

Bousset, W. *The Antichrist Legend.* London: Hutchinson, 1896.

————. *Die Religion des Judentums im späthellenistischen Zeitalter.* 3d ed. Edited by H. Gressmann. Tübingen: Mohr (Siebeck), 1926.

Box, G. H. *The Ezra Apocalypse.* London: Pitman, 1912.

————. "IV Ezra." In *APOT*, 2:542-624.

————, with J. I. Landsman. *The Apocalypse of Abraham.* London: SPCK, 1918.

Boyce, M. "Middle Persian Literature." In *Handbuch der Orientalistik Vol. 4/1*, 31-61. Leiden: Brill, 1968.

Brandenburger, E. *Adam und Christus.* Neukirchen-Vluyn: Neukirchener Verlag, 1962.

————. *Himmelfahrt Moses.* JSHRZ 5/2. Gütersloh: Mohn, 1976.

————. *Die Verborgenheit Gottes im Weltgeschehen.* Zurich: Theologischer Verlag, 1981.

Braun, M. *History and Romance.* Oxford: Oxford University Press, 1938.

Breech, E. "These Fragments I have Shored against my Ruins: The Form and Function of 4 Ezra." *JBL* 92 (1973) 267-74.

Brekelmans, C. W. "The Saints of the Most High and their Kingdom." *OTS* 14 (1965) 305-29.

Brooke, G. "Qumran Pesher: Towards the Redefinition of a Genre." *RQ* 10 (1979-81) 483-503.

Brown, R. E. "J. Starcky's Theory of Qumran Messianic Development." *CBQ* 28 (1966) 51-57.

————. *The Semitic Background of the term "Mystery" in the New Testament.* Philadelphia: Fortress, 1968.

Brownlee, W. H. *The Midrash Pesher of Habakkuk.* SBLMS 24. Missoula, MT: Scholars Press, 1979.

Buchanan, G. W. *The Consequences of the Covenant.* Leiden: Brill, 1970.

————. *Revelation and Redemption.* Dillsboro, NC: Western North Carolina, 1978.

Burridge, K. *New Heaven, New Earth.* New York: Schocken, 1969

Caird, C. B. *The Language and Imagery of the Bible.* Philadelphia: Westminster, 1981.

Cameron, R., and A. J. Dewey. *The Cologne Mani Codex: "Concerning the Origin of his Body."* Missoula, MT: Scholars Press, 1979.

Cancik, H. "Libri Fatales: Römische Offenbarungsliteratur und Geschichtstheologie." In *Apocalypticism,* edited by D. Hellholm, 549-76. Tübingen: Mohr (Siebeck), 1983.

Caquot, A. "Le messianisme qumrânien." In *Qumrân,* edited by M. Delcor, 231-47. Leuven: Leuven University Press, 1978.

————. "Remarques sur les chap. 70 et 71 du livre éthiopien d'Hénoch." In *Apocalypses et Théologie de l'Espérance,* edited by H. Monloubou, 111-22. Paris: Cerf, 1977.

Carmignac, J. "Les Dangers de l'Eschatologie." *NTS* 17 (1971) 365-90.

————. "La future intervention de Dieu selon la pensée de Qumrân." In *Qumrân,* edited by M. Delcor, 219-29. Leuven: Leuven University Press, 1978.

————. "Qu'est-ce que l'Apocalyptique? Son emploi à Qumrân." *RQ* 10 (1979-81) 3-33.

Casey, P. M. "Porphyry and the Origin of the Book of Daniel." *JTS* 27 (1976) 15-33.

————. *Son of Man: The Interpretation and Influence of Daniel 7.* London: SPCK, 1979.

————. "The Use of Term 'Son of Man' in the Similitudes of Enoch." *JSJ* 7 (1976) 11-29.

Chaine, I. "Cosmogonie aquatique et conflagration finale d'après la secunda Petri." *RB* 46 (1937) 207-16.

Charles, R. H. *The Apocalypse of Baruch.* London: Black, 1896.

————. *Apocrypha and Pseudepigrapha of the Old Testament.* 2 vols. Oxford: Clarendon, 1913.

————. *The Assumption of Moses.* London: Black, 1897.

——. *The Book of Enoch*. Oxford: Clarendon, 1893.

——. *The Book of Jubilees or the Little Genesis*. London: Black, 1902.

——. *A Critical History of the Doctrine of a Future Life*. London: Black, 1899.

——. "II Baruch." *APOT*, 2:470–526.

——, and N. Forbes. "The Book of the Secrets of Enoch." *APOT*, 2:425–69.

——, and W. R. Morfill. *The Book of the Secrets of Enoch*. Oxford: Clarendon, 1896.

Charlesworth, J. H. "The Concept of the Messiah in the Pseudepigrapha." In *ANRW* 19/2, edited by W. Haase, 188–218. Berlin: de Gruyter, 1979.

——. "The Origin and Subsequent History of the Authors of the Dead Sea Scrolls: Four Transitional Phases among the Qumran Essenes." *RQ* 10 (1979–81) 213–33.

——. "The Portrayal of the Righteous as an Angel." In *Ideal Figures in Ancient Judaism*, edited by G. W. E. Nickelsburg and J. J. Collins, 135–47. Missoula, MT: Scholars Press, 1980.

——. "The SNTS Pseudepigrapha Seminars at Tübingen and Paris on the Books of Enoch." *NTS* 25 (1979) 315–23.

——, ed. *The Old Testament Pseudepigrapha*. Vol. 1. *Apocalyptic Literature and Testaments*. Garden City, NY: Doubleday, 1983.

Clifford, R. J. "History and Myth in Daniel 10–12." *BASOR* 220 (1975) 23–26.

Cohen, S. J. D. "Yavneh Revisited: Pharisees, Rabbis and the End of Jewish Sectarianism." In *Society of Biblical Literature 1982 Seminar Papers*, edited by K. H. Richards, 45–61. Chico, CA: Scholars Press, 1982.

Collins, J. J. "Apocalyptic Eschatology as the Transcendence of Death." *CBQ* 36 (1974) 21–43.

——. "Apocalyptic Genre and Mythic Allusions in Daniel." *JSOT* 21 (1981) 83–100.

——. "The Apocalyptic Literature in Recent Scholarly Study." In *Early Judaism and Its Modern Interpreters*, edited by R. A. Kraft and G. W. E. Nickelsburg. Chico, CA: Scholars Press, forthcoming.

——. "The Apocalyptic Technique: Setting and Function in the Book of the Watchers." *CBQ* 44 (1982) 91–111.

——. *The Apocalyptic Vision of the Book of Daniel*. HSM 16. Missoula, MT: Scholars Press, 1977.

——. *Between Athens and Jerusalem: Jewish Identity in the Hellenistic Diaspora*. New York: Crossroad, 1983.

——. "Cosmos and Salvation: Jewish Wisdom and Apocalyptic in the Hellenistic Age." *HR* 17 (1977) 121–42.

——. *Daniel, 1 & 2 Maccabees*. OTM 15. Wilmington, DE: Glazier, 1981.

——. *Daniel; with an Introduction to Apocalyptic Literature*. FOTL 20. Grand Rapids: Eerdmans, 1984.

————. "The Date and Provenance of the Testament of Moses." In *Studies on the Testament of Moses*, edited by G. W. E. Nickelsburg, 15–32. Missoula, MT: Scholars Press, 1973.

————. "The Epic of Theodotus and the Hellenism of the Hasmoneans." *HTR* 73 (1980) 91–104.

————. "The Genre Apocalypse in Hellenistic Judaism." In *Apocalypticism*, edited by D. Hellholm, 531–48. Tübingen: Mohr (Siebeck), 1983.

————. "The Heavenly Representative: The 'Son of Man' in the Similitudes of Enoch." In *Ideal Figures in Ancient Judaism*, edited by G. W. E. Nickelsburg and J. J. Collins, 111–33. Missoula, MT: Scholars Press, 1980.

————. "The Jewish Apocalypses." *Semeia* 14 (1979) 21–59.

————. "Jewish Apocalyptic against its Hellenistic Near Eastern Environment." *BASOR* 220 (1975) 27–36.

————. "The Mythology of Holy War in Daniel and the Qumran War Scroll." *VT* 25 (1975) 596–612.

————. "Patterns of Eschatology at Qumran." In *Traditions in Transformation*, edited by B. Halpern and J. D. Levenson, 351–75. Winona Lake, IN: Eisenbrauns, 1981.

————. "The Persian Apocalypses." *Semeia* 14 (1979) 207–17.

————. "The Place of the Fourth Sibyl in the Development of the Jewish Sibyllina." *JJS* 25 (1974) 365–80.

————. "Pseudonymity, Historical Reviews and the Genre of the Revelation of John." *CBQ* 39 (1977) 329–43.

————. "The Sibylline Oracles." In *The Old Testament Pseudepigrapha*, edited by J. H. Charlesworth, 1:317–472. Garden City, NY: Doubleday, 1983.

————. *The Sibylline Oracles of Egyptian Judaism.* SBLDS 13. Missoula, MT: Scholars Press, 1974.

————. "The Symbolism of Transcendence in Jewish Apocalyptic." *BR* 19 (1974) 5–22.

————, ed. *Apocalypse: The Morphology of a Genre. Semeia* 14. Missoula, MT: Scholars Press, 1979.

Colpe, C. "Der Begriff 'Menschensohn' und die Methode der Erforschung messianischer Prototypen." *Kairos* 12 (1970) 81–112.

————. "Die Himmelsreise der Seele ausserhalb und innerhalb der Gnosis." In *Le Origini dello Gnosticismo*, edited by U. Bianchi, 429–47. Leiden: Brill, 1967.

————. "Ho huios tou anthrōpou." *TDNT*, 8:400–430.

Coppens, J. *La Relève Apocalyptique du Messianisme Royal. II. Le Fils d'Homme Vétéro- et Intertestamentaire.* Louvain: Louvain University Press, 1983.

Cross, F. M. *The Ancient Library of Qumran.* Rev. ed. Garden City, NY: Doubleday, 1961.

————. *Canaanite Myth and Hebrew Epic.* Cambridge, MA: Harvard University Press, 1973.

————. "New Directions in the Study of Apocalyptic." *JTC* 6 (1969) 157–65.

Cumont, F. *Astrology and Religion among the Greeks and Romans.* 1912. Reprint. New York: Dover, 1960.

Daumas, F. "Littérature prophétique et exégétique égyptienne et commentaires esséniens." In *À la rencontre de Dieu: Mémorial Albert Gelin,* edited by A. Barucq, 203–21. Le Puy: Mappus, 1961.

Davenport, G. L. "The 'Anointed of the Lord' in the Psalms of Solomon 17." In *Ideal Figures in Ancient Judaism,* edited by G. W. E. Nickelsburg and J. J. Collins, 67–92. Missoula, MT: Scholars Press, 1980.

————. *The Eschatology of the Book of Jubilees.* Leiden: Brill, 1971.

Davies, P. R. "Calendrical Change and Qumran Origins: An Assessment of Vander-Kam's Theory." *CBQ* 45 (1983) 80–89.

————. *The Damascus Covenant: An Interpretation of the "Damascus Document."* JSOTSup 25. Sheffield: JSOT, 1983.

————. "Daniel Chapter Two." *JTS* 27 (1976) 392–401.

————. "Eschatology in the Book of Daniel." *JSOT* 17 (1980) 33–53.

————. "Hasidim in the Maccabean Period." *JJS* 28 (1977) 127–40.

————. *1 QM, The War Scroll from Qumran.* Rome: Biblical Institute Press, 1977.

Day, J. "The Daniel of Ugarit and Ezekiel and the Hero of the Book of Daniel." *VT* 30 (1980) 174–84.

————. "The Old Testament Utilisation of Language and Imagery Having Parallels in the Baal Mythology of the Ugaritic Texts." Diss., Cambridge, 1977.

Delcor, M. *Les Hymnes de Qumrân.* Paris: Letouzey et Ané, 1962.

————. *Le Livre de Daniel.* Paris: Gabalda, 1971.

————. "Le Temple d'Onias en Egypte." *RB* 75 (1968) 188–205.

————. *Le Testament d'Abraham.* Leiden: Brill, 1973.

————, ed. *Qumrân: Sa piété, sa théologie et son milieu.* Leuven: Leuven University Press, 1978.

Dequeker, L. "The 'Saints of the Most High' in Qumran and Daniel." *OTS* 18 (1973) 133–62.

Dexinger, F. *Henochs Zehnwochenapokalypse und offene Probleme der Apokalyptikforschung.* Leiden: Brill, 1977.

Dieterich, A. *Nekyia: Beiträge zur Erklärung der neuentdeckten Petrusapokalypse.* 3d ed. Darmstadt: Wissenschaftliche Buchgesellschaft, 1969.

Dimant, D. "The Biography of Enoch and the Books of Enoch." *VT* 33 (1983) 14–29.

————. "History according to the Vision of the Animals (Ethiopic Enoch 85–90)." *Mhqry yrwšlym bmhšbt yśr'l* 2 (1982) 18–37 (in Hebrew).

Dunand, F. "L'Oracle du Potier et la formation de l'apocalyptique en Egypte." In *L'Apocalyptique,* 39–67. Paris: Geuthner, 1977.

Dupont-Sommer, A. *The Essene Writings from Qumran.* Translated by G. Vermes. Gloucester, MA: Peter Smith, 1973.

————. "La mère de l'Aspic dans un hymne de Qoumrân." *RHR* 147 (1955) 174–88.

————. *Nouveaux aperçus sur les manuscrits de la Mer Morte.* Paris: Maisonneuve, 1953.

Ebeling, G. "The Ground of Christian Theology." *JTC* 6 (1969) 47–68.

Eddy, S. K. *The King is Dead: Studies in Near Eastern Resistance to Hellenism, 334–31 B.C.* Lincoln: University of Nebraska Press, 1961.

Ehrlich, E. L. *Der Traum im Alten Testament.* Berlin: de Gruyter, 1953.

Eliade, M. *The Myth of the Eternal Return.* New York: Pantheon, 1954.

————. *Shamanism: Archaic Techniques of Ecstasy.* Princeton: Princeton University Press, 1964.

Ellul, J. *Apocalypse: The Book of Revelation.* New York: Seabury, 1977.

Emerton, J. A. "The Origin of the Son of Man Imagery." *JTS* 9 (1958) 225–42.

Fallon, F. T. "The Gnostic Apocalypses." *Semeia* 14 (1979) 123–58.

Farmer, W. R. *Maccabees, Zealots and Josephus.* New York: Columbia University Press, 1956.

Ferch, A. J. "Daniel 7 and Ugarit: A Reconsideration." *JBL* 99 (1980) 75–86.

Fiorenza, E. S. "The Phenomenon of Early Christian Apocalyptic." In *Apocalypticism,* edited by D. Hellholm, 295–316. Tübingen: Mohr (Siebeck), 1983.

Fischer, U. *Eschatologie und Jenseitserwartung im Hellenistischen Diasporajudentum.* BZNW 44. Berlin: de Gruyter, 1978.

Fitzmyer, J. A. "Another View of the 'Son of Man' Debate." *JSNT* 4 (1979) 58–68.

Flusser, D. "The four empires in the Fourth Sibyl and in the Book of Daniel." *Israel Oriental Studies* 2 (1972) 148–75.

————. "The Testaments of the Twelve Patriarchs." *EJ* 13:184–86.

Fowler, A. "The Life and Death of Literary Forms." *New Literary History* 2 (1971) 199–216.

Fraser, P. *Ptolemaic Alexandria.* Oxford: Clarendon, 1972.

Frye, R. N. "Qumran and Iran." In *Christianity, Judaism and Other Greco-Roman Cults: Studies for Morton Smith at Sixty,* edited by J. Neusner, 3:167–74. Leiden: Brill, 1975.

Fuchs, H. *Der geistige Widerstand gegen Rom in der antiken Welt.* Berlin: de Gruyter, 1938.

Gager, J. G. *Kingdom and Community: The Social World of Early Christianity.* Englewood Cliffs, NJ: Prentice-Hall, 1975.

Gammie, J. G. "The Classification, Stages of Growth and Changing Intentions in the Book of Daniel." *JBL* 95 (1976) 191–204.

————. "On the Intention and Sources of Daniel I-VI." *VT* 31 (1981) 282–92.

Gaster, M. "The Hebrew Text of One of the Testaments of the Twelve Patriarchs." *Proceedings of the Society of Biblical Archeology* (1893–94) 33–49, 109–17.

Gaylord, H. E., Jr. "3 Baruch." In *The Old Testament Pseudepigrapha*, edited by J. H. Charlesworth, 1:653-79. Garden City, NY: Doubleday, 1983.

Geffcken, J. *Komposition und Entstehungszeit der Oracula Sibyllina*. Leipzig: Hinrichs, 1902.

Gerhart, M. "Generic Studies: Their Renewed Importance in Religious and Literary Interpretation." *JAAR* 45 (1977) 309-25.

Gese, H. "Anfang und Ende der Apokalyptik dargestellt am Sacharjabuch." *ZThK* 70 (1973) 20-49.

Ginzberg, L. *An Unknown Jewish Sect*. New York: Jewish Theological Seminary, 1976.

Glasson, T. F. *Greek Influence on Jewish Eschatology*. London: SPCK, 1961.

Goldstein, J. A. "Jewish Acceptance and Rejection of Hellenism." In *Jewish and Christian Self-Definition 2*, edited by E. P. Sanders, A. I. Baumgarten, and A. Mendelson. Philadelphia: Fortress, 1981.

——. *1 Maccabees*. AB 41. Garden City, NY: Doubleday, 1976.

Gooding, D. W. "The Literary Structure of the Book of Daniel and its Implications." *Tyndale Bulletin* 32 (1981) 43-79.

Gray, G. B. "The Psalms of Solomon." In *APOT*, 2:625-52.

Grayson, A. K. *Babylonian Historical-Literary Texts*. Toronto: University of Toronto Press, 1975.

——, and W. G. Lambert. "Akkadian Prophecies." *JCS* 18 (1964) 7-30.

Greenfield, J. C. "Prolegomenon." In H. Odeberg, *3 Enoch or the Hebrew Book of Enoch*. New York: Ktav, 1973.

——, and M. E. Stone. "The Enochic Pentateuch and the Date of the Similitudes." *HTR* 70 (1977) 51-65.

——. "Remarks on the Aramaic Testament of Levi from the Cairo Geniza (Planches XIII-XIV)." *RB* 86 (1979) 214-30.

Greenspoon, L. "The Origin of the Idea of Resurrection." In *Traditions in Transformation*, edited by B. Halpern and J. D. Levenson, 247-321. Winona Lake, IN: Eisenbrauns, 1981.

Grelot, P. "La géographie mythique d'Hénoch et ses sources orientales." *RB* 65 (1958) 33-69.

——. "La legende d'Hénoch dans les apocryphes et dans la Bible: Son origine et signification." *RSR* 46 (1958) 5-26, 181-210.

Griffiths, J. G. *Plutarch's De Iside et Osiride*. Cambridge: University of Wales, 1970.

Gruenwald, I. *Apocalyptic and Merkavah Mysticism*. Leiden: Brill, 1980.

Gunkel, H. *Schöpfung und Chaos in Urzeit und Endzeit*. Göttingen: Vandenhoeck & Ruprecht, 1895.

——. "Das vierte Buch Esra." In *Die Apokryphen und Pseudepigraphen des Alten Testaments*, edited by E. Kautzsch, 2:331-401. Tübingen: Mohr (Siebeck), 1900.

Hallo, W. W. "Akkadian Apocalypses." *IEJ* 16 (1966) 231-42.

Hammer, R. *The Book of Daniel*. Cambridge: University Press, 1976.

Hanson, P. D. "Apocalypse, Genre," "Apocalypticism." In *IDBSup*, 27-34.

———, *The Dawn of Apocalyptic*. Philadelphia: Fortress, 1975.

———, "Jewish Apocalyptic against its Near Eastern Environment." *RB* 78 (1971) 31-58.

———, "Prolegomena to the Study of Jewish Apocalyptic." In *Magnalia Dei: The Mighty Acts of God*, edited by F. M. Cross, W. E. Lemke, and P. D. Miller, Jr., 389-413. Garden City, NY: Doubleday, 1976.

———, "Rebellion in Heaven, Azazel and Euhemeristic Heroes in 1 Enoch 6-11." *JBL* 96 (1977) 195-233.

———, *Visionaries and Their Apocalypses*. Philadelphia: Fortress, 1983.

Harnisch, W. "Die Ironie der Offenbarung: Exegetische Erwägungen zur Zionsvision im 4. Buch Esra." In *Society of Biblical Literature 1981 Seminar Papers*, edited by K. H. Richards, 79-104. Chico, CA: Scholars Press, 1981.

———, "Der Prophet als Widerpart und Zeuge der Offenbarung: Erwägungen zur Interdependenz vom Form und Sache im IV Buch Esra." In *Apocalypticism*, edited by D. Hellholm, 461-93. Tübingen: Mohr (Siebeck), 1983.

———, *Verhängnis und Verheissung der Geschichte*. Göttingen: Vandenhoeck & Ruprecht, 1969.

Harrelson, W. "Ezra among the wicked in 2 Esdras 3-10." In *The Divine Helmsman: Studies on God's Control of Human Events, Presented to Lou H. Silberman*, edited by J. L. Crenshaw and S. Sandmel, 21-39. New York: Ktav, 1980.

Harrington, D. J. "Interpreting Israel's History: The Testament of Moses as a Rewriting of Deut 31-34." In *Studies on the Testament of Moses*, edited by G. W. E. Nickelsburg, 59-68. Missoula, MT: Scholars Press, 1973.

Hartman, L. *Asking for a Meaning: A Study of 1 Enoch 1-5*. Lund: Gleerup, 1979.

———, "The Function of Some So-Called Apocalyptic Timetables." *NTS* 22 (1976) 1-14.

———, *Prophecy Interpreted*. Lund: Gleerup, 1966.

———, "Survey of the Problem of Apocalyptic Genre." In *Apocalypticism*, edited by D. Hellholm. Tübingen: Mohr (Siebeck), 1983.

Hartman, L. F., and A. A. DiLella. *The Book of Daniel*. AB 23. Garden City, NY: Doubleday, 1978.

Hasel, G. F. "The Book of Daniel and Matters of Language: Evidences Relating to Names, Words, and the Aramaic Language." *AUSS* 19 (1981) 211-25.

———, "The Book of Daniel: Evidences Relating to Persons and Chronology." *AUSS* 19 (1981) 37-49.

———, "The Four World Empires of Daniel 2 Against Its Near Eastern Environment." *JSOT* 12 (1979) 17-30.

———. "The Identity of the 'Saints of the Most High' in Daniel 7." *Bib* 56 (1975) 173-92.

Hasslberger, B. *Hoffnung in der Bedrängnis.* St. Ottilien: Eos, 1977.

Haug, M., and E. W. West. *The Book of Arda Viraf.* London: Trübner, 1872.

Hayman, P. "The Problem of Pseudonymity in the Ezra Apocalypse." *JSJ* 6 (1975) 47-56.

Hellholm, D. "The Problem of Apocalyptic Genre and the Apocalypse of John." In *Society of Biblical Literature 1982 Seminar Papers*, ed. K. H. Richards, 157-98. Chico, CA: Scholars Press, 1982.

———. *Das Visionenbuch des Hermas als Apokalypse.* Lund: Gleerup, 1980.

———, ed. *Apocalypticism in the Mediterranean World and the Near East: Proceedings of the International Colloquium on Apocalypticism, Uppsala, August 12-17, 1979.* Tübingen: Mohr (Siebeck), 1983.

Hengel, M. *Judaism and Hellenism.* 2 vols. Philadelphia: Fortress, 1974.

———. "Messianische Hoffnung und politischer 'Radikalismus' in der jüdisch-hellenistischen Diaspora." In *Apocalypticism*, edited by D. Hellholm, 653-84. Tübingen: Mohr (Siebeck), 1983.

Herr, M. D. "The Calendar." In *The Jewish People in the First Century*, edited by S. Safrai and M. Stern, 2:834-64. Compendia Rerum Iudaicarum ad Novum Testamentum 2. Philadelphia: Fortress, 1976.

Hill, D. "Dikaioi as a Quasi-Technical Term." *NTS* 11 (1965) 296-302.

Himmelfarb, M. *Tours of Hell. An Apocalyptic Form in Jewish and Christian Literature.* Philadelphia: University of Pennsylvania, 1983.

Hinnells, J. R. "The Zoroastrian Doctrine of Salvation in the Roman World: A Study of the Oracle of Hystaspes." In *Man and His Salvation: Studies in Memory of S. G. F. Brandon*, edited by E. J. Sharpe and J. R. Hinnells, 125-48. Manchester: Manchester University Press, 1973.

Hirsch, E. D., Jr. *Validity in Interpretation.* New Haven: Yale University Press, 1967.

Höffken, P. "Heilszeitherrschererwartung im babylonischen Raum." *Die Welt des Orients* 9 (1977) 57-71.

Hollander, H. W. *Joseph as an Ethical Model in the Testaments of the Twelve Patriarchs.* Leiden: Brill, 1981.

Holm-Nielsen, S. *Hodayot: Psalms from Qumran.* Aarhus: Universitetsvorlaget, 1960.

Hooke, S. H. "The Myth and Ritual Pattern in Jewish and Christian Apocalyptic." In *The Labyrinth*, 213-33. London: SPCK, 1935.

Hooker, M. D. *The Son of Man in Mark.* Montreal: McGill University, 1967.

Horgan, M. P. *Pesharim: Qumran Interpretations of Biblical Books.* CBQMS 8. Washington, DC: CBA, 1979.

Hughes, H. M. "3 Baruch or The Greek Apocalypse of Baruch." In *APOT*, 2:527–41.

Hultgård, A. *L'Eschatologie des Testaments des Douze Patriarches.* 2 vols. Uppsala: Almqvist & Wiksell, 1977, 1981.

——. "The Ideal 'Levite,' the Davidic Messiah and the Saviour Priest in the Testaments of the Twelve Patriarchs." In *Ideal Figures in Ancient Judaism*, edited by G. W. E. Nickelsburg and J. J. Collins, 93–110. Missoula, MT: Scholars Press, 1980.

——. "Das Judentum in der hellenistisch-römischen Zeit und die iranische Religion—ein religionsgeschichtliche Problem." In *ANRW* 19/1, edited by W. Haase, 512–90. Berlin: de Gruyter, 1979.

Humphreys, W. L. "A Life-Style for the Diaspora: A Study of the Tales of Esther and Daniel." *JBL* 92 (1973) 211–23.

Hunzinger, C. H. "Fragmente einer älteren Fassung des Buches Milḥamā aus Höhle 4 von Qumran." *ZAW* 69 (1957) 131–57.

Huppenbauer, H. W. *Der Mensch zwischen zwei Welten.* Zurich: Zwingli, 1959.

Isaac, E. "1 Enoch." In *The Old Testament Pseudepigrapha*, edited by J. H. Charlesworth, 1:5–89. Garden City, NY: Doubleday, 1983.

Isenberg, S. R., and D. E. Owen. "Bodies, Natural and Contrived: The Work of Mary Douglas." *RelStudRev* 3 (1977) 1–16.

Jansen, H. Ludin. *Die Henochgestalt.* Oslo: Dybwad, 1939.

Janssen, E. *Testament Abrahams.* JSHRZ 3/2. Gütersloh: Mohn, 1975.

Jarvie, I. C. *The Revolution in Anthropology.* Chicago: Regnery, 1967.

Jaubert, A. *The Date of the Last Supper.* Staten Island, NY: Alba House, 1965.

——. *La notion d'alliance dans le Judaisme.* Paris: Seuil, 1963.

Jeremias, G. *Der Lehrer der Gerechtigkeit.* Göttingen: Vandenhoeck & Ruprecht, 1963.

Jeremias, J. "Pais theou." In *TDNT*, 5:687–88.

Jones, B. W. "The Prayer in Daniel IX." *VT* 18 (1968) 488–93.

Jonge, M. de. *"Notes on Testament of Levi II–VII."* In *Studies on the Testaments of the Twelve Patriarchs*, edited by M. de Jonge, 247–60. Leiden: Brill, 1975.

——. *The Testaments of the Twelve Patriarchs: A Critical Edition of the Greek Text.* Leiden: Brill, 1978.

——. *The Testaments of the Twelve Patriarchs: A Study of their Text, Composition and Origin.* Assen: van Gorcum, 1953.

——, ed. *Studies on the Testaments of the Twelve Patriarchs: Text and Interpretation.* SVTP 3. Leiden: Brill, 1975.

——, and A. S. van der Woude. "11QMelchizedek and the New Testament." *NTS* 12 (1965–66) 301–26.

Kabisch, R. *Das vierte Buch Esra auf seine Quellen untersucht.* Göttingen: Vandenhoeck & Ruprecht, 1889.

Kallas, J. "The Apocalypse—An Apocalyptic Book?" *JBL* 86 (1967) 69–80.

Käsemann, E. "The Beginnings of Christian Theology." *JTC* 6 (1969) 17–46.

Kaufman, S. A. "Prediction, Prophecy and Apocalypse in the Light of New Akkadian Texts." In *Proceedings of the Sixth World Congress of Jewish Studies, 1973*, edited by A. Shinan, 221–28. Jerusalem: World Union of Jewish Studies, 1977.

Kearns, R. *Vorfragen zur Christologie II. Ueberlieferungsgeschichtliche und Rezeptionsgeschichtliche Studie zur Vorgeschichte eines christologischen Hoheitstitels*. Tübingen: Mohr (Siebeck), 1980.

Kee, H. C. "'The Man' in Fourth Ezra: Growth of a Tradition." In *Society of Biblical Literature 1981 Seminar Papers*, edited by K. H. Richards, 199–208. Chico, CA: Scholars Press, 1981.

———. "The Testaments of the Twelve Patriarchs." In *The Old Testament Pseudepigrapha*, edited by J. H. Charlesworth, 1:775–828. Garden City, NY: Doubleday, 1983.

Kippenberg, H. "Die Geschichte der Mittelpersischen Apokalyptischen Traditionen." *Studia Iranica* 7 (1978) 49–80.

Kittel, B. P. *The Hymns of Qumran*. SBLDS 50. Chico, CA: Scholars Press, 1981.

Klijn, A. F. J. "2 Baruch." In *The Old Testament Pseudepigrapha*, edited by J. H. Charlesworth, 1:615–52. Garden City, NY: Doubleday, 1983.

———. "The Sources and the Redaction of the Syriac Apocalypse of Baruch." *JSJ* 1 (1970) 65–76.

———. *Die syrische Baruch-Apokalypse*. JSHRZ 5/2. Gütersloh: Mohn, 1976.

Knibb, M. A. "The Date of the Parables of Enoch: A Critical Review." *NTS* 25 (1979) 345–59.

———. *The Ethiopic Book of Enoch*. 2 vols. Oxford: Clarendon, 1978.

———. "Exile in the Damascus Document." *JSOT* 25 (1983) 99–117.

———. "The Exile in the Literature of the Intertestamental Period." *Heythrop Journal* 17 (1976) 253–72.

———. "Prophecy and the emergence of the Jewish apocalypses." In *Israel's Prophetic Tradition: Essays in Honour of Peter Ackroyd*, edited by R. Coggins, A. Phillips, and M. Knibb, 155–80. Cambridge: University Press, 1982.

———. *The Second Book of Esdras*. Cambridge: University Press, 1979.

Knierim, R. "Old Testament Form Criticism Reconsidered." *Int* 27 (1973) 435–68.

Kobelski, P. J. *Melchizedek and Melchireša*̕. CBQMS 10. Washington, DC: CBA, 1981.

Koch, K. *Das Buch Daniel*. Darmstadt: Wissenschaftliche Buchgesellschaft, 1980.

———. "Esras erste Vision. Weltzeiten und Weg des Höchsten." *BZ* 22 (1978) 46–75.

———. *Ratlos vor der Apokalyptik*. Gütersloh: Mohn, 1970. English translation *The Rediscovery of Apocalyptic*. SBT 2/22. Naperville, IL: Allenson, 1972.

———, "Spätisraelitisches Geschichtsdenken am Beispiel des Buches Daniel." *Historische Zeitschrift* 193 (1961) 1–32.

———, "Vom profetischen zu apokalyptischen Visionsbericht." In *Apocalypticism*, edited by D. Hellholm, 413–46. Tübingen: Mohr (Siebeck), 1983.

———, and J. M. Schmidt, eds. *Apokalyptik*. Darmstadt: Wissenschaftliche Buchgesellschaft, 1982.

Koenen, L. "The Prophecies of a Potter: A Prophecy of World Renewal Becomes an Apocalypse." In *Proceedings of the Twelfth International Congress of Papyrology*, edited by D. H. Samuel, 249–54. Toronto: Hakkert, 1970.

Kolenkow, A. B. "The Fall of the Temple and the Coming of the End." *Society of Biblical Literature 1982 Seminar Papers*, edited by K. H. Richards, 243–50. Chico, CA: Scholars Press, 1982.

———, "The Genre Testament and the Testament of Abraham." In *Studies on the Testament of Abraham*, edited by G. W. E. Nickelsburg, 139–52. Missoula, MT: Scholars Press, 1976.

———, "An Introduction to II Baruch 53, 56–74: Structure and Substance." Diss., Harvard, 1972.

Korteweg, T. "The meaning of Naphtali's visions." In *Studies on the Testaments of the Twelve Patriarchs*, edited by M. de Jonge, 261–90. Leiden: Brill, 1975.

Kraft, R. A. "'Ezra' Materials in Judaism and Christianity." In *ANRW* 19/2, edited by W. Haase, 119–36. Berlin: de Gruyter, 1979.

Küchler, M. *Frühjüdische Weisheitstraditionen*. Göttingen: Vandenhoeck & Ruprecht, 1979.

Kuhn, H. W. *Enderwartung und gegenwärtiges Heil*. Göttingen: Vandenhoeck & Ruprecht, 1966.

Kuhn, K. G. "Die Sektenschrift und die iranische Religion." *ZThK* 49 (1952) 293–316.

———, "The Two Messiahs of Aaron and Israel." In *The Scrolls and the New Testament*, edited by K. Stendahl, 54–64. New York: Harper, 1957.

Kurfess, A. "Christian Sibyllines." In *New Testament Apocrypha*, edited by E. Hennecke and W. Schneemelcher, 2:703–45. Philadelphia: Westminster, 1965.

———, "Oracula Sibyllina I/II." *ZNW* 40 (1941) 151–65.

———, *Sibyllinische Weissagungen*. Berlin: Heimeran, 1951.

Kvanig, H. S. "An Akkadian Vision as Background for Daniel 7." *Studia Theologica* 35 (1981) 85–89.

Lacocque, A. "Apocalyptic Symbolism: A Ricoeurian Hermeneutical Approach." *BR* 26 (1981) 6–15.

———, *The Book of Daniel*. Atlanta: John Knox, 1979.

———, *Daniel et son Temps*. Geneva: Labor et Fides, 1983.

———, "The Liturgical Prayer in Daniel 9." *HUCA* 47 (1976) 119–42.

———. "The Vision of the Eagle in 4 Esdras: A Rereading of Daniel 7 in the First Century c.e." In *Society of Biblical Literature 1981 Seminar Papers*, edited by K. H. Richards, 237–58. Chico, CA: Scholars Press, 1981.

Lambert, W. G. *The Background of Jewish Apocalyptic*. London: Athlone, 1978.

———. "Enmeduranki and Related Matters." *JCS* 21 (1967) 126–38.

Lanchester, H. C. "The Sibylline Oracles." In *APOT*, 2:368–406.

Laperrousaz, E.-M. "Le Testament de Moïse." *Semitica* 19 (1970).

Leach, E. "Genesis as Myth." In *Myth and Cosmos*, edited by J. Middleton, 1–13. Garden City, NY: Natural History Press, 1967.

———. "Lévi-Strauss in the Garden of Eden: An Examination of Some Recent Developments in the Analysis of Myth." In *Claude Lévi Strauss: The Anthropologist as Hero*, edited by E. N. Hayes and T. Hayes, 47–60. Cambridge, MA: M.I.T. Press, 1970.

Lenglet, A. "La structure littéraire de Daniel 2–7." *Bib* 53 (1972) 169–90.

Levine, B. A. "The Temple Scroll: Aspects of its Historical Provenance and Literary Character." *BASOR* 233 (1978) 5–23.

Lévi-Strauss, C. *Structural Anthropology*. New York: Basic Books, 1963.

Licht, J. "Abraham, Apocalypse of." In *EJ*, 2:126–27.

———. "Taxo, or the Apocalyptic Doctrine of Vengeance." *JJS* 12 (1961) 95–103.

Lindars, B. "Re-enter the Apocalyptic Son of Man." *NTS* 22 (1975–76) 52–72.

Lindblom, J. *Prophecy in Ancient Israel*. Oxford: Blackwell, 1962.

Lohmeyer, E. *Diatheke*. Leipzig: Hinrichs, 1913.

Lücke, F. *Versuch einer vollständigen Einleitung in die Offenbarung Johannis und in die gesamte apokalyptische Literatur*. Bonn: Weber, 1832.

Luck, U. "Das Weltverständnis in der jüdischen Apokalyptik: Dargestellt am Äthiopischen Henochbuch und am 4 Esra." *ZThK* 73 (1976) 283–305.

McCown, C. C. "Hebrew and Egyptian Apocalyptic Literature." *HTR* 18 (1925) 357–411.

McGinn, B. *Apocalyptic Spirituality*. New York: Paulist, 1979.

———. *Visions of the End*. New York: Columbia University Press, 1979.

Mair, A. W. *Callimachus, Lycophron and Aratus*. LCL. Cambridge, MA: Harvard University Press, 1921, 1955.

Manson, T. W. "The Son of Man in Daniel, Enoch and the Gospels." In *Studies in the Gospels and Epistles*. Manchester: Manchester University Press, 1962.

Mansoor, M. *The Thanksgiving Hymns*. Grand Rapids: Eerdmans, 1961.

Mayer, R. *Die biblische Vorstellung vom Weltbrand*. Bonn: Bonn University, 1956.

Meeks, W. A. "Social Functions of Apocalyptic Language in Pauline Christianity." In *Apocalypticism*, edited by D. Hellholm, 685–703. Tübingen: Mohr (Siebeck), 1983.

Mertens, A. *Das Buch Daniel im Lichte der Texte vom Toten Meer*. Stuttgart: Katholisches Bibelwerk, 1971.

Metzger, B. M. "Literary Forgeries and Canonical Pseudepigrapha." *JBL* 91 (1972) 3–24.

Meyer, R. *Das Gebet des Nabonid*. Berlin: Akademie-Verlag, 1962.

Milgrom, J. "The Temple Scroll." *BA* 41 (1978) 105–20.

Milik, J. T. *The Books of Enoch*. Oxford: Clarendon, 1976.

——. "Ecrits prééséniens de Qumrân: d'Hénoch à Amram." In *Qumrân*, edited by M. Delcor, 91–106. Leuven: Leuven University, 1978.

——. "4QVisions de 'Amram et une citation d'Origene." *RB* 79 (1972) 77–97.

——. "Milkî-sedeq et Milkî-reša dans les anciens écrits juifs et chrétiens." *JJS* 23 (1972) 95–144.

——. "'Prière de Nabonide' et autres écrits d'un cycle de Daniel." *RB* 63 (1956) 407–15.

——. *Ten Years of Discovery in the Wilderness of Judaea*. London: SCM, 1959.

——. "Le Testament de Lévi en araméen: fragment de la grotte 4 de Qumrân." *RB* 62 (1955) 398–406.

Millar, F. "The Background to the Maccabean Revolution: Reflections on Martin Hengel's 'Judaism and Hellenism.'" *JJS* 29 (1978) 1–21.

Millar, W. R. *Isaiah 24–27 and the Origin of Apocalyptic*. HSM 11. Missoula, MT: Scholars Press, 1976.

Miller, P. D. *The Divine Warrior in Early Israel*. HSM 5. Cambridge, MA: Harvard University Press, 1973.

Momigliano, A. "La Portata Storica dei Vaticini sul Settimo Re nel Terzo Libro degli Oracoli Sibillini." In *Forma Futuri: Studi in Onore del Cardinale Pellegrino*, 1077–84. Turin: Bottega d'Erasmo, 1975.

Montefiore, C. G. *IV Ezra: A Study in the Development of Universalism*. London: Allen & Unwin, 1929.

Montgomery, J. A. *The Book of Daniel*. New York: Scribner, 1927.

Moore, G. F. *Judaism in the First Centuries of the Christian Era*. New York: Schocken, 1971.

Mowinckel, S. "The Hebrew Equivalent of Taxo in Ass. Mos. IX." In *Congress Volume: Copenhagen 1953*, VTSup 1, 88–96. Leiden: Brill, 1953.

——. *He That Cometh*. Nashville: Abingdon, 1955.

——. "Some Remarks on Hodayoth 39:5–20." *JBL* 75 (1956) 265–76.

Müller, H.-P. "Mantische Weisheit und Apokalyptik." In *Congress Volume: Uppsala 1971*, VTSup 22, 268–93. Leiden: Brill, 1972.

Müller, U. B. *Messias und Menschensohn in jüdischen Apokalypsen und in der Offenbarung des Johannes*. Gütersloh: Mohn, 1972.

Mueller, J. R. "The Apocalypse of Abraham and the Destruction of the Second Jewish Temple." *Society of Biblical Literature 1982 Seminar Papers*, edited by K. H. Richards, 341–49. Chico, CA: Scholars Press, 1982.

Münchow, C. *Ethik und Eschatologie: Ein Beitrag zum Verständnis der früh-jüdischen Apokalyptik.* Göttingen: Vandenhoeck & Ruprecht, 1982.

Murphy-O'Connor, J. "The Essenes and Their History." *RB* 81 (1974) 215–44.

——. "The Essenes in Palestine." *BA* 40 (1977) 100–124.

Myers, J. M. *I and II Esdras.* AB 42. Garden City, NY: Doubleday, 1974.

Neugebauer, O. *The Astronomical Chapters of the Ethiopic Book of Enoch (72–82). With Additional Notes on the Aramaic Fragments by M. Black.* Copenhagen: Munksgaard, 1981.

Newsom, C. A. "The Development of 1 Enoch 6–19: Cosmology and Judgment." *CBQ* 42 (1980) 310–29.

Nickelsburg, G. W. E. "An Antiochan Date for the Testament of Moses." In *Studies on the Testament of Moses,* edited by G. W. E. Nickelsburg, 33–37. Missoula, MT: Scholars Press, 1973.

——. "Apocalyptic and Myth in 1 Enoch 6–11." *JBL* 96 (1977) 383–405.

——. "The Apocalyptic Message of 1 Enoch 92–105." *CBQ* 39 (1977) 309–28.

——. "The Books of Enoch in Recent Research." *RelStudRev* 7 (1981) 210–17.

——. "Enoch, Levi and Peter: Recipients of Revelation in Upper Galilee." *JBL* 100 (1981) 575–600.

——. "The Epistle of Enoch and the Qumran Literature." *JJS* 33 (1982) 333–48.

——. "Eschatology in the Testament of Abraham: A Study of the Judgment Scenes in the Two Recensions." In *Studies on the Testament of Abraham,* edited by G. W. E. Nickelsburg, 23–64. Missoula, MT: Scholars Press, 1976.

——. *Jewish Literature between the Bible and the Mishnah.* Philadelphia: Fortress, 1981.

——. "Narrative Traditions in the Paraleipomena of Jeremiah and 2 Baruch." *CBQ* 35 (1973) 60–68.

——. *Resurrection, Immortality and Eternal Life in Intertestamental Judaism.* Cambridge, MA: Harvard University Press, 1972.

——. "Riches, the Rich and God's Judgment in 1 Enoch 92–105 and the Gospel According to Luke." *NTS* 25 (1979) 324–44.

——. "Social Aspects of Palestinian Jewish Apocalypticism." In *Apocalypticism,* edited by D. Hellholm, 639–52. Tübingen: Mohr (Siebeck), 1983.

——. "Structure and Message in the Testament of Abraham." In *Studies on the Testament of Abraham,* edited by G. W. E. Nickelsburg, 85–93. Missoula, MT: Scholars Press, 1976.

——, ed. *Studies on the Testament of Abraham.* Missoula, MT: Scholars Press, 1976.

——, ed. *Studies on the Testament of Moses.* Missoula, MT: Scholars Press, 1973.

——, and J. J. Collins, eds. *Ideal Figures in Ancient Judaism.* Missoula, MT: Scholars Press, 1980.

Niditch, S. *The Symbolic Vision in Biblical Tradition.* HSM 30. Chico: Scholars, 1983.

————. "The Visionary." In *Ideal Figures in Ancient Judaism,* edited by G. W. E. Nickelsburg and J. J. Collins, 153–79. Missoula, MT: Scholars Press, 1980.

Niditch, S., and R. Doran. "The Success Story of the Wise Courtier: A Formal Approach." *JBL* 96 (1977) 179–93.

Nikiprowetzky, V. *La Troisième Sibylle.* Paris: Mouton, 1970.

Nolland, J. "Sib Or 3. 265–94: An Early Maccabean Messianic Oracle." *JTS* 30 (1979) 158–67.

Nordheim, E. von. *Die Lehre der Alten. I.* Leiden: Brill, 1980.

North, R. "Prophecy to Apocalyptic via Zechariah." In *Congress Volume: Uppsala 1971,* VTSup 22, 47–71. Leiden: Brill, 1972.

Noth, M. "The Holy Ones of the Most High." In *The Laws in the Pentateuch and Other Essays,* 215–28. Philadelphia: Fortress, 1967.

————. "The Understanding of History in Old Testament Apocalyptic." In *The Laws in the Pentateuch and Other Essays,* 194–214. Philadelphia: Fortress, 1967.

Oppenheim, A. L. *The Interpretation of Dreams in the Ancient Near East.* Philadelphia: American Philosophical Society, 1956.

Osten-Sacken, P. von der. *Gott und Belial.* Göttingen: Vandenhoeck & Ruprecht, 1969.

————. *Die Apokalyptik in ihrem Verhältnis zu Prophetie und Weisheit.* Munich: Kaiser, 1969.

Patte, D. *Early Jewish Hermeneutic in Palestine.* SBLDS 22. Missoula, MT: Scholars Press, 1975.

Paul, S. "Heavenly Tablets and the Book of Life." *Journal of the Ancient Near Eastern Society of Columbia University* 5 (1973) 345–53.

Perrin, N. "Eschatology and Hermeneutics: Reflections on Method in the Interpretation of the New Testament." *JBL* 93 (1974) 3–14.

————. *A Modern Pilgrimage in New Testament Christology.* Philadelphia: Fortress, 1974.

Philonenko, M. "La cosmologie du livre des secrets d'Hénoch." In *Religions en Egypte Hellénistique et Romaine,* 109–16. Paris: Presses universitaires de France, 1969.

————. *Les Interpolations chrétiennes des Testaments des Douze Patriarches et les manuscrits de Qoumrân.* Paris: Presses universitaires de France, 1960.

Philonenko-Sayer, B., and M. Philonenko. *L'Apocalypse d'Abraham: Introduction, Texte slave, traduction et notes.* Semitica 31. Paris: Maisonneuve, 1981.

Picard, J. C. *Apocalypsis Baruchi Graece.* PVTG 2. Leiden: Brill, 1967.

————. "Observations sur l'Apocalypse grecque de Baruch I: Cadre historique et efficacité symbolique." *Semitica* 20 (1970) 77–103.

Pines, S. "Eschatology and the Concept of Time in the Slavonic Book of Enoch." In *Types of Redemption*, edited by R. J. Z. Werblowski and J. C. Bleeker, 72–87. Leiden: Brill, 1970.

Plöger, O. *Theocracy and Eschatology*. Richmond: John Knox, 1968.

Pope, M. *El in the Ugaritic Texts*. VTSup 2. Leiden: Brill, 1955.

Porteous, N. W. *Daniel*. 2d ed. London: SCM, 1979.

Pouilly, J. *La Règle de la Communauté de Qumrân: Son Evolution Littéraire*. Paris: Gabalda, 1976.

Priest, J. "The Testament of Moses." In *The Old Testament Pseudepigrapha*, edited by J. H. Charlesworth, 1:919–34. Garden City, NY: Doubleday, 1983.

Rabin, C. *The Zadokite Documents*. Oxford: Clarendon, 1958.

Rad, G. von. *Theologie des Alten Testaments*. Vol. 2. 4th ed. Munich: Kaiser, 1965.

Ramsey, I. T. *Models and Mystery*. London: Oxford University Press, 1964.

Reid, S. B. "1 Enoch: The Rising Elite of the Apocalyptic Movement." In *Society of Biblical Literature 1983 Seminar Papers*, edited by K. H. Richards, 147–56. Chico, CA: Scholars Press, 1983.

Resch, A. *Der Traum im Heilsplan Gottes*. Freiburg: Herder, 1964.

Riessler, P. *Altjüdisches Schrifttum ausserhalb der Bibel*. 1928. Reprint. Darmstadt: Wissenschaftliche Buchgesellschaft, 1966.

Ringgren, H. "Der Weltbrand in den Hodajot." In *Bibel und Qumran: Beiträge zur Erforschung der Beziehungen zwischen Bibel- und Qumranwissenschaft: Hans Bardtke zum 22.9.1966*, edited by S. Wagner, 177–82. Berlin: Evangelische Haupt-Bibelgesellschaft, 1968.

Rogerson, J. W. "The Hebrew Conception of Corporate Personality. A Reexamination." *JTS* 21 (1970) 1–16.

———. *Myth in Old Testament Interpretation*. Berlin: de Gruyter, 1974.

Rosenthal, F. *Vier Apokryphische Bücher aus der Zeit und Schule R. Akibas*. Leipzig: Schulze, 1885.

Rössler, D. *Gesetz und Geschichte*. Neukirchen-Vluyn: Neukirchener Verlag, 1960.

Rost, L. "Zum Buch der Kriege der Söhne des Lichts gegen die Söhne der Finsternis." *TLZ* 80 (1955) 205–6.

Rowland, C. *The Open Heaven: A Study of Apocalyptic in Judaism and Christianity*. New York: Crossroad, 1982.

———. "The Visions of God in Apocalyptic Literature." *JSJ* 10 (1979) 137–54.

Rowley, H. H. *Darius the Mede and the Four World Empires*. Cardiff: University of Wales, 1935.

———. *The Relevance of Apocalyptic*. London: Athlone, 1944. Reprint. Greenwood, SC: Attic, 1980.

———. "The Unity of the Book of Daniel." In *The Servant of the Lord and Other Essays on the Old Testament*, 237–68. London: Lutterworth, 1952.

Rubinkiewicz, R. "L'Apocalypse d'Abraham (en slave)." Diss., Pontifical Biblical Institute, Rome, 1977.

——. "La vision de l'histoire dans l'Apocalypse d'Abraham." *ANRW* 19/2, edited by W. Haase, 137–51. Berlin: de Gruyter, 1979.

——, and H. G. Lunt. "The Apocalypse of Abraham." In *The Old Testament Pseudepigrapha*, edited by J. H. Charlesworth, 1:681–705. Garden City, NY: Doubleday, 1983.

Rubinstein, A. "Observations on the Slavonic Book of Enoch." *JJS* 13 (1962) 1–21.

Ruppert, L. *Der Leidende Gerechte*. Würzburg: Echter, 1972.

Russell, D. S. *The Method and Message of Jewish Apocalyptic*. Philadelphia: Westminster, 1964.

Saldarini, A. J. "Apocalypses and 'Apocalyptic' in Rabbinic Literature and Mysticism." *Semeia* 14 (1979) 187–205.

——. "Varieties of Rabbinic Responses to the Destruction of the Temple." *Society of Biblical Literature 1982 Seminar Papers*, edited by K. H. Richards, 437–58. Chico, CA: Scholars Press, 1982.

Sanders, E. P. "The Covenant as a Soteriological Category and the Nature of Salvation in Palestinian and Hellenistic Judaism." In *Jews, Greeks and Christians: Studies in Honor of W. D. Davies*, edited by R. Hamerton-Kelly and R. Scroggs, 11–44. Leiden: Brill, 1976.

——. "The Genre of Palestinian Jewish Apocalypses." In *Apocalypticism*, edited by D. Hellholm, 447–59. Tübingen: Mohr (Siebeck), 1983.

——. *Paul and Palestinian Judaism*. Philadelphia: Fortress, 1977.

——. "The Testaments of the Three Patriarchs." In *The Old Testament Pseudepigrapha*, edited by J. H. Charlesworth, 1:869–918. Garden City, NY: Doubleday, 1983.

Sayler, G. "2 Baruch: A Story of Grief and Consolation." In *Society of Biblical Literature 1982 Seminar Papers*, edited by K. H. Richards, 485–500. Chico, CA: Scholars Press, 1982.

Schade, H.-H. *Apokalyptische Christologie bei Paulus*. Göttingen: Vandenhoeck & Ruprecht, 1981.

Schäfer, P. *Studien zur Geschichte und Theologie des Rabbinischen Judentums*. Leiden: Brill, 1978.

Schiffmann, L. H. *Halakhah at Qumran*. Leiden: Brill, 1975.

Schmidt, F. "Le Testament d'Abraham: Introduction, édition de la recension courte, traduction et notes." Thesis, Strasbourg, 1971.

Schmidt, J. M. *Die jüdische Apokalyptik*. Neukirchen-Vluyn: Neukirchener Verlag, 1969.

Schmidt, N. "The Original Language of the Parables of Enoch." In *Old Testament and Semitic Studies in Memory of W. R. Harper*, 2:329–49. Chicago: University of Chicago Press, 1980.

Schmithals, W. *The Apocalyptic Movement*. Nashville: Abingdon, 1975.

Schreiner, J. *Das 4. Buch Esra.* JSHRZ 5/4. Gütersloh: Mohn, 1981.

Scholem, G. *Major Trends in Jewish Mysticism.* 1941. New York: Schocken, 1961.

Schürer, E. *The History of the Jewish People in the Age of Jesus Christ (175 B.C.-A.D. 135).* Revised by G. Vermes, F. Millar, and M. Black. Edinburgh: Clark, 1973 (vol. 1), 1979 (vol. 2).

Schulz, P. *Der Autoritätsanspruch des Lehrers der Gerechtigkeit in Qumran.* Meisenheim am Glan: Hain, 1974.

Schüpphaus, J. *Die Psalmen Salomos.* Leiden: Brill, 1977.

Schwartz, D. R. "The Tribes of As. Mos. 4:7-9." *JBL* 99 (1980) 217-23.

Shaked, S. "Qumran and Iran: Further Considerations." *Israel Oriental Studies* 2 (1972) 433-46.

Sjöberg, E. *Der Menschensohn im Äthiopischen Henochbuch.* Lund: Gleerup, 1946.

Skehan, P. W. "A Fragment of the 'Song of Moses' (Deut 32) from Qumran." *BASOR* 136 (1954) 12-15.

Slingerland, H. D. *The Testaments of the Twelve Patriarchs: A Critical History of Research.* SBLMS 21. Missoula, MT: Scholars Press, 1977.

Smith, J. Z. "Native Cults in the Hellenistic Period." *HR* 11 (1971) 236-49.

——. "Wisdom and Apocalyptic." In *Religious Syncretism in Antiquity*, edited by B. Pearson, 131-56. Missoula, MT: Scholars Press, 1975.

Smith, M. "The Description of the Essenes in Josephus and the Philosophoumena." *HUCA* 29 (1958) 273-313.

——. "On the History of *Apokalyptō* and *Apokalypsis*." In *Apocalypticism*, edited by D. Hellholm, 9-20. Tübingen: Mohr (Siebeck), 1983.

——. "What is implied by the Variety of Messianic Figures?" *JBL* 78 (1959) 66-72.

Starcky, J. "Les Maitres de Justice et la chronologie de Qumrân." In *Qumrân*, edited by M. Delcor. Leuven: Leuven University, 1978.

——. "Les quatres étapes du messianisme à Qumrân." *RB* 70 (1963) 481-505.

Steck, O. H. *Israel und das gewaltsame Geschick der Propheten.* Neukirchen-Vluyn: Erziehungsverein, 1967.

Stegemann, H. "Die Bedeutung der Qumranfunde für die Erforschung der Apokalyptik." In *Apocalypticism*, edited by D. Hellholm, 495-530. Tübingen: Mohr (Siebeck), 1983.

——. *Die Entstehung der Qumrangemeinde.* Bonn: published privately, 1971.

Steindorff, G. *Die Apokalypse des Elias, eine unbekannte Apokalypse und Bruchstücke der Sophonias-Apokalypse.* Texte und Untersuchungen zur Geschichte der altchristlichen Literatur NF 2/3a. Leipzig: Hinrichs, 1899.

Stone, M. E. "Apocalyptic—Vision or Hallucination." *Milla wa-Milla* 14 (1974) 47-56.

——. *The Armenian Version of IV Ezra.* Missoula, MT: Scholars Press, 1979.

————. "The Book of Enoch and Judaism in the Third Century, B.C.E." *CBQ* 40 (1978) 479–92.

————. "Coherence and Inconsistency in the Apocalypses: The Case of 'The End' in 4 Ezra." *JBL* 102 (1983) 229–43.

————. "The Concept of the Messiah in IV Ezra." In *Religions in Antiquity: Essays in Memory of E. R. Goodenough*, edited by J. Neusner, 295–312. Leiden: Brill, 1968.

————. "Features of the Eschatology of IV Ezra." Diss., Harvard, 1965.

————. "Lists of Revealed Things in the Apocalyptic Literature." In *Magnalia Dei: The Mighty Acts of God*, edited by F. M. Cross, W. E. Lemke, and P. D. Miller, Jr., 439–43. Garden City, NY: Doubleday, 1976.

————. "Reactions to Destructions of the Second Temple: Theology, Perception and Conversion." *JSJ* 12 (1981) 195–204.

————. *Scriptures, Sects and Visions*. Philadelphia: Fortress, 1980.

————. *The Testament of Abraham*. Missoula, MT: SBL, 1972.

Strain, C. H. "Ideology and Alienation: Theses on the Interpretation and Evaluation of Theologies of Liberation." *JAAR* 45 (1977) 473–90.

Strugnell, J. "An Angelic Liturgy at Qumran—4QSerek Šîrôt Haššabbat." In *Congress Volume: Oxford 1959*, VTSup 7, 318–45. Leiden: Brill, 1960.

Suter, D. W. "Fallen Angel, Fallen Priest. The Problem of Family Purity in 1 Enoch 6–16." *HUCA* 50 (1979) 115–35.

————. "Māšāl in the Similitudes of Enoch." *JBL* 100 (1981) 193–212.

————. *Tradition and Composition in the Parables of Enoch*. SBLDS 47. Missoula, MT: Scholars Press, 1979.

————. "Weighed in the Balance: The Similitudes of Enoch in Recent Discussion." *RelStudRev* 7 (1981) 217–21.

Swain, J. W. "The Theory of the Four Monarchies: Opposition History under the Roman Empire." *Classical Philology* 35 (1940) 1–21.

Talmon, S. "Typen der Messiaserwartung um die Zeitenwende." *Probleme biblischer Theologie*, edited by H. H. Wolff, 571–88. Munich: Kaiser, 1971.

Tarn, W. W. "Alexander Helios and the Golden Age." *JRS* 22 (1932) 135–48.

Tavadia, J. *Die Mittelpersische Sprache und Literatur der Zarathustrier*. Leipzig: Harrassowitz, 1956.

Tcherikover, V. *Hellenistic Civilization and the Jews*. New York: Atheneum, 1970.

Testuz, M. *Les Idées Religieuses du Livre des Jubilés*. Paris: Menard, 1960.

Theissen, G. *Sociology of Early Palestinian Christianity*. Philadelphia: Fortress, 1978.

Theisohn, J. *Der auserwählte Richter*. Göttingen: Vandenhoeck & Ruprecht, 1975.

Thomas, J. *Le Mouvement Baptiste en Palestine et Syrie*. Gembloux: Duculot, 1935.

Thompson, A. L. *Responsibility for Evil in the Theodicy of IV Ezra*. SBLDS 29. Missoula, MT: Scholars Press, 1977.

Thorndike, J. P. "The Apocalypse of Weeks and the Qumran Sect." *RQ* 3 (1961) 163–84.

Tromp, N. J. *Primitive Conceptions on Death and the Nether World*. Rome: Biblical Institute Press, 1969.

Turdeanu, E. *Apocryphes Slaves et Roumains de l'Ancien Testament*. Leiden: Brill, 1981.

Turner, N. "The Testament of Abraham: A Study of the Original Language, Place of Authorship and Relevance." Diss., University of London, 1953.

Ullendorff, E. "An Aramaic 'Vorlage' of the Ethiopic Text of Enoch?" In *Ethiopia and the Bible*, 31–62. Oxford: Oxford University Press, 1968.

Urbach, E. E. *The Sages*. Jerusalem: Magnes, 1975.

Vaillant, A. *Le Livre des Secrets d'Hénoch, texte slave et traduction francaise*. Paris: Institut d'Etudes Slaves, 1952.

VanderKam, J. *Enoch and the Growth of an Apocalyptic Tradition*. CBQMS 16. Washington, DC: CBA, 1984.

———. "Enoch Traditions in Jubilees and other Second-Century Sources." In *Society of Biblical Literature 1978 Seminar Papers*, edited by P. J. Achtemeier, 1:229–51. Missoula, MT: Scholars Press, 1978.

———. "The Origin, Character and Early History of the 364-Day Calendar: A Reassessment of Jaubert's Hypotheses." *CBQ* 41 (1979) 390–411.

———. "The Putative Author of the Book of Jubilees." *JSS* 26 (1981) 209–17.

———. *Textual and Historical Studies in the Book of Jubilees*. HSM 14. Missoula, MT: Scholars Press, 1977.

———. "The 364-Day Calendar in the Enochic Literature." In *Society of Biblical Literature 1983 Seminar Papers*, edited by K. H. Richards, 157–65. Chico, CA: Scholars Press, 1983.

———. "2 Maccabees 6, 7a and Calendrical Change in Jerusalem." *JSJ* 12 (1981) 52–74.

Vaux, R. de. *Archeology and the Dead Sea Scrolls*. London: Oxford University Press, 1973.

Vermes, G. *The Dead Sea Scrolls in English*. Harmondsworth: Penguin, 1974.

———. *The Dead Sea Scrolls: Qumran in Perspective*. Philadelphia: Fortress, 1981.

———. "The Son of Man Debate." *JSNT* 1 (1978) 19–32.

Vermeylen, J. *Du prophète Isaie à l'Apocalyptique*. Paris: Gabalda, 1977.

Vielhauer, P. "Apocalypses and Related Subjects." In *New Testament Apocrypha*, edited by E. Hennecke and W. Schneemelcher, 2:581–607. Philadelphia: Westminster, 1965.

Villiers, P. G. R. de. "Understanding the Way of God: Form, Function and Message of the Historical Review in 4 Ezra 3:4-27." In *Society of Biblical Literature 1981 Seminar Papers*, edited by K. H. Richards, 351-78. Chico, CA: Scholars Press, 1981.

Violet, B. *Die Apokalypsen des Esra und des Baruch in deutscher Gestalt.* Leipzig: Hinrichs, 1924.

————. *Die Ezra-Apokalypse, I: Die Ueberlieferung.* Leipzig: Hinrichs, 1910.

Volkmar, G. *Das vierte Buch Esra.* Tübingen: Fues, 1863.

Wacholder, B. Z. *The Dawn of Qumran: The Sectarian Torah and the Teacher of Righteousness.* New York: Ktav, 1983.

Wacker, M.-T. *Weltordnung und Gericht: Studien zu 1 Henoch 22.* Würzburg: Echter, 1982.

Wernberg-Møller, P. "A Reconsideration of the Two Spirits in the Rule of the Community (1QSerek III,13-IV,26)." *RQ* 3 (1961) 413-41.

Widengren, G. *The Ascension of the Apostle and the Heavenly Book.* Uppsala: Almqvist & Wiksell, 1950.

————. "Iran and Israel in Parthian Times with Special Regard to the Ethiopic Book of Enoch." In *Religious Syncretism in Antiquity*, edited by B. Pearson, 85-129. Missoula, MT: Scholars Press, 1975.

————. "Leitende Ideen und Quellen der iranischen Apokalyptik." In *Apocalypticism*, edited by D. Hellholm, 77-162. Tübingen: Mohr (Siebeck), 1983.

Wilson, B. *Magic and the Millennium.* New York: Harper & Row, 1973.

Wilson, R. R. "From Prophecy to Apocalyptic: Reflections on the Shape of Israelite Religion." *Semeia* 21 (1981) 79-95.

————. *Prophecy and Society in Ancient Israel.* Philadelphia: Fortress, 1980.

————. "This World—and the World to Come." *Encounter* 38 (1977) 177-24.

Windisch, H. *Die Orakel des Hystaspes.* Amsterdam: Akademie, 1929.

Wintermute, O. S. "Apocalypse of Zephaniah." In *The Old Testament Pseudepigrapha*, edited by J. H. Charlesworth, 1:497-515. Garden City, NY: Doubleday, 1983.

Worsley, P. *The Trumpet Shall Sound.* London: Macgibbon & Kee, 1957.

Woude, A. S. van der, "Melchizedek als himmlische Erlösergestalt in den neugefundenen eschatologischen Midraschim aus Qumran Höhle XI." *OTS* 14 (1965) 354-73.

————. *Die messianischen Vorstellungen der Gemeinde von Qumran.* Assen: van Gorcum, 1957.

Yadin, Y. "Le Rouleau du Temple." In *Qumrân*, edited by M. Delcor, 115-19. Leuven: Leuven University, 1978.

————. *The Scroll of the War of the Sons of Light against the Sons of Darkness.* Oxford: Oxford University Press, 1962.

———, *The Temple Scroll.* 3 vols. Jerusalem: Shrine of the Book, 1977.

Yarbro Collins, A. *The Apocalypse.* Wilmington, DE: Glazier, 1979.

———, *The Combat Myth in the Book of Revelation.* HDR 9. Missoula, MT: Scholars Press, 1976.

———, "Composition and Redaction of the Testament of Moses 10." *HTR* 69 (1976) 179–86.

———, *Crisis and Catharsis. The Power of the Apocalypse.* Philadelphia: Westminster, 1984.

———, "The Early Christian Apocalypses." *Semeia* 14 (1979) 61–121.

———, "The Political Perspective of the Revelation to John." *JBL* 96 (1977) 241–56.

Indexes

Subjects

275

Modern Authors